PEACE STUDIES

South Asian Peace Studies

Series Editor: Ranabir Samaddar

Other Titles in the Series

Volume 2: Peace Accords and Peace Processes (edited by Samir Kr Das)
Volume 3: Women in Peace Politics (edited by Paula Banerjee)
Volume 4: Human Rights, Human Rights Institutions and Humanitarian Crisis (edited by Ujjwal Kumar Singh)

Editorial Advisory Board

Daya Varma, Professor, McGill University, Montreal, President CERAS, Montreal, Canada

Ghislaine Glasson Deschaumes, Founder and Director of the international journal of critical thought *Transeuropéennes*, Paris, France

Itty Abraham, Social Science Research Council, George Washington University, Washington DC, USA

Jyrki Kakonen, Jean Monnet Professor, Department of Political Science and International Relations, University of Tampere, Finland

Oren Yiftachel, Professor, Department of Geography, Ben Gurion University, Beer Sheva, Israel

Paul Joseph, Professor of Sociology, and Peace and Justice Studies, Tufts University, MA, USA

Rada Ivekovic, Professor, Department of Sociology, Jean Monnet University, Saint Etienne, France

Stefano Bianchini, Director, Europe and the Balkans International Network, University of Bologna-Forli Campus, Forli, Italy

Editorial Board for this Volume

Paula Banerjee
Ranabir Samaddar
Samir Kr Das
Subhoranjan Dasgupta

SOUTH ASIAN PEACE STUDIES: VOLUME 1

PEACE STUDIES

AN INTRODUCTION TO THE CONCEPT, SCOPE, AND THEMES

Edited by Ranabir Samaddar

SAGE Publications
New Delhi • Thousand Oaks • London

Copyright © Mahanirban Calcutta Research Group, 2004

All rights reserved. No part of this book may be reproduced or utilized in any form or by any means, electronic or mechanical, including photocopying, recording or by any information storage or retrieval system, without permission in writing from the publisher.

First published in 2004 by

Sage Publications India Pvt Ltd
B–42, Panchsheel Enclave
New Delhi 110 017

Sage Publications Inc
2455 Teller Road
Thousand Oaks
California 91320

Sage Publications Ltd
1 Oliver's Yard
55 City Road
London EC1Y 1SP

Published by Tejeshwar Singh for Sage Publications India Pvt Ltd, typeset by InoSoft Systems in 10 pt Century Schoolbook and printed at Chaman Enterprises, New Delhi.

Library of Congress Cataloging-in-Publication Data

Peace studies : an introduction to the concept, scope, and themes / edited by Ranabir Samaddar.
    p. cm.—(South Asian peace studies; v. 1)
    Includes bibliographical references and index.
    1. Peace. 2. Peace-building—South Asia. 3. Conflict management—South Asia. 4. South Asia—Politics and government. 5. Peace—Study and teaching. I. Samāaddāara, Raònabāira. II. Series.

JZ5538.P45   303.6′6—dc22   2004   2004004548

ISBN: 0–7619–9660–5 (US–HB)   81–7829–124–X (India–HB)
        0–7619–9661–3 (US–PB)   81–7829–125–8 (India–PB)

Sage Production Team: Jai S. Prasad, Sushanta Gayen and Santosh Rawat

IN MEMORY OF EDWARD SAID

Contents

Series Note	9
Preface	11

Section I: Defining Peace Studies

Introduction *Samir Kr Das*	19
1. Problems of Preparing a Peace Studies Reader *Ranabir Samaddar*	32
2. A Peace Audit on South Asia *Kanti Bajpai*	38
3. Neo-liberalism and Democracy in South Asia *Gautam Kumar Basu*	72
4. Legal Regime for Refugee Care *Brian Gorlick*	92
5. Self-Determination and Politics of Identity—East Europe *Subhas Ranjan Chakraborty*	103
6. Deaths, Responsibility, and Justice *Ranabir Samaddar*	119

Section II: Borders, Wars, and the People

Introduction *Paula Banerjee*	141
7. Wars, Population Movements, and the Formation of States *Samir Kr Das*	151
8. Borders as Unsettled Markers—The Sino-Indian Border *Paula Banerjee*	173

9.	Protecting the Rights of Refugees *Irene Khan*	190
10.	People and Territory: Moving Beyond Boundaries *Barun De*	206
11.	Population Movements and Interstate Conflicts *Partha S. Ghosh*	226
12.	Rehabilitation of Victims in War-torn Societies *Sanjukta Bhattacharya*	254
13.	Women Across Borders in Kashmir— The Continuum of Violence *Asha Hans*	268
14.	Nationalities, Ethnic Processes, and Violence in India's Northeast *Monirul Hussain*	292

SECTION III: CONFLICT SITUATIONS, DIALOGUE, AND PEACE

	Introduction *Subhoranjan Dasgupta*	319
15.	Building Peace in Kashmir *Tapan K. Bose*	323
16.	The Indian Nuclear Debate *Kanti Bajpai*	339
17.	Sub-Regional Dialogue in the East and the Northeast—A New Way to Cooperate *Paula Banerjee, Sanjoy Hazarika, Monirul Hussain, and Ranabir Samaddar*	368
18.	Literary Sensitivities on War, Exodus, and Partition *Subhoranjan Dasgupta*	377
19.	Between Revenge and Reconciliation *Rajeev Bhargava*	390

Further Readings on Themes in Peace Studies	413
About the Editor and Contributors	425
Index	428

Series Note

Peace has become a maximal concept, refusing to accept a minimalist version that stops with the master-idea of security. This was never so apparent than the present time, when draconian laws, outright aggression, plunder, global control of monopolies, resource wars, immigration control, and new racism—all are being justified in the West, particularly in the United States, in the name of security against terrorism and a new global order. At the same time, the world is being told that this is the pathway to peace. This series is intended to address the critical time as this. It brings together writings, which refuse to accept the dominant ideas on peace given to us by national and international security establishments.

The first volume of the South Asian Peace Studies introduces the concept, scope, and themes of peace studies. The second volume deals with peace accords in this region. The third volume narrates experiences of women in conflict and peace. The fourth volume deals with human rights institutions in this region.

This series of volumes is different from the usual conflict and conflict resolution studies that revolve around interest-based approaches and game theories. While it remains uncertain as to how much these studies have contributed to an enriched understanding of conflicts and the dynamics of their resolution, now it is reasonably clear that these while focusing on conflicts neglect the ideas and visions of peace, justice and reconciliation, and were often used as post-facto justification of the way in which a particular conflict was handled, the most well-known example in this region being the Indo-Pakistan wars over Kashmir. Conflict studies by and large divorced the idea of conflict resolution and peace from practices of democracy and justice. More important, in this kind of studies, there was little recognition of the social and political realities of the colonial and post-colonial world. Peace with justice seems to be an impossible agenda to the conflict and conflict resolution theorists and practitioners. The South Asian Peace Studies series has been planned as an exercise against that politics of excluding justice and democracy from conflict resolution and peace—by bringing into light practices of human rights, justice, dignity, reconciliation, and democracy, and lodging them at the heart of peace studies. In a world characterized by structures of dominance and inequality and the received histories of freedom, the volumes will show that peace studies will have to be of a critical nature.

Ranabir Samaddar
Calcutta Research Group, Kolkata

Preface

The series on South Asian Peace Studies begins with the publication of this anthology. The first volume introduces peace studies and is therefore a general one. The book is divided in three broad sections—selected general themes in peace studies, selected cases of conflicts and wars that have engaged the attention of peace activists and researchers in this region, and finally some of the new discussions on ways of conflict resolution that have come out of peace studies in the last decade. The first volume suggests the broad range of issues involved in South Asian Peace Studies. Each section begins with a brief sectional introduction and the volume ends with select lists of further readings on some of the themes addressed in this volume. These lists are introduced with brief editorial comments. These lists are not exhaustive; they are intended to be indicative of the literature and the general trend of research on these issues here and abroad. Of course, it needs to be remembered that we have referred to material in the English language only, while peace studies are being conducted as vigorously in many non-English speaking countries. The next three volumes will deal with peace accords in this region, women in conflict and peace, and human rights institutions in this region.

The plan to commence a series on South Asian Peace Studies requires some explanation. South Asian peace researchers are familiar with some of the journals on conflict studies and conflict resolution studies that originated from a fascination with game theories and interest-based approaches. While it remains uncertain as to how much these journals have contributed to an enriched understanding of conflicts and the dynamics of their resolution, one can notice their capacity and role in obfuscating the idea and visions of peace. Conflict studies by and large divorced the idea of peace from the agenda and politics of democracy and justice. More important, in this corpus of conflict and conflict resolution studies there was little recognition of the social and political realities of the colonial and post-colonial world. Peace with justice seemed to be an impossible agenda to the conflict resolution theorists and practitioners.

One recent example is the theory of "democratic peace" that has assiduously sought to build up the argument that western democracies have been inherently peace making, forgetting the reality of the democratic capacity to wage colonial wars and committing genocide, in other words hiding "democratic deficit" in the sunlight of conflict studies. Possibly, there is a case for acknowledging the duality of *their peace studies/our peace studies*. By this I am not suggesting a fundamentalist and a binary counter-positioning of two strands in peace studies. But certainly, ethical notions of justice, dignity, equality, reconciliation, and democracy have to be restored to their position at the heart of peace studies. In a world characterized by structures of dominance and inequality and the received notions of freedom, peace studies have to be critical. Fortunately, critical writings on peace have emerged in this region in the last decade and have built up a corpus substantial enough to justify the decision to go in for publication of a series of peace studies that will be distinct from conflict studies, though reflecting on and relating to the latter from time to time.

Why is it necessary to separate peace studies from conflict studies? Conflict is "quarrel," and the causes of war, as Thomas Hobbes had reminded us, was "quarrel." Hobbes had three origins of quarrels in mind. These quarrels were (*a*) a result of competition or pursuit of gain, (*b*) diffidence or a desire for safety, and (*c*) glory or a desire for recognition. Quarrel thus signified a broader thing, *war of every man against every man*. Self-instinct for survival leads to the quest for power. Mankind is therefore perpetually compelled to seek power because each has to go to war for self-preservation. Honor, dignity, science, technology of control, peace—are all to be understood as expressions of power. The phenomenon of power is thus basic to humankind's experience of war and peace. The "fear of death" leads man to strife, war, survival and compacts for peace. But if the instinct of self-preservation leads to war, alternatively to peace, how can mankind be sure that peace may be durable, for man by *nature* has to seek power, and therefore may relapse into war? Unfortunately, therefore, there hangs a tale about this rationality, rather about its imperfection.

The point is, if war and peace are interchangeable, then why is it that only peace condition can be visualized as *absence of war*, and not war as absence of peace? If peace is only in the mirror of war, shall we say then that war is the natural condition, and peace is what authority brings about? From Hobbes to the current arguments of *Pax Americana*, this seems the suggestion, though there is no answer to the inquiry as to why conflict, that natural product of power, fear and desire, should *naturally* lead to war and not adjustment, negotiation and understanding. The imperfection of interchangeability thus raises the basic question: must peace be seen in the light of war? In what way are these two concepts connected? Can there be a positive definition of peace that does not link to war for conceptualization? Revolt and rebellion have legitimacy in society because they override the binary, even when ushering war they become widely acknowledged as a pathway to reconciliation and peace. The rational line of argument would however put it as the "vigorous way to peace," in much the same way Hegel had spoken of the "ethical health of the people" corrupted by "prolonged calm," "corruption in nations ... the product of prolonged peace" (Section 324, *Philosophy of Right*).

Since the rational argument has only made peace an ancillary of war, it is understandable why the thinking on peace whenever it appeared in its "original form" had taken the line of *beauty, happiness,* and *goodness*. Particularly religious philosophy in its many forms has never held *reason* as a positive attribute. It is neutral faculty that may serve wicked wills. Therefore the theme of peace is lodged in a "longing," "desire" for the good, the beautiful. The immanent goodness is also crucial. So far, so good, but how do men feel happy? What is there in happiness that creates this longing for peace, a pacifist disposition, an inclination not to hurt, to understand, to appreciate, to approach quarrel with mediation? If appeals to immanent goodness have to be supplemented with logic that we have left behind, we cannot be sure that peace will be inherent to society. This is admittedly a closed circle, and peace studies will have to try break out.

The closed circle is obvious when we see that commentators like Kenneth Boulding, though not sympathetic always with the rationalist–realist argument, are forced to concentrate on the dynamic nature of peace, and therefore emphasize that peace is a state of condition in which war is absent. Given the fact that contradiction and conflict are not optional mode of social existence, the activity of peace invariably goes back to the issue of happiness. That implies *living how*, the happiness of having a vision, and therefore a capacity to exchange, interact, align, ally, and to befriend—in short to understand the difference. In an age of nuclear menace, fierce civil wars, massive migration, destitution, and a resurgence of statism, *living how* is a crucial lead to the inquiry of peace. In fact, the severity of war today has de-linked peace from war. Even the war–peace copula, which goes by the name of *security*, has broken to pieces on the ground. The psychology of conflict which is what security is all about has failed to re-anchor peace to security. Peace has become a maximal concept, refusing to accept a minimalist version that stops with the master-idea of security. This was never so apparent than the present time, when draconian laws, outright aggression, plunder, global control of monopolies, resource wars, immigration control, and new racism—all are being justified in the West, particularly in the United States, in the name of security against terrorism and a new global order. At the same time, the world is being told that this is the pathway to peace.

In selecting the essays of this volume we have relied on both published and unpublished writings, but as stated earlier, these writings are all selected from the body that has emerged in the past one decade. There is definitely a need to have a volume on how South Asian thinking on peace has developed, which would include for instance the writings of Tagore and Gandhi. But we did not include these writings in the current reader for two reasons. First, one of our colleagues in studies of international politics has planned such a volume and we did not want to duplicate the effort. Second, our purpose here has been to provide a glimpse into the various kinds of current writings. In the forthcoming volumes, we shall attempt to present select writings representative of new ideas and lines of thinking. In this volume, our selection has been dictated by the necessity to show

how the corpus has developed theme-wise and approach-wise—from conflict-management to peace, national security to human security, revenge to reconciliation and rights to justice.

In preparing this volume the editor acknowledges the readiness of the contributors and their publishers to let their writings be included in the volume. They also express gratitude for the assistance of the staff of the Calcutta Research Group in typing out and preparing the manuscript. Finally, were it not for the enthusiasm of Sage Publications, such a plan for a series on peace studies would not have become a reality.

Ranabir Samaddar

Section I

Defining Peace Studies

INTRODUCTION

Samir Kr Das

The evolution of peace studies as a discipline is much younger than mankind's abiding concern for peace. While the concern is as old as mankind's first recorded histories of war (*The Peloponnesian War* by Thucydides in the West or *The Mahabharata* in the East) it evolved into a discipline only with the advent of modernity predominantly in the West. For it is only with the advent of modernity that peace ceased to be merely a passive concern and has been made an artifact that can be brought about, engineered, and subjected to deliberate human endeavors. It does not any longer depend on divine ordination. We know that peace of the "earthly city" according to St. Augustine, depends on the "well-ordered obedience of faith to eternal law of the city of God." Since it is an article of "faith," it does not depend on what we think, feel or act about it. Nor is it merely an object to be legislated upon by a minuscule minority of "philosopher-kings" who are otherwise divinely endowed with political wisdom. The transformation of peace into an artifact means that it is the people in general who as rational and moral agents are fully entitled to enjoy it as a right and/or respect it as a moral "responsibility." Besides, the significance of a discipline rests in a large measure with its ability to reduce an otherwise vast and unwieldy mass of knowledge to some elementary and universal laws. These are potentially knowable and applicable to all contexts irrespective of their social differences. That peace is amenable to a given number of rational and moral laws is one of the great contributions by the exponents of modernity. A whole lot of game–theoretic exercises has been and is being conducted in order to explain and at the same time, avoid wars and similarly Kant's philosophy of morals has literally simplified what he calls, "the categorical imperative" into plain and intelligible "formulations."

Most of the writings on peace in South Asia are firmly grounded in the paradigm of Western modernity. They have followed either of its two mutually exclusive trajectories: first, the trajectory of instrumental rationality suggests that two (or more) actors—individuals, communities, nations or whatever, are likely to make peace only if they think on their own that they have *reasons* to make peace. Peace along this trajectory is only subservient to reasons as understood by the respective actors. Such a peace is, to say the least, of contingent character for in case the actors think that they have no reasons for making peace, there is correspondingly no peace being made by them. The early rationalists however, assigned to the contracting parties the "responsibility" of shouldering all the possible consequences of the act of making their choice even if it finally turns out to be detrimental to their changing interests. In simple terms, present-day choices according to them, are to be made within the larger parameters of the choices made in the past. But as the rationalist trajectory got entrenched, it became gradually divorced from the moral principle of "responsibility."

The first two criteria that Kanti Bajpai has taken into account in his paper while making an audit of peace in South Asia have a lot to do with the instrumental rationality. Thus, when two nations like India and Pakistan wish to avoid war between them, what they try to do among other things is to arm them in such a manner that each of them acquires a deterrent capacity vis-à-vis its adversary. The states however may simply be unable to *see* reasons on their own. It is for instance, anticipated that a South Asian Free Trade Regime would be beneficial to both India and Pakistan. Yet, the volume of international trade between them has not shot up in the way it should have for reasons best known to us. Even, what Bajpai calls "value integration"—his third criterion, may not be viewed as an end in itself and instead may be issued from the same rationale that it helps a state achieve much-needed deterrent potential or economic development for that matter. Indeed, this is also implicit in the paradox that Gorlick's paper seeks to point to. The paradox is that while peace is predicated on the international regime that he believes "replaces" national states, its establishment in the first place requires a ratification by the national states—thanks to the prevailing norm of sovereign equality that till date governs much of the formal international relations in the present-day world. His paper makes an advocacy for accession on the part of the states in South Asia to such international instruments as 1951 Refugee Convention and also the subsequent protocol of 1967. In other words, it *shows* them the reasons that they left to themselves, fail to *see* and appreciate. The argument is quite analogous to one of Rousseau's well-known moralist doctrines that, should an individual refuse to be free, he will be "forced to be free." Gorlick's advocacy suggests a quasi-moralistic position that is nevertheless subsumable under the broader liberal–rationalistic argument.

Second, according to the moral trajectory of modernity, each individual is a "morally autonomous" being. Insofar as he (Kant's writings are often accused of this gender bias) is so, he is not bound by forces external to himself. In more positive terms, he is capable of exercising "self-control" in the sense of subordinating his "desires" that clamor within him for satisfaction—due to his "finite" existence, to what Kant calls "will." A "morally autonomous" being in short, can impose his will on the varieties of his fleeting desires that otherwise might overpower him. It is this "will" that also enjoins upon him "to act in such a way that he always treats humanity, whether in his own person or in the person of another, not simply as a means, but at the same time as an end." Since "moral autonomy" makes it imperative on us to "respect" others as equally "morally autonomous" beings, not only there is peace born out of mutual respect but the peace thus born becomes both "universal" and "perpetual." Kanti Bajpai's third criterion by his own admission, is complementary to this Kantian notion.

An individual's constitution into a "morally autonomous" being makes it possible for him to move away from the "state of nature" in which we are in a perpetual state of war. Hobbes for example, describes it as "a war of all against all." It is by way of moving away from the "state of nature" that the individuals become successful in establishing the modern nation-states. While Kant welcomes this movement, he does not see it as a *sufficient* condition for peace. For the formation of modern states does not rule out war "between us as states which, though internally in a lawful condition, are nevertheless externally (in relation to one another) in a lawless condition." It is true that the modern states have provided for internal pacification within their territorial boundaries. But as the modern states take their shape and establish their monopoly control over the more or less clearly demarcated territories, the world is constantly haunted by the possibilities of war between them. Kant views his "world republic" as an artifact that has the moral power of enforcing "laws" in an otherwise "lawless" world of nation-states. John Rawls—one of his most illustrious successors describes them as "rules of people." Kant's contribution lies in seeing the history of peace as a phased and graduated, albeit irreversible, process in which peace established through the formation of nation-states does not eliminate wars between them. He makes a distinction not only between war in the state of nature and war between nation-states in the modern world but also between peace within the nation-states and peace without (internal and external peace). Observance of these rules is the *sine qua non* of joining the "world republic." The guardians of these rules have the *right* to wage a "just war" against those who flout them. Samaddar's paper "Deaths, Responsibility, and Justice" written in the wake of 9/11 questions not so much the Kantian ethic of responsibility as much as the "discriminatory" nature of carrying it out in the contemporary world. Unlike Kant, he brings in the asymmetric power relations to ruffle the otherwise serene and tranquil moral landscape of discharging the given responsibility in order to argue that "the powerless have shown responsibility" so much so that they are now invested with a "new sense of power." If power does not produce responsibility, responsibility definitely produces its own power. The traces of Gandhi are only too obvious to be lost sight of in the paper included in this section.

The inclusion of peace studies as a separate and serious discipline in academic circles of South Asia or for that matter in other parts of the world, was by no means easy. For one thing, the peace activist in her vigorous concern for actions that can bring peace has swept the rationalist and moralist assumptions, while on the other hand peace studies has been considered to be too activist to form part of any academic program. For another, while peace is usually regarded as the unit concept of peace studies much in the same way as atom defines the scope of particle physics, there has hardly been any working agreement on what constitutes its essence. Such ambiguities among other things, have always prevented peace studies from growing into a full-fledged academic discipline.

It now seems that peace studies, hitherto steeped in the paradigm of modernity, has reached a stage where its development as a discipline now hinges on a large measure on the fate of the concern over the "essence of peace." And peace studies may die a premature death—premature, because the end of the Cold War has actually led to an exacerbation of threats to peace. This section also discovers some of the early traces of an imminent paradigm-shift: peace studies today seems to be increasingly dissociated from the early Kantian concern for universal moral laws. In a world that is fiercely fragmented into a multiplicity of small and discrete universes governed similarly by a multiplicity of moral laws, any attempt at imposing universal ones is likely to be not only futile but counter-productive.

Subhas Ranjan Chakraborty's study of the Balkans provides an excellent backdrop against which the experience of the South Asian countries may be reviewed and analyzed. Globalization according to Hirst and Thompson, has only made politics "polycentric" and the disjuncture of its levels is now so nearly complete that the connection between "governance" and "government" has been severed with the effect that the latter has now become only one of the agencies among others, vying for taking up the reins of governance.[1] Thus to cite an instance from Chakraborty's paper, territorial borders of a nation-state have to reckon with a plethora of invisible and albeit officially unacknowledgeable borders of ethnic sub-territories that it supposedly encapsulates. State territoriality today is neither exclusive nor continuous. Insofar as the state has ceased to be the uncontested agency of cultural and territorial homogenization, peace at one level does not automatically ensure that at another. The state in other words, is no longer the sole organizing center of power and politics also operates at levels beyond its purview. As a result, the necessity of making peace at all levels of the society including the most local and apparently insignificant ones is more deeply felt. With globalization, every conflict—howsoever "little" and of "low intensity" it might be, acquires the highly inflammable potential of spreading across its immediate boundaries and ultimately turning into a global one. Gone are the days when peace studies was overwhelmed by the internationalist mega-projects of almost every conceivable variety ranging from humanist universalism to proletarian internationalism.

While the so-called modernist mega-projects of peace are now increasingly under fire, celebration of the so-called autochthonous micro-traditions in South Asia has by no means been easy. The tendency of celebrating them with much fanfare—whether by showcasing them as immensely valuable "museum pieces" to the outside world or by getting them rewarded with some of the world's most coveted and sought-after honors (like the Nobel Peace Prize), or both, is however very common in South Asia and even in the West. The popularity of the Hare Krishna sect or Buddhism in the West in general and the USA in particular may serve as a case in point. It is true that the renewal of scholarly interest in the autochthonous peace traditions in recent years has coincided with a certain disintegration of the mega-projects. Yet, their celebration has always proven to be difficult for us in this part of the world. For the advent of modernity has not only led to a rapid increase in the extent and intensity of social conflicts but put our so-called "very own traditions" into utter disarray. Both the articulation of "rational" self-interests and an intense individualistic desire to uphold, defend and pursue them and if necessary, in *opposition* to those of others with the advent of modernity have made it difficult on the part of the colonial as well as the post-colonial political elite to resolve the conflicts of interests. As the centralized post-colonial power gradually arrogated to itself the privileged role of resolving these conflicts as a "neutral" arbitrator and professedly in keeping with the defining principles of modern Anglo-Saxon system of Jurisprudence, the indigenous peace traditions have lost much of their relevance. The modernity project that was once initiated by the colonial state and is still being enthusiastically carried out by the post-colonial ones in South Asia was an onslaught both on peace as well as our peace traditions. Since many of these are no longer an integral part of our "living" traditions, their thoughtless and romantic re-invocation is unlikely to serve our purpose.

Introduction 25

We may note that the problematic of peace *a la* modernity was in many ways paradigmatically discontinuous with the autochthonous peace traditions: first of all, many of these traditions envisage conflicts only within a single culturally continuous space. Hindu political philosophy is usually regarded as a classic illustration of this point. As K. Satchinanda Murty and A.C. Bouquet observe:

... the Hindu political thinkers insisted that a Hindu emperor's domains should not extend beyond India, Afghanistan and Ceylon. Hindu thinkers conceived it was right to achieve a sort of unity by establishing hegemony of one state over others within the same world of culture; they prohibited aggression against states belonging to other worlds of culture; as against this some Greek, Christian and Islamic thinkers thought it was right to wage wars against alien cultures.[2]

In simple terms, since the *other* according to this philosophy, is a paradigmatic extension of the *self*, threat to peace is never interpreted as a threat to the cultural identity of the community. Both the *self* and the *other* presumably belong to the same cultural community. The policy of "non-aggression" towards the aliens may not prove to be effective, in case the latter do not reciprocate it. While modernity teaches us to view conflicts predominantly in "dualistic" terms (for the "rational" interests of the individuals like, those of the buyer and the seller, cannot but be opposed to each other), it is completely at odds with the Hindu quest for peace within a given and culturally demarcated space. The advent of modernity as J.P.S. Uberoi informs us, has resulted in a certain disintegration of all such "non-dualistic" modes of thought" as Shi'ite Islam, Sikhism and of course, Hinduism.[3] Second, modernity's inveterate rage against nature is nowhere more sharply expressed than in its conceit of exercising a no-holds-barred "mastery" over it. Peace according to this paradigm, is positioned within the matrix of inter-individual relations. Seldom is it visualized from within the problematic of man–nature relationships. Increased "mastery" over nature gives one the "happiness" that is widely recognized as the single most important prerequisite for peace. Many of the indigenous traditions on the other hand, look upon peace as both integral and indivisible. The question therefore can not be separated from the larger issue of man–nature relationships.

Most of the empirical surveys hitherto conducted on the indigenous peoples of South Asia (variously described as tribes, tribals, and *adivasis* etc.) tend to conclude that contrary to the commonplace belief, these apparently illiterate and backward groups are perfectly aware of the primary necessity of protecting the natural environment for their survival and nearly all of them trace this awareness to their cultural ethos. Moreover, while modernity measures "happiness" and peace in terms of mankind's outward "mastery" over nature, "true peace" according to Buddhism comes from within one's own self. His Holiness the xvth Dalai Lama for instance, pointed out in his speech of acceptance of the Nobel Peace Prize in 1989:

> People inflict pain on others in the selfish pursuit of their happiness or satisfaction. Yet true happiness comes from a sense of inner peace and contentment, which in turn must be achieved through the cultivation of altruism, of love and compassion and elimination of ignorance, selfishness and greed.[4]

What is called "mastery" over nature is issued from "ignorance, selfishness and greed." The same integral philosophy of peace has been propounded by some of the leading thinkers of South Asia in recent times (like Gandhi and Tagore) who challenged the western framework of modernity from a rather eclectic standpoint that draws overwhelmingly from a number of the region's most potent peace traditions. We know how both of them were influenced by Jainism, Buddhism, Vaishnavism (a pacifist sect within Hinduism) and of course, some other folk traditions lying on the margins of Hinduism and Islam. Third and as a sequel to it, we may say that what these traditions describe as "true peace" is also of *non-political* character. The already rich and rapidly growing literature on the formation of modern states whether in Europe or in South Asia (or in other parts of the world as well) establishes the connection between the advent of modernity and the emergence of "modern" states. Anthony Giddens for instance, shows how the formation of "modern" states has contributed to the "internal pacification" of territories commanded over by them.[5] Nikunja Vihari Banerjee on the other hand, argues that the patently modernist idea that peace can be brought about by the institutions of state is nothing but a "fiction." As he puts it:

The division of mankind into a multiplicity of states, each sovereign in itself and independent of others, is in the final analysis, its subjection to bondage. For what else can its bondage be except the loss of its integrity and wholeness and its reduction to parts alien to one another? And when mankind is thus in bondage what else can the sovereignty of its parts mean except a larger or smaller share of its bondage?[6]

The formation of a multiplicity of modern states not only violates the holistic principle, "integrity and wholeness" as he terms it, but by the same process, constricts their ability to "internally pacify" the territories under their command. Defining peace as "a state in which man [sic] is integrated with himself and with his fellows," he makes an important distinction between peace defined as "fiction" and peace defined as "utopia." While the former only leads to "temporary postponement of conflicts" and therefore uneasy peace, (that is why, peace under conditions of modernity cannot but be a "fiction") the latter is pregnant with the "promise of overcoming the perennial crisis of the human situation so as to herald the advent of perpetual peace." It is interesting to note that many of our traditions look upon peace more as a yet unrealized "promise" while some of them (like the philosophical system of Sankara) even question whether it is at all realizable for all. But, that we take it to be a value worth living for, makes it potent in the sense of influencing, moulding and at times, determining our social and political practices.[7] Now that the modernist mega-projects have run into rough weather, South Asia still awaits a perceptive historian to retrieve and renarrativize our multifarious and albeit fractured microtraditions of peace. There is no doubt that the demise of megaprojects has opened up in hitherto unprecedented ways, the possibilities of a new South Asian Peace historiography.

Although the peace characteristic of modernity is paradigmatically divergent from the autochthonous peace traditions of South Asia, our encounter with the West ironically forced them to engage with each other in a very complex way. The disintegration of peace traditions was never an easy affair. For instance, modernity in this region (maybe, in other parts of the world as well) for whatever reasons, has always been sensitive to the need for coming to terms with these traditions and *translate* it into their language. For the colonial and postcolonial states (as the self-appointed guardians and perpetrators of modernity in a region that is still largely dominated by pre- and occasionally anti-modern forces), this served and continues to serve as one of the most important means of acquiring legitimacy. Thus, it was possible for the pre-modern and typically western rhetoric of the "state of nature" to be freely translated into the Hindu equivalent of the *Matsyanyaya*. Similarly, the establishment of *Pax Britannica* was hailed by the subjects as the coronation of the great *Rajachakravartin* to the grand throne of power in an otherwise vast sub-continental empire. The rule was expected to put an end to the spiralling chaos and disorder that had allegedly marked the *Matsyanyaya* of the pre-colonial times. Several studies in historical anthropology have been conducted mainly in Bengal as well as in other parts of the region, to drive home the point that both modernity and the indigenous peace traditions sought to make sense of each other through the instrumentality of translation.

It is true that for some time, none of them was reducible to the other. Yet one of the major impediments of the existing peace historiography in South Asia is that its modernist–universalist claim has never allowed us to conceptualize the problem from any alternative viewpoint and in the process, wiped out the indigenous peace traditions from the pages of history. As if South Asia woke up to the concern for peace only with the advent of modernity. If any of the papers included in this collection is oblivious to these considerations, it is only because its author has seen peace as the uncontested and unproblematic contribution of western modernity. A certain kind of peace *triumphalism* marks the narratives of this kind. But, nearly all the papers included in this section point to the gray and hitherto unconquered (and often unconquerable) spaces of modernity and focus on the process of slow and irreversible disintegration of the modernist metaphor of peace. None of them, however, celebrates what we call the micro-traditions of peace. There is reason to believe that with the passing of time, our peace traditions have lost much of their steam. Most of them remain confined to some local and culturally enclosed arenas (like, the pacifist and at times, self-effacing traditions of the Jain sages) and became too weak to take on the forces of modernity on their own. The states no longer felt the necessity of reviving and extending patronage to them. Denied of patronage in an era when everything seems to depend on it, these traditions are transformed into benign and apolitical objects or "museum pieces" as we called them. Besides, their engagement with the forces of modernity entailed some modifications and transformations in their texture and character. Our peace traditions have already undergone a process of *hybridization*. The papers included in this section aptly express this dilemma.

On the other hand, there has also been a perceptible change in the modalities of peace. While it has always been tempting to define peace as the absence or postponement of war, the distinction has been considerably blurred in recent years in the wake of growing salience of war-like situations, which can be clustered neither as peace nor as war. Basu's argument that globalization has led to an extension of market principles to the ambit of the state and that the much-touted "exit" of the state from the realm of public welfare has neither put an end to "subtle militarism" exercised through the surveillance of the South Asian countries including India nor facilitated their re-democratization. Even assuming that peace and war are two mutually exclusive terms that are operationalizable for all practical purposes, the question that can still be asked is whether peace ought to be minimally defined as the absence (or postponement) of war or maximally as the entire repertoire of initiatives that prevent wars from breaking out in the first place and thereby making peace contingent and fragile. Development viewed in this light, may be strategic to peace-keeping, given that there is a widespread belief that the association of war with states at lower echelons of development still holds water in larger parts of the world. Samaddar elsewhere prefers to define the concept in rather broad terms. As he puts it, "We have to reconceptualize the notion of peace by infusing it with the issues of justice, human rights and dignity, i.e., firmly linking it with democracy in the region." Moreover, what about most of the wars that are fought by rivals ironically with the same objective of establishing peace?

Now that the binary opposition between war and peace has increasingly fallen into disuse, the hitherto practised modalities of peacemaking have obviously become circumspect. The early emphasis on the resolution of differences has proven to be counter-productive in the sense that it is based on a conception of unity that is increasingly denying legitimacy to the diversities and excluding larger segments of population from peace endeavors and in the process narrowing the social and community base of peace. In other words, we have to come to terms with a world where peace is contingent on the preservation and articulation of differences or as Samaddar puts it "the phenomenology of coexistence." Peace according to this view, is not so much "resolution of differences" as much as "resolving to understand differences." This "understanding" is not to be confused with *verstehen a la* Max Weber for it is not an instrumentality with the help of which somebody from outside a community de-cultures herself as an outsider and learns how to become an integral part of the community she is interested in studying and in our case, making peace with. Nor is it an attribute that as Tonnies pointed out, characterizes a *gemeinschaft* (community) and hence, is confined only to its members. For making peace is necessarily transcendental in the sense that it is made between actors and hence, cannot be particular to any one of them. Even when one is said to be at peace with one's own self, one is as it were split into two—both of which are making peace with each other. Second, and this is unlike both Weber and Tonnies, understanding is not altogether indifferent to the complex working of power relations in the present-day world. Because it is also an understanding that enables one to assert one's right to be different and encourages one to fight against all those designs that threaten to take this right away. Understanding is enveloped in the larger task of critiquing and changing the world. Since understanding is subservient to the requirements of preparing a critique, it cannot be essentialist. Peace as preservation of differences also implies a constant re-articulation of differences. It in other words, is a war carried through understanding of differences and peace studies as a discipline cannot but be a critique of the very disciplines of understanding the differences.

Notes and References

1. Paul Hirst and Grahame Thompson, *Globalisation in Question: The International Economy and the Possibilities of Governance.* Cambridge, 1991.

Introduction 31

2. K. Satchinanda Murty and A.C. Bouquet, *Studies in the Problems of Peace*. Bombay, 1960, p. 215.
3. J.P.S. Uberoi, *Religion, Civil Society and the State: A Study of Sikhism*. Delhi, 1996.
4. Irwin Abrams, *Peace: 1981–1990*. Singapore, 1997, p. 248.
5. Anthony Giddens, *Social Theory and Modern Sociology*. Stanford, 1987, chapter seven.
6. Nikunja Vihari Banerjee, *Towards Perpetual Peace*. Shimla, Delhi, 1988, p. 132.
7. See for instance, Helmut Reifeld and Ranabir Samaddar (eds), *Peace As Process*. New Delhi, 2001.

1
PROBLEMS OF PREPARING A PEACE STUDIES READER[1]

Ranabir Samaddar

Happily, in recent times, educationists in South Asia and India in particular, are showing concern and awareness regarding the need for a peace studies program, in the region. Here and there we have instances of peace studies programs like, the International Relations Department of the University of Dhaka has an optional paper on peace studies in its syllabus; the University Grants Commission in India is reported to be preparing to spend several crores of rupees on such a program; but in this case, critics say this will be one more way of cornering more money by some know-all elite professors and some "peace experts" and "professional peace researchers"; there are some peace foundations also (like Gandhi Peace Foundation) whose programs could not be much popularized for various reasons; finally, wherever universities have such programs under departments or special research centers, they are subsumed under strategic studies or international relations. Thus, the place of peace studies has been assigned and "shown"; it can be there, but it must not aspire for its own centrality, independence; it must remain a part of politics, strategy, and strategic consideration.

However, the growing militarization of the region, arms competition, recurrent coups, ethnic conflicts, brutal suppression of some movements and the general erosion of civil liberties and human rights, have given birth to a widespread concern for peace; this is reflected in the awareness that South Asian Peace Studies program be sooner evolved than later, if peace has to be rescued from the clutches of professional foreign policy makers. In other words, peace studies has to be linked to the peace constituencies in the society.

Yet it must be understood that a program of peace education has to cope with certain inbuilt problems, problems that inevitably emerge when a social agenda is rendered into an academic discipline. This brief note aims to draw attention to those problems.

The first question that peace studies faces is with regard to its conceptualization. Should we regard peace as just opposite to war—in other words, peace studies as the *other* of war studies, or something more, a positive discipline? As we go deeper into the question of conceptualizing our theme, it becomes clear that it is not an issue of mere semantics, but something complicated. Peace is certainly the *other* of war; but confined to that, human history shows, particularly the history of South Asia, such *pacifism*, becomes inadequate in the face of rising chauvinism, territorialism, militarism and sexist ideologies. Indeed, many of the barbaric wars have been waged and could be waged with the help of psychological support to war, where the pacifist idea was inadequate in presenting itself as an alternative noble cause worth persuing. In other words, the ideological base of war has been broader than that of peace. Thus, peace has been to seen as something more than "conflict-resolution," more than a mere management strategy with regard to conflicts. We have to re-conceptualize the notion of peace by infusing it with the issues of justice, human rights and dignity, i.e., firmly linking it with democracy in the region, realizing also the multiplex character of the notion of peace and the significance of the different elements that determine the structure of peace studies like science and technology, arts, communication and media, social sciences, law and human rights and also emphasizing the crucial role of plastic arts in aestheticizing sensitivities.

Yet, howsoever we broaden the thematic basis of peace studies, it cannot be denied that the first relevance of such studies will be in its ability to analyze war and militarization; to dissect and expose it. Otherwise, peace studies will not be a concrete, substantive discipline with its own institutional profile. Peace studies has to live, therefore, a life of an *other* of war and war studies, and as a discipline its fate will be to continuously keep on trying to break away from the shackles of an *other*, to come out of the shadow of war studies. This is an inbuilt tension which peace studies is destined to suffer as a discipline.

But such a life of *other* is not without virtues. By critiquing existing notions of security, state considerations, ethnic exclusivities, certain cultural stereotypes encouraging masochism, and practice of rigid borders peace studies can go a long way in robbing militarism of its ground. In South Asia, this critique has to extend to an investigation into the links between internal militarization and external militarism, between gender-violence and state repression, between the culture of secretiveness and defence economics, and between minority suppression and the most pervasive culture of intolerance. In other words, even as a critique it can widen its substance and constituency by realizing in its corpus the fact that power in modern societies is not only in a centralized form, known to us through the juridical notion and expression of sovereignty, it is in a dispersed shape also, permeating every layer of society, best described in Foucault's term, "the capillary form of power."

Looking at the problematic from another angle, one can say, this critique, when deepened, can pull out peace studies in South Asia from under the shadow of war studies, in other words, from its status as a "negative" discipline. One particular way will be to retrieve indigenous traditions of tolerance in South Asia by tracing the history of various ethical ideas, indigenous notions of ecological awareness and women's dignity; another way can be to demonstrate how peace is strengthened by various forms of popular movements on democratic rights.

I shall raise two cardinal questions of principle in this regard. Both are thematic posers, but as will be seen shortly, they reflect on procedural matters also. The first issue is, can there be a national peace studies in South Asia? The second, does it have to be a separate discipline at all? Let us see, briefly, what the principles involved here are.

The question of peace in the region cannot be understood without taking into account the particular conditions of postcoloniality. In other words, there is still the colonial past, a past that is still alive. It is a past when nationalistic particularities had not been predominant, and also a past that culminated into the slicing up of the region into several parts. This reality of partition has left a permanent residue, and has predicated the conditions of post-coloniality in the region. Therefore, an agenda of peace requires the evolution or a South Asian mind. Peace studies, therefore, has to be a South Asian peace studies, and not Indian peace studies, Pakistan peace studies, etc. Yet, nations are a reality today, in spite of the permanence of South Asian commonalities. And thus, peace studies to begin with, has to be Indian, Bangladeshi, Pakistani, Sri Lankan, Nepalese, etc. It is certainly an "awkward compromise." Peace studies is built on this tension. And we do not know if and how it can free itself from this inherent contradiction.

This brings us to the second question. Can it be that such contradictions will be inherent, if peace studies is conceptualized as a *discipline*, and can be tackled only if it is seen not as a discipline, but as a *field*? Discerning critics have noted the fate of women studies once it was converted into a discipline. And it has been suggested that the values of feminism have to be integrated with fundamental perspectives of history, politics, arts, and literature thereby transforming them. But once it is congealed into a discipline, it gives a chance to the conservative disciplines to ossify. Will not peace studies suffer the same fate in our region, if it is consigned to the status of a discipline? It will lose, possibly, its capacity to subvert.

These issues are raised here, as I ponder over the dynamics of preparing a syllabus, particularly a textbook. Textbook implies a definite syllabus, a defined audience or users, a defined teaching mode and a defined site of teaching i.e., a course, a degree, a group, an institution, etc. Textbook has its own order i.e., the order guiding the arrangement of matters, the sequence, i.e., chapterization. The question, therefore, is: will the conventional mode of a textbook suit peace studies at this stage? I have already hinted that much of the post-colonial rigidities have to account for the rise of a militarist psychology in the region. Its counterpoint are the flexibilities of our older history and histories. Those flexibilities are still here, in this region—but often not at the level of fact, current history, politics, diplomacy, and state-to-state relations, but at the level of *contra history*, i.e., memory, literature, and fiction. The task is, thus, how to capture this *contra history*, if at all it can be, within the rigid boundaries of a textbook. If peace studies has to be based on understanding, that is understanding differences, the flexibilities of a South Asian mind must suffuse a textbook with it. Can it be done? How do we realize the multiplex notion of peace? A discipline and a textbook, or poetics?

There are other forms of instructing material. It can be an epic, even a semi-fictive narrative, an anthology, a reader. In South Asia, the question becomes paramount—how do we find out a suitable form, or forms so that the definitive character of a discipline or "studies" can become commensurate with the task of conveying the spirit of flexibility (i.e., indigenous notions of civilizational exchanges, tolerance, shared culture, man–nature union, etc.)? Can we work out a new mode, a new pedagogy?

Let us consider, for a moment, the tensions in a reader. How do they make a reader on war, in whose shadow peace remains? I cite the example of *Oxford Reader on War*,[2] edited by Lawrence Freedman (1994), a member of the Department of War Studies of King's College, London. Now, this reader divides the issue of war into seven sections—the experience of war; the causes of war; war and military establishment; the ethics of war; strategy; total war and the great powers; and limited war and developing countries. Each section is introduced by an author, and a general introduction prefaces the whole volume. These introductions try to make the fragments disciplined and render them coherence, turn them into a coherent whole. The result is imposing an order, disciplining the unruliness of the extracts, their wayward character. War indeed demands that. Thus, the experiences of say, a Royal Naval Rating at the Battle of Trafalgar, 1805 (pp.12–15), of the end of the Warsaw Ghetto Uprising (pp. 37–39), of Vietnam (pp. 51–57), or Desert Storm (pp. 60–62) can go any direction besides the one of the book. Similarly, how does the fourth section, "The Ethics of War," sit in the whole volume—the arguments on Nuremberg and Vietnam (in one, war crimes were tried, in the other not) with the principles of realism? I can cite other examples also, of such efforts at disciplining potentially subversive extracts. It may be argued that it is precisely the aim of a reader to present before the students the width and length of a study, a theme, to show complexities, to encourage the students to go for fuller study of complexities. My hunch is, such a goal fails; instead, it neutralizes the varied reactions, anticipates the protests and numbs them, preempts violent objections. At worst, it presents a notebook. My reaction to the *Oxford Reader on Nationalism*,[3] edited by John Hutchinson and Anthony Smith (1994) is roughly along the same line. For example, in the defined sub-themes there is none on "nations and ethnicity" or "nations and minorities." These are there, but diffused, strewn as corpses throughout the book, thereby making it difficult for any one to appreciate that in the world outside, outside the reader, nationalism cannot be discussed at all without reference to ethnicity or the minority problematic. In fact, often what is understood as nationalism may be something else. The reader therefore in this case creates a myth that, as Roland Barthes would say, "deprives the object of which it speaks of all history." In this way potentially subversive pieces on war and nationalism have been tackled effectively—the complexities decently cut and tailored.

Yet it is true at the same time that this is how a theme is constructed. Similarly, then, a reader on peace cannot be understood only in its own terms, just like it cannot be understood only as a negation—a negation of war. To understand it in its own terms only is a tautology that "creates a dead, motion less world." It amounts to arguing, "peace is peaceful conditions, i.e., absence of war." To understand it is to thematize it further, vivisect it, to allow it to melt, to dissolve it.

So how about a textbook on peace studies, or a reader? We can go for all these, provided we have in mind the inbuilt complexities, provided we also try for improvization and complement the conventional modes with newer ones and make it a flexible broad ranging field that permeates many disciplines and received knowledges!

REFERENCES

1. Published in UNESCO Newsletter on Textbook Studies, George-Eckert Institute, Braunschawaig, 1996.
2. Lawrence Freedman (ed.), *War*. Oxford Reader, Oxford, 1994.
3. John Hutchinson and Anthony Smith (eds), *Nationalism*, Oxford Reader, Oxford, 1994.

2

A Peace Audit on South Asia[1]

Kanti Bajpai

If you want peace, you must prepare for peace.[2] If South Asians want peace, they must agree on the kind of peace they want and how to achieve it. Seminar after seminar in the region ends with the portentous (but vacuous) recommendation that South Asians must summon up the political will for peace and cooperation—a counsel of virtue, which we would no doubt do well to heed, but essentially tautological. The question is: what is peace and under what conditions does the political will for peace assert itself? As part of the intellectual preparation for a more peaceful region in the coming century, this paper attempts to define the notion of peace and to assess the prospects for peace in South Asia along various pathways.

Three Notions of Peace

What is peace? While there is little agreement on the answer, we can distinguish between at least three different meanings or types of peace: peace as the mere absence of war, that is, a *hegemonic* of *deterrent* peace; peace as functional and economic interaction, what could be called a *transactional* peace; and, peace as a social condition in which accommodation rather than force mediates change, in short, an *integrative* or *perpetual* peace.[3]

These three notions of peace may be derived from three basic visions of social and international life. Kenneth Boulding, in his work over several years, has used the image of threat systems, exchange systems, and integrative systems to denote the three basic ways humans relate to each other in virtually all social arenas, from the family to the international system.[4] In a compatible if not parallel way, Hedley Bull in his work on "international society" has divided Western views of international life into the Hobbesian, the Grotian, and the Kantian tradition.[5]

Boulding has argued that humans relate to each other in three ways—by means of threats, exchange, and integration. The first way in which they regulate their interactions is by the promise or actual use of punishment. In a threat system, human relations are regulated by the expectation of punishment and the desire to avoid it. Threats can serve the goal of peace, at least at a superficial level. A cold peace—the absence of war— may be achieved by two threat systems: *hegemony* and *deterrence*. A more or less generalized threat system presided over by the dominant power is *hegemony*. Hegemony is seldom an exclusively punitive system: it is preserved by a combination of carrots and sticks. But punishment is never far from the workings of hegemony. Punishment can take various forms including force. Deterrence is the threat of force to prevent unpalatable actions by another. Hegemony and deterrence may achieve a superficial peace. A hegemon can use the threat of punishment to stop others using force and thus maintain a minimalist peace. A deterrer also can practise a minimalist form of peacemaking by threatening to exact costs well beyond the gains an opponent may hope to make from an attack.

The second way in which humans regulate their relations is by means of exchange. In an exchange, both sides benefit. The prospect of future exchange for mutual benefit ensures good behavior in the present. To the extent that what is exchanged is necessary and non-substitutable, the incentive to exchange and the incentive to behave in a manner consistent with a continuation of the exchange relationship remains strong. Peace is achieved and maintained by a mutual interest in the benefits of ongoing transactions.

Beyond threats and exchange, humans can construct various integrative relationships. In an integrative relationship, humans arrive at a position of ethical respect for, and moral convergence with, others. They recognize certain obligations or responsibilities towards others. Minimally, and negatively, this entails a reluctance if not outright refusal to visit violence on others. More positively, to integrate is to invest in a continuous process of mutual communication, comprehension, and accommodation.

Three points are worthy of attention here. First of all, at any given time, most human relationships are regulated by a combination of threats, exchange, and integration. The international system, commonly, is thought to be closer to a pure threat system, at least in the view of so-called political realists.[6] Nevertheless, even international life is marked by exchange and integrative relationships.

Second, while any relationship features some combination of threats, exchange, and integration, one can think of these systems as arrayed in ascending order of stability. Threat systems are prone to instability because the promise of punishment is likely to lose credibility over time. To maintain credibility, the threatening power must not only restate but also intensify the promise of punitive action. The danger is that at some point the promised punishment may be so out of proportion to the punishable action that it will become incredible. In addition, defensive threats are not always clearly distinguishable from offensive ones. When they are not, the result is a "security dilemma" in which ostensibly defensive moves are seen as preparations for an offensive. In a security dilemma, either side may resort to preemptive force as a precaution, thus precipitating the very outcome the threat system was intended to avoid. Finally, a threat system is not an efficient system: compelling someone to act or not act in a particular way is always less efficient than having him or her do so voluntarily. Thus, threat systems are prone to periodic collapse. Exchange systems are superior: here, mutual benefit conditions behavior. However, even exchange systems have their limits, perhaps the chief of which is that when the prospects of exchange are nearing exhaustion or are exhausted the incentive to maintain certain behavioral patterns may disappear. Moreover, in an exchange system there is the constant fear that one side is profiting more than the other and will eventually turn this "relative gain" to permanent advantage.[7] If this fear persists, an exchange system can well unravel. Integrative systems are the most stable and durable. These are built not on punishment or greed, but on normative commitments issuing out of recognition of common humanity. They are not therefore liable to decay or reversal.

A third point worth reflecting on is whether there is a relationship between the three systems. Is a stable threat system—for howsoever long—a precondition of mutually advantageous exchange relations that, in turn, are the foundation for progressively higher order integrative relationships? Put more concretely: Is a stable balance of power, built on deterrence, a precondition for functional and economic cooperation? And are deterrence and functional and economic cooperation preconditions for a permanent peace? There are those, clearly, who would argue this case for South Asia and elsewhere. Others would claim that deterrence freezes relationships and thereby impedes functional or economic cooperation and progress towards integration. It is not therefore a precondition of the other levels of peace; rather, its dismantling is a precondition of the other levels. So, for instance, functional and economic cooperation may help thaw relations frozen at the level of deterrence. Or, a certain degree of integration may be prior to long-term functional and economic cooperation. If cooperation is constantly beset by concern over the distribution of gains, one way of overcoming the fear of unequal exchange is to recognize certain transcendent, integrative values in common.[8]

The Hobbesian, Grotian, and Kantian perspectives on international society, as rendered by Hedley Bull, are compatible with Boulding's schema. In Bull's view, the Hobbesian perspective is that of international relations as a threat system.[9] States are the primary actors in international affairs. As sovereign entities, they recognize no higher authority which can adjudicate disputes or enforce certain norms on behavior. Therefore, they are left with no recourse but to settle matters among themselves, in the end, by the threat or use of force. Military preponderance or balances of power and deterrence, these are the bases of peace.[10]

The Grotian view is that of international relations as a regulated exchange system. States are the primary actors in international affairs and they are sovereign, but they come to recognize and respect certain constraints on their behavior in order to pursue mutually beneficial cooperation. For Grotians, international trade and commerce not war most typifies international life, and the entanglements and benefits of these and other regulated interactions with other states is the basis for peace.[11]

The Kantian view regards international relations as a transnationally integrated system. For Kantians, the interests and values of human beings are similar and will gradually be seen to be so. The benefits of trade and commerce, the spread of education and communication, the increasing costs and miseries of war and conquest, and a deep-rooted ethical imperative will cause the convergence, diffusion, or deepening awareness of common values and interests. To the extent that they do, these will bring into being a community of mankind, over and above the community of states.[12]

Bull, like Boulding, argues that international life is at any given time a mix of the coercive, convergent, and cooperative. Thus, he notes:

> The modern international system in fact reflects all three of the elements singled out, respectively, by the Hobbesian, the Kantian and the Grotian traditions: the element of war and struggle for power among states, the element of transnational solidarity and conflict, cutting across the divisions among states, and the element of cooperation and regulated intercourse among states. In different historical phases of the states system, in different geographical theatres of its operation, and in the policies of different states and statesmen, one of these three elements may predominate over the others.[13]

The Boulding and Bull schemes suggest three pathways to peace in South Asia: hegemony and deterrence; cooperation for mutual advantage; and integration through converging values. How is South Asia poised? Has it chosen one pathway over another? What progress has it made towards peace? What is the future of the region?

Pathways to Peace I: Hegemony and Deterrence

The first pathway to peace is the coercive one of the political realists: either hegemonic power or mutual deterrence prevents the outbreak of war.

Hegemonic Peace: Are There Any Hegemons Out There?

In a regional system, there exist potentially two sorts of hegemons: powerful outsiders and powerful insiders. Either or both could impose a peace by the deployment of superior capabilities. The hegemon might simply pose an existential threat by virtue of its superior capabilities. In a hegemonic situation, lesser powers might routinely anticipate and adjust to the hegemon's wishes, including its desire for a regional peace. If not, the hegemon may construct a peace through a deliberate and careful policy of carrots and sticks. The hegemon may deploy military or economic power or even "discursive" power, that is, the power to frame the ways in which we think about problems and formulate solutions to them, to cajole and coerce regional state towards a peace settlement. The last of these, discursive power, it may be objected, sits uneasily with the notion of "threats," but the power to manipulate another's worldview is a potent instrument.

Powerful Outsiders

South Asia has a history of powerful outsiders involving themselves—or being asked to involve themselves—in regional affairs. Britain and the U.S., the Soviet Union, China, and Iran have from time-to-time intervened in regional matters. All of them except China have attempted to bring principally India and Pakistan together so as to avert polarization and war in the subcontinent. They have done so primarily in the service of their own geopolitical interests.

If one stands back from the history of the region from 1947 onwards, one can see in retrospect quite clearly that powerful outsiders were involved continuously but consecutively in trying to bring peace to the region: Britain and the U.S. from 1948–1963, the Soviet Union from 1964–1969, Iran from 1969–1979, and the U.S. once again since 1980.[14] Britain was an imperial power on its way to becoming a regional military and economic power. As a partner of the U.S. and later as an influential member of the European Community, it had greater strategic reach than most regional powers. For some years, in the aftermath of colonialism, it disposed of a certain degree of discursive power in South Asia. Iran never possessed the military, economic or discursive power of a hegemon, nor does it now 14 years after the Khomeini revolution, but its oil wealth gave it certain leverage in regional affairs. The Soviet Union possessed the military attributes of a hegemon, whereas its economic and discursive power was limited.[15] The U.S. which commanded the three attributes of a hegemon, when it was not indifferent to the region, either cooperated with the Soviet Union or was balanced by Soviet power in respect of South Asian affairs. In sum, from 1947 to 1989, no outside power quite commanded the position of a hegemon.

Have matters changed with the end of the Cold War? Britain and Iran, obviously, remain regional powers and exert little influence in South Asia. The Soviet Union no longer exists, and its major successor, the Russian Federation, is beset by enormous internal political, economic, and social problems that preclude an active role except in more or less adjacent regions. The dissolution of the Soviet Union has left but one outright superpower, namely, the U.S.: only the U.S. possesses military, economic, and discursive power of global reach. In addition, China must be reckoned a quasi-superpower, at least throughout Asia. No region in the continent can escape the shadow of Chinese military power; and in the years to come, few will escape the thrust of its economic power. One pathway to peace in South Asia, in theory, then, is for the U.S. and China, jointly or separately, to manage relations between India and its neighbors, and specifically between India and Pakistan, which is the only relationship of any great geopolitical significance for powerful outsiders.

What are the prospects of a U.S. or Chinese-powered peace in South Asia? First of all, do the U.S. or Chinese want peace in South Asia? I claim that they do. The U.S. wants peace because it is anxious to stop if not roll back nuclear proliferation worldwide. It sees the India–Pakistan conflict, now centered round Kashmir, as a situation that could lead to conventional war and even escalate to nuclear war. The India–Pakistan crisis of 1987 and the putative crisis of 1990 have been read by Washington as near-nuclear crises.[16] The Chinese since 1976 have encouraged India's neighbors, including Pakistan, to resolve their differences. Beijing's (now Peking) stand on various regional quarrels such as Kashmir and on India's internal problems especially in the Northeast has ameliorated.[17] China's interest in a South Asian peace is related to a vital security objective, namely, to reduce tensions in and around its borders. Japan, Taiwan, Vietnam, and someday a united Korea of 80 million, all these in league with the U.S. are a great source of worry.[18] Peace and stability on China's southwestern border is essential if Beijing is to concentrate on the much greater threats on its eastern flank.

Given that both the U.S. and China have an interest in fostering peace in South Asia, are they in a position to do so? Hegemons can construct a peace in three ways. They may through their superior power quite simply demand peace, with the threat that economic but also military punishment will be used to obtain compliance. On the other hand, they may promise to underwrite a peace by economic and other perhaps even military rewards (e.g., arms transfers, security guarantees). Yet another view of hegemony is that it is the power to make and enforce the "rules of the game" which encourage or constrain certain types of behavior—the ultimate threat is the threat of economic sanctions and military coercion, but in an everyday sense it is the ability to "legislate" for others that defines hegemony. Underlying this legislative ability is ideological power wherein the values, goals, rules, institutions, and practices of the hegemon are so widely diffused and legitimated that its worldview is naturalized and internalized as the correct view. Put somewhat differently: hegemons possess not just military and economic but also discursive power.[19]

What are the prospects, then, for a hegemonic peace in South Asia brokered by the U.S. and China? First of all, it is unlikely that the U.S. and China will combine to put military or economic pressure on South Asians. They have a parallel interest in a peaceful, stable South Asia, but the issue of proliferation divides them. The U.S. is aggressively antiproliferationist. It opposes the spread of nuclear weapons and missiles and sees proliferation as a powerful de-stabilizer of the region. China has joined the Non-Proliferation Treaty (NPT) but remains softer on proliferation, arguing that while it opposes the spread of weapons of mass destruction states must choose according to their security needs. Thus, Beijing has, by many accounts, helped Pakistan's nuclear and missile program, although the Chinese deny that what they have done contravenes anti-proliferation measures such as the NPT and the Missile Technology Control Regime (MTCR).

Second, while China is going to be a first-rank power in 20 or 30 years, it is not yet hegemonically placed in relation to the rest of Asia or even South Asia. It has neither the requisite military or economic might. At best, it may be in a position to play some form of mediating and persuading role. China has been a long-time Pakistani ally and has a substantial arms relationship with Islamabad. On the other side, relations with India continue to improve: over the past five years the two countries have instituted a confidence-building measures (CBM) process; they have agreed in principle to troop reductions along the border; they have liberalized border trade and increased state-to-state and open trading; and they have even made some—if small—progress on the border quarrel. China has reassured New Delhi on Kashmir, and India continues to reassure Beijing on Tibet.[20] Given its diplomatic friendship and arms relationship with Pakistan, improved relations with India, and the desire for a more peaceful and stable South Asia, Beijing could play a role in moderating Islamabad's stand on various India–Pakistan issues.

However, there are constraints on China's ability to play even this relatively modest role. Washington is unlikely to cede leadership in South Asia to China that it already views as perhaps the greatest threat to U.S. power in the 21st century. Then, while the relationship with Pakistan has endured and while the arms relationship with Islamabad gives Beijing a certain degree of leverage, its influence with Pakistani leaders has limits. Pakistan's Islamic connections and credentials are important to Beijing which is worried about the resurgence of Muslim religious feeling in Central Asia and inside its own borders, particularly Xinjiang. Moreover, any attempt to put pressure on Pakistan beyond a point may push Islamabad into Washington's arms. Given Pakistan's location on China's southwestern flank, this would be dangerous. Finally, New Delhi remains suspicious of Beijing and is fiercely opposed to Chinese meddling in what it sees as India's strategic backyard.

This leaves the U.S. as a potential hegemonic peacemaker in South Asia. While Washington has moved towards a more active role in South Asia since 1991, various factors will constrain the U.S. playing the role of a pacifying hegemon. For one thing, Washington has an enormous amount on its strategic plate: relations with Russia; economic and diplomatic relations with major competitors in Europe and Asia; security in East Asia, especially in Taiwan and the Korean peninsula; and, perhaps most of all, the economic and military growth of China. All this must be tackled by an administration that does not hide that it is more interested in "domestic" than in foreign affairs and in economic over political matters. Moreover, this heavy agenda of international issues must be engaged at a time when the U.S. no longer has a clear "grand strategy" and when it must therefore spend time inventing a basic strategic posture even as it tries to deal with day-to-day problems in various theaters.

In addition to these general constraints, there are various constraints particular to South Asia. Proliferation or not, the region remains a relatively minor U.S. concern. It is difficult to see the U.S. committing military might, diplomatic attention, and economic resources to cajole and coerce India and Pakistan in the way that it has done over 20 years or so in the Middle East—and yet nothing less than that kind of engagement will suffice for a subcontinental peace.[21] That said, India and Pakistan are not just ordinary regional adversaries. In population size, India is largest military and, in aggregate, is one of the top 10 economies in the world. Pakistan, if it were located in any other region, away from such giants as India and China, would be a regional power on the order of Indonesia or Nigeria.[22] Neither country, therefore, is susceptible to the kinds of pressure that the U.S. has been able to apply in other regions—the Middle East, southern Africa, and Korea. Finally, as U.S. power balances China's in Asia, so Chinese power will check U.S. power. Beijing is uneasy with the idea of U.S. hegemonism on China's peripheries and can be expected therefore to play a limiting role.

Not surprisingly, U.S. policy towards South Asia is not very ambitious. On proliferation, it has moved perceptibly away from the formula of "cap, rollback, eliminate." Washington seems to be coming a round to the view that any attempt to rollback and eliminate the two nuclear programs is causing India and Pakistan to dig in their heels, as on the Comprehensive Test Ban Treaty (CTBT) and as may also be the case on the Fissile Material Cutoff Treaty (FMCT). The U.S. policy is therefore more focused on capping or freezing nuclear programs. Since this is not likely within either a multilateral (e.g., CTBT or FMCT) or regional framework, Washington is attempting to engage both sides independently. Pressure on Pakistan and the resumption of the India—U.S. dialogue after the CTBT are part of the strategy of engagement with the two countries. Increasingly visibly in U.S. non-proliferation policies, especially since the North Korea agreements, is the use of a carrot and stick approach. There is caution here, but the signs are unmistakable that Washington is exploring the possibility of cutting deals with India and Pakistan even as it tightens the non-proliferation regime. In India, in particular, there is a growing recognition of the new U.S. approach and a greater willingness than before to see where this leads within the broad contours of Indian policy, namely, to stay outside the NPT and CTBT.

The second part of U.S. policy relates to Kashmir. The U.S. decision makers see a link between the Kashmir quarrel and proliferation. Continuing, and escalating, tensions over the issue could, in their estimation, reach a flashpoint. At the limit, there could be war, with the danger that nuclear weapons might come into play. Washington recognizes that if there is not greater stability in Kashmir its non-proliferation effort could well come to naught.

While the U.S. is concerned about Kashmir, there are signs that, as with non-proliferation, it has chosen to play a less obtrusive role in promoting stability. Its policy is essentially to encourage bilateral talks. Thus, it has praised the resumed Foreign Secretaries' meetings that include discussions on Kashmir. At the same time, Washington insists that it is not interested in a mediatory role. In reality, the U.S. is implicated even when it chooses to remain on the sidelines, aloofness being seen in Islamabad as a tilt towards India! As things stand, U.S. policy is indeed tilting towards India. It has stopped making statements questioning the accession of Kashmir to India (which does not mean that it has changed its official policy on the dispute) and has been restrained in its criticism of human rights violations in the state. Its naming of the Harkat ul-Ansar and others such organizations as terrorist organization is seen in India as a vindication of New Delhi's view that Pakistan is linked to the militancy.[23] This is part of an attempt to recognize India as not just a Big Emerging Market but also a diplomatic player of some consequence.

On both nuclear weapons and Kashmir, the U.S. is continuing to use its discursive power to help forge agreements. Washington is trying to shape the way South Asians think about both issues, especially proliferation. A case in point is confidence-building measures (CBMs). In the early 1990s, U.S. policy makers urged India and Pakistan to explore the possibility of CBMs as a way of stabilizing the military relationship in South Asia. U.S. experts and diplomats drew attention to the Cold War experience of NATO and the Warsaw Pact as well as the superpowers. The "Open Skies" agreement in Europe also figured in U.S. suggestions about the kind of East-West CBMs that might be emulated by South Asia. The 1990s has seen a number of track two dialogues between the U.S. and Indians and Pakistanis. Clearly, one aspect of those dialogues is the fashioning of an arms control vocabulary and sensibility within which proliferation can be discussed. On Kashmir, there is a less obvious effort to structure the discursive space. However, the frequent references to the experience of other regions, in particular the Middle East and Southeast Asia, and the dynamics of their peace processes is part of a discursive move.

Powerful Insiders

A hegemonic peace in South Asia may, alternatively, be based on Indian military, economic, and discursive power. That India has not been able to accomplish such a peace with Pakistan is obvious enough: the two countries have gone to war on three occasions (1948, 1965, and 1971). In January 1987, there was the most serious war-scare in the Subcontinent since 1971. Three years later, there was reputedly another major crisis.

With respect to the smaller states of South Asia, though, India does indeed enjoy a militarily and economically hegemonic or near-hegemonic position. Over the years various disputes have marked their relations, but India and the smaller states have not gone to war and, apart from the 1986 India-Sri Lanka war scare, there has been no prospect of war. This is not particularly surprising. Indian military and economic power is so vastly superior to the power of any combination of smaller states in South Asia that no one is in a position to confront New Delhi for very long.[24]

There is little prospect that India's hegemonic position with respect to the smaller states will change. Indeed, there is a good chance that it will increase, especially if India enjoys a spurt in economic growth. Were India, under the push of the recent reforms, to continue on a course of economic growth of 7 percent per annum, in 10 years its GNP would double. In 20 years, that is, by 2015, it would double again. This growth may of course boost military capacity in different degrees motivated by Indian concerns about Himalayan security. In return, India is responsible for the security of the smaller states. It is directly so for Bhutan and Nepal for whom New Delhi has also taken on broader responsibilities, particularly developmental. It is Bhutan's major aid donor and allows Nepalis to own property and work in India without hindrance (with no obligation on Nepal to reciprocate). After the Indian operation to save the government of Abdul Gayoom, there is an implicit recognition that India is expected to guarantee the Maldives' security as well. After the 1987 accord, India has a tacit responsibility to respond to threats to Sri Lankan security if called upon to do so.[25] India has not entered into security-related responsibilities with Pakistan (although the two sides raised the idea of a no-war/common defense pact or friendship and cooperation treaty in 1949–50, 1953, 1956, 1959, 1968, 1969, 1974, 1977, and 1980–82)[26]; but even here what is worth noting is that after the Simla Agreement of 1972, Pakistan accepted bilateralism and the normalization of relations with India.

The Gujral Doctrine is the latest attempt by India to fashion a new order in South Asia. The doctrine encompasses five principles: first, unilateralism in the sense that India will "not insist on reciprocity for any concession [it] has made"; second, vigilance in not allowing its territory "to be used against the interest of any country in the area"; third, non-interference "in the internal affairs of other countries in the area," with the expectation that others will match India's commitment; fourth, respect for the territorial integrity and sovereignty of regional states; and finally, dispute settlement through bilateral negotiations.[27]

The new turn in Indian diplomacy has contributed to a more peaceful South Asia in four ways. First, in promoting agreements with the smaller states, the doctrine has reduced the resentment and suspicion they harbor towards India. It has also reduced their incentive or desire for external reassurance and balance in their relationship with their giant neighbor. This will further reduce the friction in India's relations with the smaller states. New Delhi tends to see the smaller states as Trojan Horses for external powers, and, to the extent that these countries feel they can settle with India, their incentive to reach out to the U.S. or China is reduced.

Second, if the new diplomacy reassures Bangladesh and Nepal in particular, it invests in the political stability of the entire Northeast. As their confidence in New Delhi increases, Dhaka and Kathmandu can be expected to restrain in activities of Indian dissidents who may be operating from their territory. The doctrine is intended to be a reassurance, at the same time, that India will not support dissidents from the smaller countries.

Third, to the extent that the doctrine leads to the making and implementation of agreements such as Mahakali and Ganges water sharing, it is an investment also in the economic development of this most difficult corner of South Asia. The agreements themselves relate to the management of key resources that can in various ways strengthen the economic development prospects of Nepal and Bangladesh. One of the key potential benefits of generalized economic development in both countries will, over time, be to reduce the incentive to migrate to India. The migration of Bangladeshi Muslims in particular has led to increasing resentment not just in the Northeast and West Bengal but also in many big Indian cities and is a growing security problem. A better life in their own country should encourage potential migrants to stay put.

Agreements with India's neighbors and the new accommodating style will have a more direct economic benefit. They will help disarm critics of India who oppose Indian trade and investment. Thus, in both Bangladesh and Sri Lanka, the receptivity to trade with India is related to their liberalization efforts but also to a general warming to India. Bangladesh is already India's fifteenth largest trading partner. Indian trade with Sri Lanka will soon surpass Japan's. In sum, by promoting economic gain and benefits, it is helping pacify regional troublespots and conflict.

Lastly, the various bilateral agreements with the smaller states have threatened to isolate Pakistan. India's success on the Mahakali with Nepal and the Ganges with Bangladesh suggests that it is Pakistan, not India, which is being obdurate. This enables New Delhi to increase the pressure on Islamabad to come to terms on key issues.

The Gujral Doctrine, it should be noted, is not the act of a weak idealistic power. Rather, it is the sign of a regional hegemon. The doctrine is not a statement of unilateralist concessions. It articulates a set of responsibilities for India's neighbors as much as for India. For example, it insists on noninterference in India's internal affairs even as it promises not to interfere in the domestic politics of the smaller states. The affirmation of bilateralism has long been the cornerstone of India's approach to the region, and there is no derogation of that approach. The doctrine lays down a set of norms and practices for South Asia. It undertakes to abide by some norms and practices and in return suggests that the rest of the region do so too—with the implicit "threat" that India could always abide by some less palatable norms and practices. Here is a classic hegemonic order: reward and the withdrawal of reward. Only a hegemon has the power to promise, and do, both.

In sum, India is a full-fledged hegemon for Bhutan and Nepal and a quasi-hegemon for Bangladesh and Sri Lanka. Indian power will overshadow the region, although Pakistan will continue to challenge India. The Gujral Doctrine is a show of power, not the opposite.

The Limits of Hegemony

Let me end here by reconsidering the more general point. A peace that rests on hegemonic forces and economic power is not an efficient, lasting, and warm peace. As soon as a hegemon turns its back or appears to be losing military and economic power, hegemonically brokered agreements may unravel. Moreover, what a hegemon at one strategic moment gives, it may at another moment take away. On the other hand, a hegemony that knows how to diagnose conflict and how to conceptualize solutions will be more durable because it will fashion a psychological and intellectual shift.

Deterrent Peace: If You Want Peace, Prepare for War

A deterrent peace is a minimalist peace. It is the absence of war as a function of mutual threats. While India's relations with its smaller neighbors are hegemonic, the relationship with Pakistan is one of mutual deterrence. Since 1971, the two sides have maintained an uneasy deterrent peace.[28] With the near-nuclearization of the subcontinent, South Asia is moving closer to a deterrent system based on conventional and nuclear threats. Deterrent systems are ultimately unstable, however, and India and Pakistan need to incorporate CBMs and arms control into their military relationship in order to supplement and thereby stabilize deterrence.

Glenn Snyder has clarified that deterrence is achievable in two ways—by *denial* and by *punishment*. Deterrence by denial involves convincing a potential attacker that one has the will and means to deny it a tangible military objective (usually territory). Deterrence by punishment, on the other hand, rests on the ability to convince a potential attacker that one has the will and the means to inflict unacceptable levels of punishment.[29]

In the India–Pakistan case, deterrence has held fast at the conventional level since 1971. At the nuclear level, too, the avowed purpose of the weapons is to effect deterrence. At the conventional level, both sides have opted for a combination of denial and punishment. They have erected various forms of static defence along the border aimed at stopping armored and mobile columns from rapidly breaking through and gaining territory or moving towards key nerve centers. They have also, since 1972, attempted to refine "offensive defence" may consist of a diversionary attack or pre-emption. In 1965, India showed that diversionary attack was a viable defence when, to relieve pressure along the Line of Control (LoC) in Kashmir, it crossed the international border and sent its forces into East Punjab and Sind. The possibility that either side could use a major diversionary attack as an effective defence remains a threat and therefore potentially a deterrent.[30] Moreover, both India and Pakistan have stressed that in the next round—if there is one—they will not rest content to wait for an attack but will launch an attack if they detect preparations for a strike. The possibility that an opponent is prepared to pre-empt may also serve to deter.

While the threat of diversionary attack or pre-emption may enhance deterrence, it should be noticed that this form of deterrence is unstable and may invite the very hostilities it seeks to prevent. First, if either side cannot clearly distinguish between rehearsals for a diversionary attack (which are motivated by deterrence and defence) and rehearsals for an offensive-minded first-strike, it may be tempted to pre-empt, thus bringing on war. Second, if either side cannot distinguish between a posture of pre-emption in a defensive and deterrent sense and one that, once again, is a first-strike posture, then it may choose to "pre-empt pre-emption," leading to war.[31]

At the nuclear level, various nuclear choices are being articulated, each consistent with some form of deterrence. In India, one can identify the following: *tous azimuts, minimum, recessed, short-order weaponization, nuclear incrementalism*, and *ambiguity*.

At one end of the spectrum of choices is *outright and full nuclearization*, what the French call a *tous azimuts* or *all horizon* strategy. This would involve an ambitious program geared eventually to meeting every, and all threats—nuclear but also conventional—from rivals near and far. What such an ambitious program risks is expanding the horizon of threats. A *tous azimuts* Indian program would instill fear in Southeast Asia, the Gulf, the Middle East, the Indian Ocean rim, and, depending on missile capabilities, as far away as Europe including Russia, North America, and East Asia. These states and regions might move towards counter-capabilities, thus vastly complicating India's threat structure. Nobody responsible in India has advocated such a posture: it is evidently beyond India's technological and economic capabilities in the foreseeable future; and would seem to run against the grain of nuclear politics globally which are in recession with the U.S. and Russia making serious cuts in strategic weaponry.[32]

Minimum deterrence is a transparent posture. It does not attempt to hide the possession of nuclear weapons, indeed, quite the reverse—it advertises their availability, even their number. Moreover, it rests on assembled and reliable weapons—reliable in the sense that they have been tested. An advocate of minimal deterrence posture, K. Subrahmanyam, calculates that for India, 60 warheads on airplanes and the *Prithvi* and *Agni* missiles are enough if they are dispersed and mobile so that they cannot be eliminated in a first strike.[33] The most important problem here is how to handle the transition period between the present and a minimum deterrence future in the region.

A third set of nuclear choices is *short-order weaponization, recessed deterrence*, and *nuclear incrementalism*.[34] A general term for these may be "non-weaponized deterrence." While there are differences between these three postures, a non-weaponized posture is one in which the components of a deliverable weapon have been or are close to being assembled, and there is a high degree of confidence that when a device is fully assembled it will, if delivered on a target, detonate. These postures may not require weapons tests. The Indian test of 1974 has presumably certified a basic weapon design, and, as long as India is satisfied with a Pokharan-type bomb, further testing is probably unnecessary.[35]

Non-weaponized postures are different from a posture of ambiguity. They are different in the degree of proximity to a usable weapon and the extent of transparency in respect of the posture. The closer to a usable weapon and the more transparent, the closer one is to non-weaponized deterrence.

The fundamental question though is this: what are the costs and benefits of non-weaponization? Why not go outright nuclear, if only up to a minimal deterrent posture? What is gained through non-assembly? What is lost? This remains to be clarified beyond the assertion that it is a more economic posture and one that invites less opprobrium and anger on the part of powerful outsiders such as the U.S. It may not turn out to be financially cheaper than minimal deterrence—indeed one could argue that it may be dearer; and it may not invite less opposition from outsiders who will see it as virtual weaponization—indeed, once again, it may invite greater opposition on the argument that it is a less stable posture than outright weaponization which is the basis for arms control and confidence-building. One gain, it may be argued, is that it avoids investment in most of the infrastructure that the other nuclear powers undertook to build. But this depends on which non-weaponized posture is chosen—with or without (a) testing, (b) elaborate command and control and infrastructure, and (c) rigorous doctrine.

However, the key difficulty of answering the cost/benefit question can be seen if we ask: is the slowness a cost or a benefit? Is this a forgiving posture which slows escalation and therefore allows plenty of time for an opponent (who sees moves towards assembly) to recant, retrench, and repent; or is too forgiving and does it invite aggression and risk-taking from an opponent?

Nuclear *ambiguity* is a position wherein research and production moves towards a weapons option but leaves fuzzy how far it has gone. Thus, this position is compatible with denial of a nuclear weapons program along with carefully leaked information on progress towards weaponization. It achieves deterrence, it is argued, by playing on uncertainty. The target of an ambiguous posture can never be certain that the opponent does not possess nuclear weapons and may thus be frightened into avoiding war. The trouble with ambiguity as a strategic posture is that it is difficult to sustain beyond a point: as more and more information is leaked regarding progress towards a usable weapon, ambiguity will verge over into a non-weaponized or minimal deterrent posture; and if not enough is leaked, an opponent may doubt that a usable device exists and therefore may be tempted to challenge the would-be deterrent power. Moreover, ambiguity makes confidence building and arms control difficult. If states are unwilling to admit or deny certain capabilities, how can they enter into confidence building and arms control agreements which are premised on verifiability and transparency?

As this "debate" indicates, in India there is in motion a shift in thinking (though not as far as we know in policy)—from postures that stress ambiguity to more overt postures. From among the more overt postures, some form of short-order weaponization seems most likely wherein India and Pakistan declare and keep but do not augment their stocks of fissile material and abstain from deploying a fully assembled weapon. This more transparent nuclear environment in South Asia would be the basis for a dialogue on CBMs and arms control as a means of stabilizing mutual nuclear postures: as noted above, if states neither admit to, nor deny, possessing stocks of fissile material and deliverable or near-deliverable weapons, it is difficult to see how various stabilizing measures can be negotiated between them. Threat systems tend to degrade as the credibility of threats decline. The credibility of threats may be a function of a myriad of factors but three are fundamental: capabilities, provocability, and commitment. A deterrer must be seen to possess a reliable means of carrying out the threat of punishment; it must communicate clearly the conditions under which punishment will be visited on an adversary, that is, it must clarify its provocability; and it must demonstrate a willingness to punish infringements of those conditions, that is, it must leave no doubt about its commitment.[36] CBMs and arms control are a means of stabilizing deterrence: they can clarify that capabilities are tied to deterrence postures and not to first-strike posture and they can outlaw practices, deployment, and systems which may be seen as aggressive rather than defensive; they can help define each side's provocability and commitment; and, if deterrence appears to be decaying, they can provide structures for crisis management.

South Asia has begun a CBM process. India and Pakistan have agreed to various measures.[37] On the other hand, they have not yet begun a serious arms control process that defines mutually agreed and acceptable force structures. This is necessary both at the conventional and nuclear level and, in respect of the nuclear, will require both to move away from ambiguity to overtness. To say that it is necessary is not to say though that it will be easy or that it is likely. At least two problems face the Indian and Pakistani governments beyond the unwillingness to move away from nuclear ambiguity. First, some conventional arms control measures—such as force levels and deployments—will have to factor in internal security requirements. Second, India's concerns regarding Chinese conventional and nuclear capability will have to be addressed. Prior to these, of course, must be the recognition in both countries that arms control measures are desirable as adjuncts of deterrence and are not diplomatic surrenders to the West or to each other. In a situation where domestic opinion has been aroused against the other and where leaderships fear charges of appeasement from internal rivals, such recognition will not be easy.

Even if India and Pakistan, in spite of these problems, were to reach a state of stable mutual deterrence at the strategic levels (based on conventional and nuclear weapons), there remains the problem of deterrence at the sub-strategic level. India and Pakistan have accused each other of interference in various sub-national conflicts including Punjab, Kashmir, and Sind. Yet they have not constructed a deterrence posture that can cope with this level of aggression. In particular, India has not been able to deter Pakistan from providing arms, money, training, and refuge to Kashmiri militants. Neither conventional nor nuclear retaliation is credible at this level: there is no proportionality between the extent of aggression against India and the extent of pain that would be visited on Pakistan by conventional or nuclear war.

In the absence of a deterrence posture that is effective at the sub-strategic level, there exist instabilities. If both sides calculate that they have achieved strategic stability, there is the danger of brinkmanship at the sub-strategic level. This is ironic: the existence of stability at higher levels, may actually encourage both states to sail perilously close to the wind.[38] With nuclear weapons on both sides, conventional attack is all but ruled out. In this situation, Pakistan may feel that it can increase its support to the Kashmir militancy without fear of large-scale conventional retaliation. India, on the other hand, encouraged by the calculation that Pakistan is deterred from punishing "hot pursuit" forays into its territory, may someday choose to cross the LoC or the border. This sub-strategic brinkmanship could escalate beyond the control of either party.

If brinkmanship and the dangers arising out of it are to be avoided, it would seem that for India only two *deterrent* possibilities exist at the sub-strategic level[39]: the threat of retaliation in kind, that is, support of sub-national militancy in Pakistan (e.g., Sind, Baluchistan), and international opprobrium backed by the threat of diplomatic isolation and various types of sanctions. Pakistani leaders have long accused India of involvement in the Sind unrest. And India has certainly attempted to mobilize international opinion against Pakistan. It is worth mentioning at this point that, curiously, sub-strategic brinkmanship and sub-strategic deterrence may be related. For instance, in retrospect, one can see that the crises of 1987 and 1990 could have been the outcome of rather elaborate games of brinkmanship that were intended to draw the attention of the international community to the follies of the other side and thereby to mobilize international opinion as part of a larger deterrence game.[40]

In sum, then, South Asia has moved in the direction of a deterrent peace between its two principal military rivals, India and Pakistan. With nuclear weapons presumed to exist on both sides, there is agreement that there is deterrence at the level of nuclear and conventional war. However, paradoxically, strategic level deterrence has laid the conditions for sub-strategic instabilities. If these instabilities are not controlled, there is always the possibility that they will undo deterrence at the higher levels. South Asia can ill afford to be complacent about its nuclear status.

Pathways to Peace II: Functionalist Cooperation

David Mitrany and Ernst Haas are the most prominent proponents of what may be called the functionalist path to peace that is based on the notion of exchange and is consistent with the Grotian image of international life.

David Mitrany argues that "a working peace system," which does not abolish but rather transcends nation-states, is the route to peace. Modern states, Mitrany suggests, will increasingly be constrained to deal with various "functional" tasks in collaboration with each other. Government experts or counterparts in other countries will be forced to produce rational solutions to shared problems. This will necessitate the creation of agencies to implement and manage the agreements and, as the agencies in related functional areas group together, they will likely require budgets and an overall coordinating authority. This functional structure will eventually overlay nation-states in the sense that it will deliver services and benefits beyond the capacities of individual states to provide. In such a situation, Mitrany argues, states will continue to exist, but they will not risk war or else incur the wrath of their citizens.[41]

Ernst Haas' "neo-functionalism" suggests that spontaneously chosen functional areas, as in the Mitrany scheme, are insufficient for cooperation. In Haas' neo-functional formulation, cooperative possibilities are maximized by carefully choosing economic and "welfare" areas with "spillover" potential.[42] Neo-functionalists argues that the kind of almost spontaneous functional processes envisaged by functionalists would be too *ad hoc*, would risk being carried out in innocuous areas, and would therefore fail to create political pressure for political integration. Haas' neo-functionalism also suggests that it is not technical experts but, instead, political elites which will lead the way to peace. As elites find they cannot deliver a standard of living their constituencies desire, they will see the advantage of cooperative linkages with elites across the border, even with former enemies. Haas recognizes that the process will not be linear, that there will be plateaus, "spillbacks" and "encapsulations" in cooperation. But he suggests that periodic crises might reinvigorate cooperation by signaling the need for fresh thinking and activity, thus leading to progressively higher levels of mutual involvement and peace: elites would come to understand that earlier levels of involvement and cooperation had yielded benefits and modified relations sufficiently, so that any recursion or stagnation in the process would be too costly.

Does either the Mitrany or Haas brand of functionalism describe a pathway to peace in South Asia? Are South Asians engaged in normal exchange—functional and economic—with each other? Let me focus on the India–Pakistan relationship that is the key to peace in South Asia.

The India–Pakistan relationship is well outside the realm of normal functional and economic exchange.[43] Since 1947, the two countries have progressively disentangled themselves from each other.[44] This has happened despite the fact that the most ambitious functional agreements, the Indus Rivers Treaty (1960) and the Salal Dam agreement (1978), some grumbling notwithstanding, have been honored by both sides and have worked to the advantage of both. The disentangling of India and Pakistan reflects Pakistani preferences more than Indian. Pakistan sees exchange relations as leading to gradual assimilation to an Indian sphere of influence if not outright domination by India.

Why have India and Pakistan not entered into other functional and economic agreements? There is of course the fear of unequal gains, what cooperation theory calls the "relative gains" problem.[45] But neo-functional theory points usefully to another factor. If cooperation arises when an elite perceives an interest in exchange, could it be that such an elite has been absent in the India–Pakistan case? Hamza Alavi has argued that in many post-colonial settings the elites are what he calls a "salariat" composed of the bureaucracy, the armed forces, the intelligentsia, professionals (lawyers, doctors), and a strata of businessmen who are primarily managers (in South Asia, the "boxwallah" class).[46] This elite had no great economic stake in better relations between the two countries: it was a salary-drawing sector, and its economic linkages and preferences were with the former colonial powers or the U.S.

Recent social, economic, and political changes in India and Pakistan reflect the rise of a new elite. A new middle class is pushing upwards, whether the old salariat likes it or not. This is a middle class that is spearheaded by more entrepreneurial strata. Moreover, it is a class that did not live through Partition and, while it may share the prejudices of older generations, it is a materialistic and acquisitive sector of society. It is also outward-looking: it is not bound by the mindset of import substitution and self-sufficiency; it feels it can compete abroad; and it therefore has an eye on export markets. It is a class, finally, that has helped the push towards economic reform and liberalization in both countries, even though sectors of it oppose certain trends in the reform process.

The class could have a stake in functional and economic exchange between India and Pakistan. Its financial and economic power could be wielded to influence foreign policy. There is already evidence that in both countries there is a nascent group that has an interest in more normal economic relations between the two states. For instance, the Chambers of Commerce in both countries are beginning to argue more forcefully for trade. India and Pakistan trade, official plus unofficial, is estimated to equal $1.5 billion and could be much larger if it was encouraged. In Pakistan, the pro-trade group finds support in Nawaz Sharif, himself a new breed of businessman, one outside the traditional "twenty two" families structure.

A related trend is likely to help. Haas' work indicates that an important condition of greater exchange leading to peaceful relations is a certain plurality of social, economic, and political structure.[47] Since 1988, Pakistan has been a pluralist democracy. A democratic Pakistan reflects in part the rise of a new elite that felt suffocated by military government and by the old salariat that in large part supported military government. This new elite finds more room for dissent and for influence. In sum, Pakistan is seeing the growth of a more vibrant and confident civil society which is increasingly capable of opposing, influencing, and questioning the state and its policies, including its foreign policies.[48] In India, which has been democratic longer and where civil society has been stronger, the new elite insists on what might crudely be called "economics over politics," even in the realm of foreign policy. This sector does not want to be friends with Pakistan nor is it necessarily willing to make deals on issues such as Kashmir, but it is interested in increasing economic interactions and it wants to avoid tensions and hostilities.[49]

PATHWAYS TO PEACE III: COMMUNITY

The third, and according to Boulding the most enduring, pathway to peace is the route of community based on the evolution of common, integrating values as in the Kantian vision of international life. Here I want to turn to Karl Deutsch et al.'s work. Deutsch et al.'s *Political Community and the North Atlantic Area* describes how erstwhile enemies and rivals come to be confident that the other will not resort to force to settle mutual disputes. This is not necessarily a relationship of harmony where conflict is absent but rather one where conflict is routinely resolved short of war. Deutsch et al., argue that, broadly speaking, there are two types of peaceful relations that meet this test: an "amalgamated security community" and a "pluralistic security community." An amalgamated security community is one that has a single center of political authority and is therefore the merger of previously autonomous units. A pluralistic security community is one with two or more autonomous centers of political authority in which there exists a long-term expectation that conflict will be resolved peacefully.

Peace Audit on South Asia 63

The latter, namely, a pluralistic security community, is of interest here.[50] Deutsch et al.'s cases suggest that the "background conditions" which are essential to the establishment or success of a pluralistic security community are:

- The compatibility of major values relevant to political decision-making;
- The capacity of the participating political units or governments to respond to each other's needs, messages, and actions quickly, adequately, and without resort to violence which in turn depends on a great many established political habits, and of functioning political institutions, favoring mutual communication and consultation within each state or unit;
- the mutual predictability of behavior.[51]

The authors argue that value compatibility was "most effective when they were not held merely in abstract terms, but when they were incorporated in political institutions and in habits of political behavior which permitted these values to be acted on in such a way as to strengthen people's attachment to them. This connection between *values, institutions,* and *habits* (emphasis mine) we call a 'way of life.'"[52] With respect to Deutsch et al.'s second condition, we can read this to say that political responsiveness between states is greater when their internal political structure and institutions favor "mutual communication and consultation," that is, loosely, when they are more pluralist or democratic. Finally, if there is a convergence in ways of political life, and if political life is moving towards a pluralist and democratic conception which is more accepting of signals and communications from insiders and outsiders, there is likely to be greater predictability of behavior. By predictability, we must understand not so much a precise judgment about future behavior and dispositions but rather a reliable comprehension of what moves and motivates the other side and how the other side interprets incoming signals and communications. As noted earlier, the greater the degree of openness in the other polity, the more likely is such a comprehension.

Does the Deutschian scheme hold out any hope for a South Asian peace? Can South Asian be said to be converging on a political way of life? Is the region moving towards more pluralist and democratic political systems? Is there, commensurately, greater predictability of behavior between states and therefore a greater sense of reassurance with respect to each other?

Since 1988, South Asians have moved towards convergence in their political way of life, in two important respects—democracy, and the relationship of religion and politics. Bangladesh, Nepal, and Pakistan have turned to democratic government and have consolidated democracy, albeit differentially and not without hiccups and instabilities.[53] Sri Lanka, in spite of its devastating civil war, has maintained an open political system, and India, internal violence notwithstanding, has remained democratic. Thus, for the first time since 1947, all the major South Asian states are democratic.

Moreover, those who have come to power in the various elections since 1988 are parties of a secular character—Bhutto's Pakistan Peoples' Party (PPP) and Nawaz Sharif's Islami Jamhoori Ittehad (IJI) in Pakistan, Khaleda Zia's Bangladesh Nationalist Party (BNP) and Sheikh Hasina's Awami League in Bangladesh, and the Nepali Congress and Communists in Nepal.[54] In the Pakistani general elections, the religious parties were almost obliterated. In the Indian state elections of December 1993, Hindu forces were checked: the Bharatiya Janata Party (BJP), the political face of *Hindutva*, lost three of the states it had governed—Himachal Pradesh, Madhya Pradesh, and Uttar Pradesh. In 1996, the BJP made gains nationally, but the secular parties together polled by far the most votes, and the debilitated Congress won the highest percentage of votes of any single party. Although the BJP did come to power in 1996, its governing coalition lasted 12 days. The party's state units are increasingly prone to the kinds of infighting that have bedeviled all other major parties. In Gujarat, this led to a split in the party and the loss of power. The BJP could still come to power nationally, but probably only if it projects a moderate, secularist face.

So, one could say, to use Deutsch's terms, that a key habit on which South Asians are converging is democracy and a key value on which they are converging is secularism. Finally, institutionally, all operate mutually comprehensible political systems: all of them are familiar with and have opted for British-style parliamentary politics. Not only are they converging on a similar way of political life, that life, as suggested above, is democratic. Democracy is a system that is premised on and allows for greater internal communication and consultation. States that make a habit of greater communication and consultation internally are also more likely to be states prone to communicate and consult externally.[55] In addition, they will be prone to allow greater contact trans-nationally. With respect to the latter, it is worth noting that non-official contact between South Asian countries has scarcely been more frequent and widespread.[56]

If South Asian countries have moved closer in their political way of life and if the increasingly democratic way of South Asian political life is the condition for more communication and consultation, then one can say that over time there should be greater mutual predictability and reassurance. Specifically, one should expect that India and its neighbors—because virtually all conflicts in the region are bilateral between India and the rest—will draw closer to a pluralistic security community wherein they remain sovereign states but regulate their conflicts short of force or the threat of force.

The key bilateral relationship is of course India–Pakistan. Now, it could be argued that India–Pakistan relations have scarcely been worse—in spite of a certain degree of political convergence and growing non-official contact. Indeed, some outside the region and even some within fear that "the long peace" since 1972 may be broken over Kashmir, at least in part because populist parties, given free rein in increasingly turbulent democratic systems, will use the conflict to maneuver for domestic political advantage and thus force those in government to harden their stands.[57] While this is plausible enough, and while the history of India–Pakistan relations shows that democratic governments can be intractable and noisy, it is likely that in an open polity governments are going to be more accountable and that those who oppose war will have greater political space in which to say why they oppose it and why they should be supported.[58] There is nothing inevitable about the latter possibility (especially when we reflect on the fact that democracy is compatible with internal war such as in Sind, Kashmir, Sri Lanka), and we should not lose sight of the possibility of a populist engendered war, but accountability and organized debate and dissent over the long-haul should cause the proponents of peace to prevail over the proponents of war. The election of Nawaz Sharif in Pakistan in 1997 is a sign that the process may have begun.

Conclusion

South Asians, as all other groups of conflictual and cooperative states, have a choice of three roads to peace: a hegemonic or deterrent peace; a functional peace; and an integrative peace. The region displays advance along each road. However, hegemony and deterrence are inherently limited in their ability to bring peace beyond a point. Functionalist and economic cooperation leading to peace encounters the problem of "relative gains," but this can be overcome by cooperative agreements that protect weaker actors. Moreover, with the growth of a more vibrant civil society led by a new, more entrepreneurial middle class, the prospects of a functionalist peace have improved. The most stable, long-term road to peace is the integrative path of community building wherein force as a means of resolving conflict is more or less permanently absent. Convergence in South Asia's political way of life towards democracy, secularism and parliamentary institutions, while by no means irreversible, presages a unique moment in regional politics, one that should lead down the integrative path in the millennium to come.

Notes and References

1. Unpublished lecture at the first South Asian Peace Studies Orientation Course held by the Maulana Abul Kalam Azad Institute of Asian Studies, Calcutta, October 1997.
2. See to the contrary, the classic dictum of Vegetius (4th–5th century AD): *Si vis pacem, para bellum*—"If you want peace, prepare for war."
3. A useful anthology on peace is Raimo Vayrynen (with Dieter Senghaas and Christian Schmidt) (ed.), *The Quest for Peace: Transcending Collective Violence and War Among Societies, Cultures, and States.* Beverly Hills, CA, 1987.

4. Kenneth Boulding, "Peace and the Evolutionary Process," in Vayrynen (ed.), *The Quest for Peace*, pp. 48–59.
5. Hedley Bull, *The Anarchical Society: A Study of Order in World Politics*. New York, 1977.
6. See Kenneth Waltz, *Theory of International Politics*. New York, 1979.
7. On the relative gain problem, see Joseph Grieco, "Anarchi and the Limits of Cooperation: A Realist Critique of the Newest Liberal Institutionalism," *International Organization* 42(Summer 1988), pp. 485–507.
8. See Robert Jervis, "Realism, Game Theory, and Cooperation," *World Politics* 40(April 1988), pp. 3332–50 for the view that integrating values are important for cooperation.
9. For the argument that Hobbes and others such as Machiavelli and Thucydides are (mis)appropriated by political realists and that their thought does not lend itself easily to the realist tradition, see R.B.J. Walker, *Inside/Outside: International Relations as Political Theory*. Cambridge, 1993 and Daniel Garst, "Thucydides and Neorealism," *International Studies Quarterly* 33(March 1989), pp. 3–27.
10. Bull, *Anarchical Society*, p. 25.
11. Bull, *Anarchical Society*, pp. 26–27. For Grotius' writings, see M.G. Forsyth, H.M.A. Keens-Soper, and P. Savigear (eds), *The Theory of International Relations: Selected Texts from Gentili to Treitschke*. London, 1970, pp. 37–86.
12. Bull, *Anarchical Society*, pp. 25–26. For a selection of Kant's writings, see Forsyth, Keens-Soper, and Savigear (eds), *Theory of International Relations*, pp. 181–258.
13. Bull, *The Anarchical Society*, p. 41.
14. See Kanti Bajpai and Stephen P. Cohen, "Cooperative Security and South Asian Insecurity," in Janne Nolan (ed.), *Global Engagement: Cooperation and Security in the 21st Century* (Washington, D.C.: Brookings Institution, 1994), pp. 447–80, for a brief recovery of this history of outsider involvement in the region.
15. Stephen Clarkson shows how even at the height of its involvement with India the Soviet Union made little intellectual impact on Indians. See his "The Low Impact of Soviet Writing and Aid on Indian Thinking and Policy," *Survey* 20(Winter 1974), pp. 1–23.
16. See Kanti Bajpai, P.R. Chari, Pervaiz I. Cheema, Stephen P. Cohen, and Sumit Ganguly, *Brasstacks and Beyond: Perception and Management of Crisis in South Asia*. New Delhi, 1995 on the 1987 crisis. On 1990, see Seymour Hersh, "On the Nuclear Edge," *The New Yorker*, 29 March 1993. For the view that the nuclear dimension of the 1990 crisis and the prospect of war has been exaggerated by Hersh and by William E. Burrows and Robert Windrem, *Critical Mass: The Dangerous Race for Superweapons in a Fragmenting World*. London, 1994, see C. Raja Mohan,

"Claims on 1990 Crisis Disputed," *The Hindu*, 18 February 1994, which cites various US policy-makers to this effect.
17. Diplomatic relations between India and China were restored in 1976. The following year, the two countries resumed trade relations. In 1979, Indian Foreign Minister Vajpayee visited Beijing which lead to the reopening of border talks, and in June 1980 Beijing declared Kashmir to be a bilateral problem between India and Pakistan. See Rosemary Foot, "The Sino-Soviet Complex and South Asia," in Barry Buzan, Gowher Rizvi, Rosemary Foot, and Nancy Jetly, *South Asian Insecurity and the Great Powers*. London 1986. Manoranjan Mohanty, "India–China Relations on the Eve of the Asian Century," in Ramakant (ed.), *China and South Asia*. New Delhi, 1988), p. 73 and p. 79 refers to Chinese signals to India's neighbors to settle matters with New Delhi.
18. See Andrew J. Nathan and Robert S. Ross, *The Great Wall and the Empty Fortress: China's Search for Security*. New York, 1997 for an overview of China's security problematic.
19. Jack Donnelly, "Progress in Human Rights," in Emmanuel Adler and Beverly Crawford (eds), *Progress in Post War International Relations*. New York, 1991, p. 348 refers to this more Gramscian notion of hegemony. See also Robert Keohane, *After Hegemony*, Princeton, 1984 and Stephen Gill (ed.), *Gramsci, Historical Materialism and International Relations*. Cambridge, 1993.
20. Haroon Habib, "Kashmir Issue Should be Solved Bilaterally," *The Hindu*, 28 February 1994.
21. Stephen P. Cohen has called for an ambitious engatement with the Subcontinent in his articles on a "South Asian Regional Initiative" or SARI.
22. Stephen P. Cohen, *The Pakistan Army*. New Delhi, 1984, p. 11, has made this point.
23. See, "Harkat Ban: India Feels 'Vindicated'", *Indian Express* (New Delhi), October 10, 1997.
24. Nepal, in 1988–89, discovered that India could reshape its political choices rather effectively. New Delhi simply curtailed the number of transit points at the border and the supply of various commodities. The trouble with India ended monarchical rule and led to the resumption of democratic politics.
25. One should recall here that India came to Sri Lanka's aid during the JVP rebellion in 1971.
26. See Bajpai and Cohen, "Cooperative Security and South Asian Insecurity," in Janne Nolan (ed.), *Global Engagement: Cooperation and Security in the 21st Century*.
27. I.K. Gujral, "The Post Cold War Era," *World Affairs*, Vol. 1, No. 1 (March 1997), p. 51.
28. That it is a peace based altogether on deterrence is a hard proposition to prove. The fact that two parties have not fought is necessarily a function of deterrence. The absence of war may mean that neither was spoiling for a fight, that there were not

cassus belli. Nevertheless, certainly since the early 1980s, when India began to accuse Pakistan of involvement in the Punjab, and later, with the Kashmir troubles, there have been two potential *cassus belli*. Yet in spite of periodic crises, India and Pakistan have not gone to war. *Prima facie*, one could argue, that what has prevented war has been deterrence.

29. Glenn Snyder, *Deterrence and Defense: Toward a Theory of National Security.* Princeton, 1961.
30. For the uses of a diversionary attack in conventional deterrence, see Samuel P. Huntington, "Conventional Deterrence and Conventional Retaliation in Europe," in Keith A. Dunn and William O. Staudenmaier (eds), *Military Strategy in Transition: Defense and Deterrence in the 1980s.* Boulder, 1984, pp. 15–41. Also on conventional deterrence strategies, see John J. Mearsheimer, *Conventional Deterrence.* Ithaca, 1983 and James R. Golden, Asa A. Clark, and Bruce E. Arlinghaus (eds), *Conventional Deterrence: Alternatives for European Defense.* Lexington, 1984.
31. On this tendency to preempt the preempter, see Glenn H. Snyder, "The Conditions of Stability," in Robert J. Art and Kenneth N. Waltz (eds), *The Use of Force: International Politics and Foreign Policy*, 2nd edition. NewYork, 1983, p. 70.
32. Bharat Karnad of the Centre for Policy Research, New Delhi, has publicly advocated more or less a *tous azimuts* posture, arguing that India should be prepared to deter even the US. He made these remarks in "A Question of Answers," a weekly public affairs television show on Star TV hosted by Vir Sanghvi, which aired on October 5 and 11, 1997. Other panelists included K. Subrahmanyam, General K. Sundarji, and this author.
33. See K. Subrahmanyam, "Nuclear Force Design and Minimum Deterrence Strategy for India," in Bharat Karnad (ed.), *Future Imperilled: India's Security in the 1990s and Beyond.* New Delhi, 1994, pp. 176–95.
34. See George Perkovitch's article "A Nuclear Third Way?" *Foreign Policy*, Fall 1993, on short-order weaponization (term mine). Jasjit Singh, Director, Institute for Defense Studies and Analyses (IDSA), New Delhi, is the author of the notion of "recessed deterrence." Manoj Joshi of *The Times of India* has referred to India's missile and nuclear tests as "technology demonstrators." Joshi seems to suggest that an incrementalist program consisting of progressively-ordered demonstrations of technological competence may be enough to deter.
35. The key questions regarding short-order weaponization for deterrence are: how quickly should one be able to go from an unassembled to an assembled, deliverable weapon; how many of these should a country possess; what targets will they threaten— countervalue (cities) or counterforce (conventional or nuclear weapons); where should the different components be stored—in dispersed locations or not; who will assemble menu of targets;

and finally, should one clarify these details to one's opponents so as to leave no doubt in their minds as to one's capacity and will to punish, or should one hint and manipulate the uncertainties?
36. Alexander George and Richard Smoke summarize these in their massive study of deterrence, *Deterrence in American Foreign Policy: Theory and Practice*. New York, 1974, pp. 58–66.
37. For a survey and assessment of CBMs, see Michael Krepon and Amit Sevak (eds), *Crisis Prevention, Confidence Building, and Reconciliation in South Asia*. New York, 1995.
38. Glenn Snyder has referred to this as the "stability–instability" paradox. See his *Deterrence and Defense*.
39. I stress the word "deterrent" because India has other possibilities in respect of a solution to the Kashmir problem—an internal solution, military or peaceful; and persuading Pakistan that, even in the absence of Indian retaliation, the political, economic, social, even moral costs of its involvement are out of proportion to any possible gains.
40. There is no definitive account of the 1986 and 1990 crises as yet. On 1987, see Kanti Bajpai et al., *Brasstacks and Beyond*. Ravi Rikhye, *The War That Never Was*. Delhi, 1988 is provocative on 1987, but seems exaggerated. Hersh as well as Morrow and Windrem, *Critical Mass*, the latest attempt to explicate the 1990 crisis, have won much notoriety but little acclaim.
41. David Mitrany, *A Working Peace System*. Chicago, 1966.
42. Haas' key neofunctionalist works include *Beyond the Nation-State: Functionalism and International Organization*. Stanford, 1964, especially, chapters 1–4, "International Integration: The European and the Universal Process," *International Political Community*. New York, 1966, pp. 93–129 and, with Philippe C. Schmitter, "Economics and Differential Patterns of Political Integration: Projections About Unity in Latin America," also in *International Political Community*, pp. 259–99.
43. On the other hand, India and Pakistan have a rather impressive record of cooperation in the period from 1947–1962. See Bajpai and Cohen, "Cooperative Security and South Asian Insecurity," in Nolan (ed.), *Global Engagement*.
44. A simple indicator of India–Pakistan dis-integration is the abysmal state of trading relations: official trade between them accounts for about 2 percent of their total trading volume.
45. See for instance Joseph Grieco, "Anarchy and the Limits of Cooperation."
46. Hamza Alavi, "The State in Post-Colonial Societies," in Kathleen Gough and Hari Sharma (eds), *Imperialism and Revolution in South Asia*. London, 1973.
47. Haas, "International Integration," pp. 104–6.
48. On the transition to democracy in Pakistan, see among others David Taylor, "Parties, Elections, and Democracy," *Journal of Commonwealth and Comparative Politics* 30(March 1992),

96–115 and Kanti Bajpai and Sumit Ganguly, "The Transition to Democracy in Pakistan," *In Depth: A Journal of Values and Public Policy* 3(Fall 1993), pp. 59–86.
49. It should be added that not everyone in this sector is interested necessarily in more economic ties with the other country. What is in their general interest is a more stable economic environment and greater fiscal responsibility. War, the threat of war, heavy defense spending, these threaten stability and fiscal responsibility.
50. Deutsch et al., *Political Community*, pp. 5–9.
51. Deutsch et al., *Political Community*, pp. 66–67. I use Deutsch et al.'s work for the most part heuristically, that is, as a way of interrogating the South Asian case. Their work has been criticized on various grounds: the conditions for an amalgamater security community in particular have been challenged. Nevertheless, their findings are based on extensive case histories, the bulk of which were never published but which were drawn on the generate their general findings.
52. Deutsch et al., *Political Community*, p. 47.
53. On the transition to democracy in Nepal and Bangladesh, see Farzana Hossein, "Transition to Democracy in Nepal: The Process and Prospects," *BIISS Journal* 12(July 1991), pp. 313–35, Iftekharuzzaman and Mahbubur Rahman, "Transition to Democracy in Bangladesh: Issues and Outlook," *BIISS Journal* 12(January 1991), pp. 95–126, and Nadeem Qadir, *Bangladesh: Realities of Democracy and Crises* Dhaka, 1994.
54. I do not mean to suggest that these are the only secularist parties in the countries mentioned. Nor do I wish to suggest that their secular records are impeccable, but one can agree that they are not avowedly fundamentalist or religious parties.
55. See Bruce Russett, *Grasping the Democratic Peace: Principles for a Post-Cold War World*. Princeton, 1993, pp. 30–38.
56. A charting of non-official contacts between the two countries before and after the democratization of Pakistan would be a very useful exercise. The most thorough and recent effort to assess the non-official process in South Asia is Navnita Chadha-Behera, Paul M. Evans, and Gowher Rizvi, *Beyond Boundaries: A Report on the State of Non-Official Dialogues on Peace, Security and Cooperation in South Asia*. North York, Ontario, 1997.
57. See Edward D. Mansfield and Jack Snyder, "Democratization and War", *Foreign Affairs*, May/June 1995, pp. 79–97.
58. See Russett, *Grasping the Democratic Peace*, pp. 38–40.

3

NEO-LIBERALISM AND DEMOCRACY IN SOUTH ASIA[1]

Gautam Kumar Basu

The role of the state in the developmental processes of South Asian countries and its consequences for democratization of this region is receiving increasing attention. While the reasons for such attention are diverse, central among them is concern over the need for shift from a state-controlled economy to market economy. In some senses the adoption of market principles implies natural extension of consolidation of democratic values. The shift in preference from a state controlled planned economy to market economy by South Asian states implies two things: first, it indicates that states should offload their economic functions and assume the role of "minimalist" states and second, by embracing the concept of privatization, they should seek to reduce control over the economy and thereby try to create an atmosphere in which individual choice or freedom would reign supreme and thereby enhance democracy. We shall try to inquire into the neo-liberal policies of choice and competition, as adopted by the states of South Asia, and try to formulate certain hypotheses regarding the future of democracy in this region. The questions that appear to be crucial are: Is there something wrong with the ongoing re-democratization process? To what extent is the differentiation between civilian and military regimes valid or tenable as far as the repressive nature of the state is concerned? Is it simply a wishful thinking that force will eventually be relegated to the background?

The main purpose of this paper is to see whether the emergence of a minimalist state and the adoption of market principles will automatically lead to the establishment of liberal democratic set-up and eliminate the possibilities of militarism in South Asian countries. We shall try to argue that militarism is not necessarily going to be a phenomenon of past, but is likely to make its presence felt as and when it is required. The states in South Asian countries tend to adopt a different agenda: on the one hand, they will try to project the image of their repressive teeth in a much lighter form and on the other hand, adoption of neo-liberal policies by these states may produce what Stephen Gill has called the emergence of "disciplinary neo-liberalism" in South Asia. This paper will be divided into three parts: in the first part, we shall try to deal with the concept of militarism; the second part will try to look into the consequences of structural adjustment policies as adopted by the South Asian countries; and the third part will look into probable responses of the politics in South Asian, and an effort will be made to formulate certain hypotheses to such responses. In the concluding portion, we shall try to posit certain question's regarding the future of democracy in this region. Here, we should offer a note of caution. Given the political-economic as well as sociocultural diversity in this region and inadequacy of database, it may not be possible for us to deal with each country in detail. We shall rather try to identify the trends based on certain micro-level analysis and aggregate level data.

The term "militarism" was first used by the French Socialist Proudhon in 1864,[2] and gained currency as a political slogan in the anti-Bonapartist polemics of the republicans and the socialists in France under the Second Empire.[3] Broadly speaking, two different traditions can be identified in the process of defining the term "militarism"—the Western Liberal tradition and the Marxists tradition. The former defines militarism as "a domination of the military over the civilian, an undue preponderance of military considerations, spirits, ideals and scales of value, in the life of states. In the international spheres, militarism has provided fuel for those recriminations which were supposed to find a solution and an end in the war-guilt paragraphs of the Versailles Treaty—recriminations in which each nation charges another with building up disproportionate armaments that threaten peace and force pacific nations to follow suit.[4] The Marxist tradition, on the other hand, defines militarism as "a complex social phenomenon that comprises a system of economic, political, ideological, and directly military measures taken by aggressive capitalist nations and directed towards preparing for and conducting imperialist wars. It is utilized by the finance oligarchy to consolidate and expand its domination, to preserve the capitalist system on the one hand and to generate big profits or the other."[5] We are reluctant to agree with of either these definitions. The first definition makes a clear-cut demarcation between civilian and military affairs, but we think such a distinction is very thin and artificial. To us, military is a state apparatus, used for the purpose of fulfilling certain roles of the state, which generally tries to work on behalf of the dominant class interest in a given society. It is very difficult today to identify even a military regime to be exclusively dominated by military personnel—not only a coalition between civilian and military officials as well as politicians can be seen at the helm of a military regime, but there have been instances where military coups have been engineered by such a coalition.[6]

The second definition, on the other hand, views militarism as an integral part of the capitalist social order, and not as a structural phenomenon pertaining to various social orders throughout history. Hirtze in 1904 related militarism to feudalism and Joseph Miller argues that military spirit always sides with reactionaries—it always allies itself with non-progressive and anti-liberal movements of the time.[7] Second, this definition views militarism essentially as a war mechanism—though in the post-World War II period, the imperialist powers had intervened militarily at various places of the peripheral countries, but in most cases today, they conduct proxy wars instead of direct involvement.

A number of contemporary scholars have tended to accept Marek Thee's definition of militarism. They define militarism as "a rush to armaments, the growing roles of the military (understood as the military establishment) in national and international affairs, the use of force as an instrument of supremacy and political power and the increasing influence of the military in civilian affairs."[8] If we accept Mark Thee's definitions of militarism, the question remains: Is militarism over in the post-Cold War era? This question becomes crucial to scholars all over the world who are increasingly concerned with the question of democratic survival, rather than the processes of re-democratization. Unfortunately, militarism remains alive well under conditions of globality, with rocket propulsion and new information technologies introducing unprecedented destructive capacities into contemporary battle. Eleven major wars broke out in the "new world order" of 1991–92 while, much aided by global weapons flows, armed suppressions within countries has increased to the point that, in the 1990s, two-thirds of the world's states have used their armies against people they claim as citizens.[9] We tend to argue that the emerging neo-liberal order may not produce militarism as we understand, but tends to give way to the emergence of a "disciplined society."

II

Ever since the early 1980s, but more prominently since the early 1990s, the policy-makers in this region appear to be obsessed with a few buzzwords of a market society,[10] namely, privatization; liberalization and globalization. It seems these countries tend to accept what is known as structural adjustment policies, as prescribed by the World Bank and the International Monetary Fund. The major objective of such policies was fundamental realignment of the Third World countries' economies along free-market lines. The policies sought to ensure economic stabilization through devaluation of currencies, price liberalization and austerity measures. They also aimed at introducing structural reforms through trade liberalization, disinvestment of state enterprises, tax reforms, privatization of agricultural lands, deregulation of the banking sector as well as liberalizing capital movement. Although noble ideals like poverty alleviation and good governance were included within the scheme, the major thrusts of such policies revolved around the concepts of a minimalist state, complete elimination of subsidy, privatizing, and liberalizing economies.[11]

Privatization in the Indian context implies the following: disinvestment of public sector units, deregulation, and perhaps introduction of private sector values in state-owned enterprises. The way disinvestment has been taking place could be a matter of serious concern. In fact, it is not logically feasible that public sector units (PSUs) that are continuously incurring losses would be taken over by the private sector enterprises. Neither does it make any sense that profit-making PSUs would be disinvested. The irony is this: the Government of India is trying to sell out those PSUs that are earning profit over the years. A recent report has indicated that the Government of India has selected three PSUs in the power sector—the National Thermal Power Corporation (NTPC), National Hydro-Power Corporation (NHPC) and Power Grid Corporation Limited (PGCL)—for disinvestment. What is surprising is that the Ministry of Power was kept completely in the dark about such disinvestment.[12] This is not simply a case of lack of coordination, but also reflects the fact that the government policy lacks transparency. Take the case of Maruti Motors, which is currently in the public sector and is earning profit as a joint venture. It has been reported that efforts have been made to hand it over to Suzuki Motors.[13]

Again, in the name of privatization, the government has resorted to progressive withdrawal, and the ultimate elimination, of non-plan budget support to public sector enterprises. There is no doubt that such a policy has reduced government expenditures. But it has done nothing to ease the problem of such firms. Look at the textile mills owned by the National Textile Corporation. While no efforts have been made to modernize and make them competitive in domestic and international market, the employees continue to suffer as there is no budgetary provision for their salary. In fact, employees get salary from government ad hoc grants, given out as generosity from time to time. Those mills are supposed to go to the "market." But the government that is supposedly responsible for managing the mills does not make any attempt to make those organizations viable profit-making units. Such a policy could have two implications. First, the employees tend to get alienated, aggrieved, agitated, and simultaneously become less and less motivated. Second, not only does it generate scepticism about real intention of the government, but also erodes its legitimacy.

Apart from that, it has been argued that a Third World state can hardly establish its monopoly over large-scale and/or capital-intensive industries. In fact, the experience of public sector enterprises in Third World countries is highly dismal. Neither can such a state have greater ability to maneuver as far as the relationship between local and foreign capital is concerned because of the structural constraints within which it has to operate. One may refer to a comment, made by a former Indian M.P., A.K. Roy, who stated, "The present outcry against the public sector and planning is, therefore, not in national interest, not even in the interest of the (indigenous) private sector, but only in the interest of the multinationals and their masters abroad who seek to disturb the industrialization of the country and its self-reliant growth to make it a market for the capitalist West, now reeling under recession."[14] Just consider the statement made by a former finance minister of India while addressing a gathering of European investors; he urged them to repeat the experience of East India Company who stayed in India for more than 200 years. The implication is really dangerous.[15]

Another flaw in the government's policy of privatization is that it tends to assess each and every governmental organization in the light of how much profit it can make. Undoubtedly, this is a wrong conception. Take, for example, the cases of health and education. A study by Dr U.S. Tulasidhar has shown that the share of grants to centrally sponsored disease control program fell from 41 percent in 1984–85 to 29 percent in 1988–89 and continued to fall during 1990–91 to 1992–93 to reach an abysmal 18.5 percent. The study further shows a continuous decline "in the share of Central Grants in States' expenditure on medical and public health (from 6.7 percent in 1984–85 to 3.7 per cent in 1992–93), and family welfare (99 percent in 1984–85 to 88.6 percent in 1992–93)."[16] As far as education is concerned, a few observations will suffice. First, emphasis for alternative sources of funding has generated an unhealthy atmosphere. Education has been completely commercialized—in fact, the collection of donation amounting to several thousand rupees in prestigious schools have become a common phenomenon, second, despite rhetoric, both at the center and state levels, of higher allocations in the sphere of education, one must admit that education becomes a loser if one considers the inflationary trend. In the context of 1985–86 union budget, it has been argued that "given the rate of inflation, it means that except elementary education, all sectors of education are, in effect, losers in 1995–96 budget, higher education suffering the most."[17] The same argument has been made by Jean Drèze and Amartya Sen who observed:

> The available evidence indicates no substantial improvement in patterns of education expenditure in the 1990s. On the contrary, the growth of education expenditure has slowed down often structure adjustment measures were introduced in 1991, and education expenditure has even declined in real terms in many state.[18]

Second, the move towards market economy has created an ethos towards what we can describe "the philosophy of survival of the fittest." All schools, colleges, universities want the "best"; the mediocre students and the "less than averages" are alien to them. Higher education may be reserved for the best talent, but elementary, secondary cannot be. The question is, whether it is at all possible to identity the "best" when the system is highly unequal and biased towards the rich and wealthy—a system where wealth is acquired mainly through dubious means? If the present trend continues, it seems that in the near future money, and not merit, will be the sole criterion for admission to educational institutions—from primary to university levels. One must admit the fact that health and education constitute essential infrastructural facilities for future development. Neither should one forget that welfare activities have rarely brought profit to the government. These activities should be viewed more as long-term investment, rather than as profit maximizing activities. In fact, the Government of India has miserably failed to improve the social infrastructure of the country. The tragedy is: while the government seems proud of its foreign exchange reserves, "any attempt to inform the budget makers that India needs spending on public utilities evokes the standard response that there is no money, or that money has to be found from non-government sources."[19]

Let us raise another question regarding non-governmental sources. Two hypotheses may be formulated: first, non-governmental funding organizations have rarely come forward to invest in public spending activities. Recently, two members of an international organization, concerned mainly with humanitarian problems, visited Calcutta—while people expected that they should make certain financial commitments to alleviate humanitarian problems, they continued to emphasize the denial by the Government of India to allow their organization to visit a few sensitive zones in India. Second, people, having faith in privatization programs, continue to rely more on the government funds than on private funds. This is a very sad scenario in the sense that through such reliance on government funds, public money has been used for fraudulent purposes. One may come across non-governmental organizations (NGOs), which take money from the government and employ people at minimum wages with no benefits. Is it not exploitation? It is not clear why such NGOs be provided with financial assistance when the government itself can spend its money for welfare purpose and thereby enhance its legitimacy among the masses. We do not mean that all NGOs are performing badly or should be viewed with suspicion. Our point is: reliance of a NGO on the government for financial support—and that too at a time when "subsidy" is a dirty word—creates a paradox. There are examples when several organizations took money from the government and refused to submit accounts. It seems that a nexus has emerged between the non-governmental and the governmental sector that is diverting its own money in the name of privatization. In a class-divided society, like India, it is very difficult to keep the line of demarcation very clear and it is always possible that such distinction would remain artificial.

In fact, one of the major criticisms against NGOs is that they generate processes which are "reactionary in content, elitist in terms of interests they represent, and insensitive to the real interests of the poor and dispossessed. By claiming a universal interest, these organizations function as a mask for the interests of the dominant classes and are nothing more than another manifestation of the ideology of the ruling class."[20] One may or may not accept the argument in totality. The question however remains whether, and to what extent, such organizations can really initiate sustainable socioeconomic transformation or continue to be agents for maintaining the status quo.

Again, it is very difficult to conclude firmly that the government's policy of privatization has brought relief to the masses or has placed the Indian economy on a more solid foundation. First, foreign investment has hardly been made in the capital-intensive sector—most of the foreign investment has been made in banking as well as in the consumer goods sector. Neither did foreign technology enter the Indian market on a massive scale. It is true that foreign direct investment (FDI) in India is 15 times higher than it was before the economy was liberalized, and doubling annually since 1991.[21] But a close look will reveal that there exists a wide gap between FDI approvals and actual inflow during the period 1991–95, the Government of India has approved 21,241.3 million worth of FDI, while during the same period, the actual inflow was 18.4 percent of the approved investment.[22] Even the small inflow of FDI has pushed many Indian companies out of the market. As an estimate has shown that nearly 500,000 small units have closed down and have made nearly 2.5 million people jobless.[23] It appears that the government policy of inviting foreign multinationals to takeover vital sectors of the country's economy. Second, in a country like India where the vast majority of people depend on agriculture, it is least likely that the reforms initiated by the government will bring relief to them. The International Labor Organization (ILO) in one of its annual reports on world employment has warned:[24]

> Together with improved incentives to agri-business as a result of liberalization, they could well undermine the survival of small farms. The upshot could be the uprooting and proleterianization of small farmers and a reduction of employment as a result of an increase in capital-intensive and mechanized production.... Withdrawal of state support is unlikely to be justified on efficiency grounds since with adequate support services, the small farm sector can be competitive; experience has shown that investment there yields high economic returns. The new economic policy also generates fear over agricultural development. Such fears are over the reduction in public investment, state withdrawal from the provision of agricultural credit, and the reduction of extension service; all of these are likely to weaken the productive capacity of small farmers.

Beyond India, looking at South Asia as a whole, one will be not be surprised to see that South Asia stands on an equal footing with Sub-Saharan Africa. In both these regions human poverty affects 40 percent of the people.[25] In South Asia 50 percent of the children under 5 are underweight, 4 million people lack access to health services.[26] Nearly half the developing world's illiterate adults, about 4.7 million people, belong to South Asia.[27]

In 1993, two-fifths of the world's poor people (515 million) lived in South Asia.[28] In South Asia the per capita income of the richest 25 percent appears to be five times higher than that of the poorest 20 percent.[29] It has also been shown that in 1990, 36 percent of urban people in South Asia were living in poverty, compared with 45 percent of rural people.[30] It is difficult to say whether such a dismal scenario of South Asian countries is directly correlated to the adoption of structural adjustment policies by the countries in this region. Basic trade theory suggests that liberalization of the economy would automatically trigger alleviation of poverty, given the abundance of cheap labor and low wages, in developing countries. Reality, however, is different. It seems that "the imperative to liberalize has demanded a shrinking of state involvement in national life, producing a wave of privatization of public enterprises and, generally, job cuts. And everywhere the opening of financial markets has limited government's ability to run deficits—requiring them to slash health spending and food subsidies that benefit poor people."[31] It has been argued that the successive governments in countries of South Asia remain under constant pressure from international agencies, including the IMF and the World Bank, to cut subsidies on utility prices, staple foods, and fertilizers. In fact, "Indian fertilizer subsidies have been the subject of steady pressure from international agencies since 1991. Pakistan was forced to concede gas and other utility price rise as a condition for IMF support; and critics claim that Sri Lanka has seen water tax imposed and fertilizer subsidies cut at the instigation of the World Bank."[32] Undoubtedly, such policies erode the position of the poor.

Where do all these things lead? Probably, the following implications emerge: First, state in South Asia has moved a long way—from its role as a supposed agent of "social revolution" in an unequal underdeveloped socioeconomic system to that of a minimalist state. It seems that in this transitional process, the state seeks to reduce its role as a welfare state, becomes headstrong in reducing subsidies, shows little hesitation in opening up its economy, and tends to ignore areas like land reforms as well as redistribution of power which were preciously considered as essential for bringing about socioeconomic transformation. Second, it seems that the state has limited control over functioning of the private sector. For example, a Reserve Bank of India study group has shown that "the quality of state intervention was so poor that it had not been able to compel the private sector to deliver the goods despite vast resources having been made available to this sector and that there was no proper evaluation of the performance of the private sector."[33] It seems that private sector seeks to earn maximum profits in shortest possible time with no or little concern either for quality of goods, consumers' expectations or national well-being. The United Nations Conference on Trade and Development recognized in the early 1990s that privatization might be important, but also recommended that a one-time tax on private sector be imposed on private sector holding of financial assets. Would our private sector accept its? Or, would the Indian state be bold enough to implement it? Finally, it seems that the move by the Indian state away from the welfare state system to a minimalist state also reflects its priority for a different image of an individual. It seeks to project the individual as a utility-maximizing entity and tries to construct society as a collection of individuals with competing interests.

III

It will possibly be not wrong to argue that the states in South Asia have adopted a different agenda—the desire to establish a welfare oriented society has been replaced by a desperate move towards establishing a market society, based on the assumptions of a neo-classical political economy. Measures based on such principles might go a long way in consolidating the foundation of capitalist society, but may not be able to create society based on equity. In fact, such measures have made the poor people the real losers. The irony of market principles is that "the bounties of nature are given away at very low subsidized prices to rich entrepreneurs in the name of incentives for industrial growth, but the poor have to buy at market prices.

For instance, bamboo was earlier cheaply or freely available for making mats, baskets and roofs. With the coming up of the paper industry, it became a scarce good. The industrialists now gets it for Rs 6 per ton, the poor get it for Rs 6 per piece."[34] In other words, equity is the worst casualty in the process of transition to a market oriented society. This creates a paradox for the state: the demand for equity will continue to increase, but it will be directed to a state which seeks to reduce its functions and probably has little control as far as economic policy options are concerned. Theoretically, a minimalist state is not an ineffective state—its activities will be confined to two functions, i.e., to maintain internal law and order and to protect its territorial integrity from external aggression. In other words, its repressive teeth remain intact. The state will not hesitate to expose its teeth when the gap between the state and the civil society will be unbridgeable and the "pact of domination" is threatened.

The question is whether the states in South Asia would at all resort to repressive measures. As the situation stands, it may be argued that the gap between the state and civil society is widening. The rate of unemployment reaches an alarming position—it seems decision-makers as well as politicians are least bothered about it. Market prices are skyrocketing while decision-makers are busy in projecting the supposedly downward trend of inflation in the country. The government is championing disinvestment of PSUs, while the workers are opposing such moves. The question is: can the state resort to the use of force in case property relations become threatened in South Asia and the gap between the state and civil society becomes unbridgeable? The jubilation of the decision-makers in this part of the world over the so-called "miracle" of newly industrializing countries (NICs) should neither be overemphasized nor be completely ignored. The oft-quoted reference to development strategies of the NICs by the ruling elite clearly indicates a preference for a "strong" state. But it is difficult for the state to turn towards authoritarianism like the East Asian Tigers as their growth strategies "were the antithesis of the World Bank/IMF neo-liberal prescriptions on how best to industrialize. They were not examples of 'market friendly' plus 'minimal state' development strategies."[35] In fact, switching over to an authoritarian regime may not necessarily lead to the establishment of bourgeois hegemony and an end to its formal democratic institutional pattern. A look at the dynamics of military regimes would reveal that even they would have to take recourse to moves which one could find only in democratic countries. Such trends, combined with the trend of re-democratization all over the Third World, created a situation where the state was in dire need of establishing certain rules of the game which would establish the hegemony of the bourgeoisie and would simultaneously reorganize its repressive machineries in such a way that the application of force could appear as much lighter and subtle.

This can be done only by transferring the market assumptions, which guide and motivate the economic arena on to the political plane. This becomes more important due to the fact that without the existence of parallel market assumptions at the political level, the gap between the state and the civil society will be more pronounced, clearly visible and terribly dangerous. Once the concept of "privatization" is internalized at the societal level, the state is automatically relegated to the background, but its necessity is not ruled out. Society still needs rule-makers and rule-enforcers without which the security of property will be a myth. The solution to this problem had been stated by James Mill as far back as 1830 when he wrote in the *Westminster Review*, "Our opinion, therefore, is that the business of government is properly the business of the rich, and that they will always obtain it, either by bad means, or good. Upon this everything depends. If they obtain it by good means, the government is sure to be good. The only good means of obtaining it are, the free suffrage of the people."[36] But as we all know that the early liberals did not prescribe universal adult franchise, but recommended franchise based on property, age, educational as well as gender qualifications. In the Indian context, one business tycoon, highly wooed by the government, made this remark that "universal suffrage has proved disastrous for the Indian economy causing chaos and creating more than a dozen parties"—to him, the only way to rectify this "very system" is to introduce a system where "people without a stake in the economy" should not have any role in governing it.[37] Probably Jeremy Bentham resurfaces in the late 20th century India.

The implication is now clear. The state now sheds its entrepreneurial character and gives up its role as an agent of social revolution as embodied in the Constitution of India. Since the civil society is guided by the laws of classical political economy, neither does it participate in the community oriented activities nor does it care for such community interests; and as such, it does neither decide in which direction the state will move nor does it assess the extent to which the state has been working in community interests. This also has no grand design. The individuals, in a "privatized" society, live in isolated cells, and as such, can hardly merge with other individuals with the consequence that no political party can be formed along class lines. The question is: Who, then, will deliver the political goods? The answer lies in the establishment of mechanisms which will allow "competition" between two or more self-chosen sets of politicians (elites) arrayed in political parties, for the votes which will entitle them to rule until the next election.[38] One can see how the logic of classical political economy has been used to bridge the gap between the state and the civil society. Politicians are the entrepreneurs and voters are the consumers. The former will produce the political goods; the latter may simply express their desire, but can not produce what they actually want to. The quality of political goods will be determined in terms of the requirement of the civil society, i.e., the extent to which such goods will contribute to the preservation of the property relation in a given Third World society. Any deviation from the set norms will result in reactivating the repressive state apparatus that remains vigilant in the cloak of a civilian regime. In the Indian context, it has been observed by several scholars that idealism and vision of an ideal type society, as prevalent in the minds of politicians have started to disappear from the late 1970s and early 1980s. It has been argued, "The politicians have turned their political position into an instrument of economic gain.... The state ... is seen as an economic institution from a very different point of view, as the provider of a stock of funds over which politicians would have unaccountable control; and this unaccountability is legitimized by using part of the surplus at the state's control for distribution among their immediate supporters and social constituency."[39] In India, elections are fought either on the basis of building a

Ram mandir or projecting cardboard cut-outs of the Nehru–Gandhi dynasty. Booth-capturing is a very popular term in India's electoral politics.[40] In Pakistan, "the political 'game' of patronage, maneuvers and counter-maneuvers have taken priority over long-term policy-making."[41] In Sri Lanka, "what William Mcgowan calls the 'suppression of legitimate political dissent' outside parliament paved the way for racketeering, corruption, tax cuts and foreign investments to the gain of those domestic and foreign interests linked to the regime."[42] In Nepal, Mr Girija Prasad Koirala became the fifth Prime Minister since mid-term poll of 1994 in what may appear either as a new fashion, known as coalition politics in South Asia or simply what is now a sad commentary on Nepali politics. The fact remains: economy in Nepal is in bad shape. Several development projects have either been shelved or awaiting decisions, and 53.1 percent of people continue to live on less than $1 a day.[43]

The conscientious citizens may raise voice against it, honest officials may try to prosecute such errant politicians and self-respected academic may be cynical about it. But politicians seldom care, and the strong arm of the state is rarely mobilized against the great loot. They, in collaboration with dishonest bureaucrats and even unscrupulous academics, try to silence such dissents and criticism. But such a model of criminalizing politics has another sinister design. It can reduce the managing agency of the state to insignificance. As has been stated by C.B. Macpherson, "When the output of laws and orders is treated as a result of the input of pressures, it matters little what persons are in office as the government. The government, as the mechanism through which decisions are made, becomes in effect impersonal or anonymous as the market in the economic model."[44]

The states have adopted a different agenda: on the one hand, they seek to redefine state-civil society relations, and on the other, they try to project the repressive apparatus of the state in such a way that it may appear lighter, more rapid, more effective, and more subtle a design of coercion for the civil society. The states resort to what Bentham has described as Panopticon. At the periphery lies the civil society. Each individual lives in an isolated cell; his self-interest is the side walls which prevent him from coming into contact with his fellow individuals, and thereby the state prevents individuals from merging together and making efforts to overthrow the system. At the center, however, the state remains as the central tower with no economic function to perform but only to supervise those inside the enclosure of civil society. The individual only knows that the state is a minimalist state, but does not know whether he has been spied upon.

The uniqueness of the post-independent policy is that it did not adopt a democratic constitution just for rejecting it after a while. Probably, the worst threat to Indian democracy appeared during the emergency—but such state terrorism, proved inadequate to suppress mass movements as the end of emergency saw the emergence of a non-Congress ministry at New Delhi for the first time. The only way to counter social movements by the states was to devise a new technique of power so that individuals can be fabricated in it. They have to be separated from their fellow individuals. The concept of "privatization" has been championed by the state to develop civil society based on conflicting self-interests of individuals. Again, the states can hardly ignore the need for economic growth as it is closely connected with capital accumulation in our society. However, the crucial question is: should growth be viewed in terms of increasing GNP or should growth be associated with equitable distribution too? The latter, however, may appear to be seesaw. The state policy of equitable distribution, social justice may generate the possibility of state-alienation from the civil society, while non-recognition of those policies may generate mass movements that, in turn, may call for application of force. Thus the states require a development model that will project the image of growth, but not necessarily equitable distribution because the latter will mean state intervention, which in turn, will negate the logic of privatization. Surely the model, represented by the NICs, offers suitable and an apparently viable answer to their requirement. The question of distribution can take place through marketmechanism. But such an assumption can be valid only in a classless society, and not in a polarized society.

IV

In conclusion, it may be argued that the preference for privatization and the move towards market economy do not necessarily lead towards consolidation of democracy in South Asia. These policies might leave a sinister impact relating to the issue of survival of democracy. Though we are not drawing any definite conclusion, we can raise certain questions for further investigation: to what extent do the privatization policies result from elite initiative rather than shift in expectations of the electorate? Is such a change in policy a result of the nature of parliamentary system with concentration of power on the top political level or is a product of push-and-pull among different interest groups, which characterize a pluralist policy? To what extent, have such policies been influenced by personality and visions of our political leaders? Or, is it simply the case that liberal economic ideas become so influential that they themselves become the agents of change? To what extent, do these policies reflect "self-serving attempt of upper level state managers to enhance their power and privilege, to increase their control of policy and decrease their responsibilities for day-to-day operation."[45] Or, do such policies reflect "hegemonic strategies involved in changing the 'balance of forces' when a deep crisis of class rule has emerged?"[46]

Also we must probe into finding out (apart from through such agency and structuralist models[47]) how the states are keen on producing rules on the line of early-liberal thinking of Jeremy Bentham and James Mill, that will create an indivisible discourse for the maintenance of the status quo, normalizing order and securing domination in an otherwise turbulent society. One, however should not ignore the fact that Bentham's solution to the problems of his own society was not confined only to prescribing certain rules of the game; he also prescribed the use of an architectural design, known as the Panopticon. The purpose was to make the use of power lighter, but more rapid, and to induce a sense of conscious and permanent visibility in the civil society that assures the automatic functioning of power. At least, the tall tower of the state remains at the center in the form of a minimalist state and the capabilities associated with it. The members living inside the enclosure of the civil society may not know whether they are being spied upon, but they can be sure that they are being carefully monitored. The benefits are, as Bentham himself put in the Preface to Panopticon:

"Morals reformed—health preserved—industry invigorated—instruction diffused—public burdens lightened—economy seated, as it were, upon a rock—the guardian knot of the Poor Laws not-out, but united—all by a simple idea in architecture."[48] The message is clear: establish hegemony in a normalized form and evolve a set of techniques, strategies, and rituals by which honest and self-respected persons would be silenced, dishonesty would be legitimized, values would be destroyed, morality subverted, and domination would be violently projected.

NOTES AND REFERENCES

1. Lecture at the first South Asian Peace Studies Orientation Course held by the Maulana Abul Kalam Azad Institute of Asian Studies, Calcutta, October 1997. Some of the ideas developed here may also be found in Gautam Kumar Basu, "The Question of State-Autonomy and Regime Transformation in the Third World," *Asian Studies*. Vol. 10, 1992, pp. 6–26.
2. Ulrich Albrecht, "Militarism and Underdevelopment," in Eide et al. (eds), *Problems of Contemporary Militarism*. New York, 1980, p. 107.
3. Erickson et al., in Kernig (ed.), *Communism and Western Society: A Comparative Encyclopedia*. New York, 1973, Vol. 5, p. 436.
4. Alfred Vagts, *A History of Militarism*. London, 1938, p. 12, quoted in Skjelsback, "Militarism: Its Dimensions and Corollaries: An Attempt at Conceptual Clarification," in Eide et al., op. cit.
5. Milovidov et al. (eds), *The Philosophical Heritage of V.I. Lenin and Contemporary War*. Washington, DC, 1972. quoted in ibid., p. 84.
6. Amos Perlmutter, "The Comparative Analysis of Military Regimes: Formations, Aspirations and Achievements," *World Politics*. Vol. 33, No. 1, October, 1980, pp. 96–120.
7. Jane Oberg, "The New International Military Order: A Threat to Human Security," in Eide et al. (eds), op. cit., p. 72.
8. Marek Thee, "Militarism and Militarization in Contemporary International Relations," ibid., p. 15.
9. Jan Aart Scholte, "Beyond the Buzzword: Towards a Critical Theory of Globalization," in Eleonore Kofman and Gillian Youngs (eds), *Globalization: Theory and Practice*. London, 1996, p. 54.
10. See *Asian Development Outlook 1997* and *1998*, Asian Development Bank, New York, 1997, pp. 113–45.
11. For detail see, Michel Chossudovsky, *The Globalization of Poverty: Impacts of IMF and World Bank Reforms*. London, 1997, chapter 2.
12. *The Statesman*, 4 May 1997.

13. Gurudas Dasgupta, "Foreign Funds: No Short Cut to Self-Reliance," *The Statesman*, 30 January 1997.
14. A.K. Roy, "Dumping Nehru," *The Statesman*, 1 February 1992.
15. Arvind N. Das, "From Head to Toes," *The Telegraph*, 27 April 1997.
16. *The Statesman*, 29 August 1993.
17. J.B.G. Tilak, "Budget for Education," *The Hindu*, 15 April 1995.
18. Jean Drèze and Amartya Sen, *India: Economic Development and Social Opportunity*. Delhi, 1995, p. 123.
19. M.J. Akbar, "Dying among Dollars," *The Telegraph*, 2 October 1994.
20. Judel Ferunando and Alan W. Heston, "Introduction: NGOs between States, Markets and Civil Society," *The Annals*, Vol. 554, November, 1997, pp. 8–9.
21. *The Statesman*, 26 April 1997.
22. *The Statesman*, 14 January 1997.
23. Kuldip Nayar, "The Impact of Reforms," *The Statesman*, 26 July 1995.
24. *The Statesman*, 23 February 1995.
25. *Human Development Report 1997*, United Nations Development Programme (UNDP), New York, 1997, p. 23.
26. Ibid., p. 29.
27. Ibid., p. 30.
28. Ibid., p. 33.
29. Ibid., p. 38.
30. Ibid., p. 88.
31. Ibid., p. 88.
32. Graham Field, *Economic Growth and Political Change in Asia*. New York, 1995, pp. 80–81.
33. *The Statesman*, 24 November 1993.
34. Jaya Shrivastava, "India: Sapping Women's Roots and Resources," in *The People vs Global Capital: The G-7, TNCs, SAPs and Human Rights*, Tokyo, 1994, p. 66.
35. Achin Vanaik, *India in a Changing World: Problems, Limits and Successes of its Foreign Policy*. New Delhi, 1995, p. 56.
36. Quoted in C.B. Macpherson, *The Life and Times of Liberal Democracy* Oxford, 1977, p. 42.
37. Arvind N. Das, "From Head to Toes," *The Telegraph*, 27 April 1997.
38. C.B. Macpherson, op. cit., p. 28.
39. Sudipta Kaviraj, "India: Dilemmas of Democratic Development," in Adrian Leftwish (ed.), *Democracy and Development: Theory and Practice*. Cambridge, 1996, p. 131.
40. Graham Field, op. cit., p. 192.
41. John Bray, "Pakistan at 50: A State in Decline," *International Affairs* Vol. 73, No. 2, April 1997, p. 325.
42. Graham Field, op. cit., p. 188.

43. UNDP, op. cit., p. 214.
44. C.B. Macpherson, *Democratic Theory: Essays in Retrieval.* Oxford 1993, p. 188.
45. Joel D. Wolfe, *Power and Privatization: Choice and Competition in the Remaking of British Democracy.* London, 1996, p. 12.
46. Ibid., p. 14.
47. Ibid., pp. 8–15.
48. Quoted in Michael Foucault, *Discipline and Punish: The Birth of the Prison,* Harmondsworth, 1977, p. 206.

4

LEGAL REGIME FOR REFUGEE CARE[1]

Brian Gorlick

INTERNATIONAL HUMAN RIGHTS AS A SYSTEM OF INTERNATIONAL LAW

Human rights are freedoms that are granted equally to all persons without distinction. In a sense, human rights are universally recognized standards of behavior. The violation of these standards by states, or other agents, may give rise to situations that lead to the creation of refugees. Refugees, by definition, are victims of human rights violations.[2]

Viewing the refugee problem in the context of human rights is clearly relevant. In fact, the origin of the international system of refugee protection, as codified in international refugee law, grew out of concern for the plight of refugees fleeing the troubles of post-war Europe. Regrettably, protecting and assisting victims of human rights violations which result in forced displacement is as relevant today as it was some 50 years ago. Refugees are not simply victims of human rights violations, however, as they represent a distinct group of individuals who are without the protection of a national state. Hence, the international system of refugee law was adopted in order to replace the protection which is normally provided, or is at least the responsibility, of national governments for their citizens.

The idea of developing a system of law that protects the human rights of individuals is also nothing new. Many states have been established on the basis that individuals have certain inherent rights that must be respected by the state. The idea of establishing a system of human rights law at the international level is a more recent development for which the United

Nations has been a catalytic institution. The *UN Charter* proclaims in its Preamble that "promoting and encouraging respect for human rights and for fundamental freedoms for all without distinction as to race, sex, language or religion" is a primary purpose of the United Nations. Member states of the UN pledge themselves to take action in cooperation with the United Nations to achieve this purpose.

With the adoption of the UN Charter in 1945 and the Convention relating to the Status of Refugees in 1952,[3] a number of other international human rights instruments have been developed and adopted by member states of the United Nations. These include the *Universal Declaration on Human Rights* (1948), the *International Covenant on Civil and Political Rights* (1966), the *International Covenant on Economic, Social and Cultural Rights* (1966)—collectively known as the International Bill of Rights—the *Convention on the Prevention and Punishment of the Crime of Genocide* (1948), the *Convention relating to the Status of Stateless Persons* (1954), and the *Convention on the Elimination of Racial Discrimination* (1965). More recently, the *Convention on the Elimination of Discrimination against Women* (1979), the *Convention against Torture and Other Cruel, Inhuman or Degrading Treatment or Punishment* (1984) and the *Convention on the Rights of the Child* (1989) have been developed at the international level.

In addition to the central foundational status of the *Universal Declaration of Human Rights*, more than 186 states have ratified or adhered to at least one (or in the majority of cases more) of these international treaties, thus establishing binding legal obligations of a continuing nature. Several South Asian states are party to a number of these major human rights Conventions, in addition to the 1949 *Geneva Conventions* and their 1977 *Additional Protocols* concerning the laws of war.

Among the international human rights treaties, India is party to the two international Covenants in addition to the *International Convention on the Elimination of All Forms of Racial Discrimination, the Convention on the Rights of the Child, and the Convention on the Elimination of All Forms of Discrimination Against Women*. India has also ratified the *Convention on the Political Rights of Women*, the *Convention on the Suppression and Punishment of Apartheid*, the

Convention on the Non-Applicability of Statutory Limitations to War Crimes and Crimes against Humanity, and *Convention on the Prevention and Punishment of the Genocide.* It appears that India is also considering accession to the 1984 *Convention Against Torture.*[4]

On a regional basis, a number of human rights treaties have also been adopted including the *European Convention for the Protection of Human Rights and Fundamental Freedom* (1969), and the *African Charter on Human and Peoples' Rights* (1981). In South Asia, despite efforts in this direction, no regional human rights framework has been established. However some states, including India, have enacted national human rights legislation and have established Human Rights Commissions. In India the relevant legislation is *The Protection of Human Rights Act* (1993) which established the National Human Rights Commission (NHRC). Under this Act, the NHRC has authority to inquire *suo moto* or on petition by a victim or any person on his or her behalf into a complaint of violation of human rights. Till date, the NHRC has investigated a number of complaints involving refugees. The 1996 Indian Supreme Court case of *National Human Rights Commission v State of Arunachal Pradesh and another,*[5] in which the National Human Rights Commission was an intervening party, is hailed as a landmark judgment in the area of refugee protection in the context of India and underlines the usefulness of engaging a national human rights machinery for refugee protection.

Besides the development of legal instruments and mechanisms, whether international, regional, or national, there is increasing agreement amongst states on the universal, indivisible and interdependent nature of all human rights—civil, political, economic, social, and cultural. The 1993 Vienna World Conference on Human Rights, attended by some 5,000 delegates from 171 states, reaffirmed the importance of the international system of human rights protection. The *Vienna Declaration* included a specific section on refugees. It reaffirmed the right of everyone to seek and enjoy asylum, as well as the right to return to one's own country. The *Vienna Declaration* also emphasized the importance of addressing "the root causes" of forced displacements and identified "the responsibilities of states, particularly as they related to the countries of origins."

In the international system of human rights protection, the grant of asylum by a state to persons entitled to invoke Article 14 of the *Universal Declaration of Human Rights* cannot be regarded as an unfriendly act by another state. Similarly, and particularly in the post-Cold War context, it is widely acknowledged that international attention to human rights violations is not an interference in a country's domestic affairs, but is rather part of routine international diplomacy. Although some states will go to great lengths to avoid scrutiny or criticism before international human rights bodies, the international community has identified a need to strengthen and improve application and enforceability of the international system of human rights protection. This has been realized through, for example, the UN-sponsored human rights missions in Cambodia, El Salvador, Guatemala, Haiti, the former Yugoslavia and Rwanda; the establishment of international criminal tribunals for the former Yugoslavia and Rwanda; and technical cooperation in the field of human rights with governments and other actors. Of course, the degree varies, ranging from assistance and advice, to monitoring and reporting and direct protection.

USING HUMAN RIGHTS TO ENHANCE THE PROTECTION OF REFUGEES

In its own policies and programs the Office of the United Nations High Commissioner for Refugees, or UNHCR, has incorporated a number of human rights principles. Its protection activities in countries of asylum and countries of origin include working with states in the area of legal rehabilitation, institution building, law reform and enforcement of the rule of law and providing humanitarian assistance to internally displaced persons (IDPs). Increased cooperation with international and regional human rights mechanisms are also new areas of involvement for UNHCR. Of course, these activities add to an already overburdened agenda. Some states have expressed concern that UNHCR should not undertake tasks that go beyond its formal mandate. This concern is well taken. These activities are placing considerable strain on the limited resources of the UNHCR. Further, the question of whether UNHCR has the capacity and capability to do these tasks must be addressed. However, in this era of downsizing and reform of the UN system in general, it seems unlikely that UNHCR will be allowed to continue its activities along traditional lines.

In efforts to prevent refugee flows the UN and others, notably NGOs, are providing technical assistance to states within a general human rights framework. This includes the promotion of human rights standards through the training of judges, lawyers, and human rights activities; giving substance to educational rights by funding the construction of new schools in war-torn countries; and promoting economic rights community-based projects focused on providing assistance to returning refugees. Promoting enactment and enforceability of domestic refugee and human rights laws, promotion of national human rights institutions, and training of government authorities are other prevention-oriented activities in which the UN, governments, and NGOs are increasingly engaged.

As part of the development of human rights principles through UN Conventions, a number of international treaty bodies, or committees, have been established to investigate violations, enforce standards, and assist states in implementing their ready obligations. These bodies have authority to examine periodic state party reports regarding implementation of the treaty provisions. And with the agreement of states, some treaty bodies have the competence to investigate and decide upon individual and interstate complaints and undertake field missions in order to monitor implementation measures. During examination of state party reports, the committee may prepare formal conclusions and observations on their performance in complying with international human rights law. They may also formulate specific recommendations to governments. In recent years, some of these committees such as the Human Rights Committee, the Committee on the Rights of the Child, and the Committee Against Torture, have regularly raised issues about the treatment of refugees by state parties to the respective Conventions.[6]

In general, the UN human rights machinery has paid great attention to the plight of refugees. This raises awareness of refugee protection issues through promoting legal standards for refugees and internally displaced persons in addition to sharing information concerning incidents of violations of refugee rights. Human rights NGOs and UNHCR have played a key role in educating members of the international and domestic human rights communities on the linkages between safeguarding human rights and refugee protection. These initiatives have firmly entrenched human rights issues in relating to the refugee problem.[7]

THE NEED FOR LEGAL FRAMEWORK FOR PROTECTING REFUGEES IN SOUTH ASIA

The refugee issue is an age-old problem in India and throughout South Asia. Indeed, the formation of the modern Indian state coincided with a massive exodus and influx of displaced persons. Some 30 million persons traveled across the newly formed borders. Today, the refugee population in India is about 260,000 persons. The largest groups comprise about 100,000 Tibetans followed by 64,000 Sri Lankan Tamils, 44,500 Chakmas from Bangladesh, 19,000 Afghans and a 1,000 of other nationalities mainly from Iran, Iraq, Somalia, Sudan, and Myanmar.

While the Government of India recognizes Tibetans, Chakmas and Sri Lankan Tamils as refugees, other groups are not recognized and are considered foreign nationals temporarily residing in India. The 20,000 refugees not recognized by the Government of India are assisted by UNHCR and provided international protection and assistance under its Mandate.[8] Regrettably, given the present political turmoil in neighboring countries, particularly in Sri Lanka, Afghanistan, and Myanmar, it is expected that the number of persons seeking refuge in India will continue to increase.

The legal authority to deal with issues of citizenship, naturalization, and foreigners rests with the union legislature. In the Indian context, influxes of refugees have been handled by administrative decisions rather than through specific legislative enactments. Some specific groups of asylum seekers from neighboring countries have been accepted as refugees. In fact, India accepts large groups of refugees who are fleeing not just for reasons relating to persecution, but also due to generalized violence (e.g., Sri Lankan Tamils). It means India de facto accepts the definition of "refugee" as found in the 1969 Organization of African Unity Convention, rather than the narrower definition provided in the 1951 Refugee Convention.[9]

However, this does not hold good for all groups. The Indian government does not recognize certain refugee groups such as the Afghans, Iranians, Iraqis, Somalis, the Sudanese and those from Myanmar. Therefore the UNHCR has had to intervene through determining and granting refugee status under its mandate. This differential treatment of refugees is a fundamental problem. It negates the provision of legal rights and assistance that would normally be granted by an asylum country. Moreover, it is not clear what legal status or rights accrue to a person as a result of registration by the Government of India as a refugees, nor the relationship between "refugee" status granted by the government and corresponding national laws governing the entry and stay of foreigners.

Although a host of international human rights instruments has been ratified by India and other South Asian countries that has significantly strengthened the international regime of human rights protection in South Asia,[10] curiously, however, none of the South Asian countries has acceded to the international refugee instruments. Nor have any of them enacted a domestic legal framework in the form of a refugee or asylum law, or at least a determination procedure. Furthermore, in light of existing human rights standard in South Asia, both through accession to international instruments and domestic laws, some may argue that it is necessary to adopt a law that provides specific recognition and protection to refugees. Others have suggested that such an exercise is too burdensome and would only create another set of legal obligations that the state will have difficulty in fulfilling. Moreover, for a developing country such as India, the financial burden of hosting large numbers of refugees and ensuring that certain legal rights are fulfilled is simply too much to bear.

It is true that the international refugee instruments such as the 1951 *Refugee Convention*, in addition to defining who is a refugee, contain certain "rights" provisions. This includes protection from *refoulement* or forced return, protection against unlawful expulsion or detention, the right to employment and education, access to the courts, and freedom of movement, to name a few. In respect of many of these rights, refugees are supposed to receive the same treatment as nationals in the country of residence. Of course, certain provisions of the international refugee regime such as access to education and employment may incur financial hardship on developing countries. Many of these countries cannot cater to the basic needs of their own people. However, it is not expected that a state would be obliged to fully implement the provisions of the international treaties overnight. These particular legal obligations, in the realm of socioeconomic rights, could be progressively implemented while taking into account the economic situation of the country concerned.

Finally, an off-voiced criticism is that the international refugee regime is out of date and is being flouted by the industrialized countries. Thus, it is argued, a new legal regime should be enacted and efforts made to better enforce the international protection regime for refugees. Of course, a fundamental difficulty of international law is how to enforce it. Although the majority of the world's countries are state parties to the international refugee instruments and related human rights treaties which provide protection to refugees, it is extremely difficult for the international community or UNHCR to challenge the practices of some states who take a restrictive approach to refugees, whether through developments in the law or administrative arrangements. Unlike the human rights treaties, no supervisory committee exists in international refugee law to enforce implementation of the 1951 *Refugee Convention* or its 1967 *Protocol* through a formal process of inter-state scrutiny.

Nevertheless, given the generally positive record of receiving and hosting refugees, it may be time for South Asian countries to codify their "good practice" through acceding to the international refugee instruments and enacting national refugee laws. It is not a sound argument to suggest that as a result of an already generous approach to refugees no specific law is required. This would be like saying that because a state respects the rights of its people, there is no need for a constitution. The protection of the rights of asylum seekers and refugees through national human rights machinery is also something that should be further explored, as it is clear that the complementary nature of international refugee and human rights law in the context of national procedures could provide a suitable legal framework within which to develop principles of refugee protection.

In this context, a greater challenge for the countries of South Asia may be to accede to the 1951 *Refugee Convention* or its *Protocol* and demonstrate to the industrialized world how the spirit and scope of the refugee treaties can be implemented and respected. This would enhance South Asia's image as committed to upholding the human rights of all persons, including refugees. It would also be consistent with their broader human rights obligations as members states of the United Nations. Ironically, three South Asian countries, Bangladesh, India, and Pakistan, are members of the UNHCR Executive Committee. And yet, as noted, none of these countries have formalized their commitment to protecting and assisting refugees through adopting an international or national legal framework. Isn't it time to do so?

NOTES AND REFERENCES

1. Lecture at the first South Asian Peace Studies Orientation Course held by the Maulana Abul Kalam Azad Institute of Asian Studies, Calcutta, October 1997.
2. A key element of the refugee definition as found in the 1951 Refugee Convention is fleeing one's country of origin "owing to a well-founded fear of persecution." Persecution is not defined in international refugee or human rights law. However, one commentator has offered the following description: "... persecution may be defined as the sustained or systematic violation of basic human rights demonstrative of a failure of state protection. A well-founded fear of persecution exists when one reasonably anticipates that the failure to leave the country may result in a form of serious harm which government cannot or will not prevent," James Hathaway, "Fear of Persecution and the Law of Human Rights," *Bulletin of Human Rights*, 91(1), United Nations, New York, 1992, p. 99.
3. There are currently 132 state parties to the 1951 Convention and/or the 1967 Protocol relating to the Status of Refugees. Article 1(A) of the 1951 Convention defines a refugee as any person who: "owing to a well-founded fear of being persecuted for reasons of race, religion, nationality, membership of a particular social group or political opinion, is outside the country of his or her nationality and is unable or, owing to such fear, is unwilling to avail him or herself of the protection of that country; or who, not having a nationality and being outside the country of his or her habitual residence as a result of such events, is unable or owing to such fear, is unwilling to return to it...."

4. This was reported in *The Asian Age* on 17 August 1997. Quoting a statement issued by the Indian Ministry of External Affairs, it was noted that India's accession to the *Convention Against Torture* is part of "India's determination to uphold the greatest values of Indian civilization and our policy with other members of the international community to promote and protect human rights."

   In the refugee context, ratification of the *Convention Against Torture* is extremely important as Article 3(1) provides that: "No State Party shall expel, return ('refouler') or extradite a person to another state where there are substantial grounds for believing that he or she would be in danger of being subjected to torture." Article 3(2) further provides that: "For the purpose of determining whether there are such grounds, the competent authorities shall take into account all relevant consideration including, where applicable, the existence in the state concerned for a consistent pattern of gross, flagrant or mass violations of human rights."

5. *National Human Rights Commission v State of Arunachal Pradesh and another,* (1996) 1 SCC 295.

6. Most recently, the third periodic report of India was examined by the UN Human Rights Committee during its 60th session held at Geneva. In its "Concluding Observations" under the heading "Subjects of Concern and Committee's Recommendations," the Committee remarked as follows: "The Committee, noting that international treaties are not self-executing in India, recommends that steps be taken to incorporate fully the provisions of the Covenant into domestic law, so that individuals may invoke them directly before the courts. The Committee also recommends that consideration be given by the authorities to ratifying the Optional Protocol to the [*International Covenant on Civil and Political Rights*], enabling the Committee to receive individual communications relating to India" (Para 13). Concerning refugees, the Human Rights Committee further stated: "The Committee expresses concern at reports of forcible repatriation of asylum seekers, including those from Myanmar (Chins), the Chittagong Hill and the Chachmas [*sic*]. It recommends that, in the process of repatriation of asylum seekers or refugees, due attention be paid to the provisions of the Covenant and other applicable international norms" (Para 30). See UN Document CCPR/C/60/IND/3 of 30 July 1997.

7. A useful compilation of the various activities of the UN Human Rights bodies concerning refugees and issues of forced displacement is found in the UN Commission on Human Rights Report entitled "Human Rights, Mass Exoduses and Displaced Persons" (see E/CN.4/1997/42 of 14 January 1997).

8. UNHCR is authorized *inter alia* to "assume the function of providing international protection, under the auspices of the

United Nations, to refugees who fall within the scope of the present Statute and of seeking permanent solutions to the problem of refugees by assisting governments...." In practice, these functions include determining the status of individual applicants for refugee status, as is the case for non-government assisted refugees in India and other countries of South Asia, and seeking durable solutions to their problems which may require promoting local integration, facilitating voluntary repatriation, or resettlement to a third country. The Statute of the UNHCR is appended to UN General Assembly Resolution 428(V) of 1950.

9. In addition to the refugee definition contained in the 1951 *Refugee Convention* and its 1967 Protocol, which are the primary international legal instruments for refugee status applied by states, later international refugee instruments such as the *Organization of African Unity* (OAU) *Convention Governing the Specific Aspects of Refugee Problems in Africa* broadened the scope of the term "refugee," so as to include: "... every person who, owing to external aggression, occupation, foreign domination or events seriously disturbing the public order in either part or the whole of his or her country of origin or nationality, is compelled to leave his or her place of habitual residence in order to seek refuge in another place outside his or her country of origin or nationality...."

10. As concerns the application of international human rights standards in domestic law, the Chief Justice of India, J.S. Verma, recently noted in a speech at the SAARC LAW and UNHCR seminar on "Refugee in the SAARC Region" held in New Delhi on 2 May 1997, that: "In the absence of national law satisfying the need [to protect refugees], the provisions of the [1951 Refugee] Convention and its Protocol can be relied on when there is no conflict with any provision in the Municipal Laws. This is a cannon of construction, recognized by the courts in enforcing the obligations of the state for the protection of the basic human rights of individuals. It is more so when the country is a signatory to the International Convention which implies its consent and obligation to be bound by the International Convention, even in the absence of expressly enacted Municipal Laws to that effect [....]" For a recent judicial application of this reasoning, see the Indian Supreme Court judgment of *Vishaka et al. v State of Rajasthan et al.*, Writ Petition (Criminal) Nos 666–70 of 1992, unreported judgment of 13 August 1997.

Certain "rights" provisions of the Indian Constitution, such as Articles 14 (Right to Equality) and 21 (Right to Life and Liberty) of the Indian Constitution are available to non-citizens, including refugees. See the *National Human Rights Commission v State of Arunachal Pradesh and another*, op. cit., and *Khudiram Chakma vs Union of India* (1994) (Suppl.) 1 SCC 614.

5

SELF-DETERMINATION AND POLITICS OF IDENTITY—EAST EUROPE[1]

Subhas Ranjan Chakraborty

> If I were to accost a Yugoslav peasant and whisper to him, "In your lifetime have you known peace," wait for his answer, transform him into his father and ask him the same question, transform him in turn into his father, I would never hear the word yes.
>
> —Rebecca West, *Black Lamb and Grey Falcon*

Eastern Europe today is again an embattled region and it is appropriate that a volume on peace studies should address the history of this region. There is little doubt that enduring peace needs to return to this area; there is equally little doubt that this is an extremely difficult task, given the long history of imperial expansion and ethnic conflict in this area. However, it will not be correct to imagine that the present conflicts are necessarily the results of millennium-old hatred, though history has certainly delineated, to a large extent, the course of events in this area. The term Eastern Europe acquired a special meaning only after 1945, when it was gradually drawn into the Soviet orbit. It seemed that a new political barrier appeared that was perceived "from both sides of the fence rather like a frontier in the old Roman sense, separating civilizations that consider each other as barbarians."[2] Earlier, the term had only a limited coherence as an identity.

Historians and historical geographers have, however, recognized two great socio-political fields of east and west. Between the two fields lies a "marchland" from Scandinavia running through the north European plains to the Balkans. The region was never fully unified either within itself or through annexations by powers in the east or the west. Cultural and ethnic anomalies thrown up by a complex historical evolution have consistently impeded unification during medieval and modern times.[3] A.P. Vlasto refers to the "soft center" of Europe inhabited predominantly by the Slavs through which a frontier between the east and the west would have to be drawn. This frontier "would reflect in its oscillations the relative vitality... of east and west expressed in their bids for the spiritual allegiance of the Slav people."[4]

The history of human settlement in this region cannot be divorced from the complex physical geography of this area. Early settlement was possible because of the availability of navigable rivers, especially the Danube and the frequency of the grasslands or easily cleared woodlands and loess soil. This made the Balkans the corridor of early migrations from the Aegean Sea and the Black Sea, with westward movement possible either along the Danube or the steppe lands that gave easy access to Silesia. While the region was always congenial for settlement and economic development, it was handicapped by its remoteness from the major shipping routes. The fact of geography also makes it imperative to distinguish the northern parts of the Eastern Europe from the southern parts.[5]

The Roman Empire that incorporated greater parts of this region, exerted a powerful influence on the subsequent political developments of this area, demonstrating the essential complementarity of cultural, economic and military elements. The cultural drive came through Christianity, the economic power came through control of the great network of cities and military success was based on the establishment of an effective center. The Roman Empire, however, did not impinge directly on the northern parts. The decline of the Roman Empire was not evident in all the former parts of the empire and in Eastern Europe the imperial structure survived for another 1,000 years with its base at Constantinople. The Byzantine did not enjoy solid peace as the challenge of militarily gifted tribes proved to be an almost perennial one. Yet, it introduced the Orthodox faith and the Byzantine model was widely copied by the states that were formed in this area during the medieval period.

The migration and cross-migration of different tribes had shaped the history of this region in the early medieval period. The Germans failed to maintain effective leadership in this area and were gradually overcome by the Avars, the Magyars, the Slavs, the Bulgarians, and others. The Avars maintained their power in Pannonia for nearly 250 years, but then lost ground to the Magyars. Otto's defeat of the Magyars checked their westward advance and they, now settling in the core area of what was to become Hungary, drove a wedge between the Slavs, separating the south Slavs from the northern groups (Czechs, Poles, Slovaks etc.).[6] Political developments in Eastern Europe rested heavily on the Slavs whose original homeland extended from the Vistula eastward and southward to the Bug, Dnieper, and Pripet. The reduced tempo of east–west migration left Eastern Europe with a chance for consolidation. Such consolidation produced various larger groupings from clusters of "nations" and some of them were disposed to extreme imperial pretensions on the Roman model. The new states established a connection between the "nations" and their territories. But more significant were the emotional ties that these territories came to evoke. Ultimately, it would be impossible to separate a "nation" from the land on which it was based. Poland's perception of space, for example, cannot be understood without taking into account its long association with the Vistula river. Likewise, the link between Bohemia and the Vlatava river has been immortalized by the music of Smertana.

Several states were formed in this region between the 9th and the 14th centuries. Great Moravia, including Czechoslovakia, southern parts of East Germany and Poland and Hungary, are mentioned in documents in AD 892. The Magyars destroyed it after some time. Croatia was established towards the end of the first millennium of the Christian era and maintained its independence till the end of the 11th century. Later, it was merged with Hungary. The development of Poland is best studied in the context of *opola*, small ecological units ranging in area from 50 to 300 sq. km. The name of Poland was derived from *opola*. In the late 10th century Mieszko brought together a number of small Slav tribes east of the river Oder and founded the first Polish state. He also embraced Christianity. Poland became an important state in this area and was later involved in conflicts with neighbors to the north and east. The core of the Czech nation, a Bohemian state was formed for the first time in the 9th century.

The Magyars, who settled in the Pannonian plains in the 10th century, occupied Hungary. The Tatars devastated and Bela became virtually the second founder of Hungary. The powerful Magyar state generated a number of "Banats" or client states. In Bulgaria a state was formed as early as AD 716, but a new era began with the accession of Boria who, after his conversion to Christianity, took the name of Michael. The state forged the people of the area into a nation and resisted Byzantine attempts at assimilation. The advancing Turks gradually absorbed it in the late 14th century. Settled in the rugged upland country, the Serbs remained quite untouched by the outside world for some time. An embryonic Serb state first appeared in AD 872. The Turks later overwhelmed it. The early history of Bosnia is largely obscure. A state was formed in the early part of the second millennium. An interesting feature of Bosnian history is the Bogomil heresy, which recognized Satan (as God's rebel elder son) to be the Creator of the Universe. The cult took firm roots as heretics from Croatia and Dalmatia sought sanctuary. This might explain why, in contrast to other south Slav people, the Bosnians willingly embraced Islam after the Turkish conquest. Moldavia and Wallachia were the Danubian principalities forming the core of what was to become Romania. Albania also acquired a distinct political identity and following Turkish conquest people, already converted to Islam, settled in the area.

The construction of a new political geography in Eastern Europe was the great achievement of the medieval period. The church acted as a catalyst in the development of the states and in the creation of some sense of community in the region as a whole, providing a set of standards conducive to civilized behavior within and between nations. Different churches (e.g., Catholic, Orthodox), however, meant different cultural influences, separating Croats and Slovenes from the Macedonians, Montenegrins, and Serbs as regards mentality and national consciousness. The Christian–Muslim divide also existed in south Slav territory.

The early modern period saw the domination of Turkey established over large parts of Eastern Europe. The northern part was the theater of conflict between Poland and Russia, Poland and Lithuania, and Russia and Turkey. By the 18th century Turkey had to contend with the powerful Hapsburg and Romanov empires. As a consequence, Turkey's position in the area was on the decline. Early in the 18th century Turkey gave a part of Wallachia and a fertile part of Serbia including Belgrade to Austria. She also lost Hungary and Transylvania and Bukovina to Austria, Bessarabia and the adjacent coastland of the Black Sea to Russia. The treaty of Kutchuk–kainardji (1774) confirmed the Russian gains. Needless to say, all these centuries witnessed intermittent wars between the states in the region. The expansive tendencies of the great powers also compounded the situation here leading to the tragedy of the partitions of Poland.

In the 19th century, the instability caused by the continuing decline of Turkey was compounded by the rise of nationalism in the area. The French Revolution exercised a powerful, if somewhat indirect, influence on the region and Napoleon's advance to the Illyrian provinces even created vague hopes of liberation from Turkish rule.[7] Throughout Eastern Europe countless monuments attest to the immense emotional appeal that the idea of nationality evoked and still evokes in the region. There is enough literary evidence to suggest the growing sense of national identity that developed among almost all the nationalities in the entire region. Szechenyi, a Hungarian savant, wrote, "Poor little fatherland, how filthy you are!" in comparing the ideal with the real. A Serb student at the Heidelberg University Jevrem Grujic, left the university when a professor of history called the Serbs barbarians. The Slavic poet Kollar in his "Daughters of the Slavs" projected a resurrection of the Slavs to world leadership and glory.[8]

The emerging intelligentsia in these parts was naturally influenced by the ideas prevalent in Western Europe and craved for their emulation and implementation in Eastern Europe. Herder noted that the Serbs had "now sunk so low," but he expected them to awaken from "their long, enervating sleep." To Palacky, the Czech historian, Herder was the "apostle of humanity." The Herderian concept of national character was to leave a strong impact on the intellectuals of the small nations of Europe. It gave a fillip in particular to the growth of

Pan-Slavism.[9] Kollar acquired his Pan-Slavism through German Romanticism. Palacky and Szechenyi had their early education in Germany. The French tradition was also quite strong. Jokai, the Magyar novelist, read French. Goethe urged Karadjic to publish his epic poems of the Serb peasantry. In the process, modern Serb developed as a language. Education, particularly in universities of western Europe, played a seminal role in stimulating a quest for cultural roots. A great deal of attention was paid to the languages of the area and there was a revival of Magyar or Slovak languages as well. For example, by the 1840s the Slovaks of Hungary gave up Czech as their literary language in favor of a speech based on the living Slovak dialects. As a consequence of these developments, linguistic, cultural, and national identities were steadily emerging. Where political traditions existed, as in Hungary and Poland, the cultural revival reinforced such traditions. But as yet Slav nationalism was not seen as a great challenge by the authorities.

The year 1848 was, in Europe, a year of revolutions. Understandably, Eastern Europe did not escape the political upheaval. There were revolts in Prague, Budapest and many other towns. Liberalism was added to nationalism to provide a headier brew. Even in the areas not directly affected, the "springtime of the people" was celebrated, even though in a low key. Grujic, a student, wrote to his brother, "In the history of the world a new epoch wills itself into being ... we should found a Serbian kingdom ... restore a Serbian empire."[10] Yet, the newly acquired nationalism in the area was not without certain disturbing implications. As Robin Okey puts it, "Were the aspirations of the Germans, Czechs, Poles and Italians, of Magyars, Serbs, Croats and Romanians compatible with each other on the maintenance of a stable European polity?... Events were to show that the social issues could be resolved, but the national issues could not."[11] Indeed, the Magyars, in demanding their autonomy from the Hapsburgs, were reluctant to share it with the other national groups in Hungary. The dilemma plagues the region even today.

The revolutions of 1848 were the work of young Europe: young races, young social classes, young men. The students formed the vanguard of the movement not only in France and Germany, but also in Budapest, Transylvania, and the Serbian provinces. The apparent failure of the movements was the end of the first act, rather than of the entire drama. After 1848, the revolutionaries grew tougher, and their naïve optimism gave place to a better understanding of the psychology of the masses.[12]

The failure of 1848 also led to a period of reforms. By the late 1850s reform ideas were penetrating even areas unstirred by 1848. The Serbian philologist Danicic wrote, "Nationality without liberty can exist upon the earth, but freedom without nationality is unthinkable....The Serbian nation is in the world for no other purpose than to be the Serbian nation." The smaller nations, who were awakening to their nationhood, encountered the incompatibility with the articulate nationalism of the more developed nations. Against the rights of the larger nations, the rights of the smaller nations were presented as rights of nature. Those who represented the "nations without a history" used a liberal rhetoric and also used the question of political organization. History, however, was invariably invoked. Should the new states be organized on the basis of their historic frontier? Should a Serb state, then, have the frontiers of 1389? Likewise, should Transylvania belong to Hungary because of historic association or to Romania because of its Romanian-speaking majority? The questions of territory, and of frontier have continued to influence historical developments in the area ever since. Significantly, the post-1848 period also saw an increasing integration of the Balkan question into European politics.

The Balkans or Southeast Europe was also astir now with new ideas. The themes of Balkan politics now corresponded to those of the lands to the north of the Danube. From the mid-19th century, both Turkey and her Christian subjects were looking for European legitimacy. The Ottoman Empire tried to address the problem through the introduction of reforms. The Tanzimat reforms aimed at the creation of an efficient bureaucracy, at bringing wayward provinces under control, at introducing modern tax system and at shifting the basis of law and education from Islamic to Christian principles. But these reforms did not acquire significant roots in European Turkey. Christian peasant revolts continued during the period: in southern Serbia in 1848, in west and north Bulgaria in 1847 and 1848, and in Herzegovina in 1858 and 1862. From the early 19th century, Turkey was also obliged to grant autonomy to certain provinces.

The principality of Serbia became the focus of Balkan Slavs. Serbia became autonomous in 1829 under Milosh Obrenovic. The Karadjordjevic dynasty took over in the 1840s and a process of Europeanization proceeded apace. A secret plan was made in 1844 to create the medieval Serbian empire, but it came to nothing. After the Crimean war the duchies of Moldavia and Wallachia were united to create the kingdom of Romania. In Bulgaria nationalism developed along a somewhat different line, but was no less vehement in its expressions. Mixing Orthodox faith, folk memory and western ideas, Balkan nationalisms preached their rightful place among the nations of Europe to the exclusion of Turkey. From the time of the Serb revolt of 1804–13 and Romanian revolt of 1821, the Balkan peoples had always assisted each other. In the 1860s this cooperation took on a more formal character under Prince Michael of Serbia. He concluded agreements with Greece, Romania, Montenegro, and the Bulgarian emigres. The aim was the destruction of European Turkey.

The revolt of the Serbs in Bosnia and Herzegovina in 1875 was the signal for fresh turmoil in the area. It led to a war between Turkey and Serbia. Serbia and Montenegro were later saved from rout by the intervention of Russia. Russia defeated Turkey, who was obliged to agree to major changes in the area to the advantage of Russia. But Russia, in turn, lost most of the advantages after Bismarck, the German Chancellor, convened a Congress of European powers in Berlin. The big Russian client state of Bulgaria was cut back in size and Bosnia–Herzegovina was given to Austria–Hungary to "occupy and administer." The Congress demonstrated the heat that the mixing of nationalism and great power rivalry could produce in the area. The Austrian foreign minister Andrassy was willing to permit what he called *volkspersonlichkeiten* or ethnic identities in the Balkans provided they did not aspire to play an autonomous political role. By 1878 then there were Serbia, Montenegro, Bulgaria, and Romania as independent states. It is ironical, however, that excepting the king Milan of Serbia, Charles of Romania, Alexander von Battenberg and then Ferdinand of Saxe-Coburg of Bulgaria were all princes of German extraction.[13] Indeed, Pan-Germanism also aimed at expansion towards the Adriatic. Balkans in the *fin de siecle* era remained a veritable source of explosion. Franz Ferdinand had once described Serbia as a land of "thieves and murderers, and bandits and a few plum tree." It was this implied contempt that made nationalism in the region all the more intense. Serbia's efforts at economic improvement yielded some results. Railways were introduced and Serbia was seeking better access to the Adriatic. In 1905 the university of Belgrade was opened; in 1906 came the university of Sofia. A Serbo-Bulgarian customs union in 1905 was an attempt by Serbia to escape Austro-Hungarian economic tutelage. Serbs and Croats were also working together in Croatia and the Serbs conducted a successful campaign for the autonomy of the church and education in Bosnia. The annexation of Bosnia-Herzegovina by Austria in 1908 thus came as a great jolt to the Serb aspirations for greater Serb unity in the area.

In 1911 Serbia promoted the Balkan League, which made war on Turkey the next year. Turkey was defeated, but the Balkan war also revealed the complexity of the situation here. Earlier, unity and cohesion among the nationalities could be preserved by the construction of Turkey as the Other. But the sharing of the spoils of war after the defeat of Turkey presented a greater problem, leading to the second Balkan war between Bulgaria and the others. In spite of these developments, nationalism made significant gains in this region at the expense of Turkey. Ethnic groups in other multi-racial empires did not fare well. The explosive nature of Balkan politics was demonstrated when the assassination of Franz Ferdinand at Sarajevo, the Bosnian capital touched off the First World War. Count Czernin, the foreign minister under emperor Charles perhaps made the most fitting comment on the old order, "We had to die. We had the liberty to choose the manner of our death. We chose the most terrible."[14]

Once the existing system was called into question in Eastern Europe during the first world war, only nationalism had a magnetism strong enough to draw the dislocated elements into an alternative political order—the pattern of nation-states. During the period 1919–39 the states in the region did enjoy relative autonomy. But the post-war settlement, quite understandably, failed to provide a durable solution to the problem of nationalities. The successor states, which inherited the legacy of the heterogeneous empires, were to find the pitch queered. Poland was recreated with additional areas taken from Germany. Austria and Hungary were separate states now, with reduced territories. Bohemia, Moravia and Austrian Silesia constituted the new state of Czechoslovakia. Romania received Bukovina and Bessarabia. She also received Transylvania from Hungary; there were now 3 million Hungarians in Romania. A new south Slav state of Yugoslavia incorporated Bosnia-Herzegovina, Serbia, Croatia, Slovenia, Montenegro, and Macedonia. Bulgaria retained her 1914 frontier, but had to cede western Thrace to Greece. It was well nigh impossible to delineate the borders of the new states along strictly ethnic lines. Zones of friction appeared almost immediately in Bohemia, Moravia, in Transylvania, in Silesia, in Istria and the hinterland of Trieste. The peacemakers did provide for guarantee treaties for the minorities, but they were not enough to soothe the fractured identities of many small ethnic groups.[15] Indeed, the rationality of the creation of a compact south Slav state has been questioned in retrospect. A curious feature of these states was that although they were inspired by western nationalism, the ideology involved the East European elites, who forged an exclusivist basis for the new nation-states.[16]

To the problem of integration was added the nature of these new states. East European democracy took a distinctive form, "it was above all populist, moulded still by the romantic image of the common fate which had first stirred languishing societies a century before."[17] It was also intensely national in tone. The historical and social evolution in Eastern Europe was divergent from the west and the region was, in addition, ethnically heterogeneous and economically retarded. These features underlay "the chauvinistic element of East European nationalism, which mobilized putatively rooted ethnic identities for elite end."[18] Nationalism did play a role in cementing popular loyalties to the new state, to the detriment of sizeable ethnic minorities. In Czechoslovakia, the Germans and the Slovaks were disaffected by the strongly centralizing tendencies of Prague. In Yugoslavia, the Croat Peasant Party bitterly resented Serbian domination. Internal Macedonian Revolutionary Organization used terrorist methods to win independence. The Croats set up a separate parliament in Zagreb in 1928. The Slovenes were critical of the Serbs' monopolizing of all administrative posts.

Democracy also failed to acquire roots in the region in the years after the First World War. With the exception of Czechoslovakia, no other state could establish a functioning democratic system. Hungary's leaders repudiated democracy almost from the very beginning. Albania's few democrats faced insurmountable odds. The democratic order required time to take roots and it was precisely this time that was to be denied. The economic depression of 1929 transformed the international climate and liberal democracy was everywhere on the retreat. Economic retardation was stark reality. In Yugoslavia, 80 percent of the population were peasants, but only 20 percent of the country's investments were in agriculture. Only one-third of Bosnian children attended school in 1939; infant mortality in Romanian countryside was 20 percent; Bulgaria had 450,000 wooden ploughs to 250,000 iron ploughs; while the Dutch farmers used 311 kg of fertilizer per hectare in 1939, Yugoslavia and Romania used 0.2 kg only.[19] The main beneficiary of the political elites' failure to develop effective institutions and arrest economic decline was the far right. The Hungarian Szalasi's Arrow Cross and Romanian Codreanu's Iron Guard mobilized popular antipathy towards the traditional elite. Yet, these movements lacked the potential of their western counterparts. King Carol in Romania established a royalist dictatorship and had Codreanu shot. The Arrow Cross showed no capacity to bid for power until Hitler put them there in 1944. Before the war, king Carol of Romania, Boris of Bulagaria, Zog of Albania, and Prince Regent Paul of Yugoslavia all presided over totalitarian regimes. Communism also found a base in these societies and produced a cadre of professional revolutionaries. Milovan Djilas noted that communism's force for his generation was the promise it offered of an escape from the region's self-destroying poverty. Josip Broz as Tito became the general secretary of the Communist Party of Yugoslavia in 1937. Thus independent Eastern Europe did not quite reach its maturity in the inter-war years. Hitler's expansion towards the region ultimately produced the Second World War.

The Second World War immediately led to a drastic reorganization of the states in the area. Hitler invaded Poland from the west and Russia moved in from the east. Croatia was separate now and, along with Hungary, Romania, and Bulgaria, allied to Germany. Albania was annexed by Italy and Serbia was later taken by Germany. But after the defeat of the axis powers, the map of the area was re-drawn and remained by and large the same till the break-up of the Soviet Union led to drastic, if also violent, restructuring in Eastern Europe. The problem of minority ethnic groups was not solved even after the war. Yugoslavia's claim to have solved the Macedonian question was denied by Bulgaria; Romania resents the loss of Bessarabia to Russia and the Albanians the inclusion of a third of the Albanians in the Yugoslav state. The Hungarians had been critical of the treatment of the 2 million Magyar (minority) population in Transylvania. Milovan Djilas was always attached to his Serbian and Montenegrin roots.[20] The most important development in Eastern Europe after the war was the setting up of the communist governments between 1945 and 1949. Eastern Europe now had an ideological unity that was unprecedented in the history of the region. The effective line separating east from the west ran from the North Sea along the borders of West Germany and Austria to Italy and the Adriatic. If Hitler realized the Pan-German dream only for a very brief period, Stalin's realization of the Pan-Slav dream was to endure longer. The eastern bloc survived Stalin, but did not survive the break up of the Soviet Union. Nationalism remained a major theme here even during the Cold War period. Benedict Anderson noted several decades later, "Who can be confident that Yugoslavia and Albania will not one day come to blows? Those ... who seek the withdrawal of the Red Army from ... Eastern Europe should remind themselves of the degree to which its overwhelming presence has, since 1945, ruled out armed conflict between the region's Marxist regimes."[21] He was certainly prophetic, but it raises questions of central importance. Can ethnic and other heterogeneity within political borders be maintained only by force? Recognition of diversity and a true federal structure are likely to provide a more durable structure. This may be a pious hope, but is certainly worth trying.

We are not trying to look here at the detailed history of the region during the past half-century. That some states broke up in the early 1990s would confirm that nationalism remained a strong force in the decades after the Second World War. If the break up was what has been called the "velvet revolution" in some countries, Yugoslavia has experienced veritable hell in the process of disintegration. We may look at the outline of the history of this country after the Second World War as a case study. Yugoslavia was created as a compact south Slav state after the First World War in spite of strong national ideologies. There was an absence of clearly written rights, responsibilities, and obligations of the different nations creating Yugoslavia. This allowed the exercise of Serbian hegemony. Yet it would be wrong to believe that the Serbs and the Croats were perpetually fighting each other. They actually fought during the First World War, when Croats, as Austrian conscripts, fought the Serbian army. "This did leave some traumatic scars, but far from an all-pervasive enmity that is the central popular image in the west."[22] The other nations like the Montenegrins, Slovenes and Macedonians played a secondary role in the initial stages. The Serbs were 38.83 percent, Croats 23.77 percent, Slovenes 8.53 percent, Bosnian Muslims 6.05 percent and Macedonians 21.87 percent.[23] In spite of such heterogeneity one purpose that the new state served was to secure the international border and to bring into the new territory as many Slavs as possible This was not total, however, as many Slovenes and Croats remained within Austria and Hungary.

During the inter-war period, centralism as a form of state organization was greatly favored to the denial of national individuality of the south Slav nations. This "unitarian Yugoslavia" ran counter to the reality of a multi-racial state. "What Yugoslavia needed was a consolidation of the state and the recognition of differences within it. That would have made the state stronger, not weaker."[24] This is the view of the former Yugoslav ambassador to the European Community and needs to be noted seriously. The centralizing policies merely irritated sensibilities and helped to complete the process of national identification. The Second World War destroyed Yugoslavia as we have already seen. Serbia was now under a collaborative regime under General Nedic and the fascist Ustashi ruled Croatia. It was in Croatia that a virtual "ethnic cleansing" was launched against mainly the Serbs, but other minorities as well. This probably created a bitterness that has never been forgotten and may be seen as present in large measure even today. The estimate of Serbs killed in Croatia varies greatly. Tudjman, a historian and the President of Croatia, claims that the number was "a few tens of thousand." The Serbs believe the number to be close to a million. According to the Encyclopedia of the Holocaust an estimated 600,000 people were killed in Croatia.[25]

The Serbs organized their own national group, the Chetniks, who were active in Serbia, Montenegro, parts of Bosnia and on Serb territories in Croatia. In Bosnia there were clashes between Ustashi and the Muslims as well. A truly Yugoslav fighting force emerged in 1941 under Tito. The 5th conference of the CPY gave the call for an all-Yugoslav struggle, based on the principles of federal unity within the party. From a minor guerrilla force of 11,000 in 1941 the partisans grew to be an army of 700,000 by 1944.Thus the war, which produced intense ethnic feud in some area, also provided for the context for a united resistance movement and thus gave the federation a fresh lease of life. Tito's stature was very high after the war and he was aware of the mistakes made during the inter-war years. He gave the slogan of "brotherhood" instead of "oneness." He sought the unity of the ethnic groups rather than a symbiosis into an artificial supranational "nationality." He hoped that a policy of reconciliation would heal old wounds and, for some time, it appeared as if the approach would succeed. The hopes were belied less than a half-century later. Overall, the Tito years, reservations notwithstanding, were years of stability and respectability for Yugoslavia. The national question, except for some scattered incidents, did not become a central issue. In this respect, the situation was better than during the inter-war years. Yet, the limitations increasingly became clear only a few years after the death of Tito.

The ethnic and national dimensions of the Yugoslav crisis came out in the open after 1987. By that time economic crisis and political paralysis tended to shift the focus from the federation to the republics. Serbia was the first focus of the new national mood. The "awakening," as it were, came in stages. The lead was taken by a group of intellectuals, who wrote, in 1986, a "Memorandum on the Position of Serbia in Yugoslavia." In the second stage a group of "patriots" became the carriers and transmitters of the national ideologies. Slobodan Milosevic was the leader of this group and soon became a cult figure. In the last stage, the ideas reached the people. The crux of the Serbian contention was that the other republics had achieved a sort of national identity at the same time as they experienced development. The Serbians achieved neither. The Slovenes and the Croats had accomplished their national program mainly because of their control of the federation. The central significance of the situation in Kosovo, which continues to be a flashpoint, was brought out during this period. The exodus of Serbs from Kosovo was seen as a testimony to Serbia's historic defeat. The Serbs resolved to act and the attempt to "solve Serbia's problems opened up Pandora's box." The consequent break up of Yugoslavia, after nearly seven decades of unstable existence, was not long in coming. That it also experienced the kind of violence that it did has to be explained in terms of the complex history of nations and borders in the area and also perhaps in terms of certain developments in the international sphere.

The goals of the nationalist movements in the 19th century were: (a) the development of a national culture based on the local language and its normal use in education, administration and economic life; (b) the achievement of civil rights and political self-administration; and (c) the creation of a complete social structure on the sole basis of ethnic groups. In an ethnically mixed situation as one finds in Eastern Europe, the most "dangerous aspect of national revival is the question of national space." This often leads to, as it has probably led to in Eastern Europe, aggressive nationalism. "Claims to national space are based on appeals to two different criteria: ethnic homogeneity on the one hand and historic territory with traditional borders on the other."[26] With nationalism are invariably mixed other ingredients like the political system, the international environment, economic conditions, history and traditions. Nationalism is a necessary but not a sufficient explanation of what happened in the countries of Eastern Europe.

Borders in Yugoslavia, as elsewhere, are a major issue and one of the principal causes of the present turbulence. There are "invisible frontiers" between states and there are strong bonds transcending "visible frontiers." The new correspondence of ethnic and administrative borders made a peaceful dissolution almost unimaginable. It shows that the questions of nations and borders remain relevant and one suspects that history would always be used, and perhaps abused, to legitimize the quest for "national border."

NOTES AND REFERENCES

1. Lecture titled as "Nations, Borders and Wars in Eastern Europe" at the first South Asian Peace Studies Orientation Course held by the Maulana Abul Kalam Azad Institute of Asian Studies, Calcutta, October 1997.
2. J. Gottman, *The Significance of Territory*. Wisconsin, 1977, p. 143.
3. D. Turnock, *The Making of Eastern Europe* London, 1988, p. 81.
4. A.P. Vlasto, *The Entry of the Slavs into Christendom in Introduction of the Medieval History of the Slavs*. Cambridge, 1970, pp. 308–9.
5. D. Turnock, op. cit., pp. 5–11.
6. Ibid., pp. 115–48.
7. Ivo Andric, *The Bosnian Story*. London, 1961.
8. Robin Okey, *Eastern Europe, 1740–1980*. London, 1982, pp. 74–76.
9. Ibid., p. 77.
10. Ibid., p. 86.
11. Ibid., p. 86.
12. Francois Fetjo, *The opening of an Era. 1848: A Historical Symposium*. London, n.d., pp. 214–17; also see, R. Porter and M. Teich, *Revolutions in History* (CUP, 1986).
13. J.A.R. Marriott, *The Eastern Question*. Oxford, 1969, pp. 309–40; D. Thompson, *Europe Since Napoleon* London, 1960, pp. 428–41.
14. Quoted in R. Okey, op. cit., p. 156.
15. D. Thomson, op. cit., pp. 586–90, pp. 595–97.
16. J. Buxton, "Forward into History: The Liberalisation of Eastern Europe," in B. Brinati, J. Buxton and A. Seldon (eds), *The Contemporary History Handbook*. Manchester, 1996, p. 170.
17. R. Okey, op. cit., p. 163.
18. J. Buxton, op. cit., p. 171.
19. R. Okey, op. cit., p. 176.
20. He told a Scandinavian diplomat, "I don't like your Nordic countries, with all your wealth, your social harmony ... I want my country! Its bitterness and its poisons, its joys and its splendor." in R. Okey, op. cit., p. 232.
21. Benedict Anderson, *Imagined Communities*. London, 1987, p. 12.
22. M. Crnobrnja, *The Yugoslav Drama*. London, 1994, p. 49.
23. I. Banac, *The National Question in Yugoslavia: Origin, History and Politics*. Ithaca, 1984, p. 58.
24. M. Crnobrnja, op. cit., p. 64.
25. Ibid., p. 66.
26. Ibid., p. 5.

6

DEATHS, RESPONSIBILITY, AND JUSTICE[1]

Ranabir Samaddar

I

Counted, the murders in the sky on 11 September would probably be somewhere near 4,000, enough to make us immune to murders here, sit up and take notice; but the number is nowhere near to that of deaths at some places else. But seen on the screen, heard, and read, their effect is apocalyptic. From death in the sky in two strikes, it has transformed into a world phenomenon, which deaths of thousands and millions in the Middle East, Rwanda, and the Balkans in the last decade could not achieve. It could be achieved not by similarity, but by difference between deaths.[2] Thus, if your deaths are 50,000, they are not much; if our deaths are 6,000, they should belong to humanity. If your deaths are on the ground, they are banal; if our deaths are on the sky, they are extra-ordinary. If the killing field was in your country, then it was your country's 1,000 years' past and the present that was at fault; if the killing field is in my imaginary space of innocence for 250 years, then our innocence must outshine your culpability, for these deaths have hit the cradle of civilization. If you have demanded your way of life, you are dangerous; if we have demanded our way of life, that is because we have the inalienable right of self-determination. Your response to killings of your kinsfolk should be reconciliation; our response is retribution. Our dream of greatness is historical necessity, yours is fascism. All the rules apply to you not to us. Perhaps this is what baroque death is, a chasm between single deaths and the death ornamented, and in this way universalized—deaths that become universal not by numbers, but by the density of death achievable only by acceleration of its effects. The attacks from the sky to murder people who were literally unable to run away to the ground were a major atrocity. In scale they may not have reached the level of Clinton's bombing of Sudan destroying half its pharmaceutical supplies, and Sr. Bush's and Jefferson Clinton's blockade of Iraq killing unknown numbers of people, but in intensity, they will be more, with harsh security controls and many possible ramifications for undermining civil liberties, internal freedom, racial tolerance, and the little geopolitical sanguinity still left. This crime is a gift to the baroque art that had almost died, an art whose utility lay in making the significance of death universal, and the denial of whatever was living. In one shot, to be exact two shots, old wickedness has been wiped off the register, which had the record of American missiles smashing into Palestinian homes and U.S. helicopters firing missiles into Lebanese ambulance in 1996, American shells crashing into a village called Qana, Lebanese right-wing militia, paid and uniformed by America's friend Israel, raping, hacking, and butchering their way ahead through refugee camps, the bombing of baby food producing plant in Baghdad, the silent witnessing on one day in the summer of 1995 in Srebrenica in Bosnia when 5,000 to 7,000 were killed by the Serb militias and the UN watched, while Srebrenica was an internationally "protected area" so declared by the UN itself, the massacre at MyLai, but that is long enough past to forget, and much more.

Deaths bring new possibilities with ending existing geopolitical certainties, possibilities in form of funerary baroque. The toys of defence shields may aim at blocking the road of the Chinese to the sources of energy in the Middle East, to encircle Iran and Iraq after the American success in squeezing Syria and Lebanon between the two pro-American regional powers, Israel and Turkey. Furthermore through their influence in Afghanistan the Americans may acquire the ability to enhance their influence over Kazakhstan and Turkmenistan where a considerable amount of gold and oil were recently uncovered, also influence the internal dynamics in Iran and Iraq, which must come with the change in the political scenario in Afghanistan.

Explorations into the geopolitical ramification of the so-called terror-deaths can go far. These geopolitical ramifications suggest a new form of war, as the deaths of 11 September by themselves were of new form, wherefrom these ramifications flow, exactly as the deaths 56 years ago on 6 August and 9 August were of a new form. In forging an alliance for this new war launched by President Bush against unknown enemies (but partly defined by "our" anti-terrorist bloc against "their" terrorist bloc), all kinds of required concessions to would be allies, may well result in the sacrifice of old sanguinities such as the National Defense System (NDS), the agenda for the enlargement of NATO, and an Atlantic-based power system. Thus, India may be upgraded to the status of strategic ally, a process that has already begun, to strike at the hostile forces in West Asia and Central Asia, Pakistan downgraded to the role of peons and orderlies for strategic intrusions in the region, and a new government may have to be installed in Kabul. But here the uncertainties accelerate. For, setting up a new government in Kabul will require the cooperation, or at least positive neutrality, of Russia and all Afghan neighbors; in return concessions would have to be given elsewhere, positively a new scenario that finally draws the curtain on the Europe-centric cold war, 13 years after it had ended in 1989. To become finally Asian power with land base with required logistical support-system, the West will have to non-westernize itself, thus ending the Calvinistic campaign of democracy in Muslim-majority countries, allow countries like Iran, Uzbekistan, Kazhakstan, and Russia to have "constructive non-alignment" in response to American presence in the region, resume trade with Iran (through the lifting of sanctions imposed by the Iran-Libya Sanction Act), and strategically confront China from a direction completely unanticipated by the Chinese at least formally till now. In this new war, China too to begin with, has to remain neutral, as indeed it has been while unequivocally condemning the terrorist act, and probably expecting in vain that the West would co-operate in its stand against Uyghur, Tibetan, and Taiwanese separatisms. The Great Game, when it began, began with deaths; the new great game is on, and who could doubt that the baroque deaths were an affirmation of old power, solemn and terrific, by adding something new to it?

All the more therefore the question, what is terrorist killing and terrorist death? Not killings of terrorists not even killings by terrorists, but killings that arouse terror—a terror-death, a death that terrorizes, a terror that produces death, a death that will not be considered normal, banal, but exceptional and so different from the living as to produce terror. Therefore, part of the population in various parts of the world unable to fathom the deaths in the sky will not be terrorized at the deaths up there in the buildings touching the sky, but terrorized at the prospects of deaths that those deaths in the sky will have brought upon them. Terrors of different kinds, and this difference that the baroque cannot erase—in fact the more universal the death the more are the differences. Americans were not terrorized at the deaths in Rwanda, Tamils were not terrorized at the killings in Punjab and Bengal; death is therefore universal while terror is differential. We know that for the last half-century killings have gone on with indifference of many not affected immediately, but we also know that deaths have become now matter of concern, they produce terror, death has become a being, an act that leaps into universality. Torture of the dissenting sects in medieval times, regular throttling of infants and children to death by the Ottoman emperors, stoning of liberals to death in the rugged squares of a city, or shooting of communists by firing squads in soccer stadium—in all these death is protocol. The protocol is of establishing what should be alive, compared to the great anonymous slaughters in wars. The latter scarcely rank as events; they are not symbolic (in contrast to the deaths in the temples of financial and military power), though acknowledged as facts. They are slave massacres, unknown, collective, plebian. But paradoxically in making death a baroque act, the singularity is destroyed. Massive deaths become banal, in time what the anonymous deaths have been.

Death is an occasion always for states to come to sense, for the return of the state. Revolution needs deaths; but more than that, a statist counter-revolution needs death as the necessary protocol. The state, in order to make a come back, requires a murderous rite. The victim holds office, he is innocent, he is clean, he had no complicity with murders, he typifies the daily life of rule—he was not exceptional. His death is therefore dying at the hands of a murderer, the duration of an act, the slaughter of innocence, the catastrophe of silence, a death that requires baroque funeral—in form of wholesale incarceration of family and clan members to death, of the wife led to the pyre, of rounding up of members of a locality to the execution ground, or in form of a grand memorial, or forming a state or states. The effects outshine the occasion, or the effects outshining the cause are the occasion, the monumental *Taj* in building and destroying in honor of death. We must not eat for some days, observe certain purifying rites, force others into penance, silence, and agony, kill a few or thousands to avenge, build a mausoleum—a kind of denial of death by absorbing immediately this death into monuments of other acts that include the dying of others, an avenging angel that will make killing (of others) look like a suicide (of selves). In this way, the state returns with all controls. It returned repeatedly in Mughal India, in Ottoman Turkey, in Agrippina's Rome, in Socrates' Athens, in Sheikh Mujibur Rehman's Bangladesh, or after the killing of Prince Ferdinand in Europe when thousands and thousands followed the Austrian Prince and the cause of his nemesis, Gavrilo Princip the Serb freedom-dreamer, into dying in the second decade of the last century. In revolution, more in restoration, power needs the protocol of dying. Death by terrorist or a terrorist death is like life, for it brings so many back to life. Consider for example the following: the state that comes alive after some deaths (in Indira Gandhi's case in India or Premadasa's case in Sri Lanka, after one single death), victim who becomes the decor of life (Gandhi, Kennedy, Martin Luther King Jr.), unconcerned who become the anxious victims-to-be (Central Asia in 1990s), and the counselors who find their vocation earlier snatched away from them by the banality of life and death restored to them now (West Europeans to the Balkans). The change in the form of murderous tool does not matter. Hand (throttling), rope (tying), knife (assassinating), rifle (shooting), bombing (en masse destroying), ramming aircraft (piercing), atom bomb dropping (finishing everything in fire and smoke), chemical weapon (poisoning), death by injection (pleasant death), and guided missiles (revolutionary killing, the RMA)—all these are incidental. Essential is death achievable through killing and achievable of terror. The fundamental principle is that, this death was not certain, terror did it; it may visit me. Even after the most furious act of omission or commission, the most severe ruler like the Emperor Aurangzeb would have pardoned me, but this death may visit me any time. Therefore the ghost must be laid to rest, rubble must be turned into ashes, the corpse must be taken out of grave and given new burial—again the mode is purely instrumental, the murderous function of a killing is the protocol of the power that is living.

Death begins however with attack on life, though its function is to make at least some lives reaffirm their souls. Thus the deaths in the sky were an attack on "way of life," reinforcing old polarities, old struggles between "democracy" and "totalitarianism," "modernism" versus "backwardness," "pluralism" versus the "imposition of one opinion," and "rationality versus fundamentalism," in other words between "life" and "death." Born again Christian fundamentalists, supported by the most reactionary and religious coalition, which includes people such as the infamous Pat Robinson, avenge deaths by waging the war of modernity and rationality against fundamentalism. It has been always so, everywhere, wherever modernity had to be rescued from its own fate.

To die is then to perceive life, whence the question—how did the death come, how did the death become so liquid, how did terror become real leaping as it were to life from fantasy, what were the gods and bystanders doing when the killer was taking position—in other words does death have a structure, death that is supposed to do away with all structures? In other words, what do we mean when the philosopher says that terror-death is not "bookkeeping, but vegetation," reproduced but not repeated, death in My Lai is and is not death in the Manhattan, that death on the ground is and is not the death in the sky?

II

The whole issue here, though un-stated, is one of responsibility and ownership of means of violence. Responsibility is gone with each period of restoration when the victorious power uses violence indiscriminately, to show that the event of restoration is final. Thus the defeat of every anti-colonial uprising is followed by bloodbath. The Mutiny of 1857 in India, the Boxer uprising in China, or the uprisings in Vietnam had been drowned in the blood of genocide. Similarly, the victorious army after the Paris Commune in 1871, the state forces, hoodlums, and the gangsters in Indonesia in 1965–70, the fascists in Chile in 1974–75, and Lebanese rightist forces and the Israeli army in Beirut in 1983—all pursued a policy of deliberate terror through indiscriminate use of violence. Then came chemical warfare, gas warfare, biological warfare, and above all production of more nuclear bombs that had been dropped once on the civilians of the two defenceless cities; all these showed how spread of barbarity accompanied waves of globalization. Hitler's methods, initially considered as exceptional, quickly gained acceptance wide across the globe—from French methods in Algeria, British methods in Malay, U.S. methods in Vietnam, and Serbian methods in the Balkans to Pakistani methods in East Pakistan, and the games of the warlords in sub-Saharan Africa. Several countries not mentioned here have been no better. The issue is why and how are globalization and the spread of methods of genocide organically connected? It is here, it would be well to remember, local and the global are truly linked in a "world history," or to be more precise, linked in a world of what Sankaran Krishna terms as "mimetic histories."[3] It will be good also to remember that beneath these mimetic histories lies an almost uninterrupted but discriminatory account of responsibility. To show just one glaring example: The Geneva Convention rightly makes it an onus on the warring armed forces not to target the civilians. Therefore we consider attacks on civilians as terrorist attacks, and condemn them. But at the same time, we are scarcely aware of the absence of any norm of responsibility to be enforced on civilians of a state who collude with its authority in committing atrocities on the people of another state, another nation. We have no norm that asks us to emulate the campus protest of the 1960s in the U.S. against the conduct of the Vietnam War. One of the moral questions emanating from the reflections of holocaust is that how did the civilians owing allegiance to the power committing genocide remain silent? The question therefore is: do the civilians not have any responsibility towards norms of justice and peace, and do they have no obligation in asking their own state to stop committing crimes against humanity? Will there be no ground of considering them as accomplices of violence, granting that they will be silent accomplices? If commercial companies outside can be asked to desist from entering into relation with a state against which sanctions have been imposed, by the same logic why should not the civilians be made responsible for colluding and tolerating with their own state's colonial and murderous practices? Ironically we shall have to remember that victorious power has always enforced collective norms of responsibility. Thus, the punitive army of Great Britain hanged men of villages from trees by the side of the roads they were passing through in their expedition to quell the Mutiny of 1857 in India; American forces grouped villages in what was called strategic hamlets in Vietnam; in Algeria the French forces used to shoot dead people of a group of villages in any event of attack on the colonial army or personnel. The past account of responsibility is thus dark and intensely anti-mythical.

Spread of technology and the scientific community, diffusion of methods of coercion and of counter-insurgency, privatization and eventual breakdown of the state, and the sinister air of virtual reality, all have played their role in universalizing terror, mass murder, and in the manufacture of global silence over such genocides accompanied by selective protests. Clearly, we are witnessing the eclipse of a sense of responsibility, a decrease of the area of shame, and a rise of values that are good on pride and not on shame. The demise of ideology, we often forget, brings in the demise of the moral community also, howsoever the presence of such moral community might have conveyed at some time a sense of freedom-less-ness. In this era of virtual reality characterized by a lack of territorial constraints and mass public pressure, concentration of attack has ushered in revolution in "military affairs"—sophisticated electronic and psychological warfare as shown in Kosovo—which has not been lived up to its claims of targeted annihilation, but certainly successful to a significant extent in manufacturing global silence. They have ushered in revolution in terror-methods also as evinced in the attacks on the Manhattan. The "new wars" that we witness are products of globalization, which they in turn advance. We can advance four theses here.

First, the civil wars of mutual claims of recognition and determination have done away with every sense of responsibility, restoration of trust, and a just reconciliation of claims.

Precisely because old territorial forms of political living (territorial units such as a state, county, province, autonomous republics in a multi-national state, nation-state) are considered inadequate or irrelevant by the political classes in many parts of the world, that the grab is up for new forms of territory as a matter of life and death struggle in the politics of recognition and determination. In this sense, new wars do not signify banal geopolitics.

Second, the new wars on the basis of the RMA cannot be fought without a political consensus (G–7, new north–new south, Christian, western, Atlantic), and the RMA thus provokes globalization of confrontationist politics. It may not be preposterous to argue therefore that neutrality today is more difficult than it was in the days of cold war/long peace.

Third, a discriminatory history of responsibility encourages the global powers to wage new wars. That, responsibility too has a discriminatory history should not surprise us. Daniel Warner reminds us that when Max Weber was making the well-known distinction between an ethic of responsibility and an ethic of ultimate ends, using the figure of Martin Luther as the ultimate responsible man (in other words responsible to his own self ultimately), he was advocating irresponsibility towards others, who constituted their existence outside the universe (his person, his group, his state, or his followers) of the "mature man" to whom responsibility remained limited to his universe only.[4] Understanding why we want to know who is responsible for which deaths, and the limits of that responsibility may be as important as, if not more important than, the process of determining responsibility that is so developed in international law. It is only when we appreciate the politics of identity and its closure, which animate our desire to know, that we can begin to glimpse new possibilities of responsibility/community outside of or beyond the limitations of that desire. In this sense, we can say that even the history of responsibility and reconciliation reaches the post-colonial subjects in a determined form. As Mark Selden wrote in the report "On Asian Wars, Reparations, Reconciliation,"[5] Germany unconditionally apologized for war crimes, the U.S. did not own responsibility for war crimes in Vietnam, but went on forcing responsibility on other states for offences; none of the Latin American states have accepted responsibility for mass murders in the 1970s and 1980s, and Japan has consistently refused to own blanket responsibility for rape and enslavement of nearly 200,000 women ("comfort women"), particularly after the Nanjing massacre. This history of responsibility symbolized by a skewed war crimes tribunal at The Hague does not question the flagrant discrepancy, and is shown to be what it is by parallel trials such as the Women's International War Crimes Tribunal on Japan's Military Sexual Slavery that sat in Tokyo on 8–12 December 2000, or the trials by the citizens for deaths of thousands of people in India, Sri Lanka, and Pakistan and elsewhere in state-backed communal riots, and frenzy of the security forces. The discriminate nature of legal and moral justification for "international" war crimes tribunals, set up by resolutions of the UN Security Council to punish crimes in only two areas in the world so far—the former Yugoslavia (for which a tribunal was set up in 1993) and Rwanda (1994) is evident. The most shocking example of the tribunals' impotence has been the state of Israel, which has continued to behave in the most flagrant contempt not only of the UN, seizing tracts of territory and exploiting and enslaving the inhabiting people, but also of the most basic laws and conventions covered by the statute of the international war crimes tribunals and written into international law by Security Council resolutions such as power to prosecute persons "committing or ordering to be committed grave breaches of the Geneva conventions" including willful killing, torture or inhuman treatment, willfully causing great suffering or serious injury to body or health, and extensive destruction and appropriation of property not justified by military necessity and carried out unlawfully and wantonly. If there is any doubt about this, one has to consider only Article 3 of the Tribunals' statute that refers to the "wanton destruction of cities, towns and villages or devastation not justified by military necessity," or Article 5 that empowers the Tribunal to prosecute persons responsible for crimes against humanity, including murder, if it is "committed in armed conflict and directed against any civilian population." Or, remember in this context of Ariel Sharon's gruesome history— his role in the slaughter of over 60 Palestinians in the village of Qibya in 1953, documented by Israeli historian Benny Morris; or his responsibility as Israeli Defense Minister for the butchery of at least 2,000 people in the Lebanese refugee camps of Sabra and Shatila in 1982 (the climax of Sharon's invasion of Lebanon, denounced as illegal by the UN and even by Margaret Thatcher). Indeed, the daily breach by Israeli troops of the tribunals' own statute should pose a challenge to the tribunals' judges, prosecutors and administrators. The fact therefore is that, the emerging official discourse on responsibility and reconciliation remains completely insensitive to the truth that no healing is possible without reconciliation, no reconciliation possible without justice, and no justice is possible without some form of restitution.

Fourth, the history of wars and militarism in the Third World loses its own social and economic specificity in the global mirror. Exactly 20 years ago Irving Horowitz in a seminal work on Third World militarism showed these specificities, and the specifics of democracy there. In his words, "The Third World is faced with a set of false options.... Democracy is not addressed by politics or economics but has to do with health, education, welfare, and the social uses of the public domain." Studying "globalizing wars and integrating world systems," military nationalism and the state in the Third World, issues of legitimacy and illegitimacy of Third World rules, and "the zero-sum economics and egalitarian politics," he further commented, "The lesson is clear—While one cannot predetermine dictatorial or democratic outcomes, neither should one prejudge the possibility of outcomes simply on the basis of the military origins of many Third World Revolutions."[6] Written at the heydays of three worlds theory, Horowitz still rings true in the post-1989 age of democratic transition and restitution.

All in all, this is a specific history of globalization; and this specific history of globalization should not escape our eyes. Community, state, nation, region, civilization, and the globe, all have been dumped into the box that the current history of globalization is. They may jostle for space. But that is fine with today's global order. Similarly, the "internationalism of Microsoft's chairman" and the one "expounded by Tagore or Gandhi" both find accommodation in this current history. There is no doubt that the current phase of global politics is pushing for a new dialogue for justice. It does not mean however that, this politics will be less confrontational than the politics of the cold war. If the deaths in the sky of Manhattan are some deaths, there was another kind of death—single no doubt, but marked as much by its own specificity. I am speaking here of the death on the street in Genoa. If the protests at Genoa were an indication, rising before us are the new questions, new dialogues, new confrontations. Even though the grand statesmen of the West assembled in Genoa on 20 July 2001 would not have liked the images of conflict that their summit left in its wake, the media that they could not do without had a satisfying day with some help from the city's *carabinieri*. Carlo Giuliani, a young political activist, was shot dead at the venue of the G–8 Summit; hundreds were injured. The worldwide audience of TV onlookers since three years ago in Seattle, and then successively in Prague and Gothenburg, could not but be bemused at how this gathering of the cultured representatives of the trans-Atlantic ruling class, assembled to discuss ways and means of reducing poverty, had provoked such vehement opposition, leaving one dead, still others mutinous, and people across the globe derisive of the pomp and circumstance that accompanied the summit.

The protesters with the grassroots trade unions (SLAI-Cobas) were in a combative mood and well prepared to make the 20 July "rebellion in Genoa" a success. Among those present in the ancient mercantilist capital were delegations from Yugoslavia, Mexico, Turkey, Greece, Sardinia and elsewhere. As expected, the demonstrators represented various views and orientations—unions, political activists (including anarchists and communists), development NGOs, religious and humanitarian groups, human right activists and a whole lot of others attracted to Genoa by the assembly of Big Men. The slogans ranged from the demand to withdraw NATO from Yugoslavia and the Balkans, to the dissolution of Hague "inquisition," to support for the Palestinian *Intifada,* and opposition to the embargo against Iraq and Cuba. However, the general theme that cut across the disparate groups was in the arena of global economics and politics—the need for "globalization from below," a reduction of the current Third World debt burden, and the control of international capital flows by "civil society" rather than by the international corporations and the governments at their beck and call.

Just a week after the gathering of the big men in Genoa, a much-less-publicized anti-imperialist Camp was organized in Assisi, the medieval town of monks and mendicants, also in Italy. It was dedicated to developing political perspectives for the anti-globalization movement, which the organizers felt was at a decisive stage following the G–8 meeting and its well-publicized fallout. The violence in Genoa were seen as a signal to the movement—how to continue the protests against globalization, establish "civic control" over the emerging agenda in the wake of globalization, and stand firm to confront the forces that are pushing the one-way economic globalization. The continent most devastated by capitalism was present in Genoa as it was in Assisi: Lumumbist groups from Zaire-Congo whose country is being torn apart by Western intervention; people like Dr Bashir Kurfi, an anti-imperialist intellectual from Nigeria; and activists from Sierra Leone, Senegal, Chad, Guinea. The delegates from West Asia questioned the West's management of peace in the context of the second *Intifada*, and sought lessons from the collapse of the Oslo agreement. Other activists pointed to how the Western powers were courting Turkey for the sake of its military machine even while in Ankara's jails political prisoners were engaged in fasts unto death. In Assisi, women from Afghanistan explained their struggle against the Pakistan-backed Taliban, while the Filipino members of the "Migrante" suggested the political possibilities available to Asian migrants in the West. The Mexicans warned of how the struggle for state power could be forgotten when "civil society" issues take over the agenda, as it had in their country in these times of *neo-Zapatism*.

Just as globalization has many faces, so too does the protest in its opposition. The rebellion in Genoa as much as the murders in the sky thus raises a problematic. By embodying contradictory phenomena, it asks of politics a whole series of questions that used traditionally to be part of the elite domain. If the meeting of G–8 was a manifestation of international democracy at work, how could such pomp and glory presume to represent the majority of people on this planet? How could those who claim to care for the poor and the victims allow "humanitarian bombs" and transnational murders? Was it possible for the manifold nature of the Genoa protest to be rewritten in a coherent standard political format, making it more powerful? That is what was requiring an answer, beyond the agitation and stone throwing.

There were many images available at Genoa, starting with the ambition of the trans-Atlantic club and the failure of its rhetoric. Then there was the desperate effort of the protesters to increase their ranks through global means, and the mobs' resolve to spit on the moral indignation expressed against the agitation by the political leaders of that club. The unreality of the agenda of the super-rich to fight poverty was mirrored in the death of the protestor on the Genoa pavement. It was a hallucinatory world all right. Just as it happened in the case of Raskalnikov's murder of his landlady, in Dostoyevsky's *Crime and Punishment*, the killing of the youth in Genoa has left its clues everywhere. That lone, but symbolic, death now guarantees that henceforth the protests will continue wherever the symbols of global power present themselves. The G–8 may hereafter move their annual hermitage into the deepest forest of Canada or the furthest corner of Tasmania, but it does not look like they can easily meet amidst the glass towers and wide boulevards any longer. The docile welcome of the past will be a memory, with the protestors forcing them to remember the wealth that they represent—and not the world that they would presume to.

But an assembly of emperors away from the bustle and din of crowd—will it serve the purpose? To ask this is to ask, *what precisely is the purpose?* Again, in Dostoyevsky, punishment and crime were not events in sequel; they were one. Crime was punishment. The moment of commitment of the crime was the moment when punishment had begun. The long shadows outside the palaces and glass hotels of Seattle, Gothenburg, and Genoa are there to stay. The protestors had wanted the moments of assembly to become moments of derision and disbelief and now they have become that. An assembly deep in the forest or in a faraway island cannot attract glory. Montesquieu had reminded us more than two centuries ago, how the pursuit of glory was important for kingdoms. Modern republics, as kingdoms of today, pursue policies that promise glory, for glory brings in its wake power, wealth, and satisfaction. Hence the dilemma, how to pursue glory without murder, pomp without derision, riches without poverty, and democracy without coercion?

More than to those assembled at Assisi, this will remain a question to those who had met at Genoa. The fault-lines of this new interrogative politics are not yet clear. Possibly they suggest as I have indicated earlier different deaths, differential deaths. Perhaps, one produces a vision from top, another vision from below. Perhaps, and as I tend to believe, these deaths and the visions that stand as mausoleums to these deaths are enmeshed with each other. But there is no doubt that the death in Genoa is as much real as the deaths at Manhattan. Also there is no doubt that in this politics from below, we shall see the engagement of the principle of justice with that of claims and rights, of the ethic of responsibility with the reality of power unconstrained by responsibility, of the politics of dialogue with that of coercion, of our history of wars and peace with their history of the same, an engagement of our statelessness with their state. The early marks of these engagements are visible in the forms of new political realities in many parts of the world. They give lie to the claims of this history, already an exhibit in the curio shop after it began with the triumphal claim some 12 years ago, that globalization promotes trade, trade promotes development, development produces interdependence, and interdependence produces peace. We can use one phrase that sums up the cinema, *imperial peace*.

III

This is a perspective that raises the need more and more to explore one of the significant issues of ethics, namely *responsibility*, which is at once a notion and a virtue, and which springs from the language of ethics when the latter finds its self surrounded by realities of power. In this world of power interrogated by considerations of responsibility, more and more the terrain is shifting to the notion of justice that questions each and every form of power. To claim power on behalf of a state in order to curb violence is not enough today. To show that the claim is *just* and *responsible* is equally important. The challenge to the state from within and without is now on this new ground, which has the advantage of forcing the most reluctant power to converse and to communicate. Such a notion of justice has the added advantage of crossing the juridical limits of state reasoning. In terms of political technique, it inverts the moral fabric of the reasons of the state. And in terms of political ethic, this inversion is explosive. It replaces the state agenda with an agenda of expanding political community, violence with accommodation, revenge with reconciliation, rights with justice, and that of power with responsibility.

The potential of an ethical interrogation of political power in terms of responsibility is already evident. We thus find ourselves living in strange times when on one hand the original challengers to state theories of dominance have laid their weapons down, and on the other hand those who won the great battle of ideas of the last century are withdrawing from their positions inch by inch so that they can reformulate their positions in a moral language. The lessons to say the least are instructive in terms of examining the reworked positions from the point of the ethics of responsibility as against the reality of power. One variant of the reworking of positions is the attempt to grasp the notion of responsibility in international politics today through institutional approaches. Under the influence of great institution-setting in Europe through European Union, Council of Europe, Organization of Cooperation and Security in Europe, the European Court, various treaties, conventions, and not the least NATO, the institutional argument has become the main site of the official discourse of responsibility, and seems to suggest an almost universal efficacy of the formula that institutional processes despite lack of common governance can lead to sustained cooperation among nation-states under conditions that would be fairly defined and with the assumption that institutions are the best guarantors of responsibility. Indeed, to carry the argument little more, institutional processes can define the conditions under which the state and the international community can be responsible and will behave responsibly. There was a near unanimous opinion after the Balkan tragedy, that new institutions should be set up, institutional processes and supervision would have to be strengthened, erring nations gradually trained and disciplined in institutional behavior, and cooperation encouraged through pursuit of institutional processes. Of course, the "curious history of Europe" as the historian Eric Hobsbawm put it recently, has been the particular backdrop against which hope on institutional efficacy has soared; also the Western anxiety has led to an institutional emphasis and reinforcement.

In stepping beyond the current wisdom about the congruence between power and responsibility, received by us from neo-realism and neo-ethics, what is needed is a reconstitution of the relation between the two. Power is supposed to be accompanied by responsibility, while the experiences of the last century show, the powerless have shown responsibility, and responsible conduct has produced a different sense of power that is markedly different from the ruling domains of power. South Africa is just one instance. Close to our world, the Naga experience has been one such, or the Muslim behavior in face of the near-fascist threat of a majority-centric Hindu politics, or the Tamil behavior in Sri Lanka. If we take some of the current accounts of responsibility of the powerless, we shall find that these experiences suggest an end probably forever to the project of reconstituting empires through making power more cohesive and thereby more effective through institutional means (we can recall in this context our experience of the great reform acts of the colonial empire in India to invent the wheels of responsible government), and the need at least for the time being to deal with an irreducible non-convergence of power and responsibility—therefore of differential history, rules, conduct, and behavior not in a projected context of unlimited imperial power, but in the context of power interrogated and limited by the ethic of responsibility. The failure of the colonial administration to become responsible to the people and the near total failure of the government of today to become responsible to the desires and demands of the people mark the collapse of what I have termed elsewhere as "colonial constitutionalism."

To be sure, it is that great story of sovereignty that encouraged in us the belief that responsibility went with power, particularly if it was constitutional sovereignty and constitutionally sanctioned power. However, to understand why constitutions have failed to generate responsibility, we shall have to inquire into the ways in which modern political power is composed at state level and global level today. Responsibility comes from familiarity, a familial responsibility, which means also excluding those whom you know so much so well that you do not want them as part of your family. But a state is not formed with just everyone in the family, in that case, you would not need a state, state building means the business of including the unfamiliar in the political society to whom you do not want to be completely responsible.

In short, my plea therefore is to treat the issue of responsibility not primarily as a legal product, but to take it as the ethical opponent of legal sovereignty, which has made power irresponsible. Notions of rights, duties, entitlements, autonomy, equivalence, and subject-hood, belie the demands of responsibility, justice, and the ethics of mutual obligation. The Spanish constitutional historian Bartolomé Clavero shows how "freedom's law" that had defined the Euro-American constitutional moment in the 18th century had within it from the beginning norms of exclusion which helped it to define who would be free to what extent and therefore would legally prescribe the community of the legally free—only towards whom the state would be responsible for its conduct.[7] Therefore is the cardinal question: who enforces the norm and burden of responsibility on whom? And, if power is being questioned by the ethic of responsibility, is not the ethic itself often circumscribed by configuration of power?

This situation we are living in now at the beginning of a new century is above all marked by great power politics and law-making, exactly as it was 150 years before when states were not only establishing law and order, and introducing reforms, but were also attacking others who were not introducing responsible governance (Let us remember Great Britain's contempt for Ottoman Turkey and the virulent attack by Gladstone against Ottoman rule), at the same time securing themselves with huge armies and interventionist wars. With the same thing happening today, "a gloating and still undead Henry Kissinger" is pointing out, it is "the best thing since Metternich last dined with the Czar."[8]

Notes and References

1. Earlier version published as an essay in Ranabir Samaddar, *Three Essays on Law, Rights and Justice*, SAFHR Paper 11, Kathmandu, 1992.
2. Rajeev Bhargava in *The Times of India*, 24 September 2001, speaks of identity of pains in deaths after the carnage in New York.

3. Sankaran Krishna uses the term in his *Postcolonial Insecurities—India, Sri Lanka, and the Question of Nationhood*. Delhi, 2000, chapter 1, p. 3.
4. Daniel Warner, "Searching for Responsibility/Community in International Relations," in David Campbell and Michael J. Shapiro (eds), *Moral Spaces—Rethinking Ethics and World Politics*. Minneapolis, 1999; Max Weber's argument appears in his lecture, "Politics as a Vocation," in Hans Gerth and C. Wright Mills (eds), *From Max Weber—Essays in Sociology*. New York, 1946, pp. 77–129.
5. Mark Selden, "On Asian Wars, Reparations, Reconciliation," *Economic and Political Weekly*, 36(1), 6 January 2001, pp. 25–26.
6. Irving Louis Horowitz, *Beyond Empire and Revolution–Militarization and Consolidation in the Third World*. New York, 1982, p. 263.
7. I am indebted to Rada Ivekovic for allowing me access to this extra-ordinary essay of Bartolome Clavero, "Freedom's Law and Oeconomical Status—The Euro-American Constitutional Moment in the 18th Century" (Seminar in the Department of History and Civilization of the European University Institute, Fiesole, Italy, 28 February 2002).
8. Mike Davis, "The Flames of New York," *New Left Review*, 12, November–December 2001, p. 50.

Deaths, Responsibility, and Justice   187

Section II

Borders, Wars, and the People

INTRODUCTION

Paula Banerjee

The recent border war in Kargil has dramatically revived international attention on border politics in South Asia. South Asian borders are largely colonial holdovers that are given the appearance of permanence in the process of nation building. Utilizing the myth of national security the political elites of this region have metamorphosed these borders into areas of consuming security interest. According to one estimate, the cost of protecting the borders increased from $11.3 billion in 1989 to $14.3 billion in 1998.[1] This is an increase of almost 27 percent. Even with this increased defence expenditure efforts of the political elite to institutionalize borders are constantly interrupted by historical dynamics. Artificially created and maintained, these borders are at the center of all major conflicts and tensions in the region. Yet there is little understanding that the borders are an important and separate category for the analysis of South Asian politics/state power. Once closely studied by 19th century frontiersmen and 20th century theorists of geopolitics and foreign policy, borders provoke scant attention in current discussions of South Asian regional history of conflicts and peace. Even partition is not analyzed as an aspect of border politics, it is seen more as a fracture in the process of nation building. This has been to the detriment of peace politics and peace studies in the region. Hence there is the necessity for the inclusion of this theme in a peace reader on South Asia.

Historical discourses on borders are largely generated by the states, which present borders as natural and permanent. In the post-independence period new histories of borders are created that never were. Yet there is little understanding that the borders are the present that have never been the past. Their permanence is achieved only in state sponsored discourses. How are we to account for this distortion of history? Histories of borders have been appropriated within histories of nation formations. And histories of nations, as Etienne Balibar has reminded us, are "always already presented to us in the form of a narrative which attributes to these entities the continuity of a Subject."[2] Essentially then the states create the myth of the permanence of borders for their own interests and call it the past.

There is reluctance at the state level to see the border regions as a regional issue and such a feeling is not particular to South Asia. In South Asia such feelings are exacerbated by a marked obsession over the sanctity of borders which in recent past might not have been a part of that land. For example, the Kargil war was fought over lines that came into existence only in 1972, as a result of the Simla Agreement (see Shankarshan Thakur's article entitled "The battle is with the enemy within," in *The Telegraph*, July 7, 1999). The borders are constantly shifting which South Asian state discourses refuse to acknowledge. Yet such acknowledgements are necessary for peace in the region. Otherwise as Gautum Navlakha points out, the costs and consequences will be devastating.[3]

This section presents writings that reinterpret the formation of borders, arguing that for much of South Asian history, borders were provisional and temporary rather than immutable. The section thus offers discussions on related themes such as: discourses on borders and state formation, politics and conflicts created by borders, and questions of access. As Jean Gottman observes in another context, access has been a "central problem" in human history. And borders regulate access. By regulating access those who *man* the borders assume the power to define who belong and who does not.

Owen Lattimore once speaking of borders between China and Inner Asia pointed out that these divisions fluctuated according to the relative dynamism of systems in contact.[4] David Chappell in an essay critical for understanding the history of borders titled, "Ethnogenesis and Frontiers" shows how "expansive nationalisms generate a greater number of clients, enemies and refugees near the borders, thereby stimulate warfare and population shifts, and thus cause old groupings to redefine themselves."[5] Comparative studies on borders bring out how borders through this process become zones of transformational interaction between systems and provide insights into the process by which a cultural community distinguishes itself from perceived others.[6] Borders thus generate discourses that create the category of *us* in binary opposition to perceived/misperceived *others*. Such perceptions become the basis for exercises in state formation. To legitimate this process, new discourses bestowed with nationalist credentials evolve to define borders as unproblematic. The papers by Samir Kr Das and Paula Banerjee deal with two entirely different situations, but both show how such discourses cannot tackle the problematic of *otherness* with its intrinsic contradictions. They discuss how borders become the common site for contentions between two sets of state–discourses leading to conflict. Border conflicts, war, and war-like situations thus become the occasion for the states to reclaim the legitimacy of their discourses increasingly under attack.

Borders not only create states, the states also create borders to facilitate the division between *the others* and *we*. Control over discourses helps the state to present these barriers as invariable even when historically there were none or malleable. South Asia has witnessed uninterrupted population shifts over centuries. At times it took the form of agricultural shifts, at other times movements of population were for work, trade or religion. These movements continued until they were stymied by the Eurocentric methods of dividing people into citizens and non-citizens such as the non-state persons, refugees and migrants. These categories were not intrinsic to the region but appeared as a result of a political order brought about by foreign ruling elites and their clients. In their wake came the concept of nation-state, once again from the shores of Atlantic, spawning new forms of nationality. In the 19th and 20th centuries uncharted terrains in Asia, Africa, and Latin America were drawn into Euro-centric cartography and South Asian borders evolved. Divisions between those who belonged and those who did not were introduced and quickly reinforced. The papers by Barun De and Partha Ghosh focus on the problems of belonging and non-belonging that the borders of this region have created. In recent years the problem has been compounded increasingly by the militarism of state power, particularly in peripheral areas. Propagators of such policies create the myth that refugees threaten borders when actually the militarized borders threaten the people living on both sides of the border. Borders become the site for contests between human aspirations and political will. Political exclusivity works against the legacy of population movement and of tolerance in the region. The last 50 years bear testimony to the impossibility of maintaining boundaries of exclusion in South Asia. Yet efforts continue to exclude groups of people on ground that they threaten the existing power structure continue. And when people transgress borders political parties make maximum mileage by highlighting ethno-religious characteristics of the migrant communities to ignite primordial sentiments. In the process they increase human misery and make borders combat zones. But they fail to stop population movements.

Studies about population movements were made fashionable by social scientists during the Cold War. The super powers with their preference for realist thinking shaped much of the research and writing on refugees and migrants. In realist framework the state is the primary actor. This meant that issues of migration and refugee-flows were analyzed from the point of view of the state. Students of peace studies have sought to move beyond the traditional realist thinking about international affairs. Their works have focused on a rethinking of the situation of population flow. The papers by Irene Khan treats the refugee problem as primarily a human problem created by artificial political divisions. It situates the analysis of refugees not within a discussion of the internal affairs of a state, but within the broader framework of international affairs. Khan makes the point that the material bases of national, military and economic power of state and its geo-strategic interests cannot be the factors that can and should principally influence the formulation of policies on refugees. The South Asian states refuse to sign the International refugee convention that they rightly feel is inadequate given the massive scope of the problem. Yet it could be a starting point to move beyond the logic of "national interest" vis-à-vis refugees.

Papers in this section stress that as against considerations of militarism and security, considerations of human rights, traditions of tolerance intrinsic to the people of the region, ethics of civil societies, international law, and customs and the mandates of international humanitarian institutions can be the basis for a proper formulation of policies on refugees. The refugee problem in South Asia is thus considered here within the larger rubric of human rights issues and not as an aspect of border control. Built within such approach is the understanding that the power elites of the majority community creates the category of unwanted migrants and label them refugees through the organs of state law and bureaucracies. The border emerges as the site for exclusion and suppression of groups of people, and in such exercise national security becomes the principal justification. By moving away the problem of refugees from a security-centric approach that the state often uses to legitimize its inability to protect and enrich human life, these papers reinforce the duty of the state to bear responsibility for refugees. The policy towards building up a South Asian refugee protection regime guided by traditional humanitarian instincts, liberal administrative practices and egalitarian judicial precedents can be the only alternative to a situation marked by a domination of military security-centric policy towards matters of human development. In times of conflict it is human development that suffers most.

War creates refugees, says Sanjukta Bhattacharya in her paper on the rehabilitation of victims of conflict. She stresses the devastating effects of war on civilian populations in the post Cold War period. A decade ago states needed to focus on the enemy without to legitimize their bids for greater power. But today the state points at the enemy within. Thus wars between states are giving way to wars within states. In these wars it is the civilian population that suffer most as they face the massive destructive power of the state machinery. Common people become belligerents, but only incidentally so. Often they do not seek war, yet war comes on them. In the last decade there has been a massive increase in civilian casualties. In this context, says Bhattacharya, the issue of rehabilitation of victims assumes enormous importance. Without sustainable rehabilitation programs the roots of conflict cannot be addressed. And sustainable rehabilitation is only possible in an atmosphere of peace. Bhattacharya argues that during periods of cease-fire the state machinery should concentrate on improving the quality of lives of people in war-torn areas otherwise peace may remain a distant dream.

Among civilian non-combatants affected by war the largest section is of women. In times of conflict the men either join the ranks of combatants and guerillas or they withdraw to the jungles for fear of persecution. It is the women who swell the ranks of civil society, take care of their children, the aged and the infirm and try to give war torn lives semblance of normalcy. Yet there are few discussions in the context of South Asia about how women effect war and are affected by it. Only recently there has been an effort to reinterpret wars through feminist prisms. Asha Hans' paper on women across borders in Kashmir falls within the same genre. She feels that the language of the nationalist discourse in South Asia is exclusive and misleading where women's national identity is concerned. Women living around the border areas such as Kashmiri women, are frozen in the time wrap between the two nations without the ability to define their own positions. Their gendered roles are cast by the masculine state that has the power to define them. Many of them do not have a passport and don't understand what the state means by the *nation*. Rather than facile interpretations of nationalism to them more important questions are those of stability, freedom, and health. Hans joins her voice with Cynthia Enloe and says that nationalism has sprung from a "masculinized memory" of a masculine state. Hence women remain on the periphery of such constructions.

Women are not the only peripheral characters in discourses of borders and state formations. Monirul Hussain discusses the lives of those, who live in and form the peripheries. Hussain in his paper on the ethnic conflicts in the Northeast India discusses the Janus-faced problems of population flows. The refugees and migrants often increase political tensions that may result in war. He does not ascribe blame to the people who are compelled to move but addresses the failure of the South Asian State to provide peace in the region because of its inability to negotiate between multi-ethnic and multi-national claims of co-existence. This failure is compounded by the propensity of the post-colonial states in South Asia to use violence as means of rule and government. State sponsored violence has the unfortunate result of creating insurgents within and terrorists without borders. The state often abets and aids insurgencies across borders not realizing that borders physically bind countries sharing it. Growth or depletion on one side affects the other. With borders becoming the site of state-sponsored violence, the only outcome can be a breakdown of peace in the region and more regional instability. Hundreds perish each year in such killing fields. The set of papers in this section shows how a thorough introspection by the power elite of their security policies has become imperative.

History shows that the so-called rigid borders have not prevented the inclusion of those groups whom the power elites consider crucial for the expansion of their support base. They are then settled in conflict-areas inhabited by *others* as part of a counter-insurgency demographic technique. As pointed out by Hussain, within the borders there are those who are marked as problematic and their legitimate demands are ignored. They are deliberately excluded from resource sharing. Such exclusions create internal colonies, that is, colonies within states or borders within borders, the new ethnic boundaries. All these necessitate a re-interpretation and re-examination of old concepts and categories about refugee management and ethnic conflicts. These categories are after all not historical accidents, but formed by conscious political will.

There are a number of individual studies on issues such as politics of state discourses, state formations, border politics and population movements, the four themes addressed in this series of papers. But, as the conflict in Kargil has once again shown, these issues are intertwined and should be analyzed as such. We have very few studies that locate the issues within a common framework. State-centric discourses fail to address these issues in all their complexities and inter-connections. Peace researchers have thus turned their attention towards alternative ways of thinking on borders, population flow, and conflicts around them.

Social scientists working on issues of peace in other regions are moving away from a territory-centric approach to people-centric approach while seeking to understand borders. W. Leimgruber makes such a plea for the inclusion of psychology of human agents in the study of border issues.[7] It has to be understood that borders are human creations, they are constructs affected by our own political perceptions. The end of Cold War is marked by increased political strife in most of the former Third World and South Asia is no exception. The post Cold War era has ushered in a period of great uncertainty among states leading to skirmishes over who controls which lines. The political elite tried to explain away border wars as results of barbaric intentions of people living across the border. Our papers portray that border wars are not results of "barbaric tendencies" of one set of people against another. It is the result of a high-risk gamble that the ruling elite undertakes in its efforts to consolidate its own power over territory. What is often overlooked is that wars are never merely over territories but on people who inhabit those territories. The physical presence of these people symbolizes the borders on which they live. In the case of South Asia, they are often indistinguishable from people across the borders or the *other*. Faced with the inability to distinguish between the *us* and the *other* South Asian states tried to subsume the identity of people living in the borders within that of the majoritarian community and homogenize them. When people in the peripheries refuse to be homogenized they are marked as traitors. The state tries to contain such treachery through draconian laws of which the Armed Forces (Special Powers) Act and the Disturbed Areas Act are but two examples. As a result of this people living in the borders are alienated further.

There are more ways by which states devastate the lives of people living in these areas. While discussing the history of the bordering states of Assam and Nagaland, Udayon Misra points out how bordering areas in Assam were converted almost overnight from prosperous economic zones into check-posts and barriers.[8] This led to acute shortages of essential commodities that compounded miseries of people living in the region. By depleting the borders the state alienates the people and when they protest their often-legitimate protests are looked upon as severe threats to nation formation necessitating severe reprisals. Protestors of all hues are castigated as terrorists in the majoritarian discourses while borders remain permeable. The states continue to erect fences and check-posts to demonstrate their power but human compulsions force people to disregard borders. This is particularly so because if one side of the border is depleted economically the other side is also affected. The notion of boundary permeability is explicitly and implicitly discussed in a number of papers in this section that makes the point that all countries in South Asia still have the ability to accommodate migrants but the political will is lacking which is detrimental for peace in the region. There is a subtle plea that borders should be looked upon as zones shared by different countries and so border policies should be sub-regional rather than national. Recognition that borders form a sub-regional issue will work towards de-escalation of tension in the region.

Notions of trans-boundary cooperation are increasingly discussed in other parts of the world, especially in Europe. It is the dichotomy of our generation that while Western Europe has now ushered in a kind of "borderless world," yet the borders that they created in Sub-Saharan Africa and South Asia remain intact. Some of the essays in this section seek to remind us that for centuries this part of the world was almost borderless. For purposes of peace it is essential for us to look beyond borders into our own traditions of hospitality and accommodation. A few of the papers discuss how while borders are being constructed by the state from above the population below is constantly re-negotiating these borders. Social scientists in South Asia should now look beyond the state and its policies to understand the borders of South Asia. Even policy implementation should take in cognizance not the political will above but the reality below. When the state fails to differentiate among the *us* and *them* in the bordering areas it turns against its own people. The state tries to impose a new identity on them.

People living in margins have for centuries developed their own identities that cannot be subsumed under facile definitions of nationalism or nation-state. They have their own kin networks, local practices, and ways of governance and conceptions of democracy. If the ruling elite from the center tries to forge a new identity on them this will only induce rootless proclivities and greater fragmentation in the whole region, as is apparent from the Indian and Pakistani experiences. The state can affect social, economic, and political borders through force, but where it fails miserably is in the realm of psychological borders. Social scientists dealing with issues of borders and border formation need to address questions of identity and psychological borders. Only then will they be able to understand the tensions and linkages permeating South Asian borders and develop strategies for positive intervention for peace.

NOTES AND REFERENCES

1. P.R. Chari in *Defence Expenditure in South Asia: India and Pakistan*. Colombo, 2000.
2. Etienne Balibar and Immanuel Wallerstein, *Race, Nation, Class: Ambiguous Identities*. London, 1991.
3. Gautam Navlakha, "Kargil: Costs and Consequences," *The Economic and Political Weekly*, July 3, 1999.
4. Owen Lattimore, *Inner Asian Frontiers of China*. Boston, 1962.
5. *Journal of World History*, Vol. 4, No. 2, 1993, 270–71.
6. One can in this respect see the comparative studies collected by Howard Lomar and Leonard Thompson in their edited volume, *The Frontier in History—North America and South Africa Compared*. New Haven, 1981.
7. W. Leimgruber, "Boundary, Values and Identity—The Swiss Italian Transborder Region," in Rumley and Minghi (eds), *The Geography of Border Landscapes*. New York, 1991.
8. Udayon Misra, *The Periphery Strikes Back*. Shimla, 2000.

7

WARS, POPULATION MOVEMENTS, AND THE FORMATION OF STATES[1]

Samir Kr Das

This paper seeks to offer some very tentative and provisional hypotheses by way of establishing the inter-connections amongst such phenomena as war, population movement and formation of state system in South Asia. While individual studies focusing on any one of these phenomena are available, studies articulating them into a common frame of reference are not only rare, but almost non-existent. The importance of such a common frame can hardly be denied. On the one hand, it draws our attention to the necessity of appreciating them in their combination rather then in isolation from each other and makes them an indispensable part of contemporary political inquiry. On the other hand, it also serves as a convenient point of departure for many of the future researches that might be interested in working on the hypotheses enumerated here. Viewed in this light, the present paper is only a preliminary attempt at deciphering their inter-connections within a common frame of reference.

The task is not easy; for one thing there is no simple and foreordained way of understanding their inter-connections. The commonplace belief that modern wars are of such a scale and magnitude that they necessarily result in massive demographic displacements whether within the country or across it does not exactly hold true in a region like South Asia. Or even if it does, it certainly does not in the same manner, as is the case in other parts of the world. Contrary to popular expectations, large-scale population movements from one country to another especially after partition could not give birth to demographically homogeneous nations either in India or in Pakistan. Now with the benefit of hindsight and of course at great cost, we are slowly realizing that no amount of population movement—however gigantic and long-drawn that be, would ever contribute to such homogeneous and seamless nations and cleanse them of ethnic minorities. For another, we have also to recognize that any understanding of how these phenomena are inter-connected requires to be qualified by what I would call, an among-other-things rider. Thus, when we argue that the connection between war and population movement is so complex that the former sometimes follows the latter instead of preceding and catalyzing it—as was the case in 1971 war, we have to take account of a plethora of factors which in conjunction with that of population movement presumably due to a prolonged spell of civil war in the then East Pakistan, had triggered off the Indo-Pak war and led to the liberation of Bangladesh.

WAR AND WAR-LIKE SITUATIONS

Before we proceed, it may be instructive to sound at least three methodologically important caveats.

First, wars, especially those of South Asia, give unto themselves not just one but many "histories." As one raises this issue, one obviously reminds oneself of how the "official" history of Pakistan interprets them and how it is—to understate the point, at variance with its Indian counterpart. Besides, there is no reason to accept that the official history of whatever country is the only available uncontested history within the country—that can throw all other narratives from out of existence. What is authenticated as the official history of war is seen to be constantly engaged in a war of attrition with a multiplicity of histories that narrate the wars in their own characteristic ways. By way of engaging with the official history, they tend to assert their right to be different from it. The point has two implications. The first implication is that, these little narratives influence population movements as much as they are influenced by official histories. While exploring the possibility of writing an alternative history of two Bengals, Sudhir Chakrabarty in his inimitable style noted how the space of the

Lalan (a famous Sufi saint of the 19th century) cult in central Bengal cut across the international boundaries drawn as a result of partition. About 10 followers of the same cult belonging to Betai village of the district of Nadia now in West Bengal decided to cross the international boundary in 1955 without of course the valid papers that were and are still needed to cross it, in order to visit the holy *samadhi* (burial site) of the great saint located in the-then East Pakistan. They were subsequently arrested and taken into custody by the Pakistani authorities for having tried to violate the international boundary. This is an instance of how the notion of an alternative space runs parallel to the internationally defined space of nation-state and force the latter to compete with it.[2] The second implication is that, we may say that the role of little narratives in the formation of state-system can hardly be underestimated. It is for instance suggested that the formation of a state implies the appropriation and in its wake complete obliteration of the little narratives under reference. This "fundamentally imperial structure" of the state ideology in the words of Dipesh Chakrabarty, "never described the actual political practice in India where religious idioms and imagination had always been strongly present."[3] To my mind, the problem is much more complicated than what the scholars of state formation would have us believe. It has to do with the larger question of allowing the state to come to terms with and if necessary, to accommodate these little narratives. The unities of the state discourse are now ruptured in a way that they have lent to the little narratives a hitherto unprecedented freedom of playing a critical role in constructing the official narrative and in bringing them to bear on it. State's discourse is more a constellation of these forces than their complete obliteration. It is as we shall have occasion to see, much more porous and loose-ended than what the prevalent theories of state formation take it to be.

Second, histories of war and histories of peace are not separate or for that matter separable. They are deeply interwoven in the sense that there seems to be a vast twilight zone comprising what may be called, war-like situations that cannot be clubbed together with either of the two aforementioned categories. It is necessary to introduce this category into our frame of reference for they play an important role—much more important than that of war in setting off population movements in South Asia. Both the irreducibility of little narratives and the problematic nature of war and peace make it imperative on our part to decipher the inter-connections among war, population movement, and state formation in a primarily interpretative way rather than in any strictly empirical way. Where the world of wars is constituted in a problematic manner and gives unto itself many histories than one, we can only hope to make sense of them with the help of our own interpretation, that is to say, with our own way of "worlding" the world of wars. The exercise cannot but be interpretative.

While wars in history have attracted a good number of philosophers starting from Thucydides down to let us say, Chris Hables Gray whose *Post-Modern Wars* has created a sensation since its publication in 1997, Clausewitz's definition of it still serves as the only viable point of entry into the subject. As he points out: "War is ... an act of force to compel our enemy to do our will."[4] Viewed in this perspective, wars and war-like situations are divergent from each other on at least three major counts: First, the force employed in times of war is self-spiralling in character. Clausewitz for instance argues: "If one side uses force without compunction, undeterred by bloodshed it involves, while the other side refrains, the first will gain the upper hand. That will force the other to follow suit; each will drive its opponent toward extreme, and the only limiting factors are the counter-reprisals inherent in war."[5] In war-like situations also, one definitely compels another "to do one's will" given that there is a unitary will of the sort that Clausewitz has in mind, without "driving another to the extreme." A country while inciting and perpetuating war-like situations in another chooses not to "drive another to the extreme" because it is not willing to risk the reprisals for interests which in its perceptions are not too fundamental to warrant a full-blown war. Or it may be that the interests are considered to be fundamental but warlike situations are preferred to wars as a means for attaining them. Sumit Ganguly for instance makes the point that even in times of hot Indo-Pak wars, mutual understanding and diplomatic communication were never lost.[6] That a country is not willing to push its adversary to the extreme and is intent on keeping the exercise of violence within a tolerable threshold does not mean that war-like situations are less effective instruments of a country's foreign policy. In fact, such wars as Chris Hables Gray argues, have in a large measure been successful in calling the triumphalism of the West into question ("What makes this war so important is that it reversed the hundreds of European victories"),[7] and establishing the superiority of oriental technologies like, people's war to western technologies and cyber-war.

War according to Clausewitz, is a conflictual engagement between two "whole" communities with respective "wills" pitted against each other. One wonders whether such fully formed, homogeneous communities with their fragments knit into seamless wholes, with their wills sharply different from each other ever exist—or to say the least, pre-exist the outbreak of wars even in advanced western democracies. For wars in South Asia have also been principal vehicles of organizing peoples into fairly homogeneous nations. As Ainslie Embree informs us, "The 1962 war with China was a turning point in defining India as a nation. Nehru spoke of it as a blessing in disguise because internal disunity had been swept aside by the Chinese threat and the new mood could be used to achieve industrial advances as well as military preparedness."[8] War-like situations on the contrary imply that there may remain some fragments within what the state claims to be parts of its national body that simply refuse to be regarded as its constituent parts and join the state's preparations for coping with them. Such fragments reflect the limits of a state's nationhood and are seen to act at times at the behest of the enemy country. Hence, while coping with war-like situations, a state has to wage a war with its fragments.[9] Classical political theory also tells us that a citizen's attachment to the national body particularly in times of war is to be regarded more as an end in itself than a means to an end. Machiavelli for instance, contended that wise princes would prefer to "lose battles with their own forces than win them with others in the belief that no victory is possible with alien arms."[10] That is why, his *The Prince* underlines time and again the importance of the natives in the army structure who are likely to fight wars unto the last without asking why and whose obeisance to the nation is both unflinching and unwavering. On the other hand, a nation during war-like situations especially in South Asia reportedly includes many fragments whose attachment to it hardly contains any intrinsic worth. They consider themselves to be a part of the nation only so long as their attachment fulfills certain interests particular, if not peculiar to themselves. While referring to the "border people" who have migrated to West Bengal from Bangladesh, Ranabir Samaddar argues that for them, citizenship is very like an ordinary commodity that is freely bought and sold, in one word, transacted without any sense of moral piety, depending on the mutual interests of the parties involved in it in a world that according to him, is completely demoralized: "Citizenship has come to such a state, it means not membership of a political community, but one end of a transactional relation."[11]

Third, Clausewitz makes a clear distinction between force and political will. Although it is true that force at times especially during wars has a tendency to "usurp" political will, ideally it should be employed in order to implement the latter rather than anything else. Clausewitz's definition not only contains a strong rationalist tinge whereby force is made subordinate to will but also in the same vein sensitizes us to such situations where wars might verge on the irrational and use of force might look senseless with no apparent political will to be implemented. War-like situations serve as glaring instances where the Clausewitzean distinction between force and political will is blurred—if not already vanished, for in this case there seems to be no political will other than and independent of the use of force. A country that is keen on imposing such situation on another becomes successful and fulfills its objective the moment it imposes it, for it thereby secures a certain disarming of its enemy—one of the chief objectives of war, by way of compelling it to keep a substantial part of its armed troops busy with maintaining law and order inside the country. According to one conservative estimate, India had committed a quarter million of its armed troops to quelling armed insurrections in the former princely state of Jammu and Kashmir. War-like situations are like self-evident truths in the sense that there is no hidden truth beyond what is self-evident to us.

Several imageries of war are in currency to refer to war-like situations. Some of them are—proxy wars, (un)civil wars and low-intensity conflicts. Conversely, India has engaged in four wars of varying degrees of intensity since 1947—three of which have been with Pakistan. As Sumit Ganguly, widely acclaimed as an expert on Indo-Pak wars, maintains, "While many people quibble over definitions of war, it is safe to say that by any reasonable standard there were three wars between India and Pakistan between 1947 and 1971."[12] Wars are episodic or to borrow a Clausewitzean expression "single-short blows," but war-like situations are embedded in the state's regime of the normal.[13]

WAR-LIKE SITUATIONS AND POPULATION MOVEMENTS

None of the wars mentioned earlier, has resulted in any major trans-border population movement. None of the 12 major bilateral population movements outlined in Myron Weiner's study published in 1993—excepting only one, "the flight of Bangladeshis to India" had to do directly with war— precisely, the Indo-Pak wars.[14] In this case too, war did not precede but followed the massive population influx from the then East Pakistan to India, though of course there was a considerable return migration immediately after the war which helped India in securing at least the semblance of a demographic balance within a short while.

At this juncture, we must make a distinction—albeit of conceptual nature, between two kinds of population movements—one induced by war and the other by prolonged spell of war-like situations. First of all, the probability of return migration is as we have already noted, always higher in cases of war than in that of war-like situations. Since the latter often masquerade as the normal, they are of enduring nature and do not seem to create an atmosphere conducive to the migrants' forthwith return to their homes. Second, the country that receives the immigrants in times of war usually keeps a close watch on their movements, scrupulously counts their numbers as far as practicable, and sometimes recognizes them as refugees in need of some special treatment. It seeks to herd them together in sufficiently secluded camps so that they do not disappear into the faceless and lonely crowd called nation; it claims to enclose and represent and most importantly, garner international support in their favor with of course a varying degree of success. During Bangladesh crisis for instance, other countries assumed nearly one-fourth of the estimated costs of supporting the refugees in camps and virtually none of the costs for the larger number who had found sanctuaries outside the camps. The figure reached 9.8 million at its peak and out of it approximately 3 million did not choose to go the state-run relief camps. Richard Sisson and Leo Rose, have argued that in spite of state's attempts at isolating them and re-locating them to some far-off parts of the Northeast, they posed a major burden to the nation's exchequer and to the economy as a whole.[15] But whatever the state does as part of its humanitarian program concerning the refugees, it never allows the distinction between its citizens and foreigners to be blurred and obliterated. The making and maintaining of such distinction is always considered to be crucial to the state's nation-building project. But since much of the immigration that takes place during war-like situations are of illegal and clandestine nature, it goes on undetected and at times it becomes difficult—if not impossible on the part of the receiving country to see to it that they do not get mixed up with the faceless multitude of the nation.[16] State's failure in making and maintaining the distinction has sparked off at least two mutually opposite kinds of social reactions. On the one hand, there are attempts on peoples' part (as was the case during the Assam Movement of 1979–85) at making the state do what it does not otherwise do, that is to say, build the nation. What the state might do is not to keep a watch on the illegal entrants from across the borders for that is quite impossible, but to keep a count on its own citizens and thereby lend to the nation a face that has hitherto remained faceless and anonymous. Voters' identity cards and citizenship certificates are some of the markers that are meant for separating the citizens from the foreigners. A modern state cannot do without "enumerating" its people into a closely-knit and measurable nation.[17] On the other hand, the state's insistence on making and maintaining this distinction creates panic in the minds of some communities whose identity as Indian citizens is to say the least, ambiguous. The movement of the Gorkha National Liberation Front under the leadership of Mr Subash Ghisingh in Darjeeling (West Bengal) for their certification as Indians serves as a case in point.

Third, wars in South Asia have invariably centered on the territorial question. In other words, they were fought with motives other than dumping a country's surplus population on another country. In none of the four wars excepting that of 1971, have the population movements been too significant to cause an alarm. Conversely, war-like situations are sometimes created and perpetrated with the motive of conveniently dumping the excess population on another with the advantage of remaining unrecognized by the receiving country. It is for instance argued that the civil war in pre-war East Pakistan was a means, resorted to by the Pakistani state, of making section of its people mostly consisting of the Bengali Hindus leave the country and easing out the excess population constantly posing a danger to the country's economy and "Islamic" culture. Indeed, a theory of *lebensraum* though expressly denied by the Bangladesh state, is catching fast the imagination of the Bangladeshi intelligentsia. For instance, an eminent professor of Dhaka University has reportedly argued that tremendous population pressure is bound to take the country to the road to inevitable disaster in near future and unless the people of Bangladesh are permitted to spread out to such vast and of course sparsely populated tracts of land that just lie across her northeastern and southeastern borders comprising a substantial part of northeastern India and the Arakan Hills of Myanmar, Bangladesh would not be able to withstand the imminent disaster.[18]

STATE SYSTEM AND STATE DISCOURSE

The term state–system may be used in two relatively distinguishable senses. In the macro sense, it may be understood to mean the complex web of inter-linkages amongst different nation-states of South Asia and the inter-linkages are so intimate that "each acknowledges and to some extent guarantees others' existence." The closest approximation to such a system is the South Asian Association for Regional Cooperation (SAARC). In the strict sense, one wonders whether SAARC can be taken as an illustration of such a system for one notices here nations that acknowledge and guarantee—only grudgingly, if at all, each other's existence. The survival of Pakistan as a sovereign state depends on an explicit negation of the principles that lay down the foundations of the Indian state. The reverse is also true. In the micro sense, it refers to a process whereby a state with its intricately woven network of political institutions gets itself formed. Charles Tilly's *The Formation of National States in Western Europe* is still regarded as an excellent exposition of formation of state systems in Western Europe. The opening paper underlines four diverse processes implicit in the project of state formation—territorial consolidation, centralization, differentiation, and monopolization of the legitimate means of force and coercion. It means over and above, the establishment of a central political authority that is sufficiently differentiated from the prevailing social groups—ethnic and non-ethnic, enjoys a virtual monopoly over the legitimate instruments of coercion and the writ of which extends over the entire territory that it lays claim to. While Tilly's definition has a strong institutional bias, it does not adequately maks us sensitive to the discourse that informs and undergirds whatever the state does by way of institutionalizing itself.

The concept of state discourse has at least four significant implications that may be discussed at this point. First, what it does is to privilege those who adhere to it and to incorporate them into the national body as its "natural" constituents. By the same token, it also excludes those who do not or may be, who refuse to acquiesce to the discourse and urges them—not always implicitly, to vacate the territory that it claims to consolidate into a nation or to stay in it as ethnic minorities with an attendant denial of their rights which they consider to be fundamental to their survival as distinct cultural communities. The state discourse thereby facilitates the process of "natural" selection.[19] Partition and in its wake the birth of two nation-states in South Asia have given the people an opportunity of being "naturally" enclosed by either of the two state discourses antagonistic to each other. The opportunity also conferred on them an obligation—of making up their minds. They could not do without joining either of the two nation-states. Political geography of modern nation-states hardly leaves room for those who would like to be identified with units—larger or smaller than those of the nation-states. Hiranmoy Bandyopadhyay in a book written in an intimate, semi-autobiographical style has cited more than a dozen instances where Bengali-speaking

Muslims of post-partition West Bengal thought it unethical on their part to stay on even after the birth of a separate Muslim state.[20] When state discourse grips the masses, it does not have to exercise force in order to make the territory homogeneous. The more it rules by discourse, the less it feels the necessity of resorting to force and coercion.

In this connection, it may be pointed out that citizens' attachment to a state may be either of the two polar types or any combination of them: transactional and natural. In the first case, people who are to be incorporated into the national body are first of all assumed as outsiders whose entry into it depends on a bargain that they have to strike with the concerned state or vice versa. The relationship between the state and its people in this instance is evidently of contractual or transactional nature. The state normally does not quite encourage people to enter into a relationship of this sort partly because it is expensive as the state has to deliver what Packenham once called "political goods" like, law and order, life, liberty, and pursuit of happiness etc., and partly because peoples' loyalty to the state in this case is of a fragile and vacillating nature. As soon as the state stops for whatever reasons, delivering the goods, loyalty is or at least is threatened to be withdrawn. It is for this reason that the state always chooses to translate the first kind into the second one. In this instance, peoples' association with the state is taken to be too tacit to be actively demonstrated. This as we will see later, lends to the discourse an element of unchallengeability. M.J. Akbar's *India—The Siege Within* may be regarded as a text that accepts Kashmir's inclusion in India as an accomplished and irreversible fact and thereby keeps the question beyond the realm of negotiation. This text helps in sanitizing the issue and robs it of its problematic character. At the same time, it is a classic illustration of a paranoid text that accuses Pakistan and other vested interests of problematizing the issue and transforming it into a question.

Second, our emphasis on the state discourse enables us to appreciate its distinction from the otherwise widely used term—nationalist discourse. The postmodernist critique has called the state's claim to enclose and represent a nation into question and has drawn our attention to the challenges that it faces while building the nation both from within and also from without.

Some of the fragments the state considers to be organic to the national body are increasingly questioning the assumptions that aim at assimilating them into it and depriving them of the right to retain their cultural identities. Similarly, alongside these sub-national fragments, there are also trans-national centers of power—sometimes represented by other sovereign states which not only context the particular state's unilateral claim over the national body but stake their own claims over it. When both these forces work together, they pose a potent threat to the state. The nation in other words, has become a contested site. In that sense, the concept of state discourse confines our attention to what the state does and thereby frees us from the obligation of characterizing its activities as necessarily nationalist. Third, our distinction between state formation and state discourse instructs us to keep the opposition to the latter clearly distinct from the cases where the institutional prerequisites of the state are under attack. Such a distinction is necessary for "the new revolutionaries are concerned not so much about the political structure of the nation-state as they are about political ideology that undergirds it."[21] It is for this reason that the concept of state discourse has acquired some prominence in recent years.

Fourth, the concept is inseparably connected with that of modernity. We may even say that they advent of modernity has bestowed on the state the responsibility of holding on to and elaborating a discourse. A brief comparison of the process of state formation in modern India with that in pre-modern times may be instructive at this point. Since a plurality of states existed within a more or less culturally contiguous geographic space, any expansion, contraction or even annihilation of state's borders did not necessarily lead to any significant migration of population from one place to another in pre-modern India.[22] This does not mean that there was no migration whatsoever in pre-modern India. Migration to be precise was sparked off by factors other than the modification and transformation of political boundaries. Peasant migration within the larger Gangetic plains of undivided Bengal was a very common feature even during the colonial rule. In other words, the state did not have to elaborate a discourse; it was in the words of Rudolph and Rudolph, "an instrument for upholding and protecting the society and its values."[23] As a consequence, the cultural order of the society was not severely disrupted and the people did not feel it imperative to move over from place to place once the changes in state's boundaries came into effect. In sum, political changes would hardly touch upon the society and its values. As modernity encourages the states to organize their territories into culturally enclosed spaces and enumerate their peoples into tightly-knit, homogeneous nations, it also feels the necessity of clinging to and elaborating a discourse that as we have already argued, facilitates "natural" selection. That people are migrating from Bangladesh to the bordering states of India reveals that they could not qualify the process that the Bangladeshi state has set for its nation. Increasing Islamization, sharply deteriorating economic conditions, frequent military interventions along with many other factors have made their lives difficult in Bangladesh and push them as it were, to flee the country where they have been living for generations.[24] They are in Myron Weiner's language, "rejected" people.

WAR, WAR-LIKE SITUATION, AND THE STATE DISCOURSE

The prevailing literature on Indo-Pak wars looks upon them essentially as conflicts between two "patently antagonistic models" or state discourses as we have termed them. Partha S. Ghosh for instance observes:

> These two models (those of India and Pakistan) have not only been mutually incompatible, but having been professed in two contiguous countries with the same socio-historic experience, with no mutual boundaries, and with a record of conflictual relationship that developed immediately after independence over Kashmir, they have become patently antagonistic threatening each one's basic principles of state policy ... Islamic Pakistan and secular India became anathema to each other for the simple reason that the very survival of the states depended on an assertion on precisely those theories which had resulted in the partition, namely, the two-nation theory based on religion versus the one-nation theory based on territorial and historical concept of "Mother India."[25]

Such a view to my mind, suffers from many shortcomings two of which deserve a special mention at this point. First, it not only exaggerates the mutual antagonism between these two countries, but wrongly assumes that the discourses are fully formed and elaborated well before they take on and confront each other. It also presupposes that the strategies that the adversaries employ against each other in times of war are issued from the discourses that are both given and immutable. According to this view, the Indo-Pak wars fought almost at regular intervals till 1971 have not seemingly played any role in bringing into existence, elaborating, modifying and even transforming their respective discourses. Second, and as corollary to the first, this view freezes the discourses at a given point of their evolution—in our case at the point when the subcontinent was partitioned into two sovereign states and is unable to account for the changes that the discourses have undergone since then while adapting themselves to the changing requirements of time. In that sense, both the state discourses had to strive hard for negotiating with the "patent models" or stereotypes which have been generously used to characterize them—"the two-nation theory based on religion" and "the one-nation theory based on territorial and historical concept of Mother India." Such stereotypes also fix up the limits to states' spheres of action and negotiation. I propose to illustrate these points with reference to the elaboration of the discourse of the Indian state in course of the three major wars with Pakistan between 1947 and 1971.

The first Indo-Pak war that took place immediately after independence may be conceived of as the *moment of contingency* in its elaboration: First, India continued to interpret the Kashmir imbroglio with the terms that were directly derived from what is popularly known as, the nationalist discourse crystallized during the struggle against colonial rule since the last century. It was seen primarily—if not exclusively, as an extension of the colonial policy of dividing the Indians and "weakening the new nation and preventing her from becoming a powerful factor in Asia" through the creation of Pakistan. It is interesting to note that Great Britain continued to remain India's point of negative reference. India took time to recognize Pakistan as her principal adversary. Besides as investigative reports point out, she was not seriously interested in committing herself to any kind of long-term involvement in Kashmir: "If in the normal course, Kashmir had acceded to Pakistan, few in India would have been upset about it.... To many in India, the tribal raid was an instance of Pakistan's arrogance, similar to that displayed by the Muslims before independence, which, if not challenged immediately, would manifest itself even more blatantly in the years to come. What seemed important then ... was not the acquisition of territory by India but stopping Pakistan from enlarging its boundaries."[26] As a counter-factual argument, it has been suggested that had Sheikh Abdullah not asked for India's military assistance at that crucial hour in fighting the raiders, India in all probability would not have been involved in what ultimately turned out to be an endless war. But once she committed herself, there was no going back and her discourse bore the imprints of the involvement in a way that proved to be inerasable. What was then dismissed as too contingent a factor to engage our sustained attention came to occupy a central position in the state's scheme of things and became the be-all-and-end-all of our national identity.

The war of 1965 may be interpreted as the *moment of trial* not of course in the ordinary sense of "the one-nation theory based on territorial and historical concept of Mother India" being pitted against "the two-nation theory based on religion," but in the deeper sense that the Indian state found it extraordinarily difficult to remain steadfast to what it had decided to embrace— "the one-nation theory" itself. The war had conferred on the state the special responsibility of holding it accountable to a theory that admittedly transcended the religious and communal differences and was believed to have consolidated its citizens into the generic community of Indian nation. The depreciation of this theory was so blatant and spectacular in the everyday political practice that the state was not only busy with confronting an external enemy on the warfront but grappling with the responsibility that the rhetoric of one-nation theory has assigned to it. The Indian state was passing as it were through a particularly schizophrenic state in which more than being engaged in a war with an external enemy, it had to come to terms with what it held to be its true moral self. The transformation of "a low-key, amorphous, tolerant, and peculiarly consensual nationalism" into a highly monochromatic form which was out to throttle and emasculate the cultural diversities and steamroll them into one homogeneous type at about the same time had turned the discourse by its head and constantly reminded us that no amount of political reconstruction would be able to bring the discourse to the line of actual political practice and vice versa. The state was caught up in a terrible political dilemma: It could neither discard nor stand up to the rhetoric of one-nation theory. Besides, the minorities' natural concern for their communities located just across the borders was stigmatized as flagrantly anti-national. As Ayesha Jalal writes, "Indian Muslims have had to distance themselves from any display of concern about their predicament across the border."[27] Even M.J. Akbar notes that with Nehru's demise, "the communal Hindu element in the power structure could not be kept under control."[28] He makes a particular reference to the anti-Sikh agitation in which several communal organizations came together and joined their hands in forcing the state to assume a monochromatic form.

According to Sumit Ganguly, the war of 1965 proved beyond any doubt that "there was no ground swell of support for Pakistan's claim on Kashmir amongst the Muslim population of the state."[29] It is interesting to see how in spite of the two wars, the state discourse of India could retain its popularity even amongst the Muslims of the state. It was the promise of "secularism and socialism" held out by the discourse rather than the actual political practice, that played a key role in attracting the Sheikh and his people to veer towards India. As Sheikh Abdullah is reported to have said, "...We have joined India because of its ideal—secularism and socialism. India wanted to build a state where humanism would prevail. So long as India sticks to these ideals, our people have a place nowhere else but in India."[30] It seems that they were still prepared to give India what in juridical language may be called, a benefit of doubt and more significantly a chance to prove before the world as well as herself that her political practice was worthy of the promise embedded in the discourse.

The war of 1971 may be characterized as a *moment of unchallengeability* in the evolution of the discourse of the Indian state. It is so not because it established its unchallengeability vis-à-vis that of the Pakistani state, but because it succeeded in keeping its nationalism claims out of contention with the latter. The realm of contention is defined as a common site where one discourse challenges and in turn, is challenged by another. It is like a boxing bout where two states share a common ring. But what if the terms of discourse are fashioned in a way that they invest it with an element of certainty? This may not have (and as we know, did not) preempted the challenges, but it obviously frees it of the obligation of answering back and responding to them. In that sense, the state discourse during this period seems to have been situated outside the realm of contention underlying the war. As a result, nationalist claims were instantly read as nationalist credentials and never subjected to the test of what Ranabir Samaddar designates as "permanent plebiscite," that is to say, the test that seeks to establish the nationalist credentials of a state. This is how the discourse during this time acquired a sanitized and unproblematic character. In this connection, we may confine ourselves to an analysis of two complimentary processes through which the discourse could sanitize and de-problematize itself.

First, the nationalist character of the Indian state is too taken for granted to remain open to contestation and challenges. It is accepted as an accomplished fact—too "accomplished" to be demonstrated or constantly "displayed and presented." As Sudipta Kaviraj puts it: "This encouraged a massive pretence on the part of a national movement and later by the national state that the question of cultural construction of the nation was left behind in the past, rather than still lying in future. It made Indians believe that the imagining of the nation was an accomplished and irreversible fact: it did not have to be constantly presented and justified."[31] Thus, it is argued that the coincidence of the Indian state which the Indian nation had achieved in the past and interestingly in a past that remains not only unverified but unverifiable with the effect that the possibilities are effectively neutralized. While this coincidence is held to be pivotal to the question of state's legitimacy, effective de-problematization and sanitization were also the prerequisites for resolving successfully the question of state's legitimacy.[32]

Second, another way through which it could be achieved was to take the battle to the enemy camp and to accuse it of having failed in the task of harmonizing the state with the nation or better say, in trying to make possible what essentially is impossible. The making of the Pakistani state is such an impossible event in history and history will take its own course by way of unmaking it. Hence what happened was not history and it would assert itself by taking revenge. In other words, Indo-Pak war of 1965 was more a war of Pakistan with history than with India. While the Indian state was relieved of the responsibility of building the nation on the ground that the latter was an "accomplished fact," for Pakistan the task was not only unaccomplished, but simply un-accomplishable. Sumit Ganguly for instance has written, "As Pakistan came apart, its claim on Kashmir also eroded, in a major way. The inability of the West Pakistanis to convince their brethren in the East to remain in the same polity, made it exceedingly difficult for the Pakistani leadership to lay claim on the basis of religious composition. Naturally India took advantage of the discrepancy between fact and theory."[33] While Indian state has sought to de-problematize its own nationalist claims, it also in the same measure problematized those of the Pakistani state. Both these processes went hand in hand with each other.

To re-state our arguments very briefly: First, our analysis shows that the state discourses in South Asia are neither inflexible nor incompatible with each other, though of course frequent wars have sought to define them in patently antagonistic terms. The first Indo-Pak war serves as a classic illustration of this point. It shows how the contingent factors left their mark on the articulation of the discourse of the Indian state. Second, elaboration of the discourse on the part of the state has set forth certain limits to its nature and range of operations. The war of 1965 for instance, points out how the forces were increasingly going out of India's control and her political practice fell far short of what the rhetoric of one-nation theory demanded from her. The 1971 war on the other hand, illustrates how the state sought to master the forces through what Kaviraj calls, "massive pretence," that is to say, by way of keeping it out of the realm of contention.

Let us now see what bearing the war-like situations have on the formation and elaboration of state discourses. As an offending strategy, they are meant to subvert the terms of another state discourse. One may look at the problem in either of the two ways or even a combination of them: First, war-like situations may arise when the fragments that the state claims to represent and articulate into its nationhood may refuse to be assimilated into it and sometimes choose to act at the behest of a country that has been held responsible for the conflagration of the war-like situations. We are painfully aware of a number of nationalities strewn all over India starting from Kashmir in the north to the Nagas in the Northeast that play host to such war-like situations. The anti-statism of the United Liberation Front of Assam springs not so much from the fact that Assam has been subjected to "the internal colonialism" of New Delhi but very much from the fact that "she has never been part of India" and the Indian state has no authority whatsoever to convert her into one of its constituent units.[34] It also happens that sometimes the fragments that according to a state lie beyond its national corpus and therefore need to be excluded from it show an excessive eagerness to be encapsulated within it. It is true that in state's perceptions, their exclusion is constitutive of the nation it claims to represent; but they do not share the same perceptions.

War-like situations may also be used as a defensive strategy in the sense that the state while employing it may be interested in restoring to itself the discourse that is apparently under attack from an offending country. The reports published by such human rights organizations as Committee for Initiative on Kashmir, Peoples' Union for Democratic Rights, Peoples' Union for Civil Liberties, and Amnesty International are increasingly drawing our attention to the role of the Indian state in inciting, fomenting or for that matter, perpetrating war-like situations in Kashmir. Thus to cite an instance, a Lokshahi Hakk Sangathana report has identified as many as eight militant organizations including Muslim Liberation Front and Ikhwan-ul-Muslimoon which have been planted by the Intelligence agencies with an eye to drive a wedge in militant ranks and divide the Kashmiri people.[35] Such a role of the Indian state helps it recapture its control over the discourse that faces attack from others. It seeks first, to prove that the Kashmiris are too heterogeneous to be called a nation and that the eagerness to be included in the national body may acquire an equally militant form with the implication that militancy is no monopoly of secessionism; War-like situations in other words, may be a means through which a state chooses to negotiate its terms with the little narratives or histories of the fragments which pose a potent threat to the prevailing state discourse. That negotiation is a continuous process only establishes that the state discourse is not too strong to appropriate and completely obliterate them. These narratives and fragmentary histories are simply irreducible.

Notes and References

1. Lecture at the first South Asian Peace Studies Orientation Course held by the Maulana Abul Kalam Azad Institute of Asian Studies, Calcutta, October 1997.
2. Sudhir Chakrabarty, *Folk Histories and the Possibilities of Writing and Alternative History of the Two Bengals: A Case Study of Central Bengal* (1977).
3. Dipesh Chakrabarty, "Modernity and Ethnicity in India," in John McGuire Peter Reeves and Howard Brasted (eds), *Politics of Violence: from Ayodhya to Berhampada*. New Delhi, 1996, p. 217. Also, Bhikhu Parekh, "Cultural Diversity and the Modern State," in Sudipta Kaviraj and Martin Doornbos (eds), *Dynamics of State Formation: India and Europe Compared*. New Delhi, 1997, pp. 177–203.
4. Carl Von Clausewitz, *On War* (ed. & trans.), Michael Howard and Peter Paret. Princeton N.J., 1976, p. 75.
5. Ibid., pp. 75–76.
6. Sumit Ganguly, "Wars Without End: The Indo-Pak Conflict," in Richard Lambert (ed.), *The Annals of the American Academy of Political and Social Science*. September, 1995. Ganguly elsewhere writes "... the instances of cooperation amongst seemingly deadly adversaries does offer a scaffolding of hope upon which future generations in India and Pakistan might erect more enduring structures of cooperation." See, Sumit Ganguly, "Discord and Cooperation in Indo-Pak Relations," in Kanti Bajpai and Harish C. Shukul (eds), *Interpreting World Politics*. New Delhi, 1995, p. 411.
7. Chris Hables Gray, *Post-Modern War: The New Politics of Conflict*. London, 1997, p. 157.
8. Ainslie Embree, "Statehood in South Asia," *Journal of International Affairs*, Vol. 51, No. 1, Summer, 1997, p. 4.
9. Samir Kr Das, "National Security and Ethnic Conflicts in India: A View from the North-East," in Arun Banerji (ed.), *Security in South Asia*. Calcutta, 1998.
10. Nicollo Machiavelli, *The Prince* (trans.) with an introduction by George Bull. Harmondsworth, 1961, p. 84.
11. Ranabir Samaddar, *Marginal Nation: Report on Transborder Migration from Bangladesh to West Bengal*. Calcutta, 1996, p. 29.

12. Sumit Ganguly, *The Origins of War in South Asia: Indo-Pakistani Conflict since 1947*. Lahore, 1989, p. 8.
13. I have analyzed it in Samir Kr Das, "The Extra-ordinary Partition: The case of Post-Partition Assam," 1997, mimeo.
14. Myron Weiner, "Rejected Peoples and Unwanted Migrants in South Asia," in *Economic and Political Weekly*, Vol. 28, No. 34, 21 August 1993, pp. 1737–46.
15. Richard Sisson and Leo Rose, *War and Secession: Pakistan, India and the Creation of Bangladesh* New Delhi, 1990, pp. 178–81.
16. Samir Kr Das, *Regionalism in Power: The Case of Asom Gana Parishad (1985–1990)*. New Delhi, 1997, pp. 122–26.
17. Sudipta Kaviraj, "Religion, Politics and Modernity," in Upendra Baxi and Bhikhu Parekh (eds), *Crisis and Change in Contemporary India*. New Delhi, 1995, pp. 295–316.
18. See Sadeq Khan, "The Question of Lebensraum," in *Holiday*, 18 October 1991. Also, Abdul Momin, "Lebensraum for Bangladehis?" *Holiday*, 22 November 1991.
19. Homi Bhabha, "Narrating the Nation," in John Hutchinson and Anthony D. Samith (eds), *Nationalism*. Oxford, 1994, pp. 312–16.
20. Hiranmoy Bandyopadhyay, *Udbastu*. Calcutta, 1970.
21. Mark Juergensmeyer, *Religious Nationalism Confronts the Secular State*. Delhi, 1994, pp. 6–7.
22. See, Susanne Hoeber Rudolph, "State Formation in Asia: Prolegomenon to a Comparative Study," in *The Journal of Asian Studies*, Vol. 46, No. 4, November, 1987. Also, "Satish Chandra, "State, State Formation and Statecraft in Indian History and Tradition," in L.R. Singh (ed.), *Nation-Building and the Development Process*. Jaipur, 1994. Also, Hermann Kulke, "The Study of the State in Pre-Modern India," in Hermann Kulke (ed.), *The State in India 1000–1700*. Delhi, 1995.
23. Lloyd I. Rudolph and Susanne H. Rudolph, in *Pursuit of Lakshmi: The Political Economy of the Indian State*. Bombay, 1987, p. 67.
24. Amalendu De, "Bangladeshe Dharmeeya Janabinyas: Manchitra Paribartan," (*in Bengali*), *Parichaya*, Vol. 61, No. 10–12, May–July, 1992.
25. Partha S. Ghosh, *Cooperation and Conflict in South Asia*. New Delhi, 1995, pp. 17–18.
26. Krishan Bhatia, *The Ordeal of Nationhood*. New York, 1971, p. 286.
27. Ayesha Jalal, *Democracy and Authoritarianism in South Asia: A Comparative and Historical Perspective*. New Delhi, 1995, p. 236.
28. M.J. Akbar, *India: The Siege Within: Challenges to a Nation's Unity*. Middlesex, 1985, p. 264.
29. Sumit Ganguly, *The Origins*, op. cit., p. 146.
30. Quoted in M.J. Akbar, op. cit., p. 250.

31. Sudipta Kaviraj, "On the Structure of Nationalist Discourse," in T.V. Sathyamurthy (ed.), *State and Nation in Context of Social change*, Vol. I, Delhi, 1994, p. 330.
32. Montserrat Guibernau, Nationalisms: The Nation-State and Nationalism in the Twentieth Century. Cambridge, 1996, pp. 59–62.
33. Sumit Ganguly, *The Origins*, op. cit., p. 136.
34. See, Samir Kr Das, *ULFA: A Political Analysis*. Delhi, 1994.
35. Lokshahi Hakk Sangathana, *Voting at the Point of a Gun: Counter-Insurgency and the Farce of Elections in Kashmir*. Bombay, 1996, pp. 32–33.

8

BORDERS AS UNSETTLED MARKERS—
THE SINO-INDIAN BORDER[1]

Paula Banerjee

It was the age of the Great Game and Lord Curzon was at the helm of British affairs in India. In his now famous observation, he revealed the problem that confronted the British not just in India, but in the entire "modern" world. Frontiers, he said were indeed the razor's edge on which hung modern issues of war and peace.[2] How could the British then bring back their 10,000 troops, deployed in Chitral, Tochi Valley, Landi Kotal, and Khyber Pass? Following Curzon's principles, they could not afford to give up Quetta or any of the frontier posts. Ultimately the British constructed strategic railways up to Dargai, Jamrud and Thal, and frontiers were left to tribal levies. The borders became a problem. Many years later, Zulfikar Ali Bhutto, the great patron of Pakistan's nuclear program wrote, "Geography continues to remain the most important single factor in the formulation of a country's foreign policy ... Territorial disputes ... are the most important of all the disputes."[3]

Borders, as markers of territoriality, have reared their ugly heads once again in South Asia. Are borders then a continuous problem in this region? This paper seeks to examine the issue by taking up the Sino-Indian border as a case. The argument here is that borders are basically human constructs that become problematic at different historical junctures; the rationale behind this problem needs to be sought in the wider political context. Human history provides eloquent testimony to how trouble-free borders suddenly become troublesome, such as the Tacna-Africa in the Attacama in the 19th century, or the border between the two Koreas, or even the Malvinas Islands in South Atlantic in 1983. South Asia is no exception to this general axiom. But the crucial question is what political conditions make borders problematic in post-colonial South Asia? And how do borders, in turn, influence the politics of the region?

BACKGROUND

As with most other post-colonial constructs the origin of South Asian borders can be traced to the British. Their frontier policy between 1880 and 1920 resulted in the acquisition of a large area in South Asia, inhabited by numerous indigenous populations, without any clear-cut boundaries that separated one territory from the other. Speaking of Africa, Lord Salisbury had once made a telling comment about the principles that the British followed in general while constructing markers around territories all over the world, he said:

> We have been engaged in drawing lines upon maps where no white man's foot has ever trod; we have been giving away mountains and rivers and lakes to each other, only hindred by the small impediment that we never knew exactly where the mountains and rivers and lakes were.[4]

Symptomatic of the British way of drawing borders was the Durand Line named after Sir Mortimer Durand, who negotiated it with the Amir of Afghanistan in 1893. The Durand Line was based neither on any clear physical feature nor on any distinct political organization.[5] In the foothills of the Afghan Plateau, there was nothing to suggest that one watershed could be a better boundary than the other, especially when the main rivers flowed transverse the direction the boundary followed. The small tribal communities that inhabited the area were fiercely independent.[6] The boundary that Durand had negotiated with the Amir was demarcated with extreme difficulty by May 1896, with the exception of a section around the Khyber Pass, which was finally settled after the third Afghan war in 1921.

In the north, the British negotiated a satisfactory boundary with Nepal that was flanked by two areas in the Himalayas where they were unable to persuade China to settle for any boundary. The border remained contested. In the east, Britain persuaded China to settle for a line marking the limits of Burma, but entirely failed to prevent France from establishing posts in the headwaters of Mekong valley. With Tibet, the border issue was settled by the Treaty of Lhasa (1904). For India, perhaps the most serious British failure was their inability to persuade China to agree to any boundaries in northern Assam, east of Nepal, and the Aksai Chin. In northern Assam, India at present relies on the McMahon line, which was a product of British attempts after 1904 to limit Chinese expansion and define the precise area of British responsibility in the Himalayas. There are two versions of the McMahon line and China considers neither mandatory. The Chinese maintain that the Simla Convention is not binding on them since they never ratified it. Both India and China agree that there is traditional boundary in Aksai Chin but disagree on its location. China at times even rejects the claim that a boundary was drawn at all.[7] Unlike the Indo-Pakistan border, there is a lot more unanimity of "national sentiment" as far as the Sino-Indian border is concerned. From time to time we glibly tend to portray the Chinese as bad guys and forget the greater problem—the border issue.

The end of the empire created a new set of boundaries and borders, but old problems persisted. Partition, which was supposed to resolve all territorial issues rationally, turned out to be an edifice of complete irrationality. The governments in the region largely emulated their colonial predecessors not only in methods of governing but also in rationalizing territorial issues. The new boundary lines created political compulsions of their own resulting in a remorseless hunt for that spatial claim which would serve the political demands of sovereignty. The Great Game was not over; it was only converted into a number of smaller games waiting to erupt at any given movement.[8] The terrain where the game was played remained disputed. The great actors disappeared from the stage, but the acted upon remained confronting new specificities with outmoded methods.

THE CASE OF THE SINO-INDIAN BORDER

The border dispute between India and China epitomizes the politics of borders in South Asia. It is not a product of partition but a relic of the days of the colonial times. It may not have the same emotional appeal as the Pakistani–Indian border, but it has defied solution at any level. It is a remnant of the Great Game and yet it is at the same time a post-colonial political construction. According to the Indian view, the Sino-Indian border ran along the main crest of the Himalayas. The southern slopes of its ridges, including the independent kingdom of Nepal and the protectorates of Sikkim and Bhutan, constituted the Indian side. In the west, the boundary started from the Karakoram Pass along the watershed between the Shyok and the Yarkand, ran through the Oara Tag Pass, ascended on the Kuen Lun mountains, left the main crest along 80° 21' East, and descended in a south-westerly direction.[9] According to the Chinese, in the middle and the east their territory extended to the southern side of the Himalayan ridges. In the west, Chinese territory included an area of about 15,000 sq. miles from Lahul, the Spiti area, the Shipki Pass, the Nilang, Jhadang, and Barahoti areas, while in the east it covered the whole of the North-East Frontier Agency (NEFA) covering about 35,000 sq. miles. As for NEFA, though the Chinese did not accept the McMahon Line, the precise extent of their claim was never made clear. The Chinese refused to accept that the line was in any way legal.[10]

There are some geographical problems with the Indian claims, but the political problems seem to be more serious.[11] The western fringes of the British Empire, Aksai Chin, Kashmir and the northern borders of British India were territories that became bones of contention among three contenders—the British, the Russians and the Chinese.[12] China was the weakest of the three contenders, extremely insecure about British and Russian designs on its frontiers. The Chinese were also traditionally the most interested in creating territorial markers and the contested area was not just a colony for them. The British were apprehensive of Russia's new colonial interests on the western fringes of their empire. The more they doubted the impregnability of the Herat, Farah, Kandahar and Bolan routes, the more intransigent became their policies towards the North-West frontiers. By the time Captain Gromchevsky reached Hunza through a small route between the Pamirs and Xinjiang, as Mortimer Durand commented, the Great Game had already begun.[13] Then onwards, aggressive designs of retaining a large empire kept all the players in a scramble for more land and creation of buffers beyond boundaries. And the Great Game continued until the Great War changed the politics of territoriality.

Partition brought border questions back to the center stage of South Asian politics. Apparently partition left the Sino-Indian borders untouched, but it created new identities bringing in its wake new principles of nationalizing the peripheries that would leave their mark on all the borders of South Asia. China, from a weak third of the 1890s, emerged as a strong first in the regional power structure by the late 1940s, with a traumatic memory of encroachments on its national frontiers; and the mighty British India was severely weakened by partition. Serious disagreements with India, however, did not surface until the late 1950s. This does not mean that the Chinese were reconciled to their borders.

Official Chinese maps after 1949 continued to ignore the boundaries of the Simla Convention. The international border with India in the eastern sector was shown as lying at the Himalayan foothills. In the western sector, there were wide differences between Chinese and Indian border demarcations. China claimed a huge portion of land both in the eastern and western sectors—around 32,000 sq. miles and 10,000 to 14,000 sq. miles respectively—which India considered her own; in the central sector, the Chinese claim ran into a few hundred sq. miles. During discussions preceding the 1945 Agreement between India and China, neither side raised the frontier question nor did the Agreement specifically refer to the Sino-Indian frontier.[14] That the Chinese were serious about their border claims became apparent the same year when they protested against what they termed as the intrusion of Indian troops beyond Niti Pass into Wu-ze. Even after repeated requests from the Indian government, they did not change their maps nor did they accept the boundaries given by the British. The Indians did not seriously question Chinese actions even after they abrogated the Tibet–Nepal Treaty in 1956.[15]

In 1957, India first heard on Chinese Radio that China had built a road connecting Sinkiang and Tibet. Seeing the road demarcated on a Chinese map, questions were raised in India and the Indian government sent two search parties to find out the details. One party was taken prisoner by the Chinese and the other returned. Indians protested against the Chinese construction of a road that ran through Indian territory. In spite of these objections, China continued to advance in Ladakh and built more roads. In 1958, negotiations between India and China over border issues collapsed amid mutual recriminations. In 1959, the Chinese claimed the disputed territory. The controversy culminated in the 1962 Sino-Indian border war. India came close to fighting another war with China after 1965. Then in 1987, once again the border dispute came to the fore—this time the crisis began over the question of control of Sumdorong Chu in the Thagla Ridge.

BORDER POLITICS

How did a region located 17,000 to 20,000 feet above sea level acquire such significance in 1962? If the region had such strategic merit then why did the Indian leadership wait until the late 1950s to bring it within its political agenda? Perhaps the answer lies in the changing perception of borders in the 1950s and 1960s. During the euphoric post-Independence Nehru era, India bolstered by its own "giantism," considered itself a world power.[16] India was confident of withstanding external pressures from the Super Powers in shaping its own foreign policy. In fact, Super Power rivalry led Nehru to conclude that India's position was secure as:

> It may be that some covet her, but the master desire will be to prevent any other possessing India.... If any power was incautious enough to make the attempt, all others will combine to trounce the intruder. The mutual rivalry would in itself be the surest guarantee against all attacks on India.[17]

However, India could not remain blind to the fact that it was flanked by a hostile Pakistan and an uncertain China. It sought to neutralize regional insecurities by acquiring the garb of a world power. Such a state of affairs called for political flexibility in the region, so that the borders could remain flexible. Nehru's whole thinking and strategy at the regional level was to seek political solutions to conflict situations. "For him there was no alternative for a country like his own which, in his view, should have the ambition of playing an important role in the international system."[18] This is clearly reflected in all his actions at the regional level.

India's decision to take the Kashmir question to the United Nations illustrates its approach to the Indo-Pakistani conflict. Further, Indian openness to dialogue with Pakistan over strategic issues is also a case in point. In contrast, the Chinese "tresspass" in Bara Hoti in 1954 evoked no stronger reaction than a note to the Chinese Embassy. The following year when there was intrusion in the Dam-Zan area, the "Indian Foreign Office sent a mild note of protest saying that the unauthorized presence of Chinese soldiers ... amounted to tresspass."[19] Even as late as 1956, Nehru instructed the Uttar Pradesh government not to adopt an aggressive attitude towards China for disagreements between the two countries were being settled in conferences and "there was no major border issue."[20] One notices a similar attitude and approach with regard to the Tibet question. On Chinese actions in Tibet, India maintained benevolent neutrality. One reviewer has described India's attitude vis-à-vis China as the "doctrine of defence by friendship."[21] Coupled with this were Indian efforts to assume leadership of the newly independent Asian and African countries with the vision of developing the Nonaligned Movement. Even the Super Powers believed that Nehru was the leader of the Asian and African countries. Thus the United States first sounded India for an alliance and moved towards Pakistan only after it was made clear that India was unavailable. In 1953, Nixon advised the National Security Council to bolster Pakistan in an effort to neutralize Indian leadership of the Asian and African "block."[22] Nehru's involvement in the Korean peace process further enhanced this leadership role.

In the 1950s India's hopes of becoming a world power faced serious challenges. The increasing interest of Super Powers in South Asia and their "more intimate consultations" with other South Asian powers, deepening economic crisis in India, and finally the emergence of China as a great power led to recognition of the fact that India at best could be a regional power. In the post-Bandung era, India realized that its self-avowed leadership of the Nonaligned Movement would not go unchallenged. The Indian leadership then began to look inwards towards the region. This led to a reconsideration of the Indian political, military and strategic situation, and a concomitant interest in good fences. With this heightened interest in borders Indian leadership responded to the increasing assertion of Chinese military presence on the border. As in the 19th century, a border game began as a result of regional insecurity, but unlike in the 19th century, India was on the defensive as far as its northern frontiers were concerned. The increased number of border patrols and the constitution of a special board to complete the building of roads in these areas reflected growing interest in safe borders. The Indian leadership felt that India had to acquire regional hegemony to deal with China. The situation was further complicated by western propaganda that India had to compete with China "for the leadership of the East, for the respect of all Asia."[23] The realization that India's goal of national security could not be met effectively through only political means led to a reorientation of Indian policies towards its neighbors in the end 1950s. An important outcome of this policy reorientation was the Indian occupation of Goa by force. It was a bold signal that on territorial questions India would no longer be flexible.

Indian preoccupation with its borders was reflected in Lok Sabha and Rajya Sabha debates of the period. From 1959 onwards Nehru constantly reasserted in the Lok Sabha and the Rajya Sabha that India was not open to any discussion regarding its borders and that the borders had become a problem.[24] Indian leadership became intransigent not only about Sino-Indian borders but also about Indo-Pakistani borders. There were indications that Ayub Khan was eager to reach a settlement with India on the border issue in the East Pakistan sector that Nehru disregarded. Evidence of this changed attitude towards borders was that instead of treating exchanges with the Chinese government as confidential, the Indian leadership decided to place the entire correspondence before Parliament. The *White Papers I–III* also gave ample testimony to this changed Indian attitude. Primier Zhou's letter of 17 December 1959 carried an offer to the effect that both sides should meet and discuss the boundary question.[25] Nehru showed total unwillingness to negotiate the boundary in its entirety. His attitude is summed up by his official biographer as "a willingness to talk but an unwillingness to negotiate on the major question of the boundary as a whole, a strengthening of the Indian position in the border areas".[26] It was not just the Chinese attitude then that had made the border a problem.

Indian military leaders knew that India was in no position to defend its borders against the Chinese. General Thimayya had publicly indicated two months before the outbreak of Sino-Indian hostilities that he could not, even as a soldier, envisage India taking on China in an open conflict on its own.[27] General P.N. Thapar too had "categorically pointed out to the government the inability of India's forces to take on the Chinese and the inadvisability of such a step in NEFA and the possible repercussions in Ladakh, but Krishna Menon ignored what Thapar said." General B.M. Kaul had also advised against fighting the Chinese either in the Dhola or the Thagla region.[28] That the Indian army was pessimistic about the situation is also clear from such other sources as John Kenneth Galbraith's secret memorandum to the US Secretary of State.[29] But the Indian political leadership decided that India's "traditional boundary" and its vital strategic interests were at stake and, therefore, needed to be defended. The results of the war of 1962 are well known. India suffered a severe strategic defeat and could do nothing to stop the Chinese onslaught. Coming as a terrible jolt, this military humiliation acted as a catalyst and generated a new mood for evaluating India's concept of national security. Such an evaluation further enhanced the importance of an impregnable border if India wished to retain its regional hegemony; and in that sense the 1962 defeat made Indian leadership even more inflexible. From then onwards, the, issue of borders became a significant input in shaping India's foreign policy within the region.

Throughout 1963, most of the Lok Sabha debates on foreign policy centered on the border issue. Naturally there were clarion calls to "intensify our defensive preparations to resist any further threat to our territorial integrity," which was hardly surprising.[30] What was surprising, however, was the extent to which the leadership was prepared to go for defence preparedness. In a confidential letter addressed to the prime minister, which T.T. Krishnamachari clearly stated was "intended purely for you [Nehru] to read and to be killed thereafter," he discussed a plan to keep 16 divisions ready on the borders at all times and urged the prime minister not to slacken defense preparedness because of the Chinese ceasefire.[31] The priority that Nehru attached to the letter was apparent in that he answered it the same day. In his reply, Nehru wrote:

> China, I think, is going to be our foe or adversary for a considerable time to come ... we should ... concentrate on strengthening our defence position. I think there is not much likelihood of China attacking us militarily.... Even so...we have to strengthen ourselves to meet the Chinese menace.[32]

These letters, if nothing else, are markers of the pervasiveness of the national security lobby and the extent to which border disputes would dominate the government's policies in the 1960s and 1970s. It was argued that the only way to exercise a strong centralized control over the borders was by increasing India's military clout in the region. This was highlighted by the then Indian Defence Minister, Y.B. Chavan. During his address to the Lok Sabha on 9 September 1963, Chavan declared:

> There has not only been appreciable increase in the total quantum of Chinese forces in Tibet, all along our Northern borders, but the build [up] of these forces is concentrated at strategic points closer to our borders than they have ever done before.... Although leaders of Pakistan are well aware that our defensive preparations are meant to safeguard security against the threat from our Northern borders they are carrying on baseless propaganda that these defensive preparations are a threat to the security of Pakistan. We have also learnt recently about certain deployment of Pakistani troops on Assam and East Pakistani border.... In the current climate of hostility and tension ... we have ... to take necessary measures for defence [of] our territorial integrity against any aggressive threat.... The first programme of our defence preparedness is, one of expansion of our Armed Forces.[33]

The unresolved border disputes of the 19th century thus continued well into the present century and thereby initiated the political milieu of the South Asian region. In our times, the continuing insecurities over the borders led to the increasing importance and ultimate institutionalization of the role of the national security lobby. The innocuous Defence Committee changed into the Emergency Committee in 1962 and eventually became the Political Affairs Committee with the expanded task of looking after both internal and external security matters. India adjusted itself to "continuous tension along the border."[34] Henceforth, any border dispute was to be incessantly contested. Even the Colombo Proposals, which Nehru accepted as equitable, did not go unchallenged.[35]

The Pakistani *entente cordiale* with China heightened India's sense of insecurity about its borders and made its posture even more rigid. Kashmir became non-negotiable.[36] Even within India, there were criticisms about this changed Indian attitude. Jai Prakash Narayan's speeches are typical of such criticism. He criticized this change in Indian attitude towards Kashmir in the late 1950s as well as the so-called "legal integration" of Kashmir that began in the wake of the border disputes.[37] India was prepared to discuss the Kashmir issue even in 1962–63, but by 1965 India shifted to the stand that Kashmir could not even be on the agenda. In a discussion with Andrei Gromyko, Foreign Minister of the Soviet Union, the then Indian Finance Minister stated, "We have always held the view that Kashmir is not a matter for discussion except in regard to aggression committed by Pakistan."[38]

India's war with Pakistan may have been the result, at least to some extent, of this Indian rigidity over the border question. Even a seemingly undisputed stretch of land between Sind and Kutch that formed the international boundary between India and Pakistan was severely contested. India and Pakistan had differing views about the location of that boundary through the Great Rann of Kutch. It was agreed that the boundary extended from the mouth of Sir Creek in the west to the eastern terminus at the tri-junction of Gujarat, Rajasthan, and Hyderabad. Further, they agreed that the western sector had been defined along Sir Creek to latitude 23°58′ North and then eastward to its intersection with meridian 68°41′ East. This segment of the boundary was disputed. India maintained that it was a proper boundary and that it was only necessary to draw the boundary between the northern terminus of this extension and the eastern tri-junction. Indian authorities proposed that the northern edge of the Rann—which is a salt-impregnated alluvial tract—would be a convenient and direct boundary. Pakistan recommended a boundary that connected the meridian with the eastern trijunction via the middle of the Rann. The two countries were completely unwilling and unable to resolve the dispute and it was settled only by arbitration in 1968 much to their mutual dissatisfaction.[39] That was one of the last settlements of border disputes by arbitration, since from 1965 onward, Indian attitude towards third party mediation became extremely negative.

The connection between the Great Game and border disputes of the 1960s is borne out by the Sino-Pakistani *entente*. In October 1967, China and Pakistan signed an unpublished agreement to open the ancient silk route by building an all weather road over 500 miles from Xinjiang to Gilgit and Hunza in Pakistan occupied Kashmir. The road ran through the Mintaka Pass and the Khunjerab Pass, from where another Chinese road led to Lhasa in Tibet. India perceived this activity as a threat to its security and an infringement of its legal borders. It lodged a strong protest against the Chinese actions. Despite this, the road was formally inaugurated in 1971.[40] The unresolved Great Game thus, left the field open for smaller games. But these smaller games had logic of their own. Regional hegemonic compulsions reactivated the border issue that fostered national insecurities resulting in the growing importance of national security lobbies in the region. These lobbies could justify their existence and substance so long as the borders remained unstable. Thus there emerged vested interest groups who saw to it that border disputes were kept alive and borders remained in a constant state of flux.

There was another effect of this militarization of borders and India's northeastern border is a case in point. This region is linked to India by a narrow 70 km stretch between Bhutan and Bangladesh and shares an uninterrupted border of over 37,000 km with Bhutan, China, and Bangladesh. The majority of the population here belongs to Mongoloid groups with strong linkages with China, South and Southeast Asia. The border is porous with a long history of movements and exchanges between people, cultures, beliefs, ideas, and customs. Conviction about the sanctity of the border is weaker here than elsewhere. Such shared ecology, geography, and culture have given rise to linkages between tribes and communities on both sides of the border.[41] In fact, many of these tribes feel they have more in common with each other than with the nation-state of which they form a distant appendage. There is a growing feeling among the inhabitants that the entire Far Eastern Himalayas is peopled by marginalized communities that are peripheral groups, far away from the levers of the central government. These areas have a long history of neglect by the rest of the country. Their demands for autonomy and independence can be traced back to the time of India's independence. Enough evidence exists on the meaningful ties that most of the ethnic groups have established with neighboring countries such as China, Burma, and what was then the East Pakistan. The corporatist ideology of nation-state as articulated by the ruling *elites* failed either to counter the endemic in the development of the center/periphery syndrome. To counter insurgency movements in the region, ruling *elites* made the borders even more rigid. Here again, border disputes became an excuse for the national security lobby to militarize the entire region so that the area could become manageable. This is especially difficult in the Indian context as the colonial process created largely artificial borders in the region. Same ethnic groups inhabit both sides of the border with close cultural affinities. This has not only created porous borders but has also given rise to conflicting claims of control over bordering regions. Such militarization merely destabilized the area even further and ensured that the disputes continue to fester.

The irony of the Sino-Indian border dispute of 1962 is that it was born out of political compulsions that disregarded military clout leading to its complete domination of regional politics. In South Asia, regional politics had to address the issue of borders because unstable borders created their own politics. There was no clear regional arbiter who could dictate borders and so it had to be negotiated at every step. Once in the agenda, borders began to dominate the politics of the entire region. The situation continued until the early 1970s when India decisively emerged as the regional hegemon in South Asia. From 1969 onwards China became engrossed in another border issue— the Sino-Soviet border along the Ussuri River. India endorsed the Soviet position as a way out to resolve differences over the interpretation of the Sino-Soviet border. India also signed a treaty with the Soviet Union. China's rapprochement with the United States on the basis of the principle "the enemy of my enemy is my friend" changed the political and strategic co-relation of forces not only in the region but also in the entire world. The Chinese and Indian nuclear programs further altered the situation. The politics of borders continued, but in a different format, so different that it has to be recounted in another essay.

Conclusion

The above analysis argues that Sino-Indian relations did not create border problems. On the contrary the existence of the Aksai Chin and the McMahon lines constructed Sino-Indian relations. Whether India gave asylum to the Dalai Lama or not, the compulsions of the borders drew India and China inexorably into the vortex of a crisis. Chinese leadership understood that long before Indian leadership could. Nehru tried to wish away the border problem, but he could not do so.

The Great Game had created the situation that India and China faced later. However, the position from which they confronted it was completely different from that which their predecessors had faced. During the Great Game, the actors scrambled for more land, but during the smaller games of the 1950s and 1960s, they tried to defend the border that they considered "historically" given. But any border, either in the 19th century or even today is deliberate political and psychological construct. Otherwise how can one justify the incessant contests over either the Siachen glacier where the border dispute caused the sacrifice of about 300 men during 1996 or the Durand Line because as geographical borders they are both unfeasible and untenable? Even the northern terrains where the war of 1962 was fought are not easily accessible from either the Chinese or the Indian side. And yet, it has had enormous influence on the politics of the region.

Rigid borders in South Asia are geographically not viable, and so any policy of total demarcation is very difficult to implement. A change in the political situation carries within it a potential for change of the border situation and vice versa. The borders are active agents of politics in South Asia and the way the

British demarcated and constructed borders, mostly on the diplomatic table, has kept the issue fraught with potential conflict. Today we speak of Sino-Indian rapprochement, a thaw that has taken place since the late 1980s. Regarding the Sino-Indian talks of 1991, it was stated, "bilateral talks became possible at all because the two sides put border dispute on hold."[42] Instead of saying that the border issue has been put on hold, it is no longer crucial for regional stability and cooperation. Borders once again constructed the relation, but this time by their absence as a problem. This does not mean that borders have become non-issues in South Asian politics today. The politics of border is visible in other forms and in other kinds of relations, and the people within the region negotiate it everyday.

NOTES AND REFERENCES

1. Originally published in *International Studies*, Volume 35, No 2, 1998, pp. 179–91.
2. Lord Curzon, *Frontiers: The Romanes Lectures*. Oxford, 1907.
3. Zulfikar Ali Bhutto, *The Myth of Independence*. London, 1969, p. 11.
4. A.L. Kennedy, *Salisbury 1830–1903: Portrait of a Statesman*. London, 1953, p. 224.
5. J.R.V. Prescott, *Political Frontiers and Boundaries*. London, 1987, p. 227.
6. C.C. Davies, *The Problem of the Northwest Frontier 1890–1908*. Cambridge, 1932, p. 179.
7. A. Lamb, *The China–India Border*. Oxford, 1964.
8. I am grateful to Ranabir Samaddar for drawing my attention to this issue.
9. "China," *Annual Reports*, Ministry of External Affairs (MEA), Government of India, New Delhi, 1959–60.
10. "China," *Annual Repots*, MEA, New Delhi, 1962–63.
11. Indian claims were based on the principle of "natural boundaries." Further the McMahon Line does not consistently follow primary, secondary or tertiary watersheds, or the crests where they form watersheds. "It is thus difficult to avoid the conclusion that the alignment of the McMahon Line was result of a series of ad hoc decisions," Prescott, N. 4, p. 111.
12. Dorothy Woodman, *Himalayan Frontiers: A Political Review of British, Chinese, Indian and Russian Rivalries*. London, 1969, pp. 71–72.
13. Ispohani Mahnaz Z., *Roads and Rivals: The Politics of Access in the Borderlands of Asia*. London, 1989, pp. 151–53.

14. Subimal Dutt, *With Nehru in the Foreign Office*. Calcutta, 1977, p. 113.
15. S. Gopal, *Jawaharlal Nehru: A Biography*. Delhi, 1989, p. 475.
16. The term "giantism" is used in the same sense as John K. Lewis has used it in his article, "Some Consequences of Giantism: The Case of India," *World Politics*, April 1992.
17. Quoted in B. Prasad, "An Overview," *International Studies*, Vol. 17, Nos 3–4, 1978, p. 863.
18. Harish Kapur, *India's Foreign Policy 1947–92: Shadows and Substance*. New Delhi, 1994, p. 23.
19. Dutt, note 14, p. 115.
20. S. Gopal, *Jawaharlal Nehru: A Biography*. Vol. III, Delhi, 1984, p. 39.
21. Michael Edward, *Nehru: A Political Biography*. London, 1973, p. 270.
22. *Eisenhower Papers*, Whitman Files, NSC Series, Meeting #176, December 1953, Dwight David Eisenhower Library.
23. J.F. Kennedy, "India and China," Pre-Presidential Papers, Speech Files, 1953–1960, John F. Kennedy Library (JFKL).
24. *Lok Sabha Debates*, Second Series, vols. XXXII–XXXIX. *Rajya Sabha Debates*, vols. XXIV–XXV.
25. *White Paper, III*, pp. 52–57.
26. Gopal, note 20, p. 128.
27. Kapur, note 18, p. 25.
28. General B.M. Kaul, Oral interview with A.K. Gupta, 13 January 1972, Transcript, pp. 146–47, Nehru Memorial Museum and Library.
29. John Kenneth Galbraith to McGeorge Bundy, 22 March 1962, Department of State Papers, National Security File 106, JFKL.
30. *Lok Sabha Debates*, Fifth Session, vol. XIX, column 682.
31. T.T. Krishnamachari to Nehru, 16 December 1962. TTK Papers, No. 121/MEDC/62, Nehru Memorial Museum and Library (NMML).
32. Nehru to Krishnamachari, 16 December 1962. TTK Papers, No. 2249-PMH/62, NMML.
33. Y.B. Chavan, *Lok Sabha Debates*, Fifth Series, vol. XX, columns 5087–90; in his plans for expansion he talks of six divisions and not sixteen as Krishnamachari did and which were probably meant to be secret.
34. Gopal, note 20, p. 236.
35. Lakshmi N. Menon, Oral Interview Transcript, 20 April 1971, pp. 11–12. Nehru, *Selected Speeches*, vol. V (New Delhi, 1968), pp. 177–99.
36. Nehru, *Selected Speeches*, note 32, p. 196.
37. J.P. Narayan to S. Radhakrishnan, 25 December 1965, JPN Papers, Subject File 241, cited in ibid., p. 583.
38. "Record of Finance Minister's meeting with Mr. A.A. Gromyko, Soviet Minister of Foreign Affairs, on 16 November 1965 from 12 noon to 1 p.m." TTK Papers, Subject File 43. NMML.

39. Prescott, note 5, pp. 60–61.
40. Surjit Mansing, *India's Search for Power: Indira Gandhi's Foreign Policy, 1966-1982.* New Delhi, 1984, p. 202.
41. On 15 August 1947, many of the tribes did not know to which side of the border they belonged. The Boundary Commissions, at times, further complicated the situation. For example, the Chittagong Hill Tracts People's Association (CHTPA) petitioned the Bengal Boundary Commission, chaired by Sir Cyril Radcliffe, that since the CHTs were inhabited largely by non-Muslims they should remain within India. But on 17 August, Radcliffe awarded the CHTs to Pakistan since they were inaccessible from India. Two days later, the CHTPA resolved not to abide by the award and hoisted the Indian flat. The Pakistani army dealt with the protest but the problem has not yet been solved.
42. *The Hindustan Times*, New Delhi, 17 December, 1991.

9

PROTECTING THE RIGHTS OF REFUGEES[1]

Irene Khan

The paper examines the extent to which the basic rights of refugees are protected in Asia, and how the system can be improved, both to enhance protection and also to improve the search for solutions to the plight of refugees. After a brief introduction to the international refugee regime, the paper discusses the response of governments in Asia, which has been pragmatic and flexible, and not based on international refugee instruments or national laws. It looks at the strengths as well as the constraints of such an approach, and considers the need to develop appropriate legal and other institutional framework to protect refugees. It concludes that improving the protection of refugees as well as ensuring solutions to refugee problems will require taking a fresh look at current strategies and action at three levels: international, regional, and national.

For the purposes of this paper, refugees movements are defined, in keeping with the accepted notion in international law, as large-scale cross border population movements resulting from persecution, generalized violence or war. The paper excludes from its scope internal displacement or cross-border migration motivated by economic concerns, although the author recognizes that such a differentiation is problematic in a region where political, economic and social reasons for flight are intertwined.

THE INTERNATIONAL REFUGEE REGIME

Generally speaking, the international refugee regime is a mix of international "universal" instruments and institutions, supplemented by regional arrangements, both of which are implemented at the country level through national laws and procedures. The juxtaposition of national and international law is of particular significance because of the cross-border nature of the refugee problem, affecting at least two states, and also because the refugee, having fled his country, has lost national protection and has become an object of international protection. The term "international protection" signifies the responsibility of the international community to ensure that states respect the basic human rights of a refugee, including his/her right to return home voluntarily and safely.

The United Nations High Commissioner for Refugees (UNHCR) was established by the UN General Assembly in 1951 with a mandate to provide international protection to refugees and to assist governments to find a solution to refugee problems. The concept of international protection is fundamental to its mandate, and imposes certain obligations on states which cut into the heart of sovereign privilege and which, in practice, can lead to a degree of conflict and controversy in the relationship between governments and UNHCR.

In 1951 the United Nations adopted the Convention relating to the Status of Refugees, to which the Protocol was added in 1967. The main elements of the Convention are a definition of a refugee, and principles and standards on how refugees should be treated, including protection against forcible return to danger expulsion and detention for illegal entry. The principle of non-refoulement in Article 33, according to which a refugee cannot be returned against his/her will to a territory where his life or liberty is threatened, has received such wide acceptance that it is commonly regarded as a principle of customary international law. Under Article 35, the United Nations High Commissioner for Refugees has been given the responsibility of monitoring the Convention.

These international agreements have been supplemented by regional instruments and mechanisms that take into account concerns that exist at the regional level but are not fully appreciated or relevant at the global level. Regional mechanisms can take various forms. The *OAU Convention governing Specific Aspects of the Refugee Problem in Africa* and the Schengen and Dublin Agreements are legally binding regional treaties adopted under the auspices of the OAU and the

European Union respectively. *The Cartagena Declaration on Refugees* is a non-binding instrument adopted by NGOs and scholars in Central America, but governments have tended to follow it as a matter of policy because the Declaration reflects the consensus of practices and policies in the region. Another example of a non-binding instrument is the Bangkok Principles concerning the Treatment of Refugees adopted by the Asian-African Legal Consultative Committee in 1966. In some instances, regional arrangements have been adopted on specific refugee problems, such as the 1989 *Comprehensive Plan of Action for Indochinese Refugees in Southeast Asia* (CPA). Another interesting experiment in regionalism has been the CIS Conference, held under the chairmanship of UNHCR in 1996 and including all CIS and Baltic countries. The Conference adopted a Plan of Action or a common agenda for the region on range of issues including refugee and migration policies, nationality and citizenship laws, minority protection and projects to rehabilitate returning refugees, displaced persons and others who were forcibly relocated in the past. Although regional in nature, both the CPA and the CIS Plan of Action promoted solidarity and cooperation between the international community and the countries in the region.

Increasingly, international human rights instruments are also being used to enhance refugee protection. Basic human rights provisions, for instance in the *UN Covenant on Civil and Political Rights* (CCPR) on the right to life, liberty, and security of person, freedom of religion, freedom from torture, non-discrimination, equality before the law, etc., make no distinction between citizens and non-citizens and form an important basis for refugee protection in countries of asylum. This has been recognized by the UN Human Rights Committee, which monitors the CCPR, and which regularly asks states parties to report on how they treat refugees in their territory. *The Convention Against Torture* and the *Convention on the Rights of the Child* contain specific provisions on refugees.[2]

REFUGEE PROBLEMS IN ASIA[3]

It is difficult to speak in general terms of refugee problems in Asia, because they are diverse and vary enormously from region to region. However, two commons trends can be discerned. The first is the massive scale of displacement in the continent.[4] The second is the virtual absence of the international refugee regime in Asia. It is estimated that some 35–40 million persons have moved across international boundaries in South Asia alone since 1947. About 20 percent of the 13 million refugees in the world are to be found in Asia, not to mention much larger numbers of returnees and internally displaced persons in a refugee-like situation. Despite this fact, few countries have acceded to the 1951 Convention relating to the Status of Refugees or the 1967 Protocol and fewer still have adopted national laws on refugees.[5] Unlike Africa or Central America, there is no regional refugee instrument in Asia.

The refugee flows from outside as well as from within the region are handled by the governments in an ad hoc manner on the basis of administrative policy. Why have Asian states chosen this approach and with what consequences for refugees? Is there a need to change the approach, and how? What kind of regional and national laws and mechanisms should be considered? Are there lessons to be drawn from other regions? These are some of the issues that are examined below.

LESSONS OF HISTORY

In assessing the response to refugee problems in Asia, a historical perspective is important because many of the current concerns are rooted in past fears and perceptions, and cannot be discounted simply as water under the bridge. It is worth noting that both India and Pakistan actively participated in the committees that drafted UNHCR's mandate and the UN Convention in 1950. The two countries were keen to include the "partition refugees" under the mandate of UNHCR, so that international assistance could be provided to them. The prevailing view, however, was that the High Commissioner's task should be to provide international protection to refugees who did not receive the protection of any state, and that excluded the "partition refugees" who were treated as nationals by their receiving country.

The main focus of the international refugee regime at that time was on refugees in Europe. This became clearer when shortly afterwards refugees fled China and entered Hong Kong. The United Kingdom did not extend the 1951 Convention to Hong Kong. Instead, the UN General Assembly passed a resolution calling on UNHCR to extend its "good offices" to this group. With hindsight it would not be unfair to say that had the international community paid more heed to the refugee burden of Asia at that time, the international refugee regime might have played a greater role in the refugee situations which subsequently unfolded in that region.

It was also obvious that the international refugee regime was being used as a tool in the ideological and strategic war between the East and the West. Countries such as India that were committed to a policy of non-alignment were understandably cautious of an approach which could lead to Super Power involvement in their sub-region. To take the example of the Tibetan refugee crisis, the Government of India's policy on Tibetan refugees was governed by three considerations: the preservation of Indian security and integrity, the desire to maintain friendly relations with China, and sympathy for the Tibetan people.[6] Conscious of the political sensitivities of the situation, India did not vote on General Assembly resolutions on Tibet nor seek international assistance from UNHCR until as late as 1969 when UNHCR was permitted to open an office in New Delhi to channel funds to the Tibetan settlement program through the Red Cross.

Subsequent developments in Asia vindicated the concerns about Super Power involvement, when conflicts fueled by the Super Powers led to massive refugee flows out of Vietnam, Cambodia and Laos, and later, Afghanistan. Both the responses and the solutions were linked to the bi-polar politics of the time and part of a larger strategic game.

The very high degree of international involvement in the Indo-Chinese and Afghan refugee problems was not surprising, given the geopolitical dimensions, and had major political repercussions. Nevertheless, one should not overlook the humanitarian contribution of the international community in responding to the victims of these crises. One of the positive contributions that UNHCR made in Southeast Asia was to ensure temporary asylum for the refugees in the ASEAN countries, for instance by mobilizing international funds and finding resettlement places for the refugees elsewhere. In a bid to find a balanced humanitarian approach, even in the midst of what was a highly politicized setting, UNHCR established an early presence in the Indo-Chinese countries and maintained that presence throughout. That foresight paid off in the long run. After the end of the Cold War, UNHCR played a key role in finding solutions to the Indo-Chinese refugee problem. As part of the Paris Peace Plan on Cambodia, UNHCR helped hundreds of thousands of refugees to return home in time to participate in the elections. For the Vietnamese and Laotian refugees, UNHCR brokered the Comprehensive Plan of Action in 1989, which brought together the countries of asylum, origin and resettlement/donors in a multi-faceted operation, controlling the outflow, resettling refugees abroad and arranging for the return home of non-refugees. The last Vietnamese refugee camp in Southeast Asia was closed in June 1996.[7]

The humanitarian value of international involvement was recognized by India in the case of the refugee outflow from East Pakistan in 1971. India formally requested the assistance of UNHCR in April 1971. As the focal point for coordinating UN assistance, UNHCR channeled some US$ 220 million to the Government of India. Why did India involve UNHCR? From a humanitarian perspective, the burden was heavy and international assistance was needed if a catastrophe was to be avoided. Also, the involvement of the UNHCR involvement helped to support India's position that the issue at stake was a humanitarian one, and not, as Pakistan was claiming, a bilateral political dispute between India and Pakistan.[8]

The Afghan situation provided to be much more complex. For years the role of the UNHCR was confined to funding a "care and maintenance" program for 3 million refugees in Pakistan. After the withdrawal of Soviet troops and the Geneva Peace Accord in 1992, over 1.5 million refugees returned to Afghanistan from Pakistan and Iran with the assistance of the UNHCR. However, although the nature of the conflict has changed, the degree of violence continue, leading to new refugee outflows and massive internal displacement. International humanitarian involvement, without the concurrent political will and action to resolve the conflict, has achieved little other than limited succor to the victims.

Contemporary Concerns: Arguments Against Legal Commitments

The Cold War is over, as are the Cold War generated refugee problems (with the possible exception of Afghanistan). However, refugee problems continue unabated in Asia, though numerically on a lower scale. So does the reluctance of the Asian countries to accede to the international refugee convention.

Inadequacy of International Instruments

Underlying the reluctance is the widespread feeling that the 1951 Convention and 1967 are inadequate and inappropriate. The most common criticisms are that the refugee definition is too narrow and the scope of socio-economic rights too broad for developing countries. Also, there is no reference in the Convention or Protocol to voluntary repatriation nor the responsibility of the country of origin, which are key to solving refugee problems. The refugee problems confronting Asian countries today have less to do with the type of persecution mentioned in the Convention than with internal conflicts linked to the failures of nation-building and the disaffection or marginalization of minorities, aggravated by inequitable economic and social policies, environmental degradation and population pressure. A new dimension has also emerged in some of the situations. The inability on the one hand to control borders and the failure on the other to define clearly who is or is not a citizen are leading to refugee problems in which the nationality of the victims, and consequently the responsibility of the states concerned, is unclear, making the search for solutions to the refugee problem even more elusive.

Advantages of Bilateralism

There is also a feeling, particularly in South Asia, that accession to an international treaty or regional agreement on refugees, would internationalize the refugee issue and aggravate tensions among neighbors. Unlike Southeast or Central Asia where multilateral approaches to finding a solution to the refugee problem have been the norm, South Asian states have tended to use the bilateral channel to settle their differences within regionally recognized and historically accepted constraints. Even where international assistance for refugees has been sought, solutions have been pursued on a bilateral basis, e.g., Sri Lanka/India, Bhutan/Nepal and Bangladesh/Myanmar. In the case of Rohingya refugees, the bilateral agreement between Myanmar and Bangladesh was supplemented by separate bilateral agreements between UNHCR and the two governments respectively.

Need for Flexibility

What is significant in the case of Asia is not only the low number of accessions to the UN Convention but also an overall reluctance to enter into any legal commitment on refugees even at the domestic level, although for political and strategic reasons governments might be willing to host refugees temporarily or even for longer periods. It has been argued that dealing with refugees on an ad hoc basis gives the governments flexibility without which they could not respond effectively to highly sensitive refugee problems affecting regional stability and national security. Most of the refugees in the region are from Myanmar to Bangladesh, from Afghanistan to Pakistan or from Cambodia to Thailand. As such, the refugee problem is a major factor in bilateral relations between the host and home countries. Furthermore, because of ethnic affinities between the host community and refugees in many cases, e.g., Sri Lankan Tamil refugees in Tamil Nadu, Rohingyas in Bangladesh, Afghan Pashtoons in Pakistan or Bhutanese refugees of Nepali origin in Nepal, domestic considerations play an important role in the response to the refugee problem. Conversely, where the ethnic origin of the refugees differed from the host community, such as the Chakmas in Northeast India or the Vietnamese Chinese in Malaysia, the pressure was for a restrictive approach. It is easier to respond to such political exigencies through bilateral and ad hoc measures than within parameters set by the law.

Positive Administrative and Judicial Practice

There is also a feeling that a specific legal framework for refugees is not necessary in Asia because the region has a good humanitarian record based on administrative policy and practice. Countries have by and large responded generously to refugees. In South Asia in particular, borders have generally remained open and unlike Southeast Asia, there have been few incidents of large-scale push-backs or refoulement. A related consideration is the way in which accession to human rights instruments and constitutional guarantees, combined with a lenient attitude of the judiciary, have provided protection to refugees, e.g., in India. The National Human Rights Commission of India investigated complaints relating to the situation of Sri Lankans detained in special camps in Tamil Nadu, and the Chakma refugees in Arunachal Pradesh and Tripura, and in the case of the refugees in Arunachal, successfully petitioned the Supreme Court of India. The Indian judiciary has interpreted the constitutional provision on the right to life and liberty as protecting refugees against expulsion in one case, and, in another case upheld the principle of voluntary repatriation.

GAPS AND CONSTRAINTS: ARGUMENTS FAVORING CHANGE

Although humanitarian instinct, liberal administrative practices and judicial decisions, combined with astute pragmatism, have often provided a considerable degree of protection of refugees in Asia, there are also critical gaps and constraints, many of which can be traced to the lack of national laws and institutions and non-accession to international refugee and human rights instruments.

Precarious Nature of Protection

Experience has shown that the protection of refugees is precarious in the absence of a binding legal framework. When the asylum policy changes because of foreign policy or domestic political considerations, refugees are left without any recourse and can sometimes be forced to return to dangerous situations in their own country or be ill-treated and detained for prolonged periods in the asylum country. To take an example, when Pakistan's strategic and political interests changed in the post-Cold War period, so did its policy on asylum for Afghan refugees. Although Pakistan had an open door policy towards Afghan refugees for decades, in 1993 it closed its borders to new arrivals, who had no option but to seek tenuous refuge in the camp for internally displaced persons within Afghanistan. While political and other considerations will always play a major role in asylum policies, regardless of international or domestic legal commitments, international treaties and domestic laws can provide a more transparent and acceptable framework within which such policies can be designed.

Lack of Clarity

In the absence of refugee laws, there are no standard criteria or procedures to identify refugees or to clarify what rights they enjoy or obligations they bear. As most Asian countries do not have procedures for determining refugee status, UNHCR is obliged to recognize refugees under its mandate, but their status under national laws remains uncertain. Currently in most Asian countries refugees fall under the laws applicable to foreigners including provisions on illegal entry and overstay. The failure of the law to distinguish between refugees and other foreigners has led in some cases to detention and even deportation and refoulement of refugees. The lack of legal standards has also led to inconsistent and discriminatory treatment of refugee groups. For instance, in Pakistan, only Afghan refugees enjoy the right to residence and freedom of movement, while Iranians, Iraqis and other asylum seekers are treated as illegal aliens. In India Tibetan, Sri Lankan, and Chakma refugees do/did not have/enjoy the same legal status, privileges, and facilities. While the Sri Lankans and Chakmas are registered with the Indian authorities as refugees, the Afghans, Iranians and other nationalities have no such possibility.[9] Although liberal interpretation of the law by the judiciary can help to ameliorate the situation in individual cases, there are limits to what the courts can do when the law is silent or ambiguous.[10]

Confusion with Economic Migration

The absence of a definition of a refugee in the law as well as the lack of procedures to identify refugees is particularly problematic in a region where illegal economic migration is increasing. Popular goodwill is becoming strained by the pressure which growing migration is placing on resources and by the attendant political, socio-economic and environmental problems. The absence of clear and consistent criteria to define refugees and fair and transparent procedures to identify them not only weaken the protection of genuine refugees, they also increase the threat perception of the local population who feel that all kinds of people are being allowed to enter and remain illegally. Proper immigration control that differentiates between genuine refugees in need of sanctuary and others not in need is in the best interest of refugees as well as of social harmony.

Risk of Politicization

The lack of a legal basis for responding to refugee situations is not in the interest of good bilateral relations because it exposes the receiving state to allegations of supporting political opponents or insurgents against the neighboring home country. A legislative framework for refugee protection helps to de-politicize the response and thereby also reduce inter-state tensions.

Uncertainty over the Role of the UNHCR

In the absence of any international legal commitment, the role of the UNHCR and, in particular its access to refugees remain problematic in many parts of Asia. Its protection role, whether for refugees in the host country or returnees in the home country, is sometimes regarded by governments as being too intrusive (NGOs on the other hand accuse UNHCR of not being assertive enough). Experience has shown, however, that the presence of the UNHCR presence can provide an important, even critical, safeguard against human rights abuses for refugees in the country of asylum or for returnees after they have gone home. In Tajikistan international monitoring by UNHCR and other, and other, and close follow-up of violations gave greater legitimacy and credibility to the operation for return of refugees and displaced persons, creating confidence among the returnees and generating domestic and international support. For similar reasons, the Government of Sri Lanka has allowed

UNHCR to assist returning refugees and displaced persons in northern Sri Lanka, and the Government of India agreed to verification by the UNHCR of voluntary repatriation from Tamil Nadu.

Need to Develop a Comprehensive Approach to Protection, Solutions, and Prevention

As the complexity and size of population movements in Asia increase, the need is being felt, not only for protection of refugees, but for preventive and solution-oriented strategies to address refugee problems. Though ad hoc measures can deal with the immediate consequences of refugee flow, a more comprehensive approach is needed to tackle the underlying causes. Socio-economic factors, such as rampant poverty, uneven development, unbridled population growth, environmental degradation, and natural disasters, combined with ethno-political conflicts, are uprooting large numbers of people in the region. Many of them are on the move across borders, straining the tolerance of the receiving communities and creating security and other problems. If such issues are to be addressed properly, longer-term, more comprehensive policies need to be developed of the kind which the CIS conference promoted in Central Asia and other parts of the former Soviet Union, bringing together issues of displacement, human rights and minority protection, citizenship and socio-economic development.

Looking Ahead: Building New Institutions

The aforementioned paragraphs have sought to argue that though the response to refugee problems in Asia has been generous, it is far from adequate, and could come under serious strain in the future. The answer is to build an institutional framework to meet the following goals; (a) legal protection of refugees, including a definition, procedure for determining refugee status, and a set of standards for treatment ("rights and duties") of refugees; (b) a mechanism for states to resolve refugee problems in a manner which encourages international solidarity and cooperation while respecting refugee protection and; (c) a strategy to prevent problems from arising in the future. The experiences in other parts of the world have shown that the ideal institutional framework is a combination of national, international, and regional approaches.

Domestic Laws

Domestic laws are essential for refugee protection, because they are a means of implementing international obligations when a country accedes to the international refugee instruments. Quite apart from that, the other advantage is that a national law allows each country to respond in the manner most suited to its own circumstances and concerns. It is important, however, for the domestic legislation on refugees to reflect internationally accepted principles and standards of human rights and refugee law. Otherwise, it will not provide refugees the protection they need. In view of the reluctance of South Asian countries to accede to the existing international refugee instruments, a group of eminent persons has proposed a draft model law on refugees for the SAARC countries that would provide the basis for a similar regional approach but at the same time acknowledge each national situation.[11] Since it can be adopted without linkage to the 1951 Convention or Protocol, the drafters hope that it will be acceptable to countries of South Asia.

Regional Mechanisms

Regional mechanisms are an important means of strengthening refugee protection as well as finding solutions to refugee problems. They allow harmonization of refugee policies and practices in the region and encourage regional cooperation to solve the refugee problems. They have been used in many situations to clarify the respective responsibilities of the country of origin as well as of the country of asylum thereby ease the prospect for solutions and burden sharing. Furthermore, regional consensus on how to deal with refugee problems can help to de-politicize the issue, thereby reducing tensions between states. However, it would appear that the kind of political consensus that forged the OAU Convention on Refugees in Africa, the Schengen and Dublin agreements in Europe or led to the acceptance of the Cartagena Declaration by governments in Central America is yet to emerge in Asia. Another factor militating against a regional approach in Asia is the lack of an appropriate forum. Unlike the OAU or the EU, contentious issues have been kept off the SAARC agenda. ASEAN too does not have refugees on its agenda. Therefore, it may be premature to speak of a regional declaration, whether for South or Southeast Asia, although discussions and dialogue on the issues could help over a longer time perspective. Meanwhile, the Asian–African Legal Consultative Committee is continuing a useful dialogue with government experts on the "Bangkok Principles," with a view to developing consensus in key areas.

International Instruments

International instruments promote international solidarity and commitment to global humanitarian principles. The value of adhering to international obligations on refugees should not be ignored. The shortcomings of the 1951 Convention do not negate the universality and the continued relevance of the refugee rights it contains. One way to promote international standards on refugee protection in Asia could be to encourage accession (and adoption of implementing legislation) of a wide range of human rights instruments, which protect citizens and non-citizens alike, along with the Refugee Convention. Indeed, putting the refugee issue in a human rights context serves a broader purpose of highlighting the importance of solving and preventing refugee problems as well as protecting refugees in exile. Violations of human rights are a major cause of refugees flows, and restoring respect for human rights very often is a precondition for refugees to return home. Strengthening the human rights machinery, and particularly the protection of minorities, can help to prevent or solve refugee problems while improving the protection of those who are forced to flee.

Finally, although there is growing recognition of the need for an institutional framework, more discussion is required to clarify and build consensus on the nature, form, and content of such a framework in Asia. Governmental, inter-governmental and non-governmental actors have an important role to play in that process. The challenge is to develop a regime that protects the rights of refugees while recognizing the legitimate interests of states and the respective responsibilities of the home and host countries and the international community.

NOTES AND REFERENCES

1. Lecture at the first South Asian Peace Studies Orientation Course held by the Maulana Abul Kalam Azad Institute of Asian Studies, Calcutta, October 1997. The views expressed in this paper are those of the author in her personal capacity and do not necessarily reflect the position or policies of UNHCR.
2. Article 3 of the Convention Against Torture provides that: "No State party shall expel, return ("refouler") or extradite a person to another State where there are substantial grounds for believing that he would be in danger of being subjected to torture." This article reflects the concept of non-refoulement which is contained in Article 33 of the UN Refugee Convention, Article 22 of the Convention on the Rights of the Child provides that "States Parties shall take appropriate measures to ensure that a child who is seeking refugee status or who is considered a refugee in accordance with applicable international or domestic law and procedures shall ... receive appropriate protection and humanitarian assistance in the enjoyment of applicable rights set forth in the present Convention and in other international human rights and humanitarian instruments to which the said States are Parties."
3. This paper looks broadly at the refugee problems in South and Southeast Asia only.
4. According to the *State of the World's Refugees*, 1998, published by UNHCR, there are 4,808,624 refugees in Asia. The major locations and numbers in South and Southeast Asia are as follows: Bangladesh: 30,578; India: 233,370; Nepal: 127,000; Pakistan: 1,203,000; Thailand: 107,962, Vietnam: 34,400. Other large refugee groups are in China (290,100 from Vietnam) and Iran (2,030,539 from Afghanistan and Iraq). UNHCR Numbers 1997 estimated some 7,925,000 persons of concern to UNHCR in Asia, including refugees, internally displaced and returnees (refugees who had returned home but not yet reintegrated).
5. China, Japan, Korea, and the Philippines are parties to the Refugee Convention and Protocol and have introduced legislative or administrative procedures, in cooperation with UNHCR, to determine refugee status of applicants.
6. Press conference by Prime Minister Jawaharlal Nehru on 4 April 1959, reported in Louise Holborn, *Refugees: A Problem of Our Time*, London, 1975, p. 719.
7. The Cambodian refugee camps along the Thai border were closed in 1993, following the repatriation of the refugees. Unfortunately, political turmoil in Cambodia in 1997 and continuing

violence have led to a fresh exodus of about 45,000 refugees to Thailand.
8. Louise Holborn, *Refugees: A Problem of our Times*, p. 774.
9. See B.S. Chimni, "The Legal Condition of Refugees in India," *Journal of Refugee Studies*, vol. 7, no. 4, 1994.
10. "[I]t is as the result of judicial creativity most often, that certain basic rights, even of refugees, have been taken care of through the medium of the courts.... But this certainly cannot be treated to be a satisfactory solution": Inaugural address by Justice J.S. Verma in the Seminar report, *Refugees in the SAARC Region: Building a Legal Framework*, SAARCLAW/UNHCR, New Delhi, 2-3 May 1997.
11. The Regional Consultation on Refugee and Migratory Movement, which is a group of lawyers, judges and other eminent personalities from the SAARC countries, adopted a model national law in Dhaka in November 1997, which is published in *States, Citizens and Outsiders*, Appendix A, South Asia Forum for Human Rights, Kathmandu.

10

PEOPLE AND TERRITORY: MOVING BEYOND BOUNDARIES[1]

Barun De

Relevant to all of us in South Asia is the question of what has been called "mega-diversity," probably the principal cultural bonding which exists among us in the countries of Nepal, Bhutan, Bangladesh, Sri Lanka, Maldives, Pakistan, India and other peoples on the periphery of South Asia such as in Afghanistan, Tajikistan, the Xinjiang and Tibet regions of China and in Myanmar. I do not claim to have expertise; but only to a share in the common problems concerning the process of humanity flowing beyond national boundaries.

May I begin by invoking a passage that moved me when I first read it several years ago. It explicates the contradictions between people and territorial boundaries. An Indian scholar from Darjeeling, Dr Kumar Pradhan has written, for the Sahitya Akademi of India, a history of Nepali literature, also focusing on Nepali literature in India. He quotes and translates into English, the Nepali poet Vijay Malla's, *Chhorilai Manchitra Parhauda* (While Teaching Map Reading to Daughter).

Rato ragatle korieko Saadh Chha
khetma dil lae jhai
hera, harek rashtrako fatma,
yo ho Bharat yo ho Pakistan
Hindu Musalmanko ragatla muchieko
Yahi ho rekha mahan,
Jata hera Rato ragatle taeko chha ghera
Parevalai ganjakma banda gare jhai
Manis chha bandi yas khorma

[Drawn by red blood are these boundaries/Like enclosures in every field/Look, to delimit nation each/This is India, this is Pakistan/This is a line bold, kneaded with the blood of Hindus and Muslamans/Wherever you look drawn are the lines by red blood/Like the pigeon encaged/Men are closed in their traps.][2]

I am reminded of a poem my wife heard after the partition when she was a girl of seven or eight. It was written by the Indian Civil Servant and literatteur, Annada Shankar Ray. One of the lines in this jingle runs as follows:

Teler shishi bhanglo bole, khukhur pare raag karo!
Tomra joto burho khoka, bharat bhenge bhag karo!
Tar bela!
[Because a little child breaks a bottle of oil, you get angry with it/You infantile old dodderers—you break up India and divide it/What then?]

This is the keynote we must emphasize. When one talks of states, one is talking of these sorts of policies. When one talks of history as being dominated by states, one is talking of the history of these sorts of policies. But there is another history that is now being discovered. A generation other than mine is writing it. It is called the history of popular culture.

In the history of the popular culture of South Asia, the basic concepts are not necessarily those of ephemeral empires, which the British taught those of us who were born in British India and their dependencies, to believe were the essential elements in our subcontinent's history. Let us consider certain examples.

MYTH OF PERMANENCE: EMPIRES IN SOUTH ASIA

The Ashokan Empire was obviously the Indian government's beau ideal for the Indian state form. Adopting the symbol of the *Ashoka Chakra* or the Ashokan Lion Capital, the Nehruvian Indian state harked back to Ashokan ideas of *satyameva jayate* and *dhammavijaya* as examples of syncretism and non-aligned diplomacy. Yet, historical data tells us that the Mauryan empire hardly lasted more than a 100 years.

The shadowy Gupta Empire, which we presume from the historical evidence of the *Harisena prasasti* of Samudragupta on an Ashokan pillar in Allahabad Fort, as well as from scattered sources such as that of the Chinese traveler Fa Hsien and some Sanskrit texts, is after all only a representation of a political empire, seen as the forebearer of the Mughals, whose emperor Jahangir inscribed the date of his ascension, on the Allahabad Fort Pillar. Pre-British "imperial" India is an intellectual construct meant to validate the national integrationism of British India and the Indian state to which *inter alia* it transferred power.[3]

The Mughal Empire, as a politically stable entity is supposed even by its greatest contemporary scholars to have lasted not more than 150 years—from Akbar to Aurangzeb. The Indian composite culture was concretized at times by integrationist consolidation. But historically, its content and style has always been more coalitional and federative than purely unitary: as much "diversity in unity" as "unity in diversity." This is not to deny the fact that a strong authority ruling the bulk of the subcontinent was definitely an element of stability and authority to build a certain measure of prosperity for Indian elites. But to emphasize only this, is to ignore regional and sub-regional realities.

Obscured by the Leviathanic imperial tradition that in the Ashokan, Gupta, Mughal, and British cases, rose from or collapsed into smaller principalities or state structures, there are at least 2,000 years of political history of small principalities. The records that have been translated or interpreted are indeed often of political domination. But if one goes even into those records—the inscriptions, the manuscripts, the religious, and ethical *Sastraic* and *Puranic* texts which have been quarried for political information, one can find a great deal more information about what an eminent historian of ancient India, Brajadulal Chattopadhayaya, has called "autonomous spaces" in ancient and early medieval India. Below the Rajas were groups of people whose consensus was equal to that of classical state power. They regulated their own lives, they led cooperative lives, they led competitive lives, often autonomous of the Raja's control or even authority, provided of course they yielded up to his state and court the often large share of the surplus on which the latter maintained its regulative systems and occasionally appealed to him/her for legitimation of sanctions.[4] Not till the

Mughal period, which is only about 500 years ago, did the Indian state radically intensify its direct impingement on the life of the common people. Even then, it was like a matted latticework, or a canopy, open on all sides, suspended over the affairs of rural or inner-city quotidian life. The state in South Asia, as we define it in European terms, in the English language, the only language in which all of us seem to communicate with each other, or in French terms or in Dutch or German, is not even more than 500 years old as we now know it. What then were the other realities of traditional South Asian cultural interaction? In strict historical terms, it was a record of settlement, but also of movements.

POPULAR DIASPORAS IN HISTORICAL PERSPECTIVE

Even in the standard histories of our subcontinent, there are records of large-scale agricultural movement. The Vedic peoples were called Aryan by European historians of the past. Aryan was a term popularized by the highly statist Germans. Today it is fairly well-known that the people who spoke and then wrote the Vedas, and their Eurasian affines, spoke certain languages called Aryan, but which should on the contrary, be studied in terms of different stages of social, cultural, and material development. The Vedic peoples were a moving community, stretching all the way from southern Central Asia from Soghdiana and Bactria, called in Islamic literature *Mawar-an-Nahar* (across the river), i.e., the Oxus or Amu Darya, today the border along Turkmenistan, Uzbekistan, Tajikistan, and Afghanistan. And they moved all that way across to Bihar, Madhya Pradesh and the northern Deccan. They expanded herding, grazing, and agriculture. As they moved, they employed different forms of agriculture—slash-and-burn, hoe farming, dibbling, plough-cultivation and a range of other activities including pastoral ones.

The movement of the Vedic peoples were succeeded by other movements of settlements. British historians tended to emphasize only movements from the north-west into the south-east across the Khyber and the Bolan passes. But there were movements of the Mongoloid as well as eastern Turkic peoples across the Karakoram into the high Himalayan ranges, south of the Karakorams, in what is today Chitral, Gilgit, Hunza, Ladakh, Kashmir, and Zanskar.

There were movements later on of people from the upper Gangetic plains to western Nepal, from Tirhut into *Mades* Nepal, and from Yunnan in China and Laos into what is today called Assam, what they themselves called *Asom*. Their descendants were people who call themselves Ahom. Even today in Ahom religious functions, a language is invoked which only their priests understand. This is *Tai Ahom*, the language somewhat similar to that of the people of the Shan principalities in eastern Burma, of Chiangmai in north Thailand and of Laos and northern Vietnam. In fact some Australian scholars in the University of Canberra researching the early history of Indo-China had looked for linguistic parallels in Thailand, the Shan states and upper Assam. On the other hand there are legends amongst the Karen people of deltaic Burma, that have been interpreted as reflecting their migration in the far past from as far north of Asia as Mongolia.

Today, there is talk of an economic and cultural region that extends from eastern Nepal and upper Bihar all the way through north Bengal, Bangladesh and northeast India to Yunnan and Burma. In a broader regional perspective, there are common problems of development and prosperity from eastern UP to Upper Burma. In Bangladesh the commonalities of culture and economy in this region have been encapsulated in the SAENE concept that stands for South Asia's East and North East. Similarly there are economic and cultural commonalities between Jammu and Kashmir, eastern Xinjiang, the Badakshan regions of Afghanistan and Tajikistan, and the Balkh and Surkhan Darya/Kashka Darya regions of Afghanistan and southern Uzbekistan. These have not crystallized after late medieval times due to the exigencies of fragmented territoriality and non-existent communication. On the other hand, land highways such as the Arniko Rajpath from Tibet to Nepal, built by the Chinese and the Karakoram highway from western Tibet into Pakistan, have recreated old links.

Population movements existed within India too, but these have been greatly ignored. The *Ramayana*, for instance, is one of the greatest epics about popular transfers within our subcontinent. To me, it is a sacred text of culture since it talks of the ways, cultural, peaceful, as well as violent, indeed dialectical in all aspects, of movements from north to south. It is one of the elements in the record of domination and subordination in Indian history. One ideologically disapproves of domination and its consequences, but as a historian one has to look at this in all its social and economic aspects. One can get the best record of this in the two great epics of South Asia, the earlier, *Kshatriya*-glorifying *Mahabharata* and the later, *Brahman*-worshipping *Ramayana*. Both talk about population movements. The Mahabharata is the more violent epic. The Ramayana is more dialectically rich with a variety of cultural and ethical themes across India, of groups struggling with others to establish their own ideologies and identities in which the epic gives pride of place to the *Bharata* lineage.

I am not of course being original. I am just repeating the ideas of one of the great cultural historians of India in his 1913 Benaras and Calcutta University lectures. Dr Radha Kumud Mukherjee, in his book called *The Fundamental Unity of India* traces this fundamental unity to the domination of the concept of Bharatic lineage as kings of Ayodhya over the whole of India. He argued that the pilgrimage centers in India are interlinked in this encompassing myth. For instance, there was the idea of the 108 parts of the body of *Sati*, the spouse of *Pashupati Siva*, which fell all over India leading to temple shrines springing up.[5] There is one such shrine in Kathmandu itself in Guheswari near the ancient sanctum of Pasupatinath, another one in Kamakshya in Guwahati in Assam and another one in my own city—Kalighat in Calcutta. There are others all over India. Hindu politics of ideological domination is splayed out in locational terms. I am not arguing that this is what traditionalist historians would call, "true history" because I do not believe in the idealist concept of truth in history. History after all is a construct to be seen in relative terms, in terms of the construction of peoples' varied concepts about what they thought was a particular history of the past.

The point is to identify ways in which the popular consciousness acquired ideological forms. They are based on movements of people for a variety of agricultural shifts, a variety of forms of labor mobility and a variety of transformation of power relations. Take the emblem of the hero *Bajrangbali* or *Hanuman*, so popular nowadays among many people, including the intelligentsia. Surely, Ram, the mythological north Indian hero, did not have central Indian monkeys fighting for him. It has been argued that they were really totem-worshipping warriors with a monkey as their emblem or even a mask for ritual purposes. Again I am not saying anything new. This was said slightly before R.K. Mukherjee, around 1910–11 by Rabindra Nath Tagore in his *Bharat Varshe Itihasher Dhara* (The Course of History in India). These totemic people, Tagore hypothesized were people who fought for the dominating groups. Tagore believed that there was some sort of symbiosis between the Brahmin and Kshatriya, the typical caste-dominating combine of India. Tribal people worshipping totems, fought for the upper caste combine in their conquests.[6]

We may now turn to the idea of labor mobility. In my own state of West Bengal a tradition still persists in the areas between the hills and the plains, i.e., in the lower upland of Rarh in south-west Bengal (between the Chota Nagpur plateau and the Hooghly river) of *namal* labor. *Namal* means *jara ba ja neechey namey* (those or that, who or which, come down). They are normally Santhal, Ho or Munda tribes who have been subordinated and kept backward over the years, tribes on whom Bengalis, Biharis, and Oriyas generally established their usurious control as moneylenders. In the 19th century this led to occasional revolts that was recorded by the British and later appropriated by the leftist intelligentsia. In late 19th and early 20th century these groups were in cultural subordination. Among them are people who come down from the plateau edges, when the crop-cutting season comes. I myself saw them some 20 years ago in the then backward *thanas* of Arambagh subdivision of Hooghly district in West Bengal, coming single file, as if they were walking down a hill track, along ridges between low-lying paddies with baskets on their heads. They come, do the cropcutting and are allowed to take the gleaning and leavings from the fields. They are given a certain daily wage— increasing in the recent years—and they go back to their villages in the uplands to eke out their subsistence for the rest of the year.

If you have the *Namal* in West Bengal, you also have the *Powinda* merchants and petty usurers who came from southern

Afghanistan, the region where today the Taliban movement completely dominates, that is, Ghazni, Kandahar, and Herat from where the Taliban burst out towards Maimana and Balkh in their northward thrust against General Dostam in September 1996. Powindas would work in their upland pastures in the southern Afghan hills but every year they would come down the Bolan, Sibi, and Gomal passes into Baluchistan and then spread out to South Asia.[7] In Calcutta people like them are still called *Kabuliwallah*, because Afghanistan is known only as Kabul to us. In Bengal they would be peddling moneylenders who used, till recently, to nomadically carry money slung over their shoulders, lent at usurious rates to local labor. They would also sell housewives dates, raisins or figs, imported, they once used to boast, from Bukhara and Samarkand. But they had, historically, also acted as mercenaries in north India. There were the famous Rohilla fighters (originally from Ruh, the southern Afghan mountains) who built up the principalities of Rampur, Shahjehanpur, Bareilly or Ferrukhabad in 18th century India, leaving their name even today as Rohilkhand. Some Afghan migrants would settle on the plains, others would go back every year.

A Pakistani geopolitician, Mahnaz Ispahani, describes the impact made by roads through Afghanistan built by the Soviets and Americans during the Cold War. Americans built in southern Afghanistan, Soviets in the north, from Kushka in Turkmenistan to Herat, from Termez in Uzbekistan to Mazar-i-Sharif to Kabul through Pul-i-Khumri and the now famous Salang Tunnel where Uzbeks and Tajiks of north Afghanistan and the mullahs of the Taliban were embattled. These roads transformed the economic pattern of Afghanistan, leading Pakistan (even before the fall of the Afghan royal dynasty) to close the boundary of the Durand Line that stopped Powindas moving south. So in the last 15 to 20 years the Powinda tribes exerted pressure on the soil and became victims of economic disorder. They were unable to move across into the Pakistani border or splay out.[8]

Any Bengali will know that in the last 20 years *Kabuliwallah*s have been scarce in West Bengal. I remember meeting an Afghan ex-ambassador to India at a UNU Kyoto seminar in 1979, who had said to me that he used to have a big problem in the 1960s dealing with the *Kabuliwallahs* involved in disputes with local clients in Calcutta. Now one hardly sees recent migrant Afghans in eastern India. They have stopped moving to South Asia from Central and Northwest Asia in the way the Bengali middle class nowadays seem to be moving inexorably to England and America. And they were moving with as much of legitimacy, or illegitimacy and validity or lack of legal authority, as our present non-resident Indians move, not just to Oxford or Essex or New Jersey or Calgary in Canada but also to rocky inlets on the coasts of Greece and south Italy *en route* to a globalized and often criminally lumpenized European labor market. The question of moral judgment on such movements hardly arises. If there are any judgments, these are to be made on the pressure of consumerism that is the allure of the economy, on the fringes of which they flit. Those pressures and those market forces express themselves in open entry at certain times and in restrictive practices at other times.

One could go on multiplying examples of such professional movements. In the period of the late Mughal empire the *Peshwas* of Poona particularly from the time of Balaji Baji Rao down to Madhav Rao Narain in the middle of the 18th century, dominated Gujarat, eastern Rajasthan, Malwa, Gondwana as well as present-day Andhra, and Karnataka to the east of Maharashtra, northern Tamil Nadu, Orissa and the southwestern tip of Bengal. The Brahmins, who found very few jobs in the arid hills of the Western Ghats, since one subcaste, the *Chitpavan* Brahmins, dominated that region, felt the *Chitpavan* competition very unfair in Maharashtra. Most notably these were the *Deshastha* and the *Karhade* Brahmans many of whom migrated across the Deccan into the east Godavari basin. This was administered through the 19th century by *Deshastha* Brahmins who used the Maharashtrian surname, Rao. A book was published 30 years ago about local administration in Guntur showing Maratha migrants of a century or more migratory standing as the local elites of Guntur. There were similar migrations of Tamil Brahmins from Tamil Nadu and the east of South India to the Palghat region in the west of deep south India. A large number of Tamil Brahmins became landlords in Palghat in Kerala and even *dalawais* or *dewans* in its 18th century Nair principalities.[9] But then there were so many of this ethnic sub-community by the mid-20th century that they could not get jobs in South India, so having learnt English some became stenographers in Delhi or Calcutta. Pandit Jawaharlal Nehru's stenographers, the best in India, were a succession of Palghat Tamils. Of course now, Palghat Tamils are part of the general "non-resident" diaspora of the consumerist Indian middle class in Europe and North America.

In West Bengal we have a great name like Sakharam Ganesh Deuskar, a nationalist Bengali writer, who wrote one of the first patriotic popular tracts in Bengali—*Desher Katha*.[10] He spoke Bengali, but his mother tongue was Marathi. He was settled in Deoghar, the Santhal Parganas, where his father had come as a Marathi, working with Bengali clerks and moneylenders among the Santhal population. We had a Minister in West Bengal called Phadikar, which sounds like the Marathi Phadkar. But Shri Prabhas Phadikar lived in Daspur in Medinipur, whose folklore noted in O'Nalley's "Midnapur Gazetteer" of the early 20th century still had remnant memories of Maratha brigands of the 18th century such as *Sheo Bhat Sathe* who came to loot and stayed back to become Bengalis.

A final element of these normal movements is what I have referred to as pilgrimage routes. There is much research still to be done on the social flows and consequences of pilgrimages in South Asia. Bangladeshis who came to India, immediately after the independence of Bangladesh, would often make a pilgrimage, not to any center in West Bengal, not to *Furfura-Sharief*, for instance but would go all the way to *Ajmer Sharief*, the Mazar of Sheikh Moinuddin Chisti in Ajmer, in faraway Rajasthan. There is a tremendous novel and film in Bengali about Bengalis, among other Indians, on pilgrimage to a place in the far off deserts of the Khanate of Kalat in Baluchistan, now in Pakistan, called Hinglaj, where there is one of the 108 shrines to which I have referred to as *Avadhuta's Marutirtha Hinglaj* (the Desert Pilgrimage to Hinglaj). This was a way of cultural bonding. In my very first article written about 40 years ago, I referred to the point that Hindu, Muslim, Jain, Buddhist, Parsee, Sikh and Christian bonded themselves in what we used to call "India before 1947" by that sort of cultural diversity in unity—the diversity of common pilgrimages.

In the article entitled "A Note on the Nature of the Problem of Indian Unity" in the *Economic Weekly* in 1958, I differed from Radha Kumud Mukherjee as well as later sociologists and ethnomethodologists in the USA, like M.N. Srinivas, B. Subba Rao, Mckim Marriot and Bernard Cohn, who said that India was bonded by Hindu pilgrimages. India was indeed bonded by sacred pilgrimages but they comprised a composite variety of faiths. These could be Jain sites. There are Jain shrines in Karnataka. The present Chairman of the Indian Council of Historical Research, Prof S. Settar has written a book called *Inviting Death* about rocks opposite the Gomatesvara image in Sravana Belagola in Karnataka where Jains go to die[11] in a way that the Hindu widows are supposed to go to Kashi or Nepalis of piety are taken to Pasupathinath Ghat to die. Sikhs have shrines in Patna and in Assam, where one of the Gurus traveled and they also have a shrine incidentally in Baghdad where Guru Nanak is supposed to have gone.[12]

ENDEMIC WARS, FUZZY BORDERS AND THE REFUGEE

We may look at another element of the general problem. Normal lines of bonding are disrupted by refugee flows created by wars and violence or chauvinistic repression. The problem in general as created by wars and violence in the 19th and 20th centuries has been greatly intensified by Euro-centric concepts of refugees and uprooted peoples.

In the last 100 or 150 years Europe has been under the sway of the concept of the nation-state, described in, for instance, Benedict Anderson's simplistic *Imagined Communities*, Ernest Gellner's more sophisticated book on nationalism or Eric Hobsbawm's superb and thought-provoking survey. European imperialism ignited the concept in the shape of anti-colonial nationalism in the southern hemisphere first, as Creole independence in Latin America, in the two great Latin American Wars of Independence 1812–13 and 1825–29, when Latin American states were formed, from Mexico in Mesoamerica down to the southern cone of Argentina and Chile. These ideas indigenously developed in Asia and in different formations in Africa and were also exogenously sparked by European changes. They were explicated by emulative indigenous elites, the new nationalists of anti-colonialism and then they were replicated by the comprador groups which set up the Europeanized state system imposed on the masses "from above." It is this system which is now fragile and breaking down, for instance in, the erstwhile Yugoslavia, in Europe, in Rwanda and Burundi in Africa or in Afghanistan in Asia.[13]

This concept of the nation-state brought new forms of principality or nationality, each with a boundary "drawn by red blood," through a whole series of wars. The great cataclysms through the middle and the early modern ages in European imperial history—the Hundred Years War which led to the origins of early international law, the wars of Bourbon and Habsburg succession, the later war over North American Independence and the Napoleonic Wars, where there was a megalomaniac state seeking to dominate the whole of Europe—show that Chengiz Khan and Amir Timur in Inner Asia were not aberrations but part of a pre-modern system of *imperium*, which fascism in long-range terms still seeks to revive. In between these spurts of wars, from the time of the building of the Han, Maurya, Sassanid or Roman Empires down to campaigns of the 1980s around Iraq, there may have been only interludes when such endemic warfare did not take place.

Europeans of course had recorded delimitation of territorial boundaries for many centuries before the 19th century. Asians, Africans, and Latin Americans have been less precise for the purposes of historical record. Inferences from inscriptions or coins or dubious textual reconstruction have made the matter of historical frontiers very foggy. If one looks at the history of frontier making in the late 19th and 20th centuries in central, inner and northwest Asia, one can see how uncharted terrain was being drawn into Euro-centric cartography.

For instance, mountains here were given heights only in late 18th and 19th century maps. I keep on nagging about this to anybody who has the misfortune of being with me in a car when we go north along Wood Street in my home city of Calcutta as the Survey of India building looms up on the right side, where Radhanath Sikdar, a Bengali compradore, calculated that Sagarmatha was the highest peak in the world. The credit was given to his boss Sir George Everest, the Surveyor General. The Europeans named it as Mount Everest. A popular but scholarly biography of Sir Aurel Stein, the Hungarian scholar who settled in Kashmir, naturalized himself a Briton and died in Afghanistan, describes how he would take Indian surveyors Ram Singh and Lal Singh to survey Xinjiang, Kansu, and Ningsia—the vast inner Asian tracts of China. The reputation of this mapping of Central Asia and later of southern Iran went to men like Stein or Sir Thomas Holdich. Ram Singh went blind as a result of his tribulations and was pensioned off with a few hundred rupees annually.[14] No one knows what happened to Lal Singh and it is only recently that the far more famous "pundits" of the Rawat family of Milam in Uttarakhand trained to survey the upper courses of the Indus and the Tsanpo-Brahmaputra, by British spies have been popularized by a "British Raj" buff Charles Allan.[15] Whether done by Indian surveyors or organized by European explorers, what did happen was that inner Asia was mapped in border lines—the Durand Line between Pakistan and Afghanistan which the Afghans still do not accept, the Macmahon Line between India and China along watersheds most of which had not then been seen or walked along by Europeans or Chinese, about which the Chinese had, and still have, great doubt. Indeed in one part of it the Chinese have arbitrarily built a road through the Karakorams; thus infringing upon territory claimed by Jammu and Kashmir, even before it became part of British India creating claims of succession by the Government of India. This border delimitation has been done in the interests of imperial, national, or socialist security states.

The security states of Asia were those among which the British, with a characteristic brutal joviality said a "Great Game" was going on. As if the espionage, treachery, and intrigue between Britain and Russia through the 19th and the early 20th centuries was a "game" of cricket or even the more ferocious rugby football. Today South Asian writers, talking about rivalries in Central Asia and Afghanistan slavishly mimic North Atlantic geopoliticians in calling it a "New Great Game" although Afghans, Pathans, Tajiks, Uzbeks, and Hazaras are killing each other.

There is as yet no rigorous historical record of how peoples of the locality look at this border delimitation. In the Aurel Stein biography there is a brief account of the way in which the first Kuomintang government in China, after it came to power saw to it that Sir Aurel and his British Indian surveyors did not step on Chinese soil. The Kuomintang's new intelligentsia was keen to protect the endogenous Buddhist remains in Dun Hwang Monastery on the eastern edge of the Gobi Desert (which Stein was purloining for the British Museum's collections and also for the National Museum in New Delhi) from being taken to London in the way that the Elgin Marbles had been looted from the Parthenon in Athens and taken to form the great prizes of the British Museum. The attitude of the peoples of the locality is reflected in the way Afghan rulers resisted Aurel Stein's entry into Afghanistan which he visited only in his eighties to die in Kabul in 1943 during the Second World War[16] or the way in which Iranians, Kurds, Turks, Arabs resisted imperialist attempts at border delimitation in the interest of the old imperial and cultural trophy exhibition order.

It is interesting that Europeans themselves now are working on this theme with their access to funds, fieldwork, and linguistic and repository resources. In South and northwest Asia we need to work on the indigenous popular geopolitics of how border delimitation changed and transformed the scope of population transfers. Mahnaz Ispahani has talked of the ways in which the Powindas were choked up in Afghanistan. We need a similar description of the ways in which the Tajiks have, since the late 19th century, been divided into two, leaving what is known as lower Badakshan in the Afghan hands of Ahmad Shah Masood, the Lion of Panjshir, and High Badakshan and Gorno Badakshan (Gorno means hilly in Russian) in what is Tajikistan. After the 1924 Soviet Nationality Delimitation Law, many plains Tajiks of the north and west (past Khojent and Kurgan Tyube) were made nationals of the Soviet Republic of Uzbekistan and today are treated as Uzbeks. Yet a submerged Tajik dissidence problem persists in these southern parts of Uzbekistan.[17] Hutu refugees from Ruanda-Brundi had created similar problems in the Congo leading to the successful overthrow of President Mobutu.

Today refugee movements between the Tajiks in Afghanistan and Gorno Badakstan are fairly well known to the United Nations High Commissioner for Refugees. In 1995 summer, I talked to Olivier Roy, the eminent historian of Islamic Resistance in Afghanistan,[18] who had been the UNHCR representative in Dushanbe in Tajikistan, about instability in the region. We now hear that Shi'ite schismatic Ismailiyas in Gorno Badakstan are seeking full autonomy from plains Kuliabis and Khojentis who are mainly Sunni. In Afghanistan the attack by the Taliban on the Tajiks of the Panjshir and Faizabad means created the sort of bottling up process that we have described with regard to the Powindas of the south. Pakistan's "deep defence" strategy means considerable misery for the tribal people to Pakistan's west.

So these boundaries have brought a new heritage of war, disturbance and violence as the social structure of imperial and post-imperial state (communist as well as capitalist) concretizes.

There is no reason for us to be sentimental and deny that "actually existing socialism" in the Soviet Union was not an "internally colonialist structure." It did mean a lot more popular benefits in the shape of universal literacy and women's advancement, than under Tsarism, but it certainly was a post-imperial structure. It, too, has cracked with considerable fissures on the borders of Central Asia. This has led to refugee problems and ethnic stress.

COMMUNALISM, MILITARISM, AND GLOBALIZATION

All this forms an element in the development of communalism in South Asia. Partition of British India under imperialist aegis led to the growth of the national security state. In the 1930s and 1940s communalism existed in a symbiotic relationship with imperialism and the most feudal forms of Muslim sentiment in the Indus plains, called the Punjab School or Frontier-style authoritarianism, a landlord-cum-chieftain style authoritarianism which still prevails in junker-capitalist fashion all over Pakistan. It was also to be found, in a totally contradictory manner, in the populist petty landowner *Chaudhury* and rural cleric, *mullahs* and *pirs* who dominated parts of East Bengal and Sylhet, then in Assam. An equally obnoxious Hindu variant of nationalist historiography, racial thinking and neo-populist rhetoric in inland Deccan and central India, grew up under the influence of the Hindu Mahasabha, and the Rashtriya Swayam Sewak Sangh, and spread at the end of the Second World War. After partition and a brief interlude of a type of democracy in India as well as Pakistan which amalgamated Weimar liberalism and remnants of junkerdom,[19] these authoritarian contradictions and communalist interrelationships led to the growth of military oligarchy in Pakistan, the traumas of Bangladesh, and the highly authoritarian tendencies as well as the corruption of democracy which have engulfed India from the 1970s.

A consequence of this has been in South Asia's east and northeast where for instance, the disregard of the local and ethnic character of the Chittagong Hill Tracts has led to the Chakma or as some militants call it, the Jumma problem. Another aspect of the problem is the cynical way in which Indian ruling cliques gave arms and training to Bodo militants in the jungles south and east of Bhutan and to Eelam militants operating against the Sri Lankan regimes.[20] Then there is the ineptitude with which the genuine grievances of the Punjab were allowed to be co-opted in Sikh religious politics and Khalistani fanaticism. There have also been developments related to the *holding on to Kashmir* and the incapacity of the Pakistan and Indian regimes to think in terms of any magnanimous solution to the problems of the Kashmir Valley. These have created the milieu in which rose the demand, right or wrong, for *Azaadi* that is voiced not only by the *Hurriyat*, but also by other groups in the Valley and its western hill ramparts.

The transition after Indian independence was mishandled in Nagaland, Manipur as well as Mizoram. In Burma, a similar transition led to the Shan, Karen, and Kachin problems in upper Burma, sandwiched as they are between Yunnan and Assam with only tenuous linkages with the people of the Brahmaputra Valley or lower Myanmar.[21] Ba-ma, i.e., Burma, means union of peoples who comprise the old kingdom, dominated ultimately by the Myan, the people indigenous to the plains. They dominated the Kachin and the Shan of the northern and eastern hills, the Karen a separate ethnic group in the plains and the hills, and the Rohingyas of Arakan and other small groups in the hills. Myanmar as a name signifies majoritarian control by the plains of the hills. The Kachin, the Karen, and the Shan problems are part of a meaningful silence, if one sentimentalizes rather than rationally considers the democratic implications of Aung San Suu Kyi's tribulations. When we rightly rhapsodize about Daw Suu Kyi's stand, we do not necessarily think of the problems of the hill peasantry of Upper Burma, or the Christian Karen subaltern groups of lower Burma. They were actually Burmese subalterns, i.e., low level officers of the British imperialists, resisting the democratization of the Burmese nationalists till the end of the Second World War, beleaguered by the mafia and the warlords, as much as by the SLORC, drawn into opium cultivation and thus into the international structures of drug cartelization. This is a type of warlordism which exists also in southern and eastern Afghanistan, where poppy cultivation accounts for the bulk of cash crop income.

Problems have grown and the state, in our case the South Asian regimes, have sought to solve them, by militarizing themselves, that is, by more and more use of paramilitary formations and by the direct use of the Army. A senior officer in Fort William in Calcutta at a private dinner gathering addressed by the Indian Home Minister and the Indian Commander-in-Chief said in response to some comments made by me, "Thank you for saying what I could hardly have, the Army does not like killing its brethren in the Northeast. It would much rather be concerned with training for actual war." One doubts if the army should like training for war as distinct from frontier defence either. Whatever that may be, granted that when there is no war the army would prefer to train in their cantonments rather than be sent to the villages of Bodoland, to fight civilians in the name of encounters and missions. At Sitabaldi Fort in Nagpur about six or seven years ago, just after Prime Minister V.P. Singh had pulled the Indian troops out of Sri Lanka, I heard the same view from a non-commissioned officer, a real Indian subaltern, who was showing us round the site of a Anglo-Maratha battle fought in 1818. He had been in Jaffna. He said that he hated the business of what he called "flushing out the terrorists." He hated it absolutely and thought it a messy business unworthy of a self-respecting soldier, meant to fight in a honorable and declared war.

What people really think probably does not matter. In the last resort, national security considerations are what people *en masse* allow dominating them. And this has led to authoritarianism and the entire paraphernalia of border control by means of militarization of state power, particularly in peripheral areas of insurgency. At the same time, as authoritarianism and diplomatic bargaining grows, so also does globalization of society, economy and political culture. Globalization breaks down these petty diplomatic bargains and petty authoritarianisms in the same way as capitalism destroyed the indigenous societies of Asia in the 19th century or Chinese walls as Karl Marx figuratively called them in his articles on the China War and the East India Company's politics in the 1850s. He said in 1853 about "the future results of British rule" that whatever happens, indigenous societies will crumble before the "juggernaut wheels" of capitalism.

If globalization is not to be a battering ram but a facilitator of mass progress; if we have to indigenize it and popularly benefit from it in our own culture, then we have to think in terms of cooperative, but also enforceable, processes by means of which the popular will can become the general will.

NOTES AND REFERENCES

1. Originally published in Tapan K. Bose and Rita Manchanda (eds), *States, Citizens and Outsiders—The Uprooted Peoples of South Asia*. Kathmandu and Delhi, 1997.
2. Kumar Pradhan, *A History of Nepali Literature*. Delhi, 1984, pp. 1–2.
3. References on the 20th century construction of imperialism and counter imperialism of the colonial and nationalist ruling elite will be found in Barun De, "Unity/Diversity: An Aspect of the Construction of National Identity," in D.N. Jha (ed.), *Society and Ideology in India—Essays in Honour of Professor R.S. Sharma*, pp. 399–412.
4. Brajadulal Chattopadhyay, "Autonomous Spaces and the Authority of the State: The Contradiction and its Resolution in Theory and Practice in Early India," in I. Modelle in B. Kolver (ed.), *Recht, Staat Und Verwaltung in Klassischen Indian*. Munchen, 1977. For earlier examples of his thinking about political plurality in Indian traditional culture, see chapters 5 and 6 of Brajadulal Chattopadhyay, *The Making of Early Medieval India*. New Delhi, 1994.
5. Radha Kumud Mukherjee, *Fundamental Unity of India*. Calcutta, 1914.
6. Rabindranath Tagore, "Bharatabarshe Itihasher Dhara," reprinted in *Itihasa*, Calcutta, 1362, B.S. reprint of 1395 B.S. 19, in particular, pp. 33–34 where Tagore referred to the now common dichotomy between early text of Rama mythology where

the hero is shown as a friend of Chandalas like Guhaka and late texts like the Uttararamacharit where he orders the execution of Sudra ascetics and forsakes his wife to maintain social stability. "That a social revolution was implicit in the Ramacharita was sought to be wiped out by newer social ideals to which that earlier history was subordinated.... Yet India could not forget that he was the companion of Chandalas, worshipped by monkeys, and friend of Bibhishana. His glory was not that he destroyed enemies but that he made them his allies. He built bridges of amity between Aryas and non-Aryas. Studying sociology we find that among barbarian tribes, many worship a particular animal. Often they call themselves descendants of those animals. They call themselves by the names of those animals. Serpent dynasties are found in India in this way. The non-Aryas, whom Ramachandra subjected in Kiskindhya too were known as monkeys, indubitably for this reason. Not only monkeys but also bears were found in Ram's companies. There would be no sense in bears if monkeys were only a term of personal abuse.

7. Mahnaz Ispahani, *Roads and Rivals: The Politics of Access in the Borderlands of Asia*. London, 1988, pp. 113–14, 119.
8. Ibid.
9. R.E. Frykenberg, Guntur District, 1788–1848. *A History of Local Influence and Central Authority in South Asia*. Oxford, 1965. Ashin Dasgupta, *Malabar in Asian Trade, 1748–1800*. Cambridge, 1967, pp. 52–53.
10. Sakharam Ganesh Deuskar, (ed.), Mahadevprasad Saha, *Desher Katha*, Calcutta, new edition, 1377 B. S.
11. S. Settar, *Inviting Death: Historical Experiments on Sepulchral Hill*. Dharwad, 1986.
12. A.C. Banerjee, *The Sikh Gurus and the Sikh Religions*, Calcutta. 1983.
13. Benedict Anderson, *Imagined Communities: Reflections on the Origin and Spread of Nationalism*. London, 1983. Ernest Gellner, *Nations and Nationalism*, London, 1983. Eric Hobsbawm, *Nations and Nationalism Since 1780s: Programme, Myth and Reality*. Cambridge, 1990.
14. Annabel Walker, *Aurel Stein: Pioneer of Silk Road*. London, 1995.
15. Charles Allen, *A Mountain in Tibet: The Search for Mount Kailas and the Sources of the Great Rivers of India*. London, 1983. Indra Singh Rawat, *Indian Explorers in the Nineteenth Century*. Calcutta, 1973.
16. Walker, op. cit., vide chapters 12 and 15 entitled "The Chinese Debacle" and "Death in Some Far-off Country."
17. An interesting Tajik version of problems created by the 1924 Soviet Nationality Law has been found in a English translated version of Rakhim Masov's Russian tract published from

Dushanbe, 1991, entitled in translation, *The History of the Axe—Type Division*. It alleges "great Uzbek" discrimination of Tajiks in southern and eastern Uzbekistan.
18. Olivier Roy, *Islam and Resistance in Afghanistan*. Cambridge, 1990.
19. The amalgamation of Junker/Wiener as the dominant theme of South Asian democracy en route towards upper-caste fascism has been pointed out to me by my son, Bikramjit De.
20. Sanjoy Hazarika, *Strangers of the Mist: Tales of War and Peace from India's North-East*. New Delhi 1994, pp. 158–59 describes Bodo and Rajbangshi masses, north of the Brahmaputra, being trained, since India's 1962 border debacle, in weapons technology by India's Special Security Bureau at Chakrata and at Mahabaleshwar in covert operations; against East Pakistan and later in struggles to gain autonomy within the Indian Union.
21. Bertil Lintner, *Burma in Revolt, Opium and Insurgency Since 1948*. Bangkok, 1994.

11

POPULATION MOVEMENTS AND INTERSTATE CONFLICTS

Partha S. Ghosh

INTRODUCTION

The term "population movement" used in this paper would connote all kinds of human migrations from one part of the South Asian region to another, both voluntary and non-voluntary as well as permanent and temporary. While such movements of population are more often intra-state (for example, migrations of the rural poor to the urban centers), our concern here is not with them but only with those migrations that are cross-national.

Of all the regions in the world, South Asia has witnessed the most massive population movements in recent times in a relatively short span of time. During less than half a century after India's independence in 1947 about 30 million people have moved from one part of other kinds of persecution, or for work or food, or by drives towards ideological or racial homogenization. These movements have caused complications for interstate relationships and thwarted regional cooperation. The objective of the present paper is to underline the political dimensions of the issue and relate then to the broad contours of South Asian regional security.

POPULATION, SOCIETY AND POLITICS

There is a continuing, dynamic and intricate relationship between demographic issues on the one hand and political and sociological issues on the other. In India, however, population issues have largely been the forte of demographers who have not paid enough attention to these interaction.[1] It is only of late that these interrelationships have been recognized and academic literature has started pouring.

The Indian experience, however, is not universally true. Scholars in several other parts of the world have long recognized the interrelationship between demographic issues and sociopolitical questions. The basic premise has been that ecological demography (a partnership between demography and human ecology) promises the most systematic and comprehensive treatment of the core of sociology—the study of societies and social systems and vice versa.[2]

As far as the interaction between demographic issues and politics is concerned, it has been both theoretically and empirically proved that the demographic characteristics of a society inevitably influence the politics of that society. Nazli Choucri, one of the scholars in this field of research, while highlighting the importance of the study of population–politics interaction, writes, "many problems which are viewed as strictly political have, in fact, demographic roots. Conversely, policy interventions that are proposed with demographic intents often result in distinctly political consequences. It is this dual interaction between population and politics that has contributed to the increasing politicization of the demographic issues in the world today."[3]

Demographic variations as a factor influencing politics, however, could be of various types. It could be by internal migrations, increased birth rate and/or reduced mortality rate, cross-national migrations, or dismemberment of a country (partition of India overnight turned the Hindus into a minority in Pakistan, or, later, the secession of Bangladesh overnight turned the Punjabis into a majority in the linguistically and ethnically pluralistic Pakistan). Even such issues as abortion or sterilization can be highly sensitive political issues. The massive defeat of the Congress party in India in 1977 was largely attributed to the government's forced sterilization drives during the preceding couple of years.[4] Similarly, the issue of abortion became a major political issue in several Muslim countries on the eve of the International Conference on Population and

Development at Cairo (September 1994). In Bangladesh mass rallies were organized to force the government to withdraw from the conference.

POLITICS OF INTERSTATE MIGRATION

The phenomenon of cross-border population movements together with the interstate conflicts they generate, is increasingly becoming a major concern for the affected elites all over the world. Since the phenomenon is closely linked to the principles of self-determination, national integration, or just the ripples it causes on local politics, its nature and dimensions often become extremely complicated. The symptoms of these complexities are evidenced from the dissimilar stands taken by states with regard to questions such as ethnic loyalties, secessionist movements, and so on, within and outside their respective national boundaries. It is more a norm than an exception for a state to take a particular position with regard to these issues when it comes to dealing with them internally, but quite a different one in dealing with the same in respect to other nations. What should follow from this is that the external position of a state upon these questions is generally uniform. But even that is not so. It varies depending upon the nature of the relationship that exists at a given time between and among nations.

Within the scope of cross-national migrations two broad categories of interstate conflicts may be considered. In the first place, interstate conflicts can be caused by population pressure upon resources leading to expansionist tendencies, or, second, by clandestine population movements affecting the demographic balance of the host region to the detriment of the political future of the local elites forcing the latter to enter into a conflictual relationship with the country of origin of the migrants. Summarizing the various aspects of the migration problem vis-à-vis interstate relations, Choucri writes:

> Population size may function as a political parameter when, for example, it generates population pressures upon resources that lead to expansionist tendencies. Population composition may be a parameter of a conflict when it sets the cleavages in a society, generating

tensions that result in ethnic or religious conflict. So, too, the population distribution may be a political parameter when, for instance, tribal allegiance crosses national boundaries and generates overt conflict, or when the migration of population changes the ethnic composition of the receiving community and results in nativist reaction.[5]

Of all the kinds of demographic factors impinging upon politics, however, the most complex are probably the ones having religious and/or ethno-nationalistic roots. Since both religious nationalism and ethno-nationalism draw their sustenance from human emotions which are often irrational the interstate conflicts rooted in ethnic and religious discords are the most intractable and most violence-prone of all the issues relating to international conflict. Compared to these, resources issues, for example, seem to be much more concrete and hence conducive to compromise, if not solution.[6] This author has discussed elsewhere the religious and ethnic majority–minority cleavages that have been causing interstate conflicts in South Asia.[7]

CATEGORIES OF POPULATION MOVEMENTS

The factors responsible for population movements in South Asia fall in one or more of the following seven categories:

1. Traumatic geographical surgeries.
2. Failure in nation building leading to civil war.
3. Interethnic conflicts leading to civil strife.
4. Open or virtually open interstate boundaries.
5. Interstate developmental disparities.
6. Contractual obligations.
7. Military interventions by extra-regional powers.

GEOGRAPHICAL SURGERIES: POLITICAL FALL-OUT

Population movements that took place across Indo-Pak borders immediately before and after the partition of the Indian subcontinent belong to this category. The so-called two-nation theory created so much cleavage between the Hindu and Muslim communities that when the decision to divide the country was taken it was greeted with unprecedented communal carnage. In the wake of the partition large numbers of Hindus and Muslims migrated to India and Pakistan respectively in the midst of severe violence. It was estimated that about 15 million people were involved in this process of cross-national migration. To this figure was added a few more millions who migrated to India from Pakistan following anti-Hindu riots in Pakistan during the 1950s and the 1960s. Before the secession of Bangladesh from Pakistan in 1971, the politics and pronouncements of the Pakistani government often used to lead to communal violence in that country, causing exodus of Hindus to India. For example, in 1964 the theft of the holy relic of Prophet Mohammed from the Hazratbal shrine in Srinagar (Kashmir) led to widespread violence in East Pakistan where the Hindu population was concentrated. This led to large-scale population movements. It was estimated that the total number of refugees who arrived in India in 1964 was about a million. Earlier communal riots had led to refugee influx in India and by 1964 the total number of Pakistani refugees of this variety was estimated to be about 5.5 million.[8]

Large-scale migrations of Muslims to Pakistan and Hindus of India have resulted in serious complications for India–Pakistan relations. These complications are often not noticeable for they are indirect or are overshadowed by the strategic cleavage that is more apparent and advertized. For an analysis of the extent and nature of Indo-Pak conflict as it has been affected by cross-country migrations the issue here can be approached from two angles; one, by gauging the influence the Hindu and Muslim immigrants or refugees exercise on the politics of India and Pakistan respectively, and two, by analyzing as to how this infleunce contributes, either directly or indirectly, towards creating the enemy image of one country in another. Of course, both questions are closely intertwined.

It is estimated that about 7,200,000 Indian Muslims had migrated to Pakistan in the wake of the partition. In pre-1971 Pakistan these refugees or immigrants constituted about 10 percent (20 percent after the secession of Bangladesh) of the population of Bangladesh. The circumstance wherein Pakistan was created and the nature of pre-partition Muslim politics earned for them a unique status and purpose which otherwise is denied to an immigrant community. (The only exception probably is the case of immigrant Jews in Israel.) Having been comprised of relatively more educated people, members of the Indian Civil Service and the Indian Army, noted businessmen, and, most importantly, leaders and sympathizers of the Muslim League that spearheaded the Pakistan movement, these immigrants constituted a political force to reckon with. Actually about three-quarters of the so-called "twenty-two families" who were supposed to control Pakistan's economy were from outside Pakistan.[9] Besides, as the immigrants contributed to a rapid urbanization of Pakistan, their influences in politics were all the more apparent.[10]

The Muslim immigrants who had left their original homes in India in search of a better one in Pakistan had naturally a larger stake in the viability of Pakistan. This explains this group's insistence on strengthening forces that would help build Pakistan's unity such as Islam, Urdu, and the negation of federalism. The Muslim League both on account of its immigrant leadership as well as the large following that it had among the immigrants and refugees represented these theories of nation building. Another party that also strongly represented these ideas was Jamaat-i-Islami, again a party having a large following among the immigrants. With the gradual decline of the Muslim League it was this party which attracted most of the disillusioned immigrant Muslim Leaguers. It may be noted that Jamaat-i-Islami was originally opposed to the Pakistan movement on religious grounds like some of the orthodox *Ulema*, but once Pakistan was created it accepted the reality and moved its headquarters from India to Pakistan. It became the most vociferous champion of Islam, opposed all modernist ideas of statecraft and supported the Pakistani establishment in the eastern wing of Pakistan against what they regarded as the Hindu-tainted force of Bengal separatism.[11]

As far as the influence in India of the Hindu refugees from Pakistan is concerned, unlike in the case of Pakistan, they did never form the mainstream of Indian politics. This was partly due to their relative insignificance in terms of proportion to the vast Indian population and also to the continuance of the Congress party at the helm of affairs that refused to subscribe to a sectarian and anti-Muslim attitude that the refugees were inclined to represent. Nevertheless, these refugees contributed towards building a deep-seated distrust between the Hindus and the Muslims and this development played a not too insignificant role in souring the Indo-Pak relations.

The incidence of Hindu–Muslim riots, which is so much a familiar phenomenon in India's body politic, is largely attributable to the psychology of suspicion between the two communities generated by the division of the country and subsequent fights of millions of Hindus in the midst of violence. It may be a fact that no one possibly can establish any direct linkage between the incidence of Hindu migrations and the phenomenon of communal violence in India, as over the years Hindu–Muslim riots have taken place in many parts of the country which cannot even remotely be considered as places where immigrants or refugees got settled, still it cannot be disputed that the tendencies which breed communalism, the most important of which is the politicization of communalism and communalization of politics, have much to do with the holocaust of Hindus in Pakistan and their subsequent exodus to India.[12] The birth of the Hindu communal party Jan Sangh in 1952, one of the major constituencies of which were the dispossessed Hindus from West Pakistan, was a direct outcome of the post-independence communal strife. The linkage of Jan Sangh with the Hindu chauvinistic Rashtriya Swayamsevak Sangha (RSS) is too well known to be recapitulated here.[13]

NATION BUILDING OR NATION-BREAKING

The East Pakistan crisis and the exodus of Bengali refugees to India belong to this category. Pakistan, which owed its origin to the theory of two nations, became, ironically speaking, victim of its own thesis within less than a quarter of a century of its creation. On the same premise of national disharmony was fought the Bangladesh liberation war of 1970–71. The people of East Pakistan, claiming a distinctive linguistic-cultural identity of their own around which developed the phenomenon of Bengali nationalism, came in conflict with Pakistani, or more precisely Punjabi, nationalism. The Bangladesh liberation movement was subjected to massive repression, unprecedented in its scale and dimension, by the Pakistani military regime, causing an exodus of East Pakistan refugees to India whose number was estimated at about 10 million.

Though the presence of such a huge number of Pakistanis on Indian soil strained India's scarce resources, it gave an effective political and diplomatic handle to the Government of India to muster international support for its anti-Pakistan policies that culminated in the war of 1971 resulting in the dismemberment of Pakistan. A resolution passed in both the Houses of the Indian Parliament on 31 March 1971 declared, *inter alia*:

> Throughout the length and breadth of our land, our people have condemned in unmistakable terms, the atrocities now being perpetrated on an unprecedented scale upon an unarmed and innocent people.... This House records its profound conviction that the historic upsurge of the 75 million people of East Bengal will triumph. The House wishes to assure them that their struggle and sacrifices will receive the whole-hearted sympathy and support of the people of India.

There was hardly any concern about the drain on India's exchequer to maintain the refugees.

INTERETHNIC CONFLICTS

The Sinhala Tamil conflict which led to the arrival of thousands of Sri Lanka Tamils as refugees in India and the political conflict between the Ngalongs and the ethnic Nepalis in Bhutan which made many of the latter take refuge in Nepal and India fall into this category.

The discriminatory treatment meted out to the minority Sri Lanka Tamils by the majority Sinhalese forced large numbers of Tamils to take refuge in the neighboring Tamil Nadu in India and later in the Indian state of Orissa. The problem actually started after the unprecedented anti-Tamil riots that took place in Sri Lanka in July 1983. The anti-Tamil pogrom caused migrations of Sri Lanka Tamils to India. It was estimated that about 30,000 Tamils took shelter in India during those months. The flow continued depending upon the state of ethnic relationship. For example, during the first quarter of 1985 there was again a spurt of refugees and in February alone about 15,000 arrived in India. In May 1985, in a statement in the Indian parliament, Prime Minister Rajiv Gandhi said that there were about 100,000 refugees from Sri Lanka and that it was straining the Indian economy.[14] The flow of refugee continued unabated, and according to contemporary reports about 200 people arrived every alternate day.[15]

The Sri Lankan Tamil refugees in India presented a problem to Indian politics that was somewhat unique compared to other situations, namely, the Bangladeshi or Nepalese nationals in India or Hindu refugees in the aftermath of the partition. The number of Sri Lankan refugees was insignificant and could not cause any demographic challenge to an already over-populated India, nor were they trying to interfere with Indian politics. But on account of the nature of Tamil Nadu politics and the emotional response that the refugees evoked the problem assumed larger relevance for Indian politics (particularly so because Tamil Nadu had an earlier record of a separatist movement). Both the contenders for power in Tamil Nadu, the All India Anna DMK (AIADMK) and the DMK, rely heavily on their capacity to project themselves as champions of the Tamil cause. The Congress party ruling at the center keeps shifting its alliance with either of them depending upon prevailing political exigency. As it usually happens in this kind of situation the opposition party has an inner compulsion to assume an ultra-chauvinistic stance to which the ruling party is forced to respond to in almost equal terms.[16]

The intermeshing of the Sri Lanka Tamil politics with that of Tamil Nadu and then with that of Indian politics found its most dramatic expression in the assassination of Rajiv Gandhi during the parliamentary elections of 1991. The killing which was master-minded by the suicide quad of the Liberation Tigers of Tamil Eelam (LTTE) took place on the Tamil Nadu soil itself, causing tremors to run through the state's politics. The ruling DMK came under severe political pressure from its rival, AIADMK, which routed the DMK in the assembly elections that took place six months later in January 1992.

The ethnic conflict between the majority Drukpas and the minority Nepalis in Bhutan has caused many Nepalis to migrate into India and Nepal. In Nepal several camps have been set up for these refugees. It is the claim of the Bhutanese authorities that they have only evicted those Nepalis who had illegally settled in Bhutan. While there is some truth in this claim it is also a reality that under the garb of its citizenship laws and tackling the Nepali terrorism the Bhutan government has illegally ousted many ethnic Nepalis from its territory. According to recent reports, over 85,000 persons of Nepalese origin have left Bhutan since 1990, a majority of who have taken refuge in Nepal.[17] The situation has not gone out of control only because of the fact that the Bhutanese monarchy has a good relationship with India and the latter on its part can persuade the democratic set-up in Kathmandu not to take undue advantage of the situation.

THE OPEN BORDERS

The third category of population movements is attributable to open or virtually open international borders. Before this problem is addressed, it would be instructive to underline the fact that out of the 26 states that comprise India (including the recently created Delhi state) 17 have international borders, namely, Arunachal Pradesh, Assam, Bihar, Gujarat, Himachal Pradesh, Jammu & Kashmir, Meghalaya, Mizoram, Nagaland, Punjab, Rajasthan, Sikkim, Tamil Nadu, Tripura, Uttar Pradesh, and West Bengal. The states that do not have international borders are Andhra Pradesh, Karnataka, Kerala, Madhya Pradesh (MP), Delhi, Haryana, Maharashtra, Orissa, and Goa. For details about the demography of the states having international borders, see Table 11.1.

The border between India and Nepal is open by treaty. It is indicated by a no-man's land of 10 yards known as "Dasgaja" and stone pillars erected at every quarter mile from Mechi river in the east to Mahakali river in the west. The open border has resulted in legal Nepali migrations to India and legal Indian migrations to Nepal. About 20 years ago it was estimated that the annual flow in both directions totaled about 50,000. Some of them went to live in the country of their adoption permanently while others returned home after the purpose of their migration was served.[18] Because of the political problems associated with the growing number of Nepalis in India and the growing number of Indians in the Terai region of Nepal it is almost impossible

Table 11.1 Population Growth and Density Development Index

S.N.	State	Population Growth p.a. (India: 2.14)	Population Density (Persons/sq. km)	Population Index of Development (India: 273)	Relative Border (India: 100)	International
1.	Arunachal Pradesh	95,530	3.11	10	66	Myanmar
2.	Assam	22,295,000	2.13	285	54	Bangladesh, Bhutan
3.	Bihar	86,339,000	2.13	496	43	Nepal
4.	Gujarat	41,174,000	1.91	210.74	114	Pakistan
5.	Himachal Pradesh	5,111,000	1.79	92.88	75	China
6.	Jammu & Kashmir	7,719,000	2.63	26	135	China, Pakistan
7.	Manipur	1,827,000	2.54	82	55	Myanmar
8.	Meghalaya	1,761,000	2.80	79	54	Myanmar
9.	Mizoram	686,000	3.35	32	54	Bangladesh
10.	Nagaland	1,216,000	4.60	72	55	Myanmar
11.	Punjab	20,191,000	1.86	402	199	Pakistan
12.	Rajasthan	43,881,000	2.50	128.58	69	Pakistan
13.	Sikkim	404,000	2.51	57	73	Bhutan, China, Nepal
14.	Tamil Nadu	55,638,000	1.40	429	135	Sri Lanka (maritime)
15.	Tripura	2,745,000	2.95	262	55	Bangladesh
16.	Uttar Pradesh	138,760,000	2.29	472	72	China, Nepal
17.	West Bengal	67,983,000	2.22	767.06	97	Bangladesh, Bhutan, Nepal

Sources: Mahendra K. Premi, *India's Population: Heading Towards a Billion: An Analysis of 1991 Census Provisional Results* Delhi, 1991, pp. 6–7; Centre for Monitoring Indian Economy Pvt. Ltd., *Economic Intelligence Service: Profiles of Districts*, November 1993. Bombay, 1993.

to have hard data on the number of migrants both ways. In Nepal it was a general practice during the monarchy to exaggerate the problems arising out of growing numbers of Indians in Nepal. The Task Force on Migration which was set up in 1983 under the auspices of the Nepali National Commission on Population only referred to "some emigration" of Nepalis to India but discussed at length the problems Nepal faced from the rising number of Indians in the Terai.[19]

Indeed there has been a disproportionate rise in the population of the Terai. The annual growth rate in the region increased from 2.04 percent in 1952–54 to 2.39 percent during 1961–71 and to 4.41 percent during 1971–81, while the growth rate in the Mountain and Hill region increased only from 1.42 percent during 1952/54–61 to 1.65 percent during 1971–81. In an extreme case, the district of Kanchanpur in the Terai region registered an annual growth of 9.39 percent in contrast to which the Humla district in the mountain region showed a negative growth of 2.72 percent.[20]

Obviously this different population growth was to a considerable extent explainable by the migration of Hill people to the Terai region. But, due to the very nature of regional politics in Nepal[21] together with the Nepal King's political compulsions to project his cause as the champion of Nepali nationalism vis-à-vis its large southern neighbor, the growth in the Terai population was disproportionately attributed to migration from India. The Task Force report referred to above reflected these politics. No wonder it was subjected to acrimonious debates in the Nepali Panchayat (Parliament). Several members were ever active in highlighting the danger of India's "demographic invasion of Nepal." A survey of the *Nepal Press Digest* during the 1980s would reveal the amount of space and importance that this single issue had occupied in the Nepalese Press. And as it has been said, though in an altogether different context, that "there can be little doubt that political orientation of the press in Nepal, characterized by the more ostentatious shifts in loyalty, is determined by what the government has up its sleeves."[22] This attitude of the press was certainly indicative of the mood of the ruling elites over the question of Indians in Nepal.

The Task Force Report to which reference has already been made, said, "According to census of 1971, immigrants constituted 7.7 percent of the total population of the Terai ... [of which] 97.7 percent were born in India...."[23] It drew attention to the problems that Indian migrations were creating for the Nepali people in the Terai region and cautioned that "unrestricted flow of immigrants can have political implications affecting international relations."[24] It main recommendations were as follows:

> Indians or other foreigners should be allowed to work in Nepal only against permits. Those who are working without such permits at present should be sent back. Citizenship certificates should not be issued on the recommendation of politicians. A commission equipped with judicial authority should be formed to deal with citizenship issues. No naturalized citizen should be appointed or nominated as chief of any agency dealing with political or economic affairs, nor should he be allowed to contest elections to the National Panchayat before 12 years have passed since he became a naturalized citizen of Nepal. Only Nepali citizens should be appointed as agents for the sale of Indian goods in Nepal.[25]

In August 1983 a host of 35 legislators expressed their concern in this regard and asked the government to enforce stringent measures against fraudulent practices in granting citizenship rights. A militant Nepali organization, the *Rashtriya Samaj Sudhar Sangstha* (RSSS), spearheaded an anti-Indian campaign and propagated the theory that the 5.8 million people of Indian origin, most of who lived in the Terai, constituted 30 percent of Nepal's population and they were actually colonizing Nepal. The Nepal government did not do enough to con-trol the agitation, it rather permitted an unofficial delegation to go to China to ascertain how Beijing would react if a Sri Lanka type situation were to develop in this buffer state.[26] The Task Force Report became a sensitive issue in Indo-Nepal relations and also in Indo-Nepal diplomatic parleys. Eventually, realizing discretion the better part of valor, the government shelved the report indefinitely.[27] Like the growing number of Indians in Nepal there has been a growth of Nepalese also in India. The Nepalese emigration has largely been to the northeastern states of India and the northern districts of West Bengal and Uttar Pradesh. In 1951, Assam's Nepalese population was 101,335. It rose to 132,925 in 1961 and to 353,673 in 1971. There is also a large number of Nepalese in Tripura, Manipur, Meghalaya, Nagaland,

Mizoram, Arunachal Pradesh, and Sikkim. According to an estimate, there were nearly 5 million persons of Nepali origin permanently settled in India two decades ago.[28]

The existence of a large number of Nepalis in India has serious reverberations on Indian politics and correspondingly on Indo-Nepal relations. India's policies to restrict the flow of Nepali nationals to India have served as an irritant in the Indo-Nepali relations. In October 1976 the Government of India, probably as a response to a series of virulent demonstrations in Nepal against India's "annexation" of Sikkim in August 1975, imposed restrictions on travel of Nepalis in certain areas in India, including parts of West Bengal, Sikkim, Assam, Meghalaya, Manipur, Nagaland, Arunachal Pradesh, Tripura, and three districts of Uttar Pradesh. Considering the fact that India and Nepal had been "open" to each other from time immemorial, Nepal resented this policy. To accommodate the Nepali sentiments India introduced a system of permits. This, however, did not satisfy the Nepalese. Indeed, the restrictions caused difficulties not only to Nepalese nationals but also to about 5 million Indian nationals of Nepalese origin in the aforesaid areas who had close relatives living in Nepal. The Government of India, however, did not relent. Even the Janata Government (1977–80) that was committed to improve relations with the neighboring countries did not alter the decision. In 1980, the government introduced the system of identity cards in the state of Sikkim to control the Nepalese infiltration into the state and thereby prevented distortions in the electoral rolls that had shaken the Assam politics.

The Nepali question found its most articulated political expressions in the politics of Nar Bahadur Bhandari of Sikkim and that of Subhash Ghising, the leader of the Gurkha National Liberation Front (GNLF) of Darjeeling (West Bengal).[29] The GNLF movement assumed some international dimensions when, on 23 December 1986, Ghising wrote a letter to the King of Nepal, copies of which, 16 in all, were sent to various governments and international agencies including the superpowers, the United Nations and the governments in the South Asian region. It invoked justice for "the unpardonable historical crimes against humanity or still unresolved question of the very political existence or future states of.... Gorkhas in the Indian

Union. "It sought, fresh new treaties for a permanent political settlement of the ... victimized Gorkhas as per the provisions of the Charter of the United Nations" taking into account "the future status of their ceded land and territories."[30]

More or less similar to the problem of the Indo-Nepal border, the loosely enforced 2,000 km between India and Bangladesh has resulted in out-migration from Bangladesh. However, unlike the Nepalese situation there is no corresponding Indian emigration to Bangladesh. Although the Bangladesh government refuses to concede the fact that millions of Bangladeshis are in India yet even a casual scrutiny of the demographic evidence reveals this.[31] About a decade ago, on an average, 2,000 people were pushed back by India's Border Security Force (BSF) every month, but the number of people entering illegally was suspected be at least 10 times as high. The 1981 census revealed that in the eight border districts of West Bengal, the population had grown by over 30 percent between 1971 and 1981, whereas the remaining districts reported growth rates below 20 percent. In the extreme case of a town in northern West Bengal, the population jumped from about 10,000 to 150,000.[32]

There has also been problem of Bangladeshis entering into India with forged travel documents or with valid documents but refusing to go back after the expiry of their validity. It was revealed by the West Bengal government in 1983 that at least 400,000 passport-holders from Bangladesh, who entered West Bengal during the previous 10 years, had disappeared into the Indian community without a trace. The Bangladeshi infiltration upset the demographic balance of Assam and this was the problem at the core of the Assam crisis that rocked Indian politics from 1978 till an accord was signed in August 1985 between the agitators and the Central Government aiming at tackling the problem.[33] Evidences of Bangladeshi infiltrations are found in as distant parts of India as Delhi, Haryana, the Punjab and western UP. According to recent estimates, there were about 1.3 million illegal migrants to Northeastern states and West Bengal.[34]

The Assam accord was virtually a compromise between the positions held by the Government of India and the agitators. Neither disputed the basic fact that there existed millions of unauthorized foreigners (mostly Bangladeshis, some Nepalis) in

Assam and that they should be evicted. But over the question of the cut-off year, i.e., the year they had arrived in India, there was no agreement. For the agitators it was 1951 while for the Indian Government it was 1971. According to the accord, 25 March 1971 has been fixed as the cut-off date. It has also provided that the so-called foreigners who came between 1 January 1966 and 24 March 1971 would continue to stay in India but would become full citizens with voting rights only after 10 years.[35] Because of the very nature of the accord as well as the most difficult task of identifying the illegal migrants it was obvious from the beginning that the accord was doomed to failure. Almost a decade has elapsed after the date of signing the accord but there is hardly any evidence of illegal foreigners being actually evicted. During the initial months of Assam Gana Parishad rule in Assam there was some effect at achieving the goal but it was nominal and that too got bogged down due to the pressures of local politics.[36] In 1981, there was no census in Assam but the 1991 data tend to suggest an end of the foreigners' problem. In a recent statement the Assam Chief Minister Hiteshwar Saikia refuted the statement made in the Indian Parliament by the Home Minister S.B. Chavan that illegal immigration continued unabated in the state. Saikia said emphatically, "If anybody can identify a single foreigner in Assam, I am willing to quite politics forever."[37] Behind the chief minister's assertion was the fact that Assam had witnessed a fall in its population in the 1991 Census. Given the fact that all other northeastern states witnessed sizable growth in their population one may have legitimate misgivings about the Assam figures.[38]

Another case that can be cited in this category of migration is that of clandestine Pakistani infiltrations into the bordering villages of Rajasthan and Gujarat though data in this context is extremely sparse and that too of doubtful authenticity. About a decade ago, there were reports in the Indian press that some of the bordering villages in the districts of Ganganagar, Bikaner, Jaisalmer and Barmer of Rajasthan had registered much higher growth rates than other villages. For example, between 1971 and 1981, the population of Rajasthan's Bandha village had gone up from 172 to 5,888, of Muhar village from 9 to 247, of Kuldar from 32 to 240, of Modana from 422 to 1,198, of Mota

Kilonki-dhani from 48 to 540 and of Madasar from 445 to 1,171.[39] While part of this population growth was attributed to the construction of Rajasthan Canal, now called Indira Gandhi Nahar, which attracted people from other districts, part of it was reportedly due to infiltrations from Pakistan.[40] There was a sudden rise in number of Muslim-dominated villages along the border. In this connection it may be noted that in the wake of the 1965 and 1971 Indo-Pak wars many Indian Muslims crossed over to Pakistan and settled there. They, however, managed to continue as Indian citizens, thanks to local district politics. These people had a unique status of holding a dual citizenship, of both India and Pakistan, and continued to cross the border with relative ease.[41] There were reports of Pakistani espionage agents operating in the area and the Indian authorities nabbed some of their accomplices.[42] Lately, the Government of India has undertaken the job of barbed wire fencing the sensitive parts of the 1,044 km long Indo-Pak border in Rajasthan to prevent infiltration, smuggling and cattle movement.[43]

DEVELOPMENTAL VARIABLE

In this category of population movement we may mention the migration of Chakma tribals of Bangladesh into Tripura and some other northeastern states of India. At the root of the Chakma problem are certain developmental issues. The construction of the Karnafuli (Kaptai) hydroelectric project in 1962 submerged 54,000 acres of settled, cultivable land affecting about 100,000 people, 90 percent of whom were Chakmas. This not only destabilized the tribes economically, it also affected their social and cultural lives because of the change in the kind of economic activities that replaced the traditional ones.

Besides, the state-sponsored resettlement policies also tended to make the Chakmas alien in their homestead. These resettlement policies started during the Pakistan regime and continued even after the creation of Bangladesh. During the time of Ziua-ur-Rahman, the resettlement drive was intensified resulting in growth of militancy among the tribals. State repressions followed, causing Chakmas to seek refuge in India by the thousands. By August 1987, there were about 33,000 such refugees spread over five camps in Tripura.[44] After the restoration of democracy in Bangladesh there has been some improvement in the situation and efforts are under way to send the refugees back to their villages.

CONTRACTUAL OBLIGATIONS

There are some movements of population resulting from agreements between two nations. Into this category fall two cases, that of Indian Tamils and that of the so-called "Biharis" of Bangladesh.

According to the Sri Lankan Census of 1981, Indian Tamils were 825,233 in number, constituting 5.6 percent of the island's population. Their presence there is a legacy of the colonial period when they were brought from south India as indentured labor. This subsequently led to a controversy between India and Sri Lanka about the legal status of these people—were they Indian nationals to be repatriated to India or Sri Lankan nationals to stay on in the island? After protracted negotiations, on 30 October 1964, the Shastri–Sirimavo Pact was signed to resolve the issue. According to the Pact it was decided that of the 1953 estimate of 975,000 stateless persons of Indian origin in Sri Lanka, 300,000 (together with the natural increase in that number) would be granted Sri Lankan citizenship while 525,000 (together with the natural increase in that number) would be granted Indian citizenship. The status and future of the remaining 150,000 people (together with the natural increase in the number) would be decided later by a separate agreement. Later, in January 1974, through another agreement between the two countries it was decided that both the governments would grant citizenship to 150,000 persons left undecided by the 1964 Pact according to a 50:50 ratio.[45] For various reasons the process of repatriation was never smooth. In the first place, most of the persons granted Indian citizenship were unwilling to go to India, and second, when in India, they faced various resettlement problems. A recent study has revealed that by 31 January 1989, 116,000 families had been repatriated to India but their rehabilitation was far from satisfactory.[46]

Another case of stateless citizens was that of the so-called "Biharis" in Bangladesh. Since these people supported the Pakistani authorities in the Bangladesh liberation war they were looked upon with contempt in the liberated Bangladesh. Still, the Bangladesh government had offered them citizenship that they refused, opting to remain Pakistani nationals. After years of diplomatic wrangling between Bangladesh and Pakistan an accord was almost reached a decade ago according to which Pakistan would agree to accept them as Pakistani citizens. The number of such expatriates would be 250,000.

EXTERNAL INTERVENTIONS

Population movements have also been caused by external interventions. So far, there are two cases of this variety: Tibetan refugees in India following the Chinese annexation of Tibet and the Afghan refugees in Pakistan following the Soviet intervention in Afghanistan. Tibetan refugees started arriving in India first in 1950. It was during this year that the People's Republic of China started asserting its sovereignty over Tibet. It was, however, only in 1959 that large numbers of Tibetans fled to India and Nepal in the wake of the Chinese military action into the plateau. The reports of the International Commission of Jurists (ICJ), published in 1959 and 1966, documented several cases of religious persecution, torture, forced sterilization, destruction of families and so on, perpetrated by the Chinese authorities, which occasioned the forced migration. It is difficult to ascertain the exact number of such refugees, still it is estimated that about 85,000 Tibetans, mostly commoners, fled from their native land between 1959 and 1962. Of this number 80 percent were resettled in India with the second highest concentration in Nepal.[47]

The presence of Tibetan refugees has caused some tensions between India and China but of late after growing normalization of this relationship there is a constant effort on the part of both the governments to play down the issue. India has recognized Tibet as an autonomous region of China while the latter has virtually recognized the Indian claim over North Eastern Frontier Agency (NEFA) that is now the Indian state of Arunachal Pradesh. Insofar as domestic politics is concerned, the Tibetan refugees have not caused any tension in the places they reside in. Rather they have often contributed to the growth of the local economy. The apprehensions that the refugees were potential de-stabilizers of Bhutanese politics are also largely misplaced and exaggerated.

The Soviet intervention in Afghanistan in December 1979 resulted in a huge inflow of Afghan refugees into Pakistan. Although even before the Soviet intervention many Afghans had come to Pakistan as refugees (by Amin's time some 400,000 Afghan refugees were in Pakistan), the intervention increased the flow considerably. In spite of the fact that it was difficult to assess the actual number as many refugees created phantom families to get the $5-a-month subsistence allowance given to each person, it is estimated that by the end of 1983 the figure had reached the 3 million mark and by 1984 the inflow seemed to have settled at 10 to 15 thousand heads per month. Of the registered Afghan refugees in Pakistan some 67 percent were in NWFP, some 28 percent in Baluchistan and the rest scattered all over the country.[48]

The ecological, economic, and cultural problems that the Afghan refugees created influenced Pakistan politics, threatening the country's political stability.[49] What was, however, of even more significance was the possibility it could bring in its train of contributing to separatist tendencies that were already part of Pakistan's body politic. It goes to the credit of Zia-ul-Haq that he turned this disadvantage into an advantage. So far as Zia's troubles from democratic forces in the NWFP were concerned, the presence of refugees probably helped him. It was argued by some commentators that had it not been for the refugees who consumed so much time and energy of NWFP politicians, the Movement for the Restoration of Democracy (MRD) agitation of Sind in 1983 could possibly have received support in the province.[50] But while the refugees weakened somewhat the democratic movement in NWFP, they made the Pushtoon problem complex, viewed from a long-term point of view. The establishment of a Communist regime in Kabul indeed disillusioned the majority of the Pakistan Pushtoons about their merger with Afghanistan and made them sympathize with their ethnic cousins from across the border. But Afghan interest in Pushtoonistan did not recede. Both the Taraki and Karmal regimes celebrated Pushtoonistan days in Kabul. Given the fact that there was every possibility that all refugee would not return even if the Russian troops withdrew and a political solution was worked out the Pushtoon problem loomed large on the Pakistani horizon and it was feared that "under a different set of circumstances the issue could be revived again with the Soviet support."[51] Of course, the end of the Cold War and the collapse of the Soviet Union have now drastically altered the situation.

In Baluchistan the refugee problem had only negative consequences. On the one hand, it made the Baluchis resent the refugees who made the scarce resources of the province even scarcer, on the other hand, it emboldened the separatist forces who wanted to take advantage of Pakistan's predicament. Since the bloodiest battle the Baluchis fought against the Pakistani government during Bhutto's rule, the brunt of the fighting had been taken over by Baluchistan People's Liberation Front (BPLF), a left-wing guerrilla movement. It was reported that about 4,000 BPLF guerrillas lived in Afghanistan and got assistance from the Karmal Government in Kabul.[52] The situation provided a potential handle for the Soviet Union to encourage Baluch separatism to the detriment of Pakistan's national integrity.[53]

REGIONAL MILIEU

The enormity of the problem that cross-national migrations pose to the South Asian regional system makes one wonder how it could be tackled. At the root of these migrations lies either the economic factor, or religious or ethnic persecutions, or interstate conflict, or extra-regional interventions. Since all these factors—barring probably the last one—are potentially active, it is likely that South Asia has to live with the problem for years to come.

The factor that contributes most to the phenomenon is the diverse stages of political development in different countries of the region. The processes of nation-building which may answer the question of migrations arising out of ethnic and religious dissonances as well as the process of democratization which may address itself to the economic and political conditions responsible for cross-country migrations are dissimilar. Paradoxically, it has somewhat succeeded in India alone that has the least attributes of nationhood. It is a multi-lingual, multi-religious, multi-ethnic and multicultural society, still, it seems to have emerged as a viable state. It is difficult to provide a fully satisfactory explanation for this but what appears to be the probable explanation is its modern approach to the nation-building process and its strategic and military predominance in the region.

Unlike India, in all the other countries of South Asia, the process of nation building has been jeopardized by state patronage to particular religious, ethnic or linguistic groups. In Pakistan the emphasis has been on Islam and Urdu, in Bangladesh on Islam or Bengali, in Nepal on Nepali language, and in Sri Lanka on Buddhism and Sinhala. These particularistic tendencies have affected the process of nation building in each of these states. As far as the growth of democratic institutions is concerned, India has a better record. Except for Sri Lanka, democracy has a checkered record everywhere. Pakistan and Bangladesh have most of the time been military dictatorships, while Nepal has been ruled by an assertive monarchy. Even in Sri Lanka the democratic process has been marred by an over-emphasis on Sinhala–Buddhist nationalism to the detriment of Tamil interests. Not that Indian democracy has no weaknesses; but the factors that probably have sustained it are, in addition to secularism, its efforts towards self-sufficiency, decentralization of industries taking into account the politics of scale as well as the economies of scale, indigenous production of armaments, and the development of the institutions of participatory democracy as "a mechanism for the change of elites and the availability of counter-elites."[54]

From the above follows the complex phenomenon of mutual distrust. Belonging to the same geographical region and experiencing a conflictual interstate relationship the political system of each South Asian country has an in-built tendency to build up its credentials by highlighting the shortcomings of the others. Thus while India takes advantage of the Pakistan and Bangladesh governments' vulnerability vis-à-vis democratic forces there, these governments tend to malign India for its record on communal riots and ethnic dissonances.

FEEDING THE TEEMING MILLIONS

South Asia is one of the poorest regions of the world. Within the region, according to the latest World Development Report, India is poorer than most of the others. Still, surprisingly, the ongoing migrations are mostly towards India and not vice versa. Almost all such migrants are from Bangladesh and Nepal. What can explain this paradox? Regional development is lopsided in each of the South Asian nations. Yet, other countries such as Bangladesh and Nepal, being small in size, have an extremely limited capacity to absorb internal economic migrants. India provides a vast area somewhere within which these migrants can get their source of livelihood. No wonder that Bangladeshi or Nepali migrants travel as far as Delhi, Haryana or Punjab.

There was a time when people in order to escape poverty used to flock to less inhabited countries such as the United States. During the last decade of the 18th century Thomas Robert Malthus in his celebrated *Essay on Population* (1798) dwelt extensively upon the growth of population in England and virtually predicted its doom. Three developments, however, saved England—migration of Britons in large number; the Industrial Revolution; and the growth of the British Empire. In the 1820s more than 200,000 Britons emigrated. The figure trebled in the following decade and reached almost 2.5 million in the 1950s. Between1815 and 1914, around 20 million Englishmen left their country. In 1900 Britain's population was 41 million. Had the massive population movement not taken place this population would have numbered 70 million.[55]

For obvious reasons this cannot be the solution for South Asia, and for that matter any country of the world anymore. Not only are large-scale migrations not possible, even the small-scale ones attempted by enterprising groups and individuals to the developed countries are being resisted by the latter. In the given situation there is less likelihood graphic and technological map political instability is inherent in such a situation which would get expression in all kinds of demands for autonomy and self-determination. Not that they are the solutions to the problems, but that is how the political leaders are most likely to articulate their demands.

CIVILIZATIONAL UNDERPINNINGS

The centrality of India in the South Asian region and its long history as a civilization have created a kind of political cleavage which can be explained through the following formulations:

Indian culture being an ancient one deeply rooted to the soil provides an in-built identity to the nation which no matter how diverse the social structure is cannot be done away with. As a result it has no compulsion to project others in the neighborhood as its enemies to highlight this image. In contrast, most of India's neighbors, being small and having at some point in time been parts of the Indian civilization, have an in-built compulsion to project their distinctiveness from India lest the world ignore their existence.

What follows from this broad dichotomous reality is that many of the problems which India's neighbors find important from their respective national viewpoints are not given such importance by India for the simple reason that they are just parts of the Indian experience. Let us take the example of the sharing of the Ganga water between India and Bangladesh. The problem of sharing the river water is so much a national issue that the average Indian largely ignores its international dimensions. The Kaveri dispute between Tamil Nadu and Karnataka, the displacement of thousands of families by the Sardar–Sarovar Project in Gujarat, the conflict of interest among the states of Delhi, Haryana, Himachal Pradesh, Rajasthan, and Uttar Pradesh over the sharing of the Yamuna and Sutlej waters, and so on, are so much part and parcel of the Indian body politic that it is not surprising that Indians fail to attach the amount of importance to the Farakka issue which Bangladesh expects from it. The Kashmir problem may be seen from the same perspective. For India, neither the fact that Kashmir is a Muslim-majority state, nor its demand for self-determination is a unique situation. For a nation, 12 percent of whose population belong to the Islamic faith, (more than the entire population of Pakistan) and which from the start learnt to live with all kinds of autonomy and secessionist demands, Kashmir is just another problem in the minds of the people.

Conclusion

The movements of populations that South Asia has witnessed during the last half-century, are massive and variegated. Of late the intensity has visibly gone down although the process is going on. The migration of a couple of hundred thousands here and there into India would not affect Indian economy either way. But it is not unlikely that interested political parties may take maximum political advantage of the ethno-religious characteristics of the migrant communities to ignite primordial sentiments among sections of the masses to the detriment of India's pluralistic social fabric. The Hindu-chauvinistic parties do emphasize the Islamic dimensions of the Bangladesh infiltrations into India. The interstate problems discussed above are related to the issue of the approach to nation building. The developmental goals have to be coordinated through South Asian regional cooperation that should subsume strategies to remove intra-national economic disparities as far as possible. The task is indeed daunting but the stakes are no less high.

NOTES AND REFERENCES

1. R. Jayasree, K.B. Durup, Dominic E. Azuh and N. Audinara, "Population Research in India: 1970–1990," in P. Krishnan, Chi-Hsien Tuan and Kuttan Mahadevan, *Readings in Population Research: Policy, Methodology and Perspectives.* Delhi, 1992, pp. 485–557.
2. For more on the point and relevant literature see, N. Krishnan Namboodiri, "Ecological Demography: Its Place in Sociology," in P. Krishnan et al., ibid., pp. 321–49.
3. Nazli Choucri, "The Pervasiveness of Politics," *Populi* (New York), vol. 5, no. 3, 1978, p. 30. See also W. Howard Wriggins and James F. Guyot, "Demographic Change and Politics: An Introduction," in W. Howard Wriggins and James F. Guyot (eds), *Population, Politics, and the Future of Southern Asia.* New York, 1973, pp. 1–29.
4. V.A. Pai Panandiker and P.K. Umashankar, *Fertility Control-Induced Politics of India*, monograph, Centre for Policy Research, New Delhi, June 1994.
5. Choucri, "The Pervasiveness of Politics." For details, see her *Population Dynamics and Violence: Propositions, Insights and Evidence.* Lexington, 1974; Nazli Choucri and Robert C. North, *Nations in Conflict: National Growth and International Violence.* San Francisco, 1975; Robert C. North, *The World That Could Be.* Stanford, 1976. See also the chapter on "The Causes and Consequences of Migration," in J. Beaujeu-Garnier, *Geography of Population.* London, 1978.
6. Robert Mandel, "Roots of the Modern Inter-State Border Dispute," *Journal of Conflict Resolution*, vol. 24, no. 3, September 1980, p. 435.

7. Partha S. Ghosh, "Ethnic and Religious Conflicts in South Asia," *Conflict Studies*, No. 178, September 1985.
8. The Indian Commission of Jurists, *Recurrent Exodus of Minorities from East Pakistan and Disturbances in India: A Report to the Indian Commission of Jurists by its Committee of Enquiry*. New Delhi, 1965, pp. 309–12.
9. For an analytical and informative study of the role played by refugees in Pakistan's politics, see Theodore P. Wright, J., "Indian Muslim Refugees in the Politics of Pakistan," *Journal of Commonwealth and Comparative Politics*, vol. 12, 1975, pp. 189–205.
10. On this point, see Shahid Javed Burki, "Migration, Urbanization, and Politics in Pakistan," in Wriggins and Guyot, *Population, Politics and the Future of Southern Asia*, pp. 148, 152, 162–67.
11. Wright, "Indian Muslim Refugees," p. 198. For an analysis of Pakistan's failure in national integration, see Rounaq Jahan, *Pakistan: Failure in National Integration*. New York, 1972.
12. ICJ Report, "Recurrent Exodus," Note 8.
13. The questions have been discussed at length in Partha S. Ghosh, *Conflict in South Asia*. New Delhi, 1989, pp. 16–46.
14. *The Hindu*, 4 May 1985.
15. *India Today*, 30 September 1985, p. 50.
16. For more on this point, see Ghosh, *Cooperation and Conflict*, pp. 170–73.
17. *The Times of India*, 30 August 1994.
18. K.N. Sud, "Nepalese in India," *Hindustan Times*, 9 September 1975.
19. Nepal, National Commission on Population, Task Force on Migration, *National and International Migration in Nepal: Summary and Recommendations*. Kathmandu, August 1983, pp. 13–14, 29, cited hereinafter as *Task Force Report*.
20. Devendra Prasad Shrestha and P. Hanumantha Rayappa, "Levels of Agricultural Development and Patterns of Population Growth in Nepal," in Ashish Bose and M.K. Premi (eds), *Population Transition in South Asia*, Delhi, 1992, p. 296.
21. For details, see Ramakant and B.C. Upreti, "Regionalism in Nepal," in Urmila Phadnis et al. (eds), *Domestic Conflicts in South Asia, vol. 2, Economic and Ethnic Dimensions*. New Delhi, 1986, pp. 165–81.
22. Lok Raj Baral, "The Press in Nepal," *Contibutions to Nepalese Studies*, vol. 2, no. 1, February 1975, p. 180.
23. *Task Force*, Note 19, p. 17.
24. Ibid., p. 34.
25. Quoted in *Motherland* (Kathmandu), 11 August 1983, as reproduced in *Nepal Press Digest*, vol. 27, no. 23, 16 August 1983, p. 337.
26. *The Hindu*, 6 September 1983.
27. See Lok Raj Baral, *Regional Migrations, Ethnicity and Security*. New Delhi, 1990, pp. 128–34.

28. Sud, "Nepalese in India," A.C. Sinha, "Immigrants from Nepal," *The Statesman*, 17 April 1982.
29. For details, see Ghosh, *Cooperation and Conflict*, pp. 110–18; Baral, *Regional Migrations*, pp. 55–64.
30. For the complete text of the treaty, see *The Hindu*, 24 December 1986.
31. Noted Indian demographers like Ashish Bose and B.K. Roy Burman have testified to this. See *India Today*, 15 June 1984, p. 136; B.K. Roy Burman, "Points and Counter-Points in North East India," in Akhtar Majeed (ed.), *Regionalism: Development Tension in India*. New Delhi, 1984, pp. 65–74.
32. Ashis K. Biswas, "The Unchecked Influx," *The Hindu*, 17 February 1982.
33. For a summary of the Assam Accord, see *India Today*, 15 September 1985, p. 27. For a fairly detailed analysis of the Assam problem, see Citha Dorothy Maass, "The Assam Conflict," *Internationales Asienforum*, vol. 15, 1984, pp. 219–59.
34. S. Mukerji, "Migration in Eastern India: How Much of It Is Illegal," *The Journal of Family Welfare* vol. 37, no. 3, September 1991, p. 71. For a detailed study of Bangladeshi immigration into Tripura, see Gayatri Bhattacharyya, "Refugee Rehabilitation and its Impact on Tripura's Economy," Ph.D. dissertation, University of Calcutta, 1978, pp. 19–20.
35. *India Today*, 15 September 1985, p. 27.
36. Baral, *Regional Migrations*, pp. 117–18.
37. *The Times of India*, 22 August 1994.
38. For details of the census data, see Raghubir Chand and Mahabir Chand Thakur, "Changing Population Profile," *Seminar*, no. 378, February 1991, pp. 19–23; Mukerji, "Migration in Eastern India" pp. 71–73.
39. *India Today*, 15 September 1985, p. 53.
40. The facelift that the canal has effected to the local economy has been discussed in B.G. Verghese, *Winning the Future: From Bhakra to Narmada, Tehri, Rajasthan Canal*. New Delhi, 1994, pp. 67–73.
41. *Sunday*, 10–16 November 1985, pp. 15–22.
42. *India Today*, 15 September 1985, pp. 53–54.
43. *The Hindu*, 22 August 1994.
44. Ibid., 3 August 1987.
45. For details, see Ghosh, *Cooperation and Conflict*, pp. 155–61.
46. L. Vedavalli, *Socio-Economic Profile of Sri Lankan Repatriates in Kotagiri*. New Delhi, 1994, pp. 38–39, 46–49, 154–55. See also Partha S. Ghosh, "The Other Tamils," *The Statesman*, 8 September, 1990.
47. Dawa Norbu, "Refugees from Tibet: Structural Causes of Successful Settlement," paper presented to the Fourth International Research and Advisory Panel Conference on Forced Migration, Oxford University, 5–9 January 1994, pp. 1–3. See also K.P.

Population Movements and Interstate Conflicts 253

Saksena, "Problems of Refugees. The Indian Experience," paper presented at the Tenth Course of International School on Disarmament and Research on Conflict (ISODARCO), Venice, 17–27 July 1984, pp. 14–16.
48. Ali T. Sheikh, "Afghan Refugees," paper presented at the Tenth Course of ISODARCO, Note 47.
49. Hafeez Malik, "The Afghan Crisis and its Impact on Pakistan," *Journal of South Asian and Middle Eastern Studies*, vol. 5, no. 3, Spring 1982, pp. 45–50.
50. Mohammad Ayoob, "Dateline Pakistan: A Passage to Anarchy?" *Foreign Policy*, no. 59, Summer, 1985, pp. 159–60.
51. Malik "The Afghan Crisis and its Impact on Pakistan," *Illustrated Weekly of India*, 3 November 1985, p. 51. For a study of the Pak–Afghan conflict over Pustoonistan, see Mujtaba Razvi, *The Frontiers of Pakistan: A Study of Frontier Problems in Pakistan's Foreign Policy*. Karachi, 1971.
52. Jamal Rasheed, "All Eyes on Baluchistan," *Middle East International*, 15 January 1982, p. 10.
53. For an analysis of the Baluch separatism and the Soviet connection, see Selig Harrison, *In Afghanistan's Shadow: Baluch Nationalism and Soviet Temptations*. Washington, 1980; Inayatullah Baloch, "Afghanistan–Pakistan–Baluchistan," *Aussenpolitik* (English Edition), 3rd Quarter 1980, pp. 283–301; Inayatullah Baloch and Hans Frey, "Pakistan and the Problems of Subnationalism," *Journal of South Asian and Middle Eastern Studies*, vol. 5, no. 3, Spring 1982, pp. 60–69; Urmila Phadnis, "Ethnic Movements in Pakistan," in Pandav Nayak (ed.), *Pakistan: Society and Politics*. New Delhi, 1984, pp. 182–211.
54. Rajni Kothari, "Political Reconstruction of Bangladesh: Reflections on Building a New State in the Seventies," *Economic and Political Weekly*, 29 April 1972, pp. 882–85.
55. Paul Kennedy, *Preparing for the Twenty-First Century*, New York, 1993, pp. 4–5.

12

REHABILITATION OF VICTIMS IN WAR-TORN SOCIETIES[1]

Sanjukta Bhattacharya

> What is that sound high in the air
> Murmur of maternal lamentation
> Who are those hooded hordes swarming
> Over endless plains....
>
> —T.S. Eliot[2]

War brings unimaginable devastation not only to people, but also to the land and the environment. With the invention of modern means of mass destruction and the instruments for targeting them at points far off from immediate battlefields, the scope of damage has increased immeasurably. Bacteriological, chemical and nuclear weapons, anti-personnel land mines and napalm bombs can not only wipe out populations and cause incalculable injury to people but damage the environment and make land unfit for habitation for long periods of time. Sophisticated aircraft and short and long-range missiles can carry destruction to the heart of non-combatant civilian population areas. According to data collected by the United Nation Children's Fund (UNICEF), 90 percent of all victims of war since World War II have been civilians, and it is estimated that in the not too distant future, the ratio of soldiers to civilians killed in war will be 1:100.[3]

The nature of wars, too, is changing in recent time. Wars between states, territorial, border, resource and even ideological conflicts are giving way to wars within states, ethnic, religious and minority conflicts and conflicts generated by a desire for regional autonomy or independence or for a greater share of power at the center. Common people rather than regular armies are very often involved in these wars. Sabotage and subversive activities in civilian areas are hallmarks of these types of conflict where guerrilla groups operate in populated urban and rural districts. Civilian casualties are therefore increasing, means of livelihood are being affected, and mass displacements of populations in conflict-prone areas are becoming more frequent.

In this context, the issue of rehabilitation of victims of conflict in war-torn societies becomes a complex one involving large sections of the resident population, internally displaced persons (IDPs), refugees, local communities, and demobilized members of regular armies and guerrilla organizations at one level and the land and productivity, at another. According to the *Oxford Dictionary*, "rehabilitation" means "restoration of a normal life or good condition." "Normal life" in any given society may not entail "good condition"; on the contrary, it may have contained the germs of conflict that caused the devastation in the first place. Rehabilitation, therefore, does not imply merely resettlement, repatriation, relocation, and reintegration of people in their traditional habitats. It also means rebuilding of bridges, houses, educational institutions, and hospitals, repair of roads, water and sanitation facilities, reforestation and improvement of the productivity of farmlands and industries, de-mining of all areas—in short, a total reconstruction of the economy which includes survival strategies to help ensure long-term benefits without which peace can become jeopardized. This is especially true of Third World countries, because wars have been taking place more and more frequently in the poorest of poor societies or in countries already ravaged by conflicts during the Cold War period. Here, rehabilitation can imply building rather than rebuilding, construction rather than mere re-construction, the country itself being a victim of conflict.

THE ISSUE OF PROTECTION AGAINST EFFECTS OF WAR

The issue of large-scale rehabilitation of victims of war, however, would not arise if international laws regarding the protection of civilian populations were fully honored during wartime. The legal basis of protection can be found in international humanitarian and human rights concepts and refugee law. Humanitarian law has its roots in Jean-Jacques Rousseau's *The Social Contract,* in which he pointed out that "War is no way a relationship of man with man but a relationship between states, in which individuals are only enemies by accident not as men but as soldiers," and at the end of the war, soldiers "again become mere men" and their lives must be spared.[4] Inherent in this is the distinction between soldiers and civilians and that the purpose of war is not to destroy but to overcome the enemy forces.

The four Geneva Conventions of 12 August 1949, however, marked the real beginning of humanitarian law and extended protection under this law to the victims of civil war. The Fourth Convention provided specific protection for the first time to civilians who have fallen into enemy hands from arbitrary treatment and violence. On 8 June 1977, two Protocols additional to the Geneva Conventions were also adopted. The Geneva Conventions and their additional Protocols distinguish between "combatants" and "protected persons." The latter group included civilian internees, civilians on the territory of the enemy and civilians in occupied territories as well as the wounded, sick and shipwrecked members of armed forces and civilians and prisoners of war. All these have the right to special protection. The Geneva Conventions also emphasize humane treatment especially for civilians without distinctions based on race, color, sex, language, religion, political opinion, national origin, wealth, birth or other status. The First Convention insists on women being treated "with all consideration due to their sex." The Fourth Convention prohibits the use of civilians as a shield to protect certain areas or installations from military attack. The collective punishment of civilians and measures aimed at intimidating or terrorizing civilian populations, pillage, hostage taking and reprisals against civilians are also forbidden. To protect civilians, specially vulnerable people, safety zones may be set up with the consent of both sides during conflict or in times of peace and these may not be subjected to attack. According to Additional Protocol I, refugees and stateless persons must also be treated as protected persons. It also redefined conditions in which children can be evacuated from dangerous areas.

To protect means of survival during war, Article 23 of the Fourth Convention lays down that here should be free passage of relief for civilians in need. Consignments of essential foodstuffs, medicines, clothing, and tonics for children and expectant mothers are not subjected to any conditions. In the case of occupation, the occupying power is obliged to ensure that the population is not deprived of food and medical supplies.

These Convention and Protocols are further supplemented by the *Universal Declaration of Human Rights* (10 December 1948) that ensures for everyone the right to life, liberty, and security of person whatever the status of the country. Articles 13(2) and 14(1) also legitimize refugee flows, specially during emergencies and the right of refugees to resettlement. The *International Covenants on Civil and Political Rights and on Economic, Social and Cultural Rights* (16 December 1966) further supplement the human rights document. The *Convention on the Prohibition of the Development, Production, and Stock-piling of Bacteriological (Biological) and Toxin Weapons and their Destruction* (10 April 1972), the *Chemical Weapons Treaty of 1993*, the *Convention on the Prohibition of Military or any other Hostile Use of Environmental Modification Techniques* (10 December 1980) as well as the recent efforts to ban anti-personnel land mines (5 December 1997), if respected, would limit damage to the environment and large scale injury to civilians.

There are regional instruments, too, like the *European Convention for the Protection of Human Rights and Fundamental Freedom* (4 November 1950) and its Protocol of 16 September 1963, the *African Charter on Human and People's Rights* (27 June 1981) and the *American Convention on Human Rights* (22 November 1969), which guarantee specific basic rights. In addition, legal instruments regarding refugees have protection clauses for refugees.

However, during armed conflict, belligerent parties pay little heed to humanitarian laws or human rights, creating the need for large-scale rehabilitation after wars. Moreover, while laws regarding international armed conflict are extremely codified and have means of international supervision, the laws on non-international armed conflicts consist only of some generally worded rules and have no internalized supervision.

Non-internationalized armed conflict can be of two types—internationalized civil war which includes wars of national liberation and other internal armed disputes. To the first only Common Article 3 of the Geneva Convention and Protocol II are applicable. Article 3 prohibits violence to life and person, the taking of hostages, outrages on personal dignity and the carrying out of arbitrary executions while Protocol II lays down fundamental guarantees of humane treatment. Internal armed disputes or non-internationalized civil wars are outside the scope of international humanitarian law, though Common Article 3 is also applicable here.[5]

What is important that in the post-Cold War period, the last mentioned type of conflict is the order of the day. Though human rights laws offer adequate protection if regarded, they are often violated. Further, some human rights protections can be curtailed in wartime under provisions relating to a state of emergency. Therefore, human rights guarantees are incomplete. As a result of breach of protection under international law, armed conflicts at different periods of time have created huge numbers of victims in various parts of the world who need to be relocated, resettled, repatriated and rehabilitated. A quick look at rehabilitation efforts in different region can provide examples on which South Asian countries can draw.

REHABILITATION EFFORTS IN REGIONS OTHER THAN SOUTH ASIA

One of the largest rehabilitation efforts was in Europe after World War II. Many of the victims of war were Jews who needed relocation and a significant number were rehabilitated in America and later in Israel. But what was important was that European countries were devastated and their economies needed support, without which lives could not be reconstructed. This came in the shape of the Marshal Plan, which was designed to reinforce the peace that had already been established. It amounted to some $110 billion in 1989. Its greatest success, however, was the impetus it gave to regional planning. According to one author, Michael Hogan, the American focus on "fusing separate economic sovereignties into an integrated market capped by super-national institutions of economic planning and administration" helped to generate the European integration we see today.[6] The emphasis was on productivity and long-term macroeconomic policies and thinking in regional terms. This had a trickle down effect leading to a general improvement in living standards as people were integrated into booming economies. The end product was peace and war between West European countries is unthinkable today.

In West Asia, on the other hand, the seeds of war were sown with the creation of Israel that led to the formation of a new diaspora: the Palestinian diaspora. Over 700,000 fled the erstwhile Palestinian territory after the 1948 and later wars created more displaced persons. Arab states that lacked the resources were reluctant to integrate them specially because this would have implied the recognition of the permanence of Israel. So, many Palestinians were forced to live in dreary United Nations' refugee camps under the auspices of the UN Relief and Works Agency (UNRWA), camps that grew into permanent communities in Jordan, Syria, and Lebanon. There have been numerous attempts at settling the refugee problem, but negotiations broke down again and again because Israel did not wish to receive Arab refugees or pay compensation for their properties, and Arabs opposed any refugee settlement that would recognize a Jewish state. The result has been a series of armed conflicts, the militarization of refugee populations and general breach of peace. Even after the 1993 peace accord, one of the major points of discord is refugee rehabilitation, especially because the refugee population has grown too large (estimated at around 4 million) to be resettled only in the Palestinian Authority areas.

In other parts of the world where major rehabilitation efforts have taken place, it is important to note the economic content of the programs. In Africa specially, reconstruction efforts and economic rehabilitation have always been given a priority. In the 1960s the UN High Commissioner for Refugees (UNHCR) organized rural resettlement schemes by which rural refugees would be able to re-establish themselves in their accustomed way of life and simultaneously contribute to the economies of host countries. "zonal development" schemes were started in Zaire, Burundi, and Uganda to make refugees self-sufficient at a standard of living comparable but not better than that of the local population and urban refugees were encouraged to join these rural communities. However, with the escalation in the numbers of displaced persons in the following decades, integrating refugees into the host country's economy was no longer feasible and repatriation became the preferred solution. In war-devastated regions, rehabilitation also entails reconstruction work and UN agencies often pooled their resources and expertise for all round relief. Operation South Sudan was an important precedent where help was provided to not only returnees but also IDPs on a large scale.[7] In Mozambique, rehabilitation efforts included removal of mines and the demobilization of 60,000 government and 19,000 RENAMO troops. A legal framework was drawn up before repatriation between Mozambique and the UNHCR in March 1993 where it was noted that returnees would not be punished or discriminated against and the government agreed to make land available for cultivation and settlement. Steps were taken to repair roads, water supplies, and health facilities and some relief supplies were stockpiled in areas where refugees were likely to return. Thus, sufficiently stable conditions were created to help displaced persons to re-establish themselves. Quick Impact Projects (QUIPs) were introduced to make re-integration of the victims of war sustainable.

UN agencies have also attempted mid-term reconstruction during war, the 1989 Cross Border Operation in Somalia being an example. Sectoral development strategies were introduced and operationalized within regions in Somalia that were then under UN protection. Relief and reconstruction were integrated in 386 QUIPs and as a result thousands of Somali refugees in Kenya decided to return to their habitual residences.

In Central America, peace efforts were promoted by neighboring and extra-regional powers and their is a political will on the part of these countries to sustain peace through economic and political rehabilitation. In fact, it was here that Quick Impact Projects were first introduced by the UNHCR. These are small-scale projects involving returnees, IDPs, and local residents, and are based on proposals drawn up by the community concerned. In Nicaragua QUIPs were used for repairing schools, health centers, roads and bridges as well as boosting the agricultural sector through the provision of tools, seeds, processing machinery and transport. Small businesses were also set up and the special needs of women and vulnerable groups were taken into account. In some areas, QUIPs were planned and implemented in clusters to maximize their effect.[8] All this helped production to increase and marketing of surplus began in areas where long periods of war had destroyed the economy. However, certain discrepancies in the rehabilitation efforts do exist. For instance, the Indian population of Guatemala is not treated at par with other groups, thus creating the cause for future conflicts. Moreover, during the wars, there had been large-scale urban migration as well as loss of assets through disinvestment, de-capitalization and even sale. Large numbers of the entrepreneurial class moved abroad. On the other hand, almost an entire generation was recruited into armies or guerrilla groups at an early age and now they lack skills for civilian work.[9] All this makes reconstruction and rehabilitation work difficult.

Another important region for rehabilitation is Indo-China. Resettlement in Third World countries was a major option here perhaps for political reasons. This was specially true for the Vietnamese who were covered by the comprehensive Plan of Action for Indo-Chinese Refugees (CPA).[10] For those who were not eligible for resettlement, $360 was given as a one time grant to each voluntary Vietnamese returnee to help resettle themselves in Vietnam. When many refused to leave the camps, the camps were ordered to be closed down by the end of 1995 and a diminishing incentive was used, the grant being cut down to $240.[11]

The rehabilitation program in Cambodia included QUIPs which were designed to help returnees reintegrate in their societies and reach self-sufficiency, simultaneously benefiting the local population through the repair and fresh construction of roads, bridges, health centers, water points, schools, etc. Agricultural programs were launched to rehabilitate 8,000 ha of land and provide seeds for 60,000 families. At the same time, the UN Transitional Authority in Cambodia (UNTAX) and a non-governmental organization (NGO), Handicap International, tried to clear mines from farm lands. Returnees were initially offered 1 to 2 ha of land each, but this proved impracticable. So, other options were also offered like a smaller plot of land and a house, or $50 for each adult and $25 for each child under 12 and each returnee family was also given a 400 days supply of food, utensils, and agricultural tools.

A more recent case of conflict and rehabilitation is Bosnia. Much is left to be desired in the rehabilitation efforts. In Bosnia, Muslim victims in concentration camps were systematically tortured and killed and women were sexually violated.[12] In such cases political and economic rehabilitation may not be enough; psychological rehabilitation as well as freedom from fear are also very necessary. The damage is done to the body, mind as well as the soul.

SOUTH ASIA

In South Asia, several conflicts have occurred since 1947 entailing large scale rehabilitation efforts afterwards. Some however come under the category of internal disturbances rather than war, like the problems in Kashmir and Northeast India, and will not be discussed here. Massive displacement of population did take place in India in 1947–48 and in Bangladesh following the 1971 war. There was a political will behind the rehabilitation efforts because displacement was the result of disturbances or war connected with national liberation. People were willing to accept and integrate persons with whom they had ethnic and religions ties and employment was available as a result of the departure of the erstwhile rulers.

An estimated 20 million crossed the India–Pakistan borders between 1947 and 1950 and the Nehru–Liaquat Pact, 8 April 1950, formalized migration specially in the eastern sector. Both nations were new and rehabilitation became a part of state formation. In India, the government decision regarding the West Pakistan refuges was taken in 1947, while the corresponding decision for EastPakistanis was taken in 1955–56. Large sections of West Pakistan refugees were settled in and around Punjab, Uttar Pradesh, Delhi, Patiala East Punjab States Union (PEPSU) and the North East Frontier Agency (NEFA). Facilities in cash and kind were provided in accordance with former avocation and central and state governments gave aid in setting up cooperatives, cottage and small-scale industries. About 202,000 West Pakistan refugees were employed in central government offices by 1964–65. An amount of Rs 19.12 million was given to 4.07 million refugees from West Pakistan in 1947 by way of compensation, provident fund dues, pensions, and in response to other claims. In the east, rehabilitation started late and cash compensation for lost property was given only from 1972. Some of them procured homesteads and farmlands or started businesses partly on their own initiatives, but many stayed in camps for long periods of time. It was only later that schemes were floated for state-sponsored resettlement and as a result colonies like Harekrishnapur, Rasikpur, Rahmatpur and Kanthalia in Nadia and Keleghai and Garbeta in Midnapur came up. In 1987, the West Bengal government decided to offer freehold titles to refugees still living in squatter colonies with funds provided by the center. Short-term relief, emergency cultivation schemes, various types of loans, irrigation projects to provide water, poultry projects, supply of tools and milk-cows to non-agricultural families and other projects were employed to help rehabilitate East Pakistani refugees. Many were also sent to Assam, Tripura, Maharashtra, Andamans, Madhya Pradesh the NEFA, Bihar, Andhra Pradesh, Uttar Pradesh, Manipur, and Orissa. The largest rehabilitation scheme was at the Dandakaranya where a systematic effort was made to reclaim forestland for cultivation, set up planned villages and follow an integrated pattern of development. About 50,000 families were sent to Dandakaranya but an estimated 24,800 were resettled, the rest having deserted according to official estimates. Despite all these efforts, however, the rehabilitation of refugees from East Bengal is not complete partly because the migration still continues. The refuge and Rehabilitation Department is still active and a central rehabilitation branch office has been set up in Calcutta by the Union Home Ministry to monitor the work of the state government.[13]

In Pakistan, too, a concerted effort at rehabilitation was made. Under the Registration of Claims (Displaced Persons) Act, 1956, a detailed procedure for the registration and verification of claims by displaced persons was established. The displaced persons (Compensation and Rehabilitation) Act, 1958, laid down procedures for the allotment and transfer of evacuee property in favor of refugees who had abandoned properties in India. The resettlement problem was solved in both Pakistan and India without any outside assistance.

Rehabilitation by itself is, however, not enough. The Mohajir issue in Pakistan proves that it is important for a person to be integrated into the local society. The Mohajirs are Urdu-speaking Muslims who migrated from India in 1947 and were rehabilitated mainly in Sindh, where they established their dominance in urban areas but felt discriminated against. Their grievances took a political turn when they organized the Mohajir Quami Mahaz (MQM) in 1978 and from the 1980s their movement has been becoming more and more violent.

Apart from the early India–Pakistan migration, a large influx of Tibetans to India and Nepal occurred between 1959 and 1962. Today there are an estimated 133,000 Tibetan refugees, 80 percent of whom have been rehabilitated in India. The Indian government has had several Integrated Development Plans for their rehabilitation, the latest being for 1992–97. The Tibetans are considered to be a model refugee community and their rehabilitation has been quite successful. When they came, they faced trauma and fatigue as well as problems of cultural and physiological adjustment in the new low lands climate. Most of them were monks. Farmers and petty traders and came from pre-industrial and purely traditional cultures. In India, immediate rehabilitation meant dispersal to colder Himalayan regions where many were temporarily absorbed in road construction in 95 camps. The elderly lamas were settled in Dalhousie and a residential lamasery for 1200 junior lamas was set up in Buxa. In 1960–63, five major agricultural settlements in India and several smaller ones in Bhutan were initiated. Mysore state agreed to settle 3,000 Tibetans in a 3,000-acre tract, and in June 1962, Bhutan granted land for 3,000 more in two settlements, with funds from the Indian government. By 1965, these settlements had become self-sufficient.[14]

The Government of India has followed a deliberate policy of non-assimilation in the case of the Tibetans, especially because one of the causes of their forced migration was the fear of loss of cultural identity and religious institutions. However, the creation of separate settlements means that Tibetans are not really integrated into Indian society. Though a generation has been born here, they retain their separate identity as Tibetans and wish to return to their homeland sometime in the future.

So far as Bangladesh is concerned, it has had to deal with massive rehabilitation at two different periods of time. After the formation of Bangladesh in 1971, millions of refugees returned from India. At this point not much special effort at rehabilitation was made since most returned to their former homes and employments. The major issue was building a new state from the devastations of war and rehabilitation efforts were integrated into it. The second attempt is the ongoing Chakma rehabilitation process. According to the Chakma Accord of May 1993, Bangladesh promised to return their legitimate properties and assured them of security. Incentives like a cash relief of 10,000 Taka, six months' rations, educational facilities and the writing off of loans up to 5,000 Taka were also provided. However, the resettlement efforts were half-hearted and returnees faced harassment. A fresh 20-point agreement was signed between Bangladesh and the Parbatya Chattagram Jumma Saranarthy Kalyan Samity on 10 March 1997 which again ensured security to life and property and short-term relief. For instance, each repatriated family would be given 15,000 Taka, adequate rice, pulses, oil, and salt and nine months money to buy bullocks or cows, loans for house-construction, general amnesty, preference in employment in the CHT Development board, etc.[15] However, total commitment of the country to Chakma rehabilitation is lacking as can be seen from the political disturbances which have followed the Chakma Accord of 2 December 1997 which promises to end the 22 years old insurgency and given wide powers to the tribals and boost their self-governing rights.[16] Again, a lack of political will may lead to incomplete rehabilitation efforts and further conflict.

In Sri Lanka, the continuing warfare makes immediate rehabilitation impossible. There is, however, a current notion that rehabilitation will be easier to accomplish if a refugee exodus does not take place. The problem is that villages and towns have become battlefields and people often cannot live safely in their own homes. Of 600,000 IDPs in Sri Lanka in 1994, 250,000 were sheltered in some 473 government sponsored holding centers or camps, while others reportedly stayed with relatives or friends. The government provided food rations and in 1988 initiated a resettlement program called "Unified Assistance Scheme which included clearing and controlling areas, then resettling displaced persons on a voluntary basis with money grants, three-month food rations and some help in rehabilitating the infrastructure, as well as guarantees of security. Recently, the government also allowed people to resettle in areas controlled by the Tamil rebel guerrillas, but did not extend its full assistance package to this program.[17] this resettlement took place amidst continuing conflict so it may be assumed that it was geared more to military and political objectives than humanitarian imperatives. In 1990, the UNCHR too, started Open Relief Centers to provide a safety net system as an alternative to flight to India. The aim was, however, not to rehabilitate people but to provide humanitarian relief.

Conclusion

Rehabilitation is not possible in the face of continuing warfare. After wars, long-term development programs should accompany rehabilitation. Traditional approaches of providing people with seeds, tools, and a small cash grants have proved to be inadequate. There should be a link between repatriation assistance to individuals and development aid to communities, which should encompass not only the returnees but the local residents who had not moved during wartime but were nevertheless affected. The needs of special groups like women and children who are particularly adversely affected by war, and the disabled and elderly, should be borne in mind for rehabilitation to be successful.

The key word, however, is peace. Lasting peace provides stable conditions for sustainable rehabilitation. Peace, among other thing, involves respect for human rights, which is the domestic responsibility of sovereign states. Rehabilitation efforts should therefore also ensure social, economic, and political rights to ensure the removal of causes of friction, which create internal conflicts. For all this what is important, specially for countries of South Asia, which are characterized by internal conflicts over the issues of minority rights and empowerment, is political will.

Notes and References

1. Lecture at the first South Asian Peace Studies Orientation Course held by the Maulana Abul Kalam Azad Institute of Asian Studies, Calcutta, October 1997.

2. T.S. Eliot, "The Waste Land," from his *Selected Poems*. London, 1986, p. 65.
3. Ruth Seifert, "War and Rape: A Preliminary Analysis," in Alexander Stiglmayer (ed.), *Mass Rape: The War Against Women in Bosnia-Herzegovina*. London, 1994, p. 63.
4. Quoted in Hans–Peter Gasser, *International Humanitarian Law: An Introduction*. Haupt, 1993, p. 7.
5. Ibid, pp. 66ff.
6. Michael J. Hogan, *The Marshall Plan: America, Britain and the Reconstruction of Western Europe, 1947–52* New York, 1987, p. 19.
7. Gil Loescher, *Beyond Charity—International Cooperation and the Global Refugee Crisis*. New York, 1993, pp. 81–85.
8. UNCHR, *The State of the World's Refugees, 1993*. London, 1993, p. 115.
9. Benjamin Crosby, "Central America," in Anthony Lake (ed.), *After the Wars*. New Brunswick, 1990, pp. 103ff.
10. John Fredriksson, "Revitalizing Resettlement as a Durable solution," *World Refugee Survey*, 4 June 1997, p. 49.
11. *Time*, 2 May 1995.
12. Fredriksson, n. 8, p. 50.
13. See Santosh Kumar Biswas, *The Rootless People*. Calcutta, 1995; U. Bhaskar Rao, *The Story of Rehabilitation*. Delhi, 1967; and R.N. Saksena, *Refugees: A Study in Changing Attitudes*. Bombay, 1961.
14. Dawa Norbu, "Tibetan Refugees in South Asia: A Case of Peaceful Adjustment," in S.D. Muni and Lok Raj Baral, *Refugees and Regional Security in South Asia*. New Delhi, 1996, pp. 78–98.
15. Saleem Samad, "Impact of Political Crisis on Demographic Migration of the Ethnic Minorities of Chittagong Hill Tracts," paper presented at a seminar on *Human Rights and Security*, 26–27 March 1997, Jadavpur University, Calcutta.
16. *The Statesman* Calcutta, 3 December 1997.
17. Office of the UNCHR, *UNCHR's Operational Experience with Internally Displaced Persons*. Geneva, 1994, pp. 47–48.

13

WOMEN ACROSS BORDERS IN KASHMIR—THE CONTINUUM OF VIOLENCE[1]

Asha Hans

An inquiry into the place of women in the nationalist discourse of a Partitioned India has emerged in recent years.[2] This partial filling-in of a vacuum in Indian history has been an important step in our understanding of women's history in the subcontinent. More specifically, both Menon and Bhasin, and Butalia, who spoke to women who crossed borders from the newly-formed state of Pakistan to India during Partition in 1947, have brought to light memories long suppressed. These memories needed to be revealed so that the language of the nationalist discourse would not continue to be exclusive and misleading where women's national identity is concerned. As this discourse is not static and is linked to a political language that is ever changing, their excellent work enables us to understand both the continuity and the present discourse in India.[3] I would like to use this backdrop of history to understand women's position in the border areas of India relating to the Kashmir conflict.

In recent feminist interpretations of Partition and women on the borders, Kashmir has found little space. Butalia, confines herself to the Punjabi odyssey while Menon and Bhasin mention only of Azad Kashmir. One cannot blame them, as Kashmir has long been one of the intricate questions confronting history, which has defied every attempt at resolution. The latest conflict in 1999 is a part of the history of turbulence in the state.[4]

Understanding Women's Position in the History of Kashmir

Fours wars have been fought between Indian and Pakistan (1948, 1965, 1971, and 1999) where Kashmir has been a significant if not a direct causal factor. In the process Kashmir has been dismembered into three parts, and borders shifted. Today the northern part is known as Azad Kashmir and is under Pakistani control, the southern part, the state of Jammu and Kashmir, is under Indian control, and the eastern in China. In each change and conflict the civilians have suffered, yet the written histories only document the national hostilities and negotiations and bargains between states.[5] Male-centered narratives have no place for feminist action and evaluation. This absence of a feminist viewpoint is not surprising. Women's exclusion from historical chronicling is universal. Combined with a male construction of female roles, it has made the task of a feminist historiography difficult.

Recounting the Past

Among the well-known female rulers in India is Queen Didda of Kashmir. The following passage is reflective of the current male-oriented historical analyses. Dhar,[6] chronicling Kashmiri history, writes:

> In 950 AD, Khemgupta ascended the throne of Kashmir, a man of mediocre ability who married princess Didda. Queen Didda was the de-facto ruler of the state, as she was very dominating and exercised immense influence over her husband. In 980 AD Didda ascended the throne after the death of her husband. Before her, two other queens had ruled Kashmir namely Yashovati and Sugandha. Didda was a very unscrupulous and wilful lady and led a very informal life. But in spite of these drawbacks, she was an able ruler, who firmly ruled the valley. She died in 1003 AD (p. 19).

In the documenting of ruler's in Kashmir's history, women are mentioned only in this one paragraph. Dhar notes two other female rulers besides Didda, but no narrative of their lives exists. Above all, in Dhar's analysis, Didda's immorality precedes her ability as a ruler. Women's power here is not perceived as power. Furthermore, universal sexual ethics are not applicable to women. Didda's sexuality is a barrier to her finding a place in history equal to male sovereigns of the period.

Nationalist interests have perceived women as objects to be controlled. Nevertheless, we have to recognize that different historical understandings have produced different constructions of female roles. Dhar implies that Queen Didda transgressed the role circumscribed to females and, therefore, presents her as a target of contempt and ridicule. As the historiography of pre-independence years in India from a feminist point of view has yet to be explored, for a more authentic rendering, older histories would need to be examined. This exercise is essential for understanding not only the past but, also for understanding our identity (Sen).[7] The exclusion of women from these shared memories of history influences women's place in the current nationalist discourse.

PARTITION AND SHIFTING IDENTITIES

During Partition, Kashmiri women suffered along with other women of Partitioned India. Menon and Bhasin explain this with a story from Azad Kashmir. In October 1947, tribal intruders who forced all Hindus to leave invaded Muzzafarabad (now across the border from India and the capital of Pakistani-occupied Azad (free) Kashmir. The medical assistant distributed poison to all the women who feared sexual assault at the hands of the invaders. Many women took the poison and died. The rest jumped over a bridge into the river. Those who did not take their own lives were raped. When a woman chose to commit suicide, often her husband and/or brother helped her. If they were not able to strangle her, they threw her into the river (p. 52). Menon and Bhasin's story from Azad Kashmir is one of the many covered-up stories of mass rapes, sucides, abductions, sale, and honor killings. Most are of women who have become refugees twice over, once in 1947–48 and then again in 1990. During Partition, the women were considered sexual objects and of no use to the *Qwam* (the nation) if they lost their purity. Their purity had to be protected even if it meant death. The Partition drew a red bloodline of violence in women's lives. Women's vulnerability relegated her to a lower place in this *Qwam*.

The history of wars and negotiations after independence relating to Kashmir, therefore, make no mention of women. Women were invisible factors in the negotiations that took place between India and Pakistan either on a bilateral or at the international level. Women were only given a critical place in the political mosaic of Kashmiri history, which was documented after 1989, when the current state of conflict started. As in all conflicts, even here, it is women's sexuality that has taken center stage, whether from the angle of the state security forces or the *mujahideen* (a guerrilla group, whose members believe themselves to be the true defenders of Islam and wage a war to please God).

To understand the post-Partition phase, it is important to understand the ethnic composition of the state. Jammu and Kashmir, the constituent part of Kashmir, which is Indian, is not Muslim as is generally indicated. The state is currently divided into four largely loose religious groups and sub-groups. The majority of the Buddhists are confined to Leh and Ladhak, Hindus to Jammu, Shia Muslims to Kargil, and Sunni Muslims to the Valley. The history of these ethnic divisions and sub-divisions is long. Kashmir was a Hindu state from the second millennium BC. Part of it converted to Buddhism in the third century BC. A resurgent Shivaite Hinduism ended Buddhism in Kashmir as it did in other parts of India.

Central Asian incursions introduced Islam. Islam changed in the 12th century as it began to be related to the Sufi school of Persia (modern-day Iran). In the Valley, the 700 years old *kashmiriat* tradition blended Sufi Islam's egalitarian spirit with a more liberal Hinduism. An easy relationship existed between Buddhists, Muslims, and the Hindus. The Mughal rulers 400 years ago did not replace this culture with the practice of a strict Islam as they had done in other parts of India. Therefore, it remained a liberal Islam different from the proselytizing of fundamentalist Islam (p. 21).[8] It gave relatively greater freedom to Muslim women, as triple *talaq* (an Islamic practice which gives Muslim men the right to divorce a wife in the form of three repudiations used by saying the word *talaq* three times to formalize a divorce) and the practice of four wives were not adopted. Widow remarriage has been common. Today, the non-violence and secular ideals of *kashmiriat* have been destroyed in Kashmir and replaced with a newly-imported Islamic order which has no place for Hinduism or Budhism, and which has a strictly circumscribed code of conduct for women.

"My Green Valley has Turned Khaki"

The present Kashmir problem started on 19 January 1990. Half-a-million Hindu families were displaced after loudspeakers broadcasting from mosques asked them to leave the Valley within three days or face dire consequences. The majority of the Hindus in the Sunni-dominated valley were forced to live in camps in non-Muslim areas of the state and in other parts of the country. Women left all that is familiar and secure to adapt to a new life of uncertainty. There is no safety even in other areas of Kashmir, outside the Valley, as conflict has entered Kashmiri lives in every part of the state. Women, wherever they are, remain targets of militancy and state controlled force.[9]

Since 1990s the violence and its consequent effects on the lives of Kashmiri women are comparable to those experienced by women in any other global conflict situation. Conflict, displacement, and the new and fundamentalist character of Islam have changed not only social but also physical structures. The Line of Control (LoC), a boundary dividing Kashmir, and agreed to by both India and Pakistan by the Simla Agreement of 1972, has again become a center of conflict creating a new Hindu–Islam divide. The Valley is, thus, demanding freedom from the State of India. Hindus who lived in peace with their neighbors since the second millennium BC have been forced to vacate the Valley. This shifting of the LoC, though physical, has created new boundaries in women's lives. A Kashmiri–Hindu woman, displaced by the conflict, questions the "freedom"—a freedom in which women pay the cost by being restricted to play a role of the outsider or spectator—as well as her own and her community's position in this search for a new national identity.

Azadi (Freedom) 1989–1995
What nation
Does not have a dream
Like that?
History is a nightmare

From which we cannot wake:
We cannot arise.

I have heard a house to house
Searches for young men with beautiful
Hair who hide frightful weapons
In their sister's hope chests.

To the women who love them
They tell nothing except that
One day Azadi will arrive
At everyone's doorstep.
Life will become prettier, more
Honourable, more pious.

Who are these men?
I would like to ask you.
I would like to know
Why their dream of Azadi
Excludes me (and my people).

—Pandit, June 30, 1999[10]

Hindu women find themselves completely excluded from this quest for a new Kashmiri national identity. This search for freedom is only perceived in the context of Islamic vs non-Islamic positioning. As Hindu women are extraneous to this search we are compelled to confine ourselves in this article to women restrained by Islamic boundaries.

In the late 1980s, clerics coming from outside Kashmir pushed strict Islamic schools for children, the wearing of veils for girls and women, undermining the liberal Sufi ethos. The veil is a new phenomena introduced by the strict codes of Islam and imposed by the new Islamic leaders with links to Pakistan and Iran.[11] Women's lives have been inevitably affected, as they are perceived to be the representatives and emissaries of culture. The politics of culture and the presence of Border Security as well as the Armed Forces have had had a profound effect on the lives of women in Kashmir. For example, Kunaan Poshpora in Kupwara, near the border, has come to be known as the "raped village." On the night of February 22–23, 1991, over 30 women and children were supposed to have been gangraped by the soldiers of the Fifth Rajputana Rifles. This village, like many other villages, has lost its honor. All its women remain unmarried and are shunned by the community (recounted during a visit in 1992).

Present-day Kashmiri nationalism traces it origins to the political–cultural interventions of Islam. Those excluded from the search for a "new" Kashmiri identity try to negotiate with the Indian state to counter the strategies of their rejection from mainstream Kashmiri politics. This maneuvering for ending the politics of exclusion has not worked. The state is unable to support their pleas or even prevent the further dismembering of its own body. Pandit, in her poems, poignantly chastizes the policy-makers for the plight of the Kashmiri diaspora:

> Kings and king-makers play dice,
> Bet on their mother, not the wife.
>
> —Pandit, May 30, 1998

In the Hindu epic *Mahabharata*, Draupadi, the common wife of the Pandavas, was lost in a game of dice in a political battle for a kingdom. When Duryodhan, the Kaurav price, ordered her stripping in public, she was saved by divine intervention in the form of Krishna, the incarnation of Vishnu. The "betting" was then on the wife and, in the Hindu social order; it remains so toady. In any nationalist debate it is the "mother" as nation whose honor has to be protected and during Partition it was a major strategy employed by the state.[12] This strategy, however, did not work as Partition has dismembered the "mother" (p. 51).[13] This cry of a patriarchal system, signifying the preservation of the purity of the national order at all costs, returns at the heightening of tensions between the two nations but remains as unsuccessful now as it was then.

In her work, Pandit reveals a significant shift as she perceives the rulers and policy-makers of a modern India staking their "mother" in a battle. The enemy is not responsible for the dismembering; the rulers themselves have created the shifting borders. The "mother's" purity and sacred identity becomes a victim of state intertia and the moral corruption of the public sphere. What Pandit does not see, however, is that "womanhood" in her poems is all inclusive as neither mother nor wife escapes the violence of the state. All women, including the "mother" figure, find themselves caught within a continuum of violence. This change takes place in the political strategic field and, therefore, has political connotations.

To date, there has been little scope for academic work in the politics of violence. The curtain around Kashmir is dense and very little information escapes except what the state, or the militants, desire. What is indisputable is that the onset of violence a decade ago in Kashmir has engulfed the entire community of Kashmiri women.

Two rare studies provide insight into women's situation in Kashmir today.[14] In the first, the Women's Centre of Bombay University spoke to women in Kashmir in 1994 and the consequent report highlighted the abuse of women during conflict. The report documented large-scale rape and other forms of gender-specific violence that took place over the years as a result of the conflict. Consequently, the mosques, traditional centers of male power and dominance, have become centers of women's collective. Women have sought assistance from a fundamentalist Islam, an exploitative agency, to create solidarity. This step takes them within the cloisters of conservatism where they have had to sacrifice the limited freedom they enjoyed under Sufism in order to protect themselves from violence.

The canons of the new Islamic order demand the continuation of progeny. Injunctions of the new regime require that remarriage of widows continue. It is common, even for widows who already have children, to remarry and leave their children with their former husband's family. The militants positing family planning as un-Islamic have threatened doctors who practise in the field of reproductive and child health (RCH) care. Abortion is not allowed even in cases when the pregnancy has occurred as a result of rape by security forces.

Women though questioning the ban, cannot act against the militants, but do question their different positions towards sterilization and rape. While sterilization is considered as un-Islamic and banned, no such action is taken as far as rape is concerned. Resentment exists particularly in areas where the militants are trained in Pakistan—where reproductive health services including family planning is allowed—while the trained militants in Kashmir refuse RCH services to their own women.[15] Women's health has, thus, become a major casualty of the conflict.

Contextualizing Women's Position in the Kargil Conflict

The Kashmir crisis is a complex issue that has defied solutions over the past 50 years. This complexity is clearly discernible in the approximately 100 km of the disputed border areas covering the Kargil, Drass, and Batalik sectors on the LoC, which form the nucleus of the latest conflict. Like Kashmir in general, the Kargil region in which the conflict initiated does not have a homogenous ethnic composition. There are five ethnic communities: the Balti, Ladhaki, Zanzkari, Purki, and Dard Shin. In Drass the people are mainly of the Dard stock, an Aryan race believed to have originally migrated to the high valleys of the western Himalayas from the Central Asian steppes. They speak Shina which, unlike the Tibetan-originated Ladakhi dialects spoken elsewhere in Ladakh region, belongs to the Indo-European linguistic family. One of the "Minaros" (or *Brokpas*), tribal inhabitants said to be descended from the army of Alexander of Macedonia, is an endogamous tribe that continues to practice its own ancient rites and rituals.

In 1948, during the post-Partition conflict, Kargil and Drass were captured by Pakistan, but were regained by Indian forces.[16] As Pakistan retained the surrounding area between 1948 to 1965, the Kargil area was specifically targeted by Pakistani artillery fire from the overlooking peaks. In 1965, Indian forces gained control of the hills aroung Kargil, but these were returned to Pakistan as part of the Tashkent peace process brokered by the former Soviet Union. The firing on Kargil continued and in 1971, when the hills overlooking Kargil were taken from Pakistan, peace came to the region for a short time with the demarcation of the LoC in 1972 between the two countries. As militancy in the Sunni-dominated Valley increased, and Shi'ite Kargil did not support the militants, and Pakistani forces resorted to increased shelling.[17] Civilian casualties in Kargil over the years have resulted in the relocation of numerous people to Buddhist-dominated Leh. Ethnic conflict has increased in this peaceful region as Buddhists resent this encroachment on their cultural and territorial homogeneity.[18]

In February 1999, India initiated a new diplomatic process to end the conflict with Pakistan.[19] The peace process did not last long, as in May 1999, while the diplomatic initiative was still underway, hundreds of new posts had been set up by armed raiders on the Indian side of the LoC. The borders are poros and it has been easy for armed combatants to cross them. The issue is complicated as the intruders are a combination of mercenaries, Afghan and Pakistani *Mujahideen* as well as Pakistani army regulars.[20] Kargil was not a civil insurgency but a bilateral conflict. The border war intensified on May 26, 1999, when a full-fledged Indian army action took its place on the LoC. By the third day, India had deployed more troops to the Kargil region bringing the total to an estimated 30,000. India launched air strikes in Kashmir for the first time in 20 years. By July 11, 1999, a pullout was agreed upon and there was a subsequent reduction in the level of intensity in the conflict, although, it did not end.

The multiethnic and multinational composition of the border represents a unique political identity not shared by the rest of the state. Villages lie on both sides of the LoC. Here it is culture that mediates relations within the borders and outside them. For instance, a confusing situation exists in a village called Hundermann. Situated directly on the LoC, it is sometimes in Pakistan and sometimes in India. In 1948, it was part of Pakistan. In 1971, the Pakistanis destroyed the village and the Indian army occupied it, and overnight the villagers became Indians.[21] Since then, the people of Hundermann have had to live with intermittent shelling. The physical violence of bombing and the multi-psychological situational pressures, make the life of women in this village and many others in Kargil constantly traumatic.

As the war-like situation never actually ceases, violence in the lives of these people is a continuous oppressive component that decreases and increases at will. When the conflict intensifies, the boundaries of the LoC are extended to include all women who come into contact with it—the women living on the LoC, those crossing it, and those distanced by physical space but located in the center by virtue of their very identity. The LoC transforms these women's lives during heightened tension by the use of different systems of control. Control is exerted through the use of language and over women's movements, and therefore there identities and sometimes their economies are affected. For the women who live on these borders, as well as the women who have never seen the LoC because of its physical distance but are nevertheless tied to it, the LoC embodies an all-pervasive identity, which they can neither denounce nor adopt.

The war has affected women's lives in these villages profoundly, as their location on the borders has enclosed them in different nationalisms at different stages of their lives. Conflict creates in the life of all these women a new language of nationalism, which acts as a control mechanism. Their autonomies and agencies are both objectified in the larger national cause. Fortunately not all women associated with the LoC are completely subsumed by the male ideological order. Some manage to discover windows left open where they can pursue avenues of empowerment and personal or group autonomy.

FEMALE COMBATANTS FROM ACROSS THE BORDER AND A RECEPTION BY HOURIS

The LoC, in a feminist context, provides not only the demarcating of a political boundary but it also engenders a language of its own. This language uses women's bodies in the nationalist dialogue. For instance, in the Tuloling assault in the Drass Sector, three-storied bunkers were found with the bodies of four women who had been armed, same as the men. An Indian army captain who found the bodies, interviewed by the media, was asked what women were doing at this high altitude. He replied: "Well, probably to look after their personal *adam* (administration), he said with a wink."[22] Who were these four women? Insurgents, mercenaries, or women recruited by the Pakistani armed forces? What was their role in the Kargil conflict? The answers may never come. Indian soldiers in some posts have spotted women as well as found the bodies of women killed during air strikes. Some have suggested that the Afghan mercenaries have brought in women.[23] There is no proof that this information is true and the women's identity remains hazy.[24]

What is relevant here is the male adversary's perception of their roles. The female crossing of borders symbolizes the violation of not only political but also social and cultural boundaries. The adversary's construction of the insurgent woman's identity is being called into question.

The female representation of the enemy becomes a symbol of the body politic. These women kept faith with the male martyrs and opted for death rather than capture. Their reconstructed identity, however, transforms the female warrior into a powerless sexual object, denying her full status as fighter/soldier. As, there is no one to uphold her community honor, the language pursued in the cultural context acquires violence and the "line of control" becomes a line of violence—an attempt to violate their bodies through this control. It is certain that women in nationalist struggles do not achieve the status of their male counterparts. Whoever these women holding rifles are, the response of their male adversaries is to attack them through the undermining of their national "honor."

When male combatants cross borders they provoke a different response, even as adversaries. For instance, another view presented of women's role in this conflict is that of *houri*—women sent by the God's to tempt mortals. Pakistani soldiers are seen as being tempted by tantalizing, nubile nymphets waiting for them on the Indian side of the border, promising them entry to God's own "dancing hall." By all accounts, as an Indian newspaper correspondent suggests, our forces are firmly set on the path to a glorious victory, matched by the boundless ignominy of the adversary who have been foolish enough to believe that the barren Kargil hills are crawling with *houris*. It is a tribute to the Indian soldiers that they did not mow down the fleeing enemy—that is not the style of this side of the line that divides Hindu civilization from Islamic barbarism.[25]

The difference evident in the two examples presented above lies in the construction of "theirs" and "ours." "Theirs" are sexual objects—whether as *houris* of a sexual fantasy or insurgents that administer to men's sexual gratification—while "ours," by default, are not. Women are seen as objects of sexual fantasy or mundane providers of sexual favors. Through the women, the purity and cultural inferiority of the other nation is attacked.

Controlling the "Identity": Displacement and the Violence of Conflict

With resurgence of the conflict each time, victims of Partition settled on many parts of the border are faced with displacement and fear of being uprooted once again. Control over mobility of populations is an inevitable part of war. In this context, people living on the LoC have lived under the shadow of the guns since Partition and, with each conflict, have shifted to safer places. The Partition and the new boundaries have meant an extended violence, which has become a routine and inescapable part of daily life. In the Kargil conflict the number of persons rendered homeless are somewhere in the region of 278,601 and the majority who have moved are women and children. The displaced are from Kargil, Drass, Batalik, and the border areas of Punjab and west Jammu and Kashmir. Kargil has a very low-density population and, even if the conflict is in Kashmir, most of the displaced are from the Punjab sector of the border.

The displaced in Kashmir have resettled in places such as Kupwar, Uri, Gurez in Kashmir and Pura, Akhnoor, Poonch, and Rajouri in Jammu and Pallanwala. Most women and children have left their homes to find safer places on their own. In neighboring Himachal Pradesh in the Chham region more people have joined the exodus for safety.[26]. The most unsettled are the people on the Punjab border. The Inspector General (Border) of Punjab Police, J.P. Birdi, estimates that over a quarter-of-a-million people left their homes on the Punjab border. The numbers given out by the Indian government and Birdi are different, as here as in most refugee situations, due to incessant movement enumeration is difficult. It was noted by Birdi that, the worst affected areas are the Khem Karan and Khalra sectors. Most of the people from these sectors have moved to Taran Taaran, Amritsar, and other places. People living in these sectors suffered heavily in the 1965 and 1971 conflicts because they had to vacate their lands and homes in a hurry which were looted when they fell into enemy hands. This time around they were prepared and the women and children moved to distant and safer places.[27] Often, in these areas the man will stay back to look after his house and fields. Since Partition, the violence associated with displacement has not diminished. While the majority of women in this region have been forced to move in with friends and family during the war. On the LoC where there are army operations the women face complete dislocation and exclusion.

In Kargil, Drass, and Batalik it has not only been the shelling from the Pakistani side which has forced people to leave their homes, but also the occupation of villages by the Indian army which has temporarily inducted men into the army while shifting women and children to "safe places." For reasons of "security" women and children of villages on the LoC have been loaded into small trucks and "relocated to safer areas." As the army moves into the village, the men are inducted as temporary workers in the armed forces specifically to carry heavy guns up into the mountains. The women already removed to "safer" places are moved again, this time to unknown places. The men are not told where the women are, and at the end of their forced servitude in the army, the men move from village to village searching for their once-united families.

Toko, a small village with a population of about a little over 100 and about 500 m from the Srinagar–Leh road towards the LoC in Kashmir, is a ghost town as the Indo-Pak artillery exchanges have caused large-scale migration.[28] Many women and children have been relocated to Somat. The village of Chaukyal, is another village from where people have been moved to "safer areas." Gagangeer, on the Srinagar–Leh road, has been host to an increasing number of displaced.[29] All the displaced in Gagangeer are from Pandrass, a village near Drass and ethnically close to Baltistan. Families live in tin sheds provided by the government each measuring 1800 sq. ft and each housing approximately 20 families.[30] The 400 displaced, mostly women and children, live without adequate cooking facilities and clothing. As the army trucks, which brought them here, were too small and too few to carry their belongings, they arrived without clothing, bedding, or cooking utensils. The government provided only some rice and cooking oil. With temperatures falling below 5°C, the coming winter threatens their very survival.

In Kargil, Drass, and Batalik the state has been responsible for the dislocation of the family life of its citizens as well as the loss of honor of the male. Men lose not only their homes but also their rights as citizen as they are forced to become unpaid slaves in the army. This loss of autonomy as a head of family, in the eyes of their communities, is a loss of honor. Simultaneously, by keeping the women in their families out, these men have also lost control over their homes and personal lives. For the women, it is a dispossession of their ownership of goods and the autonomy they exercised within their own homes. Unlike other women on the border, the women on the LoC have been removed not only from their homes, but also from their family and communities, and find themselves without any support. The women of Kargil live in a vacuum with no links to anyone else in the country. Unwanted, unheard, and disregarded they are excluded from the nationalist undertakings, and their nationalism always remains suspect.

Though unheard and isolated by the state, many women have however managed to support themselves and their children in the unknown places where they have been relocated. They learn to network with local communities in an attempt to solidarity. They master the art of negotiating with local bureaucracies, and in a very short time, strive to position themselves within the mainstream.

Widows of Freedom and the Iconization of Social Displacement

The LoC controls all women who encounter it—the women on the borders, those who have crossed over, and those whose husbands are stationed there as soldiers. War treats all women alike whether they are of suspect nationalities or not. This war in India eulogized only the wives and mothers of "martyrs." This group has been used by the state to create war hysteria and gain sanction and sympathy for its war-like actions. The symbolism of honor and the war widow as victim, projected by the state, challenges the autonomy of the war widow and sends her back to a privatized existence within the family.

At the funeral of Squadron Leader Ajay Ahuja, his widow Alka, clutching her fidgety child, presented a perfect picture of bereavement and sacrifice. The government promised her a house, pension, and compensation. This was the beginning of a process where the state manipulated the image of the war widow as sacrificing herself at the altar of the nation. The colonization of women's bodies for exploitation is a historical tradition and women are at the mercy of the subjugator and their supporters. In this case, it is the dominant authority of the state that exploits them, assisted by the community, which carries out its directives. The imperatives of colonialism require that these women be iconized as widows of freedom. Their bodies, in the process, are used to further the cause of the nation. As most of the men who died were between the ages of 19 to 35, war widows are usually young and find themselves manipulated by both the state and their families.[31]

A soldier's death leaves behind a windfall and a divided family. At stake are a compensation of usually Rs 2–3,000 (about US $75—a large sum when spent in Indian currency), a job, a gas agency, and a plot of land provided by the state. The money meant for the widow rarely reaches her. Most women have to hand over the money to other men in the family for safekeeping and proper use. Some have been brutally beaten for not agreeing to the demands of a dead husband's family. This matter is further complicated by the fact that, for most part, widows in the villages are illiterate. They are not aware of the financial assistance that is owed to them. They do not know where to go, nor do they know how to complete any necessary forms. Some husbands' families have even been known to force a widow not to sign the official papers so that she does not get the money, as it will provide her freedom to marry someone else. In many cases where there are male relations, force is used to marry her off to them, so that the money remains within the family.[32] The lump sum paid out at the time of a husband's death and the monthly pension belongs to the soldier's widow, but widows are too often victimized, blackmailed, and exploited, their attempts at empowerment are threatened as they remain dependent on their husbands' families.

As money is collected by the state from public contributions in the name of the war widows, political parties are not left behind, making promises that "we will look after our own." The media recounts earlier stories of war widows to feed temporary war hysteria. Soon these stories of Kargil war widows will be buried in oblivion like Major Batra's wife whose husband died in the 1971 conflict. A park and a road were named after Major Batra, but his widow today is homeless. Another 1971 war widow, Indra Sood's gas agency in Agra was revoked. Mohini Giri, former Chairperson of the National Commission for Women found a war widow crying outside a private school as the child born after husband's death was denied admission.[33] In Bihar, a flat and land promised to war widow Balamdina Ekka, as well as land to another widow, Jeera Devi, are yet to materialize.[34] Only 20 percent of widows actually benefit as a result of bureaucratic obstructions.[35] The war widows of 1971 have lived with years of financial uncertainty, social ostracism, and daily needs that remain unmet. They know the nation has a short memory.

The war widow becomes the longest suffering casualty of war.[36] The systemic banishment of these women to the outskirts of society begins from their own homes. Upon widowhood, tradition demands that the woman's *mangalsutra* (a gold and black bead chain worn as a sign of marriage) be removed. Her bangles are broken, her *bindi* (red dot on forehead signifying auspiciousness) is wiped off, and she is obliged to dress in white. She remains in white dress, a symbol of purity, for the rest of her life. She is inauspicious, barred from wearing colored clothes and ornaments. To be a true "Indian woman" one must be a *Sati Savitri*, a mythical character whose husband died but was pulled back from hands of *Yama*, the God of death, by her love and dedication, thus saving her from widowhood. *Savitri* is the epitome of a sacrificing womanhood and not *Sati* (self-immolation) as usually represented. Savitri is willing to sacrifice herself (by going with *Yama*). To escape this public shame of widowhood, a woman must die before her husband.

The state, and sometimes the society, temporarily suspends this tradition of inauspiciousness, especially during war, by allowing a widow to remarry. However, despite the newly defined national identity of Indian womanhood, the patriarchal order remains entrenched. A war hero's death bequeaths his widow with deprivation and societal discrimination. A 15-year-old widow, Ranjita, the wife of Jyoti Kumar, cries for the death of a husband she barely knew. Her marriage was conducted during a one-day leave granted to the soldier. The marriage is unconsummated as her husband was summoned away by a call of duty. She cries not for her husband, but for her fate—a widow trapped in a hostile environment. She will have to spend a lifetime suppressing her sexuality. It will be a life robbed of any vestige of self-esteem under the guise of sympathy.[37]

Some attempt to challenge the Hindu constructions of widowhood, which bars their participation from social life, has been made. There are a few stories of empowerment and acceptance, where a mother of a slain son accepts her daughter-in-law as a daughter and treats her as a son.[38] In a patriarchal society this is an achievement of the highest order that a daughter-in-law can hope for, and that a mother-in-law can bestow. In Punjab, the custom of marrying a dead husband's younger brother still exists, and this makes it easy to control the widows. As women try to break these barriers, excuses are made that the objective is to protect their honor, which becomes tainted especially when they are living in a joint family with other males. Usually, however, these marriages ensure that compensation stays within the family. Twenty-two-year-old Sunita, pregnant and barely widowed for 15 days, is expected to marry her 18-year-old brother-in-law. She wants to find a job and look after her child. Her mother-in-law disapproves and feels that if she uses force, Sunita may call in the *Panchayat* (local elected leadership), creating a rift in the family structure.[39] The potential empowerment of women is seen as a threatening force that will break the traditional forms of control.

The widows therefore, become similar to the women living on the LoC and those crossing it as victims of conflict.

CONCLUSION: WOMEN ACROSS BORDERS AND THE NATIONALIST DISCOURSE

I began with the nationalist discourse of a Partitioned India, situating Kashmir in the context of the borders and boundaries in peoples lives created by the state. Considering that nationalism has a language of its own, and that this language is gendered, one can assume that it is reconstructed with each change in the political structures. To uncover the journey of nationalist discourse in Kashmir, it is important to question of nationalist discourse is the sum total of a people's perceptions, views, and concepts, or is it something more? Does it include women?

We realize that the nationalist discourse in Kashmir today cannot be discussed in a homogenous setting of territorial space and gender. Women across contested borders are in zone of a nowhere land. In this vacuum, the production of gender in the discourses and practices of nationalism, as elsewhere, constructs women as subordinate to men.[40] The answer to Enloe's questions of whether nationalism has sprung from a "masculinized memory" (p. 3) is affirmative.[41] In the history of the Kashmiri "nation," it is the men who have constructed not only the ideology of freedom but also women's space (and place) within it.

Women remain on the sidelines, dominated by men, whether in exile, or as widows, or as women living on the LoC. Since 1947, nothing has changed in terms of Kashmiri women's rights, responsibilities, and equality, frozen in a time wrap at the borders of two nations. The widow of Kargil symbolizes the dignity, the sacrifice of the nation, and the *hourie* of attaining the non-achievable. The widow's place in the nationalist discourse is related to the government's use of methods to retain ascendancy of power, and remaining within the cultural strategy of the party.

Women's most significant attributes have been seen as signifiers of ethnic differences and in the reconstruction of the Kashmiri ethnic national category. Veena Das's questioning of the commitment to cultural rights which leads to empowering the community against the state, but in which the individual is totally engulfed by the community, applies to Kashmiri women.[42] The nationalist discourse acquires great significance in the shifting of identities and of cultures.[43] The women in the Kargil war are currently positioned between the state and community, their identities merged in one or the other as necessitated. The Kargil conflict has confirmed the pattern of Kashmir in general where what counts are class, caste, and ethnicity, but what cuts across all these factors is the marginalization of women in Kashmiri politics.

In the Kargil conflict, the Kashmiri narrative of nationalism has little meaning, as the historical origins of the two are different. Where do the women of Kargil stand in this widespread narrative of violence for the achievement of a Kashmiri nation? We find that they neither fit into the Hindustan, land of the Hindus, Pakistan of the Sunni Muslims, or Ladkhak of the Tibetan Buddhists. Ideologically closer to Iran (Khomeini's) of the Shia Muslims, they are nevertheless physically distanced from them.[44] Linking their nationalism with Iran fulfils Benedict Anderson's conception of a nation belonging to "a kinship" or religion rather than an ideology (p. 5),[45] but one is tempted to ask whether the hanging of Khomeini's photographs in their houses does not contradict this understanding of nationalism. Only in assuming that adherence to Khomeini's thoughts is not ideology but religion, can one understand Khomeinism as a religious cult that fulfils these people's needs for a barrier against Sunni nationalism on the other side of the border, where the *jihad* is not only against the Hindu or Buddhist, but also the Shia. I would argue that perhaps it would be better to understand them, as Perry Anderson has perceived them—that theirs is a nationalism, which is yet not born, because it has not been opposed. Presently we can assume that this nationalist space is filled by the nations on both sides of the border, which are the "other" and, therefore, incompatible with their feelings of nationalism. Khomeini, thus, fills the space until they discover their own identity.

Ultimately the rise of religious or cultural nationalism is a cause of concern for women but unsettled borders question the very belonging of women. To borrow from Menon and Bhasin's observation, the first can be explained in terms of a tendency to impose an idealized notion of womanhood. Their second observation of women across borders is much more complicated as it is related to women's identity in a volatile situation of continuing wars and violence. Women's emergence as full-fledged citizens of any country is countered by their very being on a border that is not acknowledged and a genered-national boundary in which they are not provided a space.

For women living on the LoC, attaining a national identity is not easy. For instance, in 1971, most of the village women and children afraid of the war moved deeper into Pakistani and Indian territories. Zebunissa, from a small village on the LoC, was originally from Pakistan and married to an Indian. Borders did not mean anything to her. Her perception of nationhood has been mediated by kinship relationships. An outsider from across the border, she has lived under the shadow for fear. At risk is her body, which the Border Security Force can occupy at any time. A Shia in a Sunni-dominated country, she is also at risk in her former homeland of Pakistan. Do women on borders share in nationalism/national projects? Zebunissa has no answer. For her, nationalism is gendered and she has a role to play only if the male order of the state and the society allow her to. Border areas have little room for parliamentary democracy. Zebunissa, a Pakistani national, is today in India. What is her nationality? She has no passport, and her name is not in the voting list.

Women across borders have a difficult role to play. The duality of women's role can be assessed from the Pakistani side, which constructed them as freedom fighters, and from the Indian side, which interprets their role as objects of sexuality. A woman of Kargil, steeped in poverty and a Shia Islam, replies that nationalism for her means stability in her life. It means keeping the *mullahs* away from her domain. It means freedom to education and health services. It means that nationalism is mundane and steeped in the everyday life.

Notes and References

1. Originally published in *Canadian Women's Studies*, vol. 19, no. 4, Winter, 2000.
2. Swarna Aiyar "August Anarchy: The Partition Massacres in Punjab 1947," *South Asia Journal of South Asian Studies*, Special Issue on North India: Partition and Independence, vol. 18, 1995, pp. 13–36; Urvashi, Butalia. *The Other Side of Silence: Voices from the Partition of India.* New Delhi, 1998; Ritu, Menon and Kamla Bhasin, *Borders and Boundaries: Women in India's Partition.* New Delhi, 1998.
3. Sumantra Bose, "Hindu Nationalism and the Crisis of Indian State," in Sugata Bose and Ayesha Jalal (eds), *Nationalism, Democracy and Development.* Delhi, 1998, pp. 104–64. I would use the nationalist discourse in Kashmir as a part of an India discourse going by Bose's description that the conflict in Kashmir is not of a Muslim-majority state against a predominantly Hindu state, but of a people against the brutally coercive power of the state as a whole. From a feminist perspective, where women are at the receiving end of state-controlled and militant induced crime, this paradigm is useful.
4. The complexity of Kashmir's history has been documented mostly from a political angle. The best book written to date is Sisir Gupta's, *Kashmir: A Study in India-Pakistan Relations.* New Delhi, 1966; which provides a detailed analysis of the post-Partition phase in an objective manner. Later writings have included Prem Shankar Jha, *Kashmir, 1947: Rival Versions of History.* Delhi, 1996; B. Puri, *Kashmir: Towards Insurgency.* Delhi, 1993; and Sumantra Bose, *The Challenge in Kashmir: Democracy, Self Determination and a Just Peace.* Delhi and London, 1996; which have tried to provide unbiased views but

the Indian perspective is more detailed. Victora Schofield, *Kashmir in the Crossfire*. London, 1996, provides a Pakistani perspective. Mushirul Hasan's, *Legacy of a Divided Nation: India's Muslims Since Independence*. Delhi, 1997; and *India's Partition: Process, Strategy and Mobilization*. Delhi, 1993; and Satya Rai, *Partition of Punjab*. Bombay, 1965; in general have analyzed Partition extremely well. There is some reference to abduction and sale of Kashmiri women by the raiders of 1948, in Menon's history on the integration of Indian states (cited in Misra, K.K. *Kashmir and India's Foreign Policy*. Allahabad, 1979.
5. Sisir Gupta, op. cit.; Prem Shankar Jha, op. cit.
6. Dhar, L.N. "An Outline of the History of Kashmir," in *Kashmir— The Crown of India*. Kanyakumari Vivekananda Kendra, 1984, 1–28.
7. Amartya Sen in his, "On Interpreting India's Past," in Sugata Bose and Ayesha Jalal (eds), op. cit.; argues that in India, the limits of national identity can be compared with the identities associated with first, the more restricted boundaries of community and groups within a nation, and second, the more inclusive coverage of broader categories. The latter, for instance, could be an Asian or even that belonging to the human race. Some identities, he argues, can go beyond the nation, and yet within the nation define a part of it. For instance, the identity of a woman as a Muslim, which is clearly not confined to the limits of a nation, and yet exists within a nation (such as India), will be a correspondingly circumscribed identity (such as being an Indian woman, or an Indian Muslim) (pp. 10–11).
8. Virendra Kumar, *Rape of the Mountains: Kargil (The Untold Story)*. New Delhi, 1999.
9. Kamakshi Bhatay, Saumintra Kitu Rani and Haseena. "People's Human Rights," *Kashmir Times* 4 July 1997.
10. Lalita, Pandit, *Sukeshi Has a Dream and Other Poems of Kashmir*. May 30, 1998 (unpublished).
11. Robert Marquand, "Kashmiris, Forgotton in Conflict," *Christian Science Monitor*, September 6, 1999.
12. The Partition had little legitimacy in the eyes of the majority Hindu state. The dismemberment of the body of "Mother India" was an attack at its honor. The Indian war cry as projected by the soldier remains *Dharti ma ki kasam* (Hindi: I swear in the name of the mother earth) for *Madre Watan* (Urdu: Mother Nation). The Hindus state becomes significant today as the ruling party, the BJP, has been very closely linked ideologically to the RSS, a rightwing Hindu nationalist party which has refused to accept the Partition and the orgins of an Islamic state carved out of Indian territory.
13. Sugata Bose, "Nation as Mother: Representations and Contestations of 'India' in Bengali Literature and Culture," in Sugata Bose and Ayesha Jalal (eds), op. cit.

14. Kashmir University, "National Seminar on Gender and Discrimination in Kashmir Valley," Srinagar, Dept. of Sociology, Kashmir University, August 2–4, 1997; Women's Initiative. *Kashmiri Auroton ka Bayan: Khaki ban gain hain sabz vadhiayan.* Bombay, 1994.
15. Ashima Kaul Bhatia, "Militants Force Sterilization," *New Time* January 5, 1999.
16. K.K. Misra, op. cit.
17. M.K. Akbar, *Kargil: Cross Border Terrorism.* New Delhi, 1999.
18. *The Hindu.* 27 June 1999.
19. The Prime Minister of India with a large group of officials drove across the border in a bus into Pakistan to meet Nawaz Sharif and his colleagues. This diplomatic initiative, after nuclear testing by both states, was seen as the beginning of a peace initiative.
20. The two major groups are Lashkar-e-Toyeba made up of non-Kashmiri Sunnis, and Harkat-ul-Mujahideen which is composed mainly of Afghans, Pakistanis, and even some Arabs.
21. "A Village Between Two Nations," *Outlook,* September 6, 1999.
22. Gaurav C. Sawant, "Three Storey Bunders and Armed Women," *Indian Express,* 15 June 1999.
23. M.K. Akbar, op. cit.
24. There are some other views as provided by army sources that these women are porters forced to bring in weapons and other essential items because, unlike men, they would face less of a threat from Indian armed forces then men.
25. Gupta, Kanchan. Online. www.rediff.com/news/1999/july/6inter.com
26. *The Hindu,* op. cit.
27. J.P. Birdi, Online. www.rediff.com/news/1999/jun/25inter.com
28. Chindu Shreedharan, Online. www.rediff22diary.htm
29. *Indian Express.* 5 June 1999.
30. Tapan K. Bose, "The Other Face of War," *Himal* July 12, 1999.
31. M.K. Akbar, op. cit.
32. Patnaik, Elisa. "Martyrs Kin Locked in Family Battle," *Asian Age,* September 4, 1999, pp. 1, 11.
33. Bishkha De Sarkar, "The Answer is Blowing in the Wind," *The Telegraph.* 25 July 1999, p. 19.
34. M. Prasad, "In Bihar, Widows of 1971 War Still Wait for Compensation," *Indian Express.* 28 June 1999, p. 5.
35. M.K. Akbar, op. cit.
36. Margaret Owen, *A World of Widows.* London, 1996; provides an incisive analysis of the status of widows of South Asia.
37. V. Mohan Giri and Meera Khanna, "Prisoners for Life: The Sorry Plight of War Widows," *The Times of India,* 21 July 1999, p. 14.
38. M.K. Akbar, op. cit.
39. Nandini R. Iyer, "Chinks in the Armour," *The Sunday Statesman,* 11 July 1999, p. 2.

40. Sitralega Maunaguru, "Gendering Tamil Nationalism: The Construction of 'Woman' in Projects of Protests and Control," in Pradeep Jeganathan and Qadri Ismail (eds), *Unmaking the Nation: The Politics of Identity and History in Modern Sri Lanka.* Colombo, 1995.
41. Cynthia Enloe, *Bananas, Beaches and Bases.* Berkeley, 1969.
42. Veena Das, *Critical Events: An Anthropological Perspective on Contemporary India.* Delhi, 1995.
43. I take the nationalist discourse here as Sudipta Kaviraj in "On the Structure of Nationalist Discourse," in T.V. Satyamurthy (ed.), *State and Nation in the Context of Social Change.* Vol. 1, Delhi, 1994; refers it—an intellectual process through which the conception of an India (read Kashmiri) nation is gradually formed and the discourse that forms it is in favor of it and gives it historical shape (p. 301).
44. Khomeini in 1980 ordered *Hijab* (curtain) Law and ordered women working in the state sector to veil. In Kargil, the women always covered their heads but the veil was never in practice. The Mullahs took up Khomeini's diktat though their power to implement the law was limited.

14

NATIONALITIES, ETHNIC PROCESSES, AND VIOLENCE IN INDIA'S NORTHEAST[1]

Monirul Hussain

The Northeast is a generic term, which includes seven Indian states, that is, Arunachal Pradesh, Assam, Manipur, Meghalaya, Mizoram, Nagaland, and Tripura. These seven states are also commonly called "Seven Sisters." Except for the former princely states of Manipur and Tripura, all other states were parts of British colonial Assam. The political map of Northeast/Assam transformed very significantly during the post-colonial period. In this process of transformation—the post-colonial Indian state, nationalism and ethnicity played very decisive role. It affected all the communities and propelled modification in the structure, identity, self-definition, and the definition of the *other*. Admittedly, the nationality question and in a wider sense the ethnic question is very complex in India's Northeast. We have tried to comprehend this question elsewhere in more details.[2] The Northeast is a very distinctive geopolitical entity in India having an area of 255,083 sq. km with more than 31 million population as per the Census of India 1991. The Northeast accounts for 7.7 percent of India's total area and 3.73 percent of India's vast population. The objective of this paper is to report the national and ethnic question and its resultant conflicts in India's Northeast in general and Assam in particular. Though the objective looks simple, the reporting is unlikely to be so as the phenomena involved here are very complex, wide, heterogeneous, uneven, subtle, and sensitive.

Geographically speaking, this region has both hills and valleys. The hill areas cover nearly 70 percent and the plains cover the remaining 30 percent of the total area of Northeast. Apart from hills, Assam has two valleys—the Brahmaputra and the Barak. These two valleys are divided by the Barail range of hills in which two of Assam's remaining hill districts (Karbi Anglong and North Cachar Hills) are located. Manipur has a small valley called the Imphal valley. The remaining areas of the entire Northeast are covered by hills. The peculiar topography of Northeast has been favorable for various insurgent outfits that have been fighting for secession from the Indian Union. Needless to say the valleys are densely populated and the hills are sparsely populated. Whereas in the hills, the indigenous tribal people are in majority and in the valleys the non-tribal population is in majority. Out of seven states of the region, four are predominantly tribal and the remaining three have substantial Scheduled Tribe population. Arunachal Pradesh has more tribal population than it has been shown in the census data if we include the non-indigenous tribal groups particularly the Chakmas and the Hajongs who have been living there since 1964. In fact tribal population in Assam is much higher than it has been shown because non-indigenous tribal people such as like the Santhals, Oraons and Mundas etc. living in Assam have not been "Scheduled" in Assam unlike West Bengal, Bihar, Orissa, and Madhya Pradesh etc., Besides, quite a few "Other Backward Classes" are demanding for scheduling of their community into "official" tribal category. In addition to tribals, the Ahom, Koch-Rajbongshis and Chutiyas etc., belong to South Asia, the culture complex of the entire region has significant elements of South-East Asian region. Distinctively, like South-East Asia, the large majority of population of Northeast racially belongs to the Mongoloid groups. A perceptive journalist observes vividly:

> The girls of Imphal in Manipur who ride cycles and scooters, resemble their Thai and Lao counterparts. They could easily be placed either in Bangkok or Vietnam. The seductively swaying Manipuri dances are similar to the gentle rhythms of the Khmers and Laotians as well as the Thais and Indonesians. The distinctive shawls of Nagaland, Manipur, and Mizoram each colorful strand proclaiming a tribe, a lifestyle and identity, share a commonality with communities across the borders of Myanmar and Thailand.[3]

It would be pertinent to point out that society in Northeast is fundamentally a multi-religious and its religious composition is relatively different from the rest of India. In terms of religion, Meghalaya, Mizoram, and Nagaland are Christian majority states wherein most of the tribals have been Christianized. However, in tribal majority Arunachal Pradesh, most of the inhabitants follow their traditional tribal religion and others follow either Tibetan or Myanmarese variety of Buddhism. Though in Assam majority of the people belong to Hinduism of two different sects (*Shaktas* and *Vaisnavas*), here the caste is practised in a very loose form. Manipur and Tripura are also Hindu majority states with a substantial Muslim, Buddhist, Christian and other population. Assam has a substantial Muslim population i.e., 28 percent of the total population of the state. In terms of percentage of Muslim population among the Indian states, Assam stands only next to the state of Jammu and Kashmir. Besides, the linguistic composition of Northeast is also very complex and different from the mainland India. Apart from three non-tribal Scheduled Languages such as, the Asamiya, Bengali, and Manipuri, the people of Northeast use more than 200 languages and dialects.

Contrast to valley's settled agriculture, the dominant mode of agriculture in the hills is *jhum*—the slash-and-burn method of agriculture. In the wake of penetration of capitalist mode of production in agriculture since early 1970s, many parts of India experienced the "Green Revolution" but the hills of Northeast are still trapped viciously in the primitive mode of agricultural production. The slash-and-burn method even cannot generate the bare minimal subsistence level of the community involved in such practice. Even the areas where settled agriculture is dominant, for example, the Brahmaputra valley, its agricultural production is far below the demand of the valley. It is estimated that Assam has to pay Rs 100 million annually to import food grains. All this demonstrates the precariousness of agricultural production in Northeast and its weak position in India's growing agricultural economy.

During the post-colonial period some regions/states in India have developed very rapidly, for example Punjab, Haryana, Karnataka, Gujarat, Maharashtra, Western Uttar Pradesh and the Capital Region of Delhi. Here, we must note that the entire Northeast has remained economically backward even by Indian standard with severe unevenness among seven states and various communities living therein. It virtually lacks industries to boost its economy. Besides, the region has remained demographically the fastest growing and most heterogeneous in India, culturally diverse, politically very sensitive and volatile, socially highly plural and located away from the mainland India in its northeast. Obviously, its location has its own strategic importance. This region is surrounded by China, Myanmar, Bhutan, and Bangladesh. No region in India other than the Northeast is surrounded by four foreign countries. The Northeast is connected with the mainland India through a narrow corridor between southeast of Nepal and south of Bhutan and north of Bangladesh.

We conceptualize the Northeast as a periphery within a larger periphery (India) in the global context. The Northeast suffers from being both far from the center and decisively dependent on it. Consequently, this region's integration with the post-colonial Indian nation-state has remained problematic. Several aberrations have already strained the process of integration with India. It has been questioned and at times challenged from the below against the dominant discourse of national integration. The popular consciousness and culture of Northeast today posits significantly away from India's *Cowbelt/ Aryavarta/Akhand Bharat*.

Historically speaking, substantial parts of this region, particularly its hill areas, were neither a part of pre-colonial Assam nor of pre-colonial India. Even the Brahmaputra valley stood at the periphery of the Indian economy and polity till the British colonized it. The colonial incorporation of the Northeast took place much later than the rest of the Indian subcontinent. Significantly, the British took much more time, stretching from the second quarter of the 19th century to the end of it, to complete the region's colonization process. While pre-colonial (Ahom) Assam was annexed in 1826, its neighboring Bengal had been annexed as early as 1763. The colonial rulers had to wait until 1873 to bring the Garo tribal population under their control, while the annexation of the Naga hills was completed only in 1889.

Similarly, though the British rulers established their control over the Mizos, then known as Lushais, between 1871–89, they could form the Lushai Hills district only in 1898. Amlendu Guha has rightly pointed out that "The boundaries of the British power in Northeast India were in fact always moving, always in flux right up to its last days in India."[4] Neverthless, the British province that came to be known as Assam took shape more or less by 1873.

It is pertinent to point out that the pre-colonial society in Assam was fundamentally semi-tribal and semi-feudal in nature, with a mix of more than one classical mode of production. It generated a very limited surplus and obviously had a very limited market. Although an oppressive system—even by Mughal standards—with its resultant backwardness, it must be admitted that its economy was largely self-sufficient, enabling it to maintain its distance from India. This, together with its geographical factors, help us in explaining the perpetuation of Ahom rule for as long as 600 years, beginning from 1228 and ending in 1826, when it was annexed by the British. The Asamiyas as a nation or nationality did not emerge in pre-colonial Assam. However, it should be noted that the Asamiya language and literature developed substantially in a myriad-tongued society. Even the ruling Ahom clan gave up its Tai/Thai language and accepted Asamiya, as did the Hindus and the Muslims who came from northern India/Bengal. The art of writing was known in Assam since the 6th century AD and the present Asamiya script had taken shape by the 12th century AD. The development of the Asamiya language and literature and performing arts, particularly with the emergence of Vaisnavism, and the resistance by the people of Assam, irrespective of religion and race, against the Mughal, substantially contributed in cementing the unity and stability of the Asamiyas as a pre-national collectivity in pre-colonial Assam.

The colonization gradually broke the isolation of Assam by linking it with the colonial capitalist world economy, a break that was historically very significant for Assam and the Asamiyas. Initially, Assam was made a new division of Bengal. However, in 1874, it became a new province of British India. Very significantly, this new province included the thickly populated Sylhet region, which historically and ethnically belonged to Bengal. This arrangement ended only with the partitioning of the country in 1947, when Sylhet opted to join East Pakistan.

The creation of the new province was obviously designed to weaken both the Asamiyas and the Bengalis and to pave the way for Asamiya–Bengali competition and conflict under the colonial aegis. Nearly all the hill areas of the Northeast with their innumerable tribal groups, as well as the Cachar areas, became part of colonial Assam, in addition to what was traditionally Asamiya homeland which the Asamiyas had been sharing with many autochthon tribals like the Bodos, Mishings, Rabhas, Lalungs, and Deuris, as well as other Mongoloid groups like the Morans, Motaks, Ahoms, Borahis, and Chutiyas. Though the province was named Assam, it was in fact "an amalgam of Asamiya-speaking, Bengali-speaking and myriad-tongued hill tribal areas in which Asamiya was claimed the mothertongue of less than a quarter and Bengali of more than 40 percent of population."[5]

The size of pre-colonial Assam swelled significantly in colonial Assam wherein the Asamiyas became a minority and the second largest group after the Bengalis. However, they remained demographically strong in Assam proper i.e., the Brahmaputra valley. The drastic changes in its territory, the new political situation and colonial economy opened the floodgates of social and demographic transformation of the hitherto stagnant and unchanging Assam with serious social implications.

We know that nations are products of historical development covering long periods of time beginning with the decline of feudalism and the emergence of capitalism. In the Indian context, however, neither the decline of feudalism nor the emergence of capitalism from within played a decisive role in the rise of Indian nationalism. Rather, it was the penetration of British colonialism and the response of the Indian people to this colonialism/imperialism that gave birth to Indian nationalism. Although the process of nationality formation among the Asamiyas under the colonial situation started late in the Indian subcontinental context, it would be improper to isolate it from the operative trend of general Indian nationalism. In India, since the beginning of the 19th century:

> Nationalism has been developing at two levels—one all India on the basis of pan-Indian homogeneities and an anti-imperialism shared in

common; and another regional (Bengali, Marathi, Asamiya, etc.) on the basis of regional cultural homogeneities. From the very outset, the two nationalisms are found intertwined and dovetailed. Traditionally, an average Indian identifies himself with both the nationalisms except in some peripheral areas (e.g., Nagaland and Mizoram) untouched by the railways and by the Indian national movement.[6]

In fact, in the context of the Northeast, the Asamiyas were the first group to integrate with the rest of India economically, politically, culturally, and emotionally. Guha has rightly pointed out that like an average Indian, an Asamiya, too, is simultaneously aware of both his regional and Indian identities.[7]

By Asamiya we very specifically mean the people who have accepted the Asamiya language as their mothertongue. Needless to say, the term also includes neo-Asamiyas such as Na-Asamiya Muslims, assimilated autochthon tribals of the Brahmaputra valley and the black tribals who have accepted the Asamiya language and nationality. We would also like to clarify why we are calling the Asamiyas a nationality and not a nation. Though it is very difficult to strictly separate nationality from a nation, even then, we have preferred to call Asamiya a nationality mainly because it has not grown fully and it is still growing. Besides, it is relatively small in size compared to major nations like the Bengalis, the Marathis, the Tamils of the multinational Indian society.

Both the trends—the pan-Indian nationalism and the regional nationalism are largely secular in content and spirit. In Northeast, the Asamiyas are the largest national group with a state of their own, the second being the Bengalis living in the region. However, after Independence, in the absence of an all powerful "colonialism" regional nationalism has sharpened—a Tamil became more Tamil, an Asamiya became more Asamiya, though in the context of post-colonial nation-state he remained an Indian at the same time. Besides certain subaltern groups at the margin of the Indian society and history, for example the various tribal groups of Northeast experienced ethnic nationalism during the post-colonial period. This in other words may be called nationalism of national minorities of India. When we talk of ethnicity here in this paper we are in fact referring specifically to the ethnicity of tribal groups living in Northeast/Assam.

COLONIAL TRANSFORMATION

Though Assam had a rich tradition of *Buranjis* (chronicles) since the arrival of the Ahoms in AD 1228, the pre-colonial aristocracy had neither the knowledge nor experience of keeping written and formal administrative and land records. As a consequence, it did not fit into the new system based on the colonial bureaucratic principles of maintaining written and formal records of administration, justice, and land revenue, etc. Besides, western education became a pre-condition for obtaining jobs in the new colonial administration. The colonial state had no intention of educating/training the Asamiyas so soon after colonization. This led to a decline of the pre-colonial Asamiyas in colonial Assam. This also explains the colonial rationale of importing Bengali *babu* to man colonial bureaucracy.

We have already noted that the British had colonized Bengal much earlier than Assam. As a result, a new, western educated middle class emerged from among the high caste Bengali Hindus, and consolidated its position in the Bengal Presidency.[8] It was thus possible for the colonial rulers to avoid investment in western education in Assam, and avail instead of the services of the already surplus, educated-unemployed persons from Bengal Presidency.[9] In the absence of an indigenous Asamiya middle class for a long period of time, the Bengalis virtually monopolized nearly all the jobs in the colonial administration. In addition, many more Bengalis came to Assam as lawyers, teachers, private doctors, shopkeepers, jewellers, traders, tailors and so on. Not surprisingly, they became very conspicuous in the colonial administration and emerging urban centers of Assam.

Besides the Bengalis, the Nepalis also came to Assam as part of the colonial army.[10] Many Biharis came in as laborers. In the absence of an indigenous business caste or class, the migrant Marwaris filled up the vacuum in business, trade, and banking. Apart from Sylhet, Assam is a naturally rich though thinly populated province. The colonial rulers therefore openly encouraged massive migration of various groups into Assam in order to augment their land revenue by bringing more land under cultivation and habitation. In order to avoid the dual oppression of colonialism and feudalism in East Bengal, many poor peasants migrated to the Brahmaputra valley. Again, in the absence of a local labor force, the colonial state patronized and created conditions for massive migration of tribal population, mainly from the Jharkhand areas, to meet the growing demands of cheap labor for the British-owned tea plantations in Assam. In other words, the colonial situation propelled massive migration into Assam and, in the process, changed its demographic structure radically. The colonial state provoked and patronized the Asamiya-non-Asamiya conflict in colonial Assam though colonialism itself had created the conditions of massive migration to Assam. It did not allow the Asamiya nationality to grow and hindered the assimilation process of various groups. It encouraged national hostility and exclusiveness in Assam.

By and large, education was badly neglected in colonial Assam. The response to western education among the Asamiyas was crippled by the colonial suppression of the Asamiya language from 1837 to 1874. It took more than a decade to reintroduce Asamiya as the language of school and courts in the Brahmaputra valley. The colonial suppression of Asamiya in its own homeland and its replacement by another language of a neighboring province, Bengali, created the conditions for reactionary conflict between the speakers of the two sister languages. Thus, while the suppression of Asamiya to a large extent delayed the popular urge for western education, the existence of an already large number of educated unemployed in Bengal meant that the colonial rulers could well afford to ignore the expansion of education in Assam.

The first and the second high schools in Assam were started in as late as 1835 and 1841 respectively. Bengal got its first university (of Calcutta) in 1857, but Assam had to wait for a university until after the collapse of colonial rule: the first university (Guwahati) of Assam was officially started only in 1948. Even the first college of the Brahmaputra valley was established only at the beginning of the 20th century. All these factors point to the belated development of education in Assam and its relative educational backwardness compared to Bengal.

However despite such colonial constraints, a new Calcutta-oriented Asamiya middle class gradually emerged in the late 19th century. Obviously, it was a weak and very small middle class located in the colonial hinterland. This incipient Asamiya middle class composed of high castes like Brahmins, Kayasthas, Kalitas and a few Asamiya Muslims, took special interest in developing the Asamiya language and literature. Gradually, the language became an important and perhaps the most sensitive symbol of the Asamiya middle class and nationality.

The colonial situation imposed on the Asamiya middle class stiff competition from the migrant Bengali middle class. Initially, this class responded by collaborating with the colonial rulers. However, with the emergence and consolidation of the national movement for freedom, the growing popularity of the Congress party and the consolidation of the Asamiya middle class in the 20th century, a large section of this class could gradually outgrow its collaborative role. This Assam `.ssociation, which was the first valley-wide political organization, helped mould the Asamiya national consciousness. And with the merger of the Assam Association with the Indian National Congress in 1920, the Asamiya middle class in particular and the Asamiya masses in general became part of the pan-Indian nationalism with a distinct regional identity. However, a section of the Muslim middle class was attracted towards the Muslim League. They formed the provincial government for five times within a period of seven years (1938–45). This contributed significantly in the growth of anti-Muslim feeling among the Asamiya Hindu middle class. Significantly, many middle class Muslims such as Fakhruddin Ali Ahmed (who became the fifth President of India) and Maulana Tyabullah were among the top ranking Congress leaders.[11] The colonial Assam witnessed both secular and communal political mobilizations.

Compared to the Brahmaputra valley, the hill areas of present-day states as Nagaland, Mizoram, Arunachal Pradesh, became part of colonial India much later. By and large, the colonial state maintained a policy of *status quo* and isolation for the tribal people of the Northeast virtually insulating them from the plainsmen and the national movement for freedom. The enforcement of an "Inner Line" system in 1873 in most of the hill areas reflected their policy. In addition, the Government of India Act of 1935 made most of the hill areas of the Northeast "excluded areas," wherein provincial legislature had no jurisdiction. A.C. Bhagabati pertinently pointed out that the

"... tribal communities of this region thus remained virtually isolated from social and political developments taking place elsewhere in the country. There was little scope for the hill tribal people's participation in the electoral processes which commenced elsewhere well before independence."[12] However, we must note that though the colonial state took an apparently non-interfering line, its ally, the Christian missions, penetrated the hill tribal population and succeeded in converting a good number of them to Christianity. It is the missionaries who introduced them to modern medicine and western education.

However, the situation in the Brahmaputra valley was different. The tribal people of the plains like the Bodos, Rabhas, Sonowals, Lalungs, Mishings, and Deuris were well integrated with both pan-Indian as well as Asamiya nationalism. They, too, participated in the freedom movement. Significantly, most of the plains were Hinduized long before Assam was colonized. We have noted earlier that racially, the majority of the people of Assam belonged to various Mongoloid groups. The Ahoms, Koch-Rajbongshis, Chutiyas, Morans, Motaks, Borahis, etcetera, who came from Mongoloid stock, integrated well with the Asamiya nationality and pan-Indian nationalism.

So did the high caste, minority Hindus—Asamiya Brahmins, Grahabipras, Kayasthas, Kalitas and Keots—and other low caste Asamiyas and Asamiya Muslims comprising the Syeds, Goria, Moria, and Julahas. However, two large migrant groups—the black tribals engaged as plantation labor and the oppressed Muslim peasants who came from East Bengal—were not well integrated with the Asamiya nationality in colonial Assam. By the time India attained independence, the Asamiyas were the most advanced nationality in the Northeast and among the Asamiyas, the high castes were the most advanced group in an economically backward, multi-racial, multi-religious, multi-class and multi-lingual regional society.

Post-Colonial Transformation

India attained independence and British colonialism collapsed in the subcontinent in 1947. However, the neo-colonial/imperial hegemony continued through its control over the oil and tea industries. As a result of independence and partition, Assam lost its Muslim and Bengali dominated and thickly populated Sylhet district to East Pakistan. This substantially reduced the number and percentage of both Muslims and Bangalis in post-colonial Assam. However, the predominantly Bengali speaking Cachar district in Barak Valley remained with Assam. Except for NEFA (now Arunachal Pradesh), Manipur and Tripura, the entire hill region of the Northeast remained with Assam, in addition to Assam proper, i.e., the Brahmaputra valley.

Independence and partition thus made the Asamiyas numerically and politically stronger in post-colonial Assam. For the first time, they became the single largest group in Assam. The Bengalis declined and gradually lost their dominance. The Muslims, who were enthusiastically involved in Muslim League's divisive politics in Assam, also lost their political relevance. The tribal groups, both in the hills and the plains, remained largely backward, as did all other non-caste Mongoloid groups like the Ahoms, Koch-Rajbongshis, Chutiyas, Morans, Motaks and Borahis. In such a situation, the Asamiya middle class composed mainly of Asamiya high caste Hindus consolidated their position. They started dominating state politics, exercising their hegemony over the Asamiyas, the neo-Asamiyas and non-Asamiya groups in post-colonial Assam. The exertion of this hegemony, and the response to it of various groups, together with the nature of socio-economic and cultural development, very significantly determined the nationality and ethnic question in the hills and plains of Assam during the post-colonial period.

The nature of the political system and the composition of the ruling class were transformed after independence. It is therefore necessary to understand the nature and composition of the Indian ruling class and its role in resolving and accentuating the nationality question. The Indian ruling classes are composed of the bourgeoisie and landlords. Obviously, the big Indian bourgeoisie plays the most dominant role in the coalition of these two classes. Recently, Rudra has argued very forcefully that the intelligentsia too has become a partner of the Indian ruling class.[13] In a country like India with federal structure, there are also state-level depositories of power.[14] The ruling class in India obviously operates at two levels—the all-India and the state/regional levels. Though the ruling class at the state level is a part of the Indian ruling class, at times it tries to assert its limited autonomy/identity at the state/regional level in order to wrest some concessions to ensure its survival, growth, and power.

Assam, too, has its state-level ruling class. The Asamiya ruling class has been playing a very significant role in determining and influencing the national question in the Northeast together with the Indian ruling class. Obviously the Asamiya ruling class includes a very small and weak Asamiya bourgeoisie composed of a few tea-planters, owners of powerful regional presses, transport operators, contractors, professionals, the middle class, and the rural gentry. The majority of them belong to Asamiya high caste groups. They plunder the state in their private interest and exert their hegemony over the entire regional society. It is true that the Asamiya ruling class in not bourgeois in a clearly productive sense, but is inclined towards it ideologically and culturally.

Without a clear role in production and in a weaker position vis-à-vis the Indian ruling class, it is forced by the objective situation to enforce its hegemony through its control over the government apparatus in the state. Because of its caste and class limitations, the Asamiya ruling class has always been very reluctant to share power and benefits even with other oppressed sections of the same nationality, leave alone non-Asamiyas. It has been fairly successful in projecting its own class interest as the interest of the Asamiya nationality or of the people of Assam. It has also been able to pass off its own identity crisis as the crisis of the Asamiya nationality or of Assam as a whole.

In order to exploit its natural resources and markets more profitably, the Indian ruling class needs an ally in Assam and for this it is prepared to grant some concession to the Asamiya ruling class. This class in its turn neither led nor participated in any movement for Assam's economic development. However, this class very enthusiastically participated and led the Assam movement 1979–85.[15] Because of its class interest and very sectarian approach, it even failed to reach the goals of the movement. Like other ruling class movements, this movement also encouraged national exclusiveness and hostility, oppression, violence, and riots forcing the common Asamiyas, Na-Asamiyas and non-Asamiyas living in Assam to suffer immensely. This movement created conditions for the emergence of the United Liberation Front of Asom (ULFA)—an insurgent outfit to challenge the integration of Assam with India. Despite this, the horizon of the Asamiya nationality expanded significantly after independence. Notwithstanding the massive migration during the colonial and post-colonial period, the Asamiyas have not lost their identity. Significantly, most of the oppressed migrant groups, particularly the black tribals, Santhals, Mundas, Oraons, etc., who work mainly as tea-plantation labor, and the migrant East Bengal peasants have identified themselves with the Asamiya nationality. Although they have already adopted Asamiya as their mother tongue, they naturally need more time in order to become fully Asamiyaized. However, we must point out that the new generation is more Asamiyaized than the earlier generation. The process of Asamiyaization is thus likely to become more consolidated in the coming years.

Over the years, the Asamiyas have grown faster than any other group in Assam, maintaining their numerical dominance in the state. This shows the historical capacity of the Asamiya nationality to absorb and accept migrant groups into its fold. The Asamiya language too, has firmly consolidated its position. It is both the official language of the state, and the medium of instruction upto graduate level (together with English) in Assam's two universities. It is also the most popular and advanced language backed by a rich literature.

However, the fact remains that a substantial number of people belonging to several groups are yet to merge fully with the Asamiya nationality. In fact, some of the groups who have already been assimilated are now seriously trying to revive their old identity because of their oppressed status and hatred against the Asamiya ruling class. While, at the present stage of political development, the black tribals and the Na-Asamiya Muslims have by and large accepted their own oppressed status and the dominant status of the Asamiya high caste ruling class, the autochthon tribals of Assam are not prepared to do so. This is one of the reasons behind the forceful emergence of tribal movements in Assam immediately after the institutionalization of the Assam movement of 1985.

Tribals of Brahmaputra Valley After Independence

We have noted earlier that the plains' tribal populations have been sharing their traditional homeland—the Brahmaputra valley—with the Asamiyas. It is therefore almost impossible to isolate the rich tribal elements from the composite Asamiya society, culture, and nationality. According to the last census, the Scheduled Tribes constituted 13 percent of the total population of Assam. The Bodos, Mishings, Sonowals, Ravas, and Tiwas demographically occupy the first, second, third, fourth, and fifth positions respectively. Needless to say, the tribal people were the first natives of Assam's plains and hills. Unlike the hill tribal people, the plains' tribal people own land individually, not communally. They could not make any significant progress in colonial Assam. And while they did make some progress during the post-colonial period, other groups progressed even further, thereby increasing the social distance between them and the plains' tribal population.

In addition, the Asamiya ruling class has successfully kept the plains' tribal people from acquiring even the limited benefits that have accrued to the hill tribal ones. The Indian constitution provides the hill tribal population some autonomy in managing their own society through the provision of the Sixth Schedule. This was not, however, extended to the plains' tribal population. It would be worthwhile to state that the tribal people are perpetually experiencing the problem of land alienation, poverty, indebtedness, severe unemployment, economic exploitation, and cultural and political oppression. At the time of independence, the plains' tribal dominated areas were classified as "tribal blocks" and "tribal belts," ostensibly to protect the tribal population from the penetration of non-tribal population into their areas. The Asamiya ruling class, which was responsible for these schemes, made a mockery of them by allowing non-tribal people to purchase land and property in tribal areas.

In colonial Assam, the tribal dialects/languages remained neglected. During the post-colonial period, however, with the growing consciousness of their identity among the plains' tribal population and the support they have received from the progressive and democratic sections of the non-tribal population, some attention has recently been paid to the development of their dialects/languages. For instance, the Bodos have developed their language in the Devnagri script and it is now the medium of the instruction up to the secondary level in Bodo-dominated areas. The Mishings have adopted the Roman script for developing their language that, from 1986, has been the medium of instruction at the primary level in Mishing-dominitated areas. The Deuris, the Tiwas, and the Ravas have adopted the Asamiya script for developing their respective languages. It should be pointed out that all these tribes not only stand at uneven levels among themselves in terms of social economic and political development, they also stand unevenly in terms of their assimilation with and exclusion from the Asamiyas. For example, the Sonowal and the Meches of Upper Assam have completely assimilated and identified with the Asamiyas.

In the absence of a well-developed/developing language of their own, the plains' tribal people accepted Asamiya voluntarily as the medium of instruction/education. As a consequence, they were regarded as sub-nationalities within the composite Asamiya nationality. However, the official imposition of the Asamiya language in 1960 had resulted in a severe backlash from the tribals both in the hills and plains. In addition, from the late 1960s onward, the plains' tribals became more conscious and articulate about their ethnic identity, using it to gain political power and overcome their socio-economic backwardness and oppression. The problems regarding their right to traditional land, their language and script, identity, culture, economic development, discrimination, exploitation and, more significantly, their demand for political autonomy are yet to be resolved to their satisfaction.

HILL TRIBAL POPULATION AFTER INDEPENDENCE

By the time India entered the post-colonial phase, a very small but distinguishable group of educated tribal elites emerged among the Nagas, Mizos, and Khasis as a result of their exposure to Christianity and western education, largely under the aegis of the Christian missions. This small group acted as motivators of social and political change in their respective societies. They were exceedingly conscious of their distinct ethnic identity, which they vociferously articulated in order to fulfill their political aspirations under the changed situation. They were also acutely conscious of their oppressed status in the Asamiya ruling class-dominated Assam as an integral part of India. Some of them even felt that India should grant them sovereignty and recognize them as friends rather than a part of India. It was this feeling, fuelled by their incomplete integration with India that led to the rise of insurgency in the Naga hills during early 1950s and in the Lushai (Mizo) hills during the mid-1960s.

Despite severe state oppression on the one hand, and a liberal policy of appeasing and corrupting the tribal elites on the other, insurgency and secessionist tendencies have not died down fully even today. By the time one group comes over-ground, another group goes under. Earlier, one was used to hearing about Naga and Mizo insurgency. Now, several other groups have emerged—the Peoples' Liberation Army (PLA), the Peoples' Revolutionary Party of Kangleipak (PREPAK), the United Liberation Front (of Meiteis), the National Socialist Council of Nagaland (NSCN), the Tripura Volunteer Force (TVF), and the United Liberation Front of Asom (ULFA). These organizations do not only represent the frustration of the youth of various ethnic groups; they also represent the failure of the post-colonial Indian state to resolve the nationality/ethnic question in the Northeast.

In order to meet the aspirations of the hill tribals, the Sixth Schedule of the Indian Constitution granted them some autonomy in the form of Autonomous District Council in addition to other protective measures. Accordingly, the major hill tribal groups—Nagas, Mizos, Khasis, Jaintias, Garos, Karbis, and Dimasa-Kacharis—got limited autonomy regarding internal matters. However, it was gradually realized that the autonomy granted to them through the statutory provisions was not adequate enough under the Asamiya-dominated state legislature and government. The intransigent language policy of the state government alienated the hill tribal people from the Asamiyas.

It was under such a situation that the question of Assam's reorganization came up. Eventually, the Naga Hills district became Nagaland in 1963, the United Khasi and Jaintia Hills and Garo Hills districts together became Meghalaya, an autonomous state within the state of Assam[16] which was later elevated to a full-fledged state in 1972. The Lushai Hills became Mizoram, a union territory that later achieved full statehood. Only the Karbi and the Dimasa-Kachari dominated Karbi-Anglong and the North Cachar Hill districts decided to stay with Assam. Now, even in these two hill districts, the tribals are agitating for an autonomous state within the state of Assam. What is important to note is that the separation of hill tribals was largely guided by their hatred of the Asamiya ruling class and their incomplete/weak integration with India along with a consciousness of their identity that sharpened very significantly during the post-colonial phase.

The Mizos have got Mizoram, the Nagas have got Nagaland and the Khasi-Jaintias and the Garos have together got Meghalaya in their traditional homeland. The dominant majority of these tribals are Christians. However, the nature of ethnic coalition in these tribal states differs significantly. Nagaland is fundamentally a state of about a dozen tribal groups with a pan-Naga identity. The same is true of the Mizos in Mizoram. However, it was a political coalition between the Khasi-Jayantias and the Garos who was responsible for the formation of the state of Meghalaya. It is appropriate to point out here that many Naga groups are living outside Nagaland, i.e., in Assam, Manipur, Arunachal Pradesh, and Burma (now Myanmar). Similarly, there are demands for a unification of ethnically contiguous parts of India, Burma and Bangladesh to create a "Greater Mizoram."

In the same way, there are Khasi and Garo inhabited areas in Assam and Bangladesh. Manipur has a large hill tribal population besides the Meities. There are serious problems of adjustment.

ETHNIC CONFLICT AND VIOLENCE: THE PRESENT SITUATION

Our discussion on the nationality and ethnic process will remain incomplete if we fail to situate the link between these processes and with the emergence of political violence. Sharpening of nationality and ethnic identity has manifested in the emergence of violence. Besides, the state too played a crucial role in creating conditions for violence. Over the years political violence has virtually come to occupy the center-stage from its fringe. Needless to say violence has been a part of social transformation in Northeast. Both sociology and history point to the fact that traditional and modern societies are less vulnerable to violence and instability than a society in rapid transition like Northeast.

The Nagas were the first to revolt against their integration with the post-colonial nation-state in India. The Indian state too responded violently against a small ethnic group when there were scopes for dialogue. A section of Mizos took up arms in 1966 and state too responded with its arms. The Mizo insurgency ended in 1986 after an accord with the Government of India. This was the only successful political accord signed by the leadership of an ethnic-insugent movement and the Government of India. But surprisingly, when dominant Mizos gave up arms a minority ethnic group the Hmars took up arms in order to press for their ethnic demands. Today, Mizoram is the only state in the Northeast where a peaceful situation exists.

The Naga insurgency still continues with periodic lull notwithstanding the creation of Nagaland as a state for the Nagas in 1963. The area of operation of Naga insurgents has widened significantly despite security operations. The National Socialist Council of Nagaland (NSCN) today operates far beyond Nagaland. Besides, it trains the other insurgent groups of the Northeast —the United Liberation Front of Asom (ULFA), the Bodo Security Force (Bd.SF), Peoples Liberation Army etc. It has been able to form an apex body to coordinate the activities of various insurgent groups. The insurgents in Nagaland are virtually running parallel government there. And, now they have started a parallel administration in Assam's North Cachar Hill district too.

In Manipur today, the ethnic situation is very grim. Conflict exists between the Meities and non-Meities. Recently Hindu–Muslim conflicts also surfaced. The perennial Naga–Kuki conflicts have resulted in killing thousands. Besides insurgency and inter and intra-tribal conflicts, the society in Manipur is threatened by dreaded AIDS. The spread of AIDS in Manipur has its roots in the nexus between insurgents and the drug peddlers.

In Tripura too the situation is far from normal. The tribal insurgents have been fighting against the migrant/refugee

Bengalis. The violence against the migrants has been continuing in Tripura since the beginning of massacre of Mandai in 1980. The Left Front government in the state tried seriously to end the conflict and provided some autonomy to the indigenous tribal population. However, the Congress Government made mess of it by using the insurgency against the Left forces. Tripura is an example where the migrants and refugees of East Pakistan, i.e., the Bangali Hindus became the majority in the aftermath of partition and the indigenous tribal population became the minority in their traditional homeland.

Meghalaya attained statehood through a remarkably peaceful political movement with a stable coalition of three major tribes, that is, the Khasis, the Jaintias, and the Garos. Now the society in Meghalaya is not in peace—the tribal people are now becoming increasingly restive though the tribals run the state government. There exists strong resentment against the Hindu Bengalis who have permanently settled down in Khasi Hills/Shillong. Most of the Bengalis of Shillong came from East Bengal/East Pakistan as migrants/refugees.[17] Even here, some of tribal youths have taken up arms for insurgency and violence against the migrants.

In Arunachal Pradesh the situation is peaceful but there exists a serious threat to peace and order. An ethnic movement led by the All Arunachal Pradesh Student's Union (APSU) has been demanding the expulsion of Chakma, Hajong, and Tibetan refugees/stateless people from the soil of Arunachal Pradesh. The Tibetans came with the Dalai Lama when he fled Tibet to India through Arunachal Pradesh (then NEFA). The Chakmas and the Hajongs numbering 66,000 came to India during the mid-1960s in the wake of India–Pakistan war of 1965. The Government of India settled them in NEFA when it was in deep slumber. With NEFA's transformation into Arunachal Pradesh and growth of ethnicity among the indigenous tribals the Chakmas and the Hajongs who are in fact tribal people of non-indigenous origin became the *persona-non-grata* in the state.[18]

In Assam the situation is much more complex today. During the entire post-colonial period Assam has been experiencing a series of unending social and political movements and its resultant violence repeatedly. Apodictically, the society in Assam has transformed into a notoriously violent one without any tangible sign of abnegation. This has not happened very abruptly—it has a long history of growth and maturity. Apart from the communal violence in the wake of India's partition, particularly in districts of lower Assam, society again experienced violences during the two important movements based on the linguistic and cultural identity of the Asamiyas in 1960 and 1972. Further, since the beginning of Assam Movement (1979–85), Assam has been churned in the cauldron of communal, ethnic, and state violence. Some instances of them are the North Kamrup pogrom of 1980 in which a large number of people belonging to the linguistic and religious minorities were massacred.[19] Similar massacres took place again in 1983 at Chaulkhowa Chapori and Silapathar in 1983. The infamous Nellie massacre of 1983 witnessed the killing of more than 5,000 people mostly women and children belonging to a religious minority community. This massacre exposed very brilliantly the nature and hidden goals of the Assam Movement. Everyone in Assam thought that peace had a chance in the aftermath of the Assam movement. But it was not to be. Peace in Assam was disturbed by two subsequent movements i.e., ULFA movement for an independent Assam and the Bodo movement for Bodoland. Both these movements led to killing and counter-killings. And this continues unabated.

In early 1993, an accord was signed between the government and the leadership of the Bodo movement, which granted some autonomy to the Bodos in the form of an interim Bodoland Autonomous Council (BAC). But lack of a clear-cut boundary and presence of a significant non-Bodos in the proposed BAC areas created a problem. In order to cleanse the proposed Bodoland areas from the non-Bodos, selective massacres started from 1994. The Bodo militants organized systematic massacres of Na-Asamiya Muslim peasants in Kokrajhar, Bongaigaon and Barpeta districts in 1994.[20] In Barpeta district alone about 1,000 people were killed, thousands injured and about 60 villages burnt down to ashes. The Barpeta massacre gained limelight mainly because the militants not only killed the innocents in their homes, fields, forests, and villages, they even did not spare those who took shelter at the Banhbari relief camp run by the state. Like earlier massacres in Assam, none was punished for such crimes against humanity.

The Bodo militants were again involved in violence, this time against another very oppressed group—the Santhals of Kokrajhar and Bongaigaon districts in May and June 1996 in which about 4,000 people have been killed and 0.2 million rendered homeless. Till the writing of this paper about 0.15 million people were still in the relief camp scared to go back to their home without adequate security. It seems the killing was fundamentally to cleanse the Bodoland area from the non-Bodos. However, unlike the Barpeta massacre, here the Bodo militants equipped with sophisticated arms had to encounter a stiff resistance from the Santhals equipped with their traditional bows and arrows.

During the last two months the ULFA has increased its violent activities and the army in turn has started counter insurgency operations in Upper Assam. The insurgents have also threatened some distinguished Asamiya intellectuals, who neither support their demand for secession nor their violent methods. A young journalist sympathetic to the cause of ULFA was gunned down in broad daylight in Guwahati by a member of Surrendered ULFA (known as SULFA). ULFA's death list included an army officer who was killed at the doorsteps of Assam's famous Kamakhya temple and an IPS Officer of Tinsukia district along with his several bodyguards, an ex-Minister of Hiteswar Saikia's Government with his seven Asamiya security guards and two other police sub-inspectors. The army in turn gunned down two and the police gunned down one SULFA member in the course of their operations. The situation in Assam is very fluid and grim even if we do not include the routine extortions, kidnappings, and threats to life and property.

It seems the post-colonial state in India has not been successful in resolving the nationality and ethnic question of Northeast India and its resultant conflict and violence. The state violence too has affected the ordinary masses. The insurgents become more ruthless once they experience state violence. Anthony Giddens[21] has rightly observed "Although the governments oppose the activities of terrorists within their own border, they none the less often encourage guerrilla movements using identical tactics in other regions of the world." This also applies to the South Asian countries. Each country of the region, if involved, should introspect very seriously against aiding and abetting the insurgents across the border. The same moral standard should be applied to both the insurgents from inside and outside the border. The insurgent should also realize that importing secession from a neighboring country is a historical impossibility.

One of the causes of ethnic conflict in Northeast is migration. It is impossible to stop migration but it is definitely possible to control it very significantly. The other major cause is desire for economic development of the region. Most insurgents and their supporters in Northeast view their own society or motherland as a colony of Delhi/India. They want to "de-colonize" their society and their dream of de-colonization situates them against the mighty Indian state. Peace package or amnesty aiming at rehabilitating the insurgents/ex-insurgents without removing the present structural conditions that generate conflict and violence in the Northeast can at best give a very temporary respite. Both short-term and long-term strategy is needed to overcome the impasse and to minimize the conflict and violence. The long-term strategy in the days of globalization/liberalization is going to be very arduous in the wake of the retreat of state in India. The state must address itself to the questions raised by national and ethnic movements of the Northeast. The Indian state should not retreat from its responsibility towards the Northeast. We are sure the alienated people of the Northeast will respond positively if some positive initiative comes from the state. This is the time for the Indian state to come closer to the people of Northeast and try to understand them from below rather than from Delhi or from market situation.

Notes and References

1. Originally published in the *Indian Journal of Secularism*, vol. 1, no. 2, July–September, 1997.
2. Monirul Hussain, "Refugees in the Face of Emerging Ethnicity in Northeast India," *Studies in Humanities and Social Sciences*, vol. 2, no. 1, 1995.
3. Sanjay Hazarika, *Strangers of the Mist: Tales of War and Peace from Indian Northeast*. Delhi, 1994.
4. Amalendu Guha, *Planter Raj to Swaraj: Freedom Struggle and Electoral Politics in Assam*. New Delhi, 1977.

5. Amalendu Guha, "Little Nationalism Turned Chauvinist: Assam's Anti-foreigners Upsurge," *Economic and Political Weekly*, vol. XV, nos 41, 42, 43 and 44, 1980.
6. Ibid.
7. Ibid.
8. B.B. Misra, *The Indian Middle Classes: Their Growth in Modern Times*. New Delhi, 1961; also see J.H. Broomfield, *Elite Conflicts in a Plural Society*, California, 1968.
9. Guha, op. cit., 1977.
10. Monirul Hussain, "Nepalis in Assam and Asamiya Nationality Question," *Mainstream*, vol. XXXVII, no. 29, 1989.
11. Monirul Hussain, *The Assam Movement: Class, Ideology and Identity*. Delhi, 1993.
12. A.C. Bhagabati, *Tribal Transformation in Assam and Northeast India: An Appraisal of Emerging Ideological Dimensions*. Calcutta, 1988.
13. Ashok Rudra, "Emergence of Intelligentsia as a Ruling Class in India," *Economic and Political Weekly*, vol. XXIV no. 3, 21 January 1989.
14. Ibid.
15. Hussain, *The Assam Movement*.
16. Monirul Hussain, "Tribal Movement for Autonomous State in Assam," *Economic and Political Weekly* vol. XXI no. 32, 1987.
17. Hussain, op. cit., 1995.
18. Ibid.
19. Hussain, op. cit., 1993.
20. Hussain, op. cit., 1995.
21. Anthony Giddens, *Sociological Consequences of Modernity*. Cambridge, 1989.

Section III

Conflict Situations, Dialogue, and Peace

INTRODUCTION

Subhoranjan Dasgupta

Peace is a living, human condition more often aspired for than actually attained. It is difficult to define peace in either absolute or normative terms because even a so-called period of peace, unmarked by actual hostility or war, may carry and nurture the seeds of violence. At best, peace can be described or relativized in relation with and in opposition to war. This can be attempted with the "politics of understanding" which, depending on the efficacy of dialogue, charts the progress or regress of reconciliation among nations and peoples. But once we try to concretize this approach, unknowingly perhaps, we raise a theoretical paradigm sustained by the basic human desire to live and let live. In fact, this desire attests to the elemental aspiration for harmony and not discord and its acceptance as a principle prompts further theorization, which Rajeev Bhargava's paper—the last one of this section—raises and that has often gone unnoticed in black and white grand narratives of peace and war. Peace, therefore, emerges from the multiplicity of the human condition and its language is nourished by reflection and dialogue which accommodate differences in an ambience of many-layered understanding.

In discussing the real, detrimental role and the imagined need of nuclear weapons in South Asia, Kanti Bajpai in his paper (the second in this section) chooses the very art of dialogue—question, proposition, and rejection—to dissect each and every argument in favor of nuclear weapons. Is India's nuclear program an actual deterrence as far as the "threat" posed by the two adversaries (Pakistan and China) is concerned? Do nuclear weapons reduce the cost of militarism? Is nuclearization in consonance with the goals of economic justice and social dignity? The moment we raise these queries, having or not having nuclear weapons is no longer limited to the narrow and dangerous question of national pride. The argument breaks the crust formed by the dubious claims of security and vanity and flows into other channels that coalesce later to phrase the genuine counter-claim, namely, nuclearization would lead to "over-centralization, hyper-secrecy, gigantism, bureaucratism and militarism." While Bajpai's paper was written before the Buddha smiled for the second time in Pokhran, the war in Kargil after the publication of the paper has proved how faultless his prediction has been. Instead of fortifying peace, or better said, instead of acting as deterrence, Pokhran and Chaghai, together, led to the two-month long battle in Kargil, the biggest and most destructive flare up between India and Pakistan since 1971.

Along with nuclear weapons, Kashmir also provoked Kargil. Probably, it will continue to foment more Kargils if the intractable problem is not resolved. In short, the essential question of peace and concord in South Asia is tied to Kashmir and the aspirations of its people. Once we regard these aspirations as legitimate, the rigid national ideologies of both India and Pakistan vis-à-vis Kashmir are bound to lose their razor sharp edges. In his paper on Kashmir Tapan Bose has highlighted this desire of the people of Kashmir which constitutes the ignored though indispensable *other* to India and Pakistan's nation-state engineered mutual intransigence. The latter is so blind and obsessive argues the writer that it fails to pay even a minimum concern and respect for the wishes of those that live and suffer in Kashmir. As opposite to this the jointly authored note on cooperative border management based on the instance of the Indo-Bangladesh border shows how a democratization of border management can be achieved on the basis of social and economic realities. Peace, after all, is a matter of the people.

In the last paper of this section, "Literature, Peace and Creativity," the theory and praxis of peace are refracted through the prism of creativity. Situated in the South Asian context, this paper evaluates the expressions of creative writers on War, Partition, and Exodus. The texts, meticulously selected, voice the anguish of the writers protesting against war and its causes as well as suggest a redemptive realm where peace and human dignity aspired and fought for challenge the actuality. This quest for peace, ironically enough, is uttered unambiguously in those very epics that are commonly labeled "heroic poetry" or "veergathas." The most sublime epic of South Asia *Mahabharata* ends with the joyous celebration of peace when Yudisthira embraces his Kaurava cousins in Paradise. Prior to this blissful "Family Reunion" which, by itself, is a castigation of war, we discover the language of reflection and dialogue in Krishna's impassioned advocacy for peace. Indeed, that consummate diplomat questions, proposes and rejects war as an avoidable curse.

This paradigm established in the "veergatha" becomes an integral part of the creative tradition and we find its variegated expressions in modern South Asian literature. Inspired by the dedicated western critique of war spearheaded by thinkers and writers such as Henri Barbusse, Romain Rolland, Erich Maria Remarque and others, writers of the Indian subcontinent reacted to the wars launched by oppressors and fascists by scripting unqualified condemnation. In this sphere too, Rabindranath Tagore led the creative protest by writing that immortal line, "Serpents are exhaling poisonous breath everywhere." The thinker in the poet traced the source of the breath to the feeling of blind and aggressive nationalism, to that suicidal "self-locked" position which erases the scope of dialogue and reconciliation. Hence, there is no doubt that both creative writers and social scientists in their dissections of the cause of war have emphasized the overarching role of the self-justifying nation-state as the fountainhead of evil. When this hungry nation-state attempts to crush the peace-loving citizen with its national anthem and war drums, a poet like Birendra Chattopadhyay seeks his rebellious refuge in another planet where there are neither borders nor armies. The logic and worldview of reflexivity receives its intense, lyrical and almost utopian "poetizing" when the poet appeals:

> Let us go to the moon
> If there is time let us offer moon,
> More valuable than gold, a national anthem.

There is a categorical link between the politics of understanding and this genre of creativity because both, in their own ways, predict a human condition built on faith and friendship. No wonder, political scientists, activists, and writers cross the boundaries time and again with their thoughts and words to define and determine the same undifferentiated quest for a just peace. Indeed, the literary aestheticization of the entire endeavor grants to the vision of and struggle for peace a "timeless permanence." In the words of Raymond Williams, "Creative practice (becomes) our practical consciousness" in the material social sense and the poet and the analyst come to represent two sides of the same coin. This protesting public sphere was and is being created in the East and the West ceaselessly. The antifascist movement of the 1940s in the Indian subcontinent was led by poets, painters, dramatists and singers like Ali Sardar Jafri, Somenath Hore, Bijon Bhattacharjee, Salil Chaudhuri and many others. Their prime enemy was war launched by Nazi Germany and imperialist Japan. While they drew their sustenance from comrades in the West, the West also readily accepted inspiration from the East, from the subcontinent in particular. This writer was in the heartland of Europe, in divided Germany, when the peace movement there against nuclear stockpiling attained its climax. In those days of protest, young men and women marched on the street carrying placards of Mahatma Gandhi. A political scientist teaching at the University of Heidelberg went one step forward and quoted from *Mahabharata's* "Udyog Parva" to denounce the installation of Cruise and Pershing missiles. In short, in contrast to the rigidity of border-bound nationalism, the struggle for peace repudiates and obliterates national borders. It brings people together who pronounce the same verse.

Finally, we phrase the question what acts as the cementing medium between social science, on the one hand, and aesthetics and creativity, on the other? What has prompted us to end with an article on creativity and its relation to peace? The answer is simple—ethics brings the two together. When both the disciplines are infused by that Kantian sense of ethics, which is the precondition of peace, we proceed in the words of Michel Foucault, towards "ethics as a form of aesthetic practice or an aesthetics of existence." Based on the critical ontology of our own selves, this existence combines social science and poetry to articulate the same protest.

15

BUILDING PEACE IN KASHMIR[1]

Tapan K. Bose

PROLOGUE

In August 1947, the British left, after partitioning the Indian subcontinent into two independent nation-states, India and Pakistan on religious–communal lines. There were 562 "princely states" in the British Indian Empire. Maharajas, Rajas, and Nawabs ruled over these territories under the suzerainty of the British Crown. On the lapse of British paramountcy, these rulers were "legally" free to decide whether to join either of the two new states or remain independent. This legal choice of independence was essentially a hypothetical one. The religious composition of the subjects and the geographical location of these princely states dictated their merger with the newly emerged successor nation-states of India and Pakistan. No princely state could become independent.

Maharaja Hari Singh, the Hindu ruler of the mountain kingdom of Jammu and Kashmir, however was anxious for independence. The princely state of Jammu and Kashmir embracing over 128,000 sq. km was uniquely placed as a buffer territory between India and Pakistan and had common borders with Afghanistan and China. Neither Pakistan nor India was ready to accept an independent Jammu and Kashmir. They kept on pressing the Maharaja to accede to either of the new states. Pakistan claimed this territory, as 72 percent of the Maharaja's subjects were Muslim. India wanted the Muslim majority territory of Kashmir as an emblem of her secularism. Sheikh Mohammed Abdullah, the most popular leader of Kashmir's anti-monarchy movement of the 1930s and the 1940s, had encouraged the Indian leaders to believe that Kashmiri Muslims wanted to merge with a secular India. However, the Maharaja had put the Sheikh and other leaders of the Kashmir democracy movement behind the bars. He offered a "stand-still" agreement to India and Pakistan, as he wanted some more time to make up his mind. Pakistan signed the agreement but India refused.

As the Maharaja continued to dither, violence broke out in the Jammu and Punch regions where sections of the local Muslim population wanted to merge with Pakistan. There was a similar revolt in the northern hill territory of Gilgit. In violation of the "stand-still" agreement, Pakistan stopped the passage of food and other essential commodities to Jammu and Kashmir through her territory. In September 1947, tribal raiders backed by Pakistan army invaded the valley. The Maharaja requested India to send in its armed forces. India made it contingent upon his signing the instrument of accession in favor of India. The ruler signed the instrument of accession, and India accepted it with the proviso that after the restoration of normalcy, the final political status of the territory would be decided through a referendum. Indian soldiers were airlifted to Srinagar on October 27, 1947. India and Pakistan began their first war in less than three months of coming into being as independent states.

In January 1948, India appealed to the Security Council of the United Nations to restore peace in Kashmir. On January 20, 1948, the UN Commission on India and Pakistan (UNCIP) was constituted (UNSC Resolution S/654). In April 1948, the UN adopted the first Plebiscite Resolution. The resolution called upon Pakistan "to withdraw all its armed personnel including the tribesmen from the territory of Jammu and Kashmir." It asked India "to reduce its armed forces to the minimum level needed to maintain law and order" and to hold a plebiscite as soon as possible on the question of accession of Jammu and Kashmir to India or Pakistan. The Plebiscite Administrator was to be nominated by the UN Secretary General (UNSC Resolution S/726, April 21, 1948). A UN crafted ceasefire was implemented on January 1, 1949. The Plebiscite Resolution was reaffirmed.

Between 1949 and 1958 UNCIP made several attempts to implement the plebiscite resolution. Even partition of the territory along the ceasefire line with limited plebiscite in the valley was proposed at one stage. The intransigence of India and Pakistan defeated every effort of the UN. India and Pakistan created two separate political entities on the disputed territory—"Government of Jammu and Kashmir State" (India) and "Government of Azad Kashmir" (Pakistan) under the stewardship of their yes-men. The emergence of these political entities altered the ground situation as these new "stake holders" started manipulating the people of the divided territory on the command of their masters in Delhi and Karachi. The Kashmiris, who disagreed with New Delhi or Karachi, were soon put behind the bars. By 1958, within 10 years of having taken the Kashmir dispute to the United Nations, and having asked for international intervention in the resolution of the dispute, India changed its position on outside mediation in Kashmir. As a result, during 1960 and 1964 India turned down the offers of mediation by President Nasser of Egypt, President Kennedy of the United States of America and the Prime Minister of the United Kingdom.

The second Indo-Pakistan war on Kashmir took place in 1965. The third Indo-Pakistan war of 1971, which began on the soil of former East Pakistan and present Bangladesh, spilled over onto the territory of Kashmir. For the last 52 years, India and Pakistan have been virtually at war with each other. At times this war has been fought with guns, but most of the time it has been a verbal duel. The so-called "Kashmir dispute" lies at the very core of this enmity. Both India and Pakistan feel incomplete without Kashmir. Because of this enmity the people of the former princely state of Jammu and Kashmir have been living under virtual war conditions. The ceasefire line of 1949, which became the Line of Control (LoC) after the third Indo-Pakistan war of 1971 continues to be violated by both sides. These intermittent armed conflicts have taken a heavy toll on the lives of Kashmiris over the last five decades.

In 1989 sections of Kashmiris began a militant movement for national self-determination. In retaliation, Indian government let loose a reign of terror in Kashmir valley. Pakistan aided and abated this armed struggle and tried to use it to further its own agenda in Kashmir. While India calls the movement in Kashmir, "Pakistan's proxy war"; Pakistan says that it is merely providing moral support to the Kashmiris in their struggle for a just cause.

Since 1948, India and Pakistan have held several rounds of "official dialogues" to resolve the Kashmir dispute and other "outstanding" conflicts. However, these were the dialogues of the deaf, where both sides merely asserted and reasserted their respective positions. As a result of this stalemate, the two governments have often resorted to military means for resolving disputes.

The first meeting of Indian and Pakistani Defence Secretaries on the dispute over Siachen glacier began in January 1986. The talks continued for three years, culminating in the meeting of the prime ministers of India and Pakistan in Islamabad in July 1989 where the "broad parameters of Siachen agreement" were worked out. However, when the military commanders of both countries met in New Delhi in August 1989 "to determine the position of their respective forces in Siachen," the talks failed. Despite, the agreement on "broad parameters" by prime ministers, Siachen dispute remains unresolved till date. Similarly, the talks on the Wuller Lake Barrage that had begun in 1987 after eight unsuccessful rounds ended in a stalemate in 1992. After a break of nearly two years, during which India and Pakistan indulged in the most violent form of verbal sabre rattling, the official dialogue was resumed in 1994. The Lahore Declaration of February 1999 was the culmination of this process. It seemed that the prime ministers of India and Pakistan had agreed to shun military means and resolve all the disputes through negotiations. The Lahore Declaration lent vigor to the voices for peace on both sides of the border. The people of India and Pakistan began to hope for meaningful cooperation and peace. This opening created by the Lahore Declaration once again was closed by the latest war in Kargil.

INDIAN POSITION ON KASHMIR

- The state of Jammu and Kashmir is now and has been since its accession to India on 26 October 1947 an integral part of the Indian Union. Nothing agreed to by India in the UN

Security Council of August 13, 1948 and January 5, 1949, or in any subsequent instrument, alters this status or in any way modifies Indian sovereignty over the state.
- The only component of the Kashmir issue legally admissible in the talks between India and Pakistan on the future status of the state pertains to Pakistan vacating the territories illegally occupied by it. The future status of the state is otherwise an exclusively domestic matter to be resolved, within the Four Corners of the Indian Constitution.
- Talks between India and Pakistan in regard to the future status of the state should be held within a strictly bilateral framework and in conformity with the Simla Agreement of July 1972.

PAKISTANI POSITION ON KASHMIR

- The state of Jammu and Kashmir is now and has been since the end of British rule over undivided India, a disputed territory. The state's accession to India in October 1947 was provisional. This understanding is formally acknowledged in the UN Security Council resolutions of August 13, 1948 and January 5, 1949 to which both Pakistan and India agreed and which remains fully in force today, and cannot be unilaterally discarded by either party.
- Talks between India and Pakistan over the future status of the state should be focused upon securing the right of self-determination for the Kashmiri people via conduct of a free, fair and internationally supervised plebiscite, as agreed in the aforementioned UN Security Council resolutions.
- The plebiscite should offer the people of Jammu and Kashmir the choice of permanent accession of the entire state to either Pakistan or India.
- Talks between India and Pakistan in regard to the future of the status of the state should be held in conformity both with the Simla Agreement of July 1972 and the aforementioned UN Security Council resolutions. An international mediation in these talks should not be ruled out.

The Current Situation: Kargil War, Indians, Pakistanis, and Kashmiris

The war in Kargil is apparently over. The soldiers and other waring parties have pulled back. Indian and Pakistani citizens have heaved a sigh of relief. Yet, peace remains a distant objective. According to latest reports, guns have already started booming across the LoC in Kupwara and Jammu. Several lives have been lost after the ceasefire in Kargil. The sordid saga of sibling rivalry continues.

According to newspaper reports, the Indian army has pulled out 52 battalions from counter insurgency operations in Kashmir in which it has been engaged for the past 10 years. It seems the Indian army has decided to disassociate itself from the day-to-day counter-insurgency operations in the Valley and other areas of Jammu. However, the Director General of Police of Jammu and Kashmir has said that he anticipated an increase in the activities of the militants after the Kargil ceasefire. He has asked for more paramilitary forces to deal with the situation. Between July 16 and 27, 1999, about 60 persons, including women, children, and migrant workers from outside Kashmir were killed by suspected terrorists in Jammu region of Kashmir.

While the ceasefire in Kargil brought a temporary respite to the citizens of India and Pakistan, for the people of Kashmir it meant a mere shift in the venue of war. The supporters of the *mujahideens* in Pakistan threatened to turn their guns against Prime Minister Nawaz Sharif because of his remark that India and Pakistan should try to move away from their hard-line positions on Kashmir in order to resolve the Kashmir dispute through negotiations.

In 1982, the Indian forces had established effective military control over the undemarcated Siachen glacier area by occupying the heights of Saltoro ridge on the western edge of the glacier. Since the failure of Siachen talks in 1989 Pakistan has been trying to capture the high mountain posts in Kargil sector to offset its disadvantage in Siachen. In 1997 there was a major confrontation between Indian and Pakistani forces in Kargil that claimed several civilian lives and caused large-scale damage to civilian property. During the November 1998 round of official talks between India and Pakistan, the Indian side is reported to have reneged from the 1989 understanding of demilitarization of Siachen glacier through mutual withdrawal of forces. India apparently refused to pull back from Saltoro ridge. Instead, offered a ceasefire that would consolidate its effective control over the entire glacier.

NUCLEAR WEAPONS INCREASE THE STAKE

The war in the Kargil sector of Kashmir, which began in the first week of May 1999, was one of the many skirmishes on the LoC in which the armies of the two countries have been engaged during the last three decades. Normally, such border skirmishes did not get widespread media attention. It was seen as routine clashes in the distant hills of Kashmir. The governments did not bring back "body bags" of dead soldiers to bring the war nearer to the homes of the ordinary citizens. However, this time the stakes were higher. Since the induction of nuclear weapons in their arsenal a year ago, the two countries had acquired greater self-image as "invincible military powers."

This time, Pakistan pushed the "intruders" much deeper into the Indian controlled territory across the LoC in Kargil and Drass than before. India upped the ante by unleashing its air force at an early stage of the skirmish. Both sides threatened to use "all" weapons. The fear of a nuclear holocaust became real. It was frightening to see how sections of the media of both India and Pakistan manipulated news, as if the press had become the force multiplier of the military. The newspapers and electronic media were competing with each other in portraying their patriotic ardor. On the front pages of the newspapers there was no space for peace. Stories about citizens groups calling for peace and holding of peace rallies were either not published, or buried deep inside. The only other news from Kashmir that appeared in the Indian newspapers was stories of activities of militants. In all these stories while the criminal activities of the militants were highlighted, virtually nothing was reported about the excesses committed by Indian security forces. The media's reluctance to report Indian government's callous handling of the refugees of Kargil was yet another example of its politics and priorities.

Voices of Peace, Voices of Sanity

During the past five years, the voices for peace and normalization of India–Pakistan relations have gained considerable momentum. The increasing demand on both sides of the border for lifting the ban on India–Pakistan trade, the growing viewership of Pakistan television in India and Indian satellite television channels in Pakistan, the lengthening queue of people seeking visas outside the embassies of India and Pakistan and the starting of a bus service between Lahore and Delhi are indications of the fact that the peoples of India and Pakistan want and need peace.

Indian and Pakistani civil society institutions and public forums have already started working on humanitarian issues together. The growing popularity of Pakistan–India Peoples' Forum for Peace and Democracy, the partial success of the joint campaigns for the release and repatriation of prisoners and the joint campaign for the protection of human rights defenders in both countries are evidence of a growing alliance. These are the building blocks for a sustainable peace. They show that the civil society of the two countries is slowly moving towards reconciliation, that together they will be able to heal the scars and the wounds of the partition of 1947.

When guns start blazing and soldiers die, it is natural that patriotic passions will rise. Under these circumstances, ordinary people who do not want war, feel compelled to support the soldiers fighting on the front and the war efforts of the government. In such situations the voices for peace become feeble. Unlike the days of 1965 and 1971 Indian–Pakistan wars, this time the ordinary peoples of the two countries showed far less jingoistic fervor. In both countries significant sections of citizens continued to call for caution and asked for end of hostilities. This had a restraining effect on the war hysteria that was being whipped up by the ultra nationalists through the media and on the streets.

Weak and small as they might have been, at the time of crisis these voices represented the urge of society to live in peace. It was heartening to note that Pakistan–India Peoples' Forum for Peace and Democracy and other democratic organizations throughout the 10 weeks long Kargil war remained active in both countries. Joint statements were issued calling on the two governments immediately to end hostilities, demilitarize the LoC and to begin dialogues for resolution of all outstanding disputes, including Kashmir. The members of the Forum in several cities of India and Pakistan in collaboration with other civil society organizations and NGOs held public meetings and peace rallies to mobilize public opinion for peace. While the statements of the Forum and news about its activities were published by only a few of the leading newspapers in India and Pakistan, majority of them ignored it.

THE IMPORTANCE OF KARGIL

As newspaper reports indicated, the people of the Valley were least bothered about the ongoing war in Kargil. They were more concerned about the loss of business due to lack of tourists, and the fate of the refugees and apprehensive of brutal reprisal by security forces on suspicion of helping the enemy. The loud claims of Pakistan that it was Kashmiri freedom fighters who were waging a liberation war in Kargil and that Pakistan army was not involved, found very few takers in the Valley. Other than a section of the leaders of the All Parties Hurriyat Committee no Kashmiri had come forward in support of the "freedom fighters" in Kargil. The average persons in the Valley were neither excited by the activities of the so-called "freedom fighters" nor were they sympathetic to the Indian soldiers. It seemed that they were patiently waiting for this current crisis to blow over.

No peace rally was held in Srinagar or elsewhere in Kashmir. The Kashmiri intellectuals and other civil society actors who support the work of Pakistan–India Peoples' Forum for Peace and Democracy were afraid to express their support in public because of the threat of the guns. In the prevailing gun culture of Kashmir, "peace" has become a dirty word. It is risky for the moderate Kashmiris to speak out for peace as they have been targeted by Indian and Pakistani war machines as well as by the militants and *mujahideen*.

Kashmiriyat—Kashmiri Nationalism

Kashmiri nationalism or *Kashmiriyat* was the main source of inspiration of the political reforms movement in the 1930s in the princely state of Jammu and Kashmir. The movement was anti-monarchy, anti-colonial, and pro-democracy. *Kashmiriyat* represented human dignity, social justice, freedom of conscience, and religion and economic security for the common masses. It is obvious that in their endeavor to create a broad coalition of peoples, the leaders of Kashmiri national movement did not adequately address the issues of minority rights, ethnicity and regional autonomy. The linguistic, cultural, and religious diversity of the princely state of Jammu and Kashmir was subsumed in the overarching concept of *Kashmiriyat*. It was essentially a political alliance, which attempted to build a secular democratic national liberation movement. It tried to build alliances with the anti-colonial national liberation movements in the subcontinent.

Unfortunately, while the leaders of Kashmiri national movement were trying to build a partnership on the basis of equality, the Indian National Congress and Indian Muslim League wanted the Kashmiris to submerge themselves in either of the "two nations" of which they had become the self appointed brokers. Under this dual pull, Kashmiri national movement finally split on ethno-religious lines. The non-Kashmiri speaking Muslims of Punch, Rajouri, and the Northern Areas who had closer linguistic, social, and economic ties with west Punjab remained with the Muslim Conference. This section, which was led by religious preachers, a section of the land owning classes and traditional tribal chiefs, supported Muslim League's call for the creation of Pakistan as the homeland of Muslim "nation" on the subcontinent.

Sheikh Mohammed Abdullah and his supporters, the majority of whom did not belong to the landed gentry and the upper classes formed the National Conference. It had a great following among the Kashmiri speaking, predominantly Muslim populations of the Valley. While a small section of the Kashmiri Pandits, the Hindu minority of the Valley joined the National Conference, the majority of the Kashmiri Pandits, and the Hindus of Jammu as well as Buddhists of Ladakh were organized on religious and ethnic lines under the banners of Kashmir Hindu and Buddhist Mahasangh and Praja Parishad. Despite these differences, Kashmiri national movement had remained broadly united in its struggle against the autocratic rule of the Dogras. National Conference's commitment to radical land reforms, economic support to the dispossessed and establishment of a democratic system of government had inspired the masses of Kashmir.

The Muslim League and the Congress ignored the strength of Kashmiri nationalism and its appeal to the common masses of the region. This ignorance had led Pakistan in 1947 to believe that Kashmiris would rise in support of their armed actions in the Valley. India's interpretation of the resistance put up by the Kashmiris against the invading forces as a sign of their desire to become an integral part of India was equally faulty. Kashmiris have resisted both in their own manner and have paid a very heavy price for it.

KASHMIRI CIVIL SOCIETY

For the last five decades, Kashmiris have lived under virtual war conditions. According to conservative estimates, more than two million Kashmiris have been uprooted from their homes during the last 50 years. The so-called LoC has remained a war zone. Not a year goes by without major exchanges of fire across this line. Every skirmish has taken its toll on Kashmiris. On both sides of the divide, be it the Indian administered three-fifth of the territory of the former princely state or the two-fifth of the territory controlled by Pakistan, Kashmiris have been ruled by puppet governments imposed by rulers in New Delhi and Islamabad.

Pakistan and India have been dealing with the two halves of Kashmir under their respective control like colonial masters. Their efforts to create pro-India and pro-Pakistan Kashmiris have fractured the civil society of Kashmir. Emergence of India or Pakistan-sponsored interest groups and the usurpation of political power at local levels by these groups have deepened social and political fissures, alienating vast sections of Kashmiri masses from the local ruling elite. The highhandedness of the states and their local agents, rampant corruption, ruthless suppression of democratic movements and all dissent, gave rise to violence.

Civil society is the terrain of democratization. It is the sphere of social interaction between state and society and between communities. For obvious reasons India and Pakistan did not want a vibrant civil society in Kashmir. They deliberately controlled the growth of citizens' initiatives and public associations through legal and administrative measures. The Kashmiri society today has become polarized on ethnic and religious lines. Kashmiriyat or Kashmiri nationalism, which inspired all sections of peoples and communities of the region in the 1930s, has lost its appeal.

INDIAN JAMMU AND KASHMIR

In Indian Jammu and Kashmir, during the last 50 years, the three principal ethnic communities, Kashmiris, Dogras, and Ladakhis have had very little social and cultural interaction. The Kashmiri Pandits and the Kashmiri Muslims have drifted further and further apart. The Indian state's policy of divide-and-rule, and the practice of empowering one community to the disadvantage of the other, created, deepening rift between classes and communities. The inability of the emerging Kashmiri Muslim middle class to look beyond its self-image as the "majority" and its clamor for the lion's share of all benefits and concessions was one of the major reasons for the alienation of minority communities from *Kashmiriyat,* the all-embracing nationalist identity of the 1930s.

The militant movement that began in the Valley in 1988–89, has only one agenda today, right of "self determination." It is yet to develop its social, economic, and cultural policy. The failure of the movement to broaden its agenda has resulted in the loss of its democratic characteristics. This is why there is virtually no support for the ongoing Kashmiri self-determination movement in Jammu and Ladakh. This is also the reason for the final departure of Kashmiri Pandits from the Valley. Moreover, today there seems to be little scope for reconciliation as the Kashmiri Pandits who left the valley feel "self-determination" means merger with Pakistan.

Pakistani Azad Kashmir

The situation in Pakistan held parts of Kashmir is not very different. Ethnically divergent communities of Sudans, Jats, and Gujjars inhabit Muzaffarabad, Rawalakot, Mirpur, and Kotli regions that are known as "Azad" Kashmir. Gilgit, Baltistan, and the northern areas, are the home of the Dardic people. The entire population of Pakistan controlled Kashmir is Muslim. The majority of the population belongs to the Sunni sect of Islam. However, the depth of the appeal of Kashmiri nationalism can be gauged by the fact that though the majority of the people in Pakistan-held Kashmir are non-Kashmiris and do not even speak Kashmiri language, most of them still want to be known as Kashmiris. Perhaps there is another explanation. It is the ethnic divergence that has made it necessary for these communities to cling to the common identity of "Kashmiri."

In Pakistani Kashmir too, dissent is not tolerated. The northern areas comprising Gilgit-Baltistan are virtually under direct colonial rule. They do not even have the most basic democratic rights. Pakistan government has ruthlessly crushed the popular movement for democracy in Gilgit and Baltistan. The entire region is virtually controlled by Pakistan army and its Inter Services Intelligence (ISI).

In the early 1970s, when the Mangla Dam was constructed in Mirpur district of Pakistan controlled Azad Kashmir, thousands of acres of fertile land of the Jat peasantry of the district were inundated. Virtually no compensation was paid to the farmers who lost their land. Mirpur derived no benefit from the Mangla project. All the water and electricity went to Punjab. Unable to get justice from Pakistan, the Mirpuris finally turned against Pakistan. During the 1970s large number of Mirpuri Jats had migrated to England. Today, they form the mainstay of Kashmir independence movement abroad.

All newspapers in Azad Kashmir and northern areas are controlled by Pakistan's ISI. Intelligence departments harass all dissenters, they are arrested under false charges, tortured and detained for long periods without trial and dubbed as Indian agents. In Pakistani Kashmir, Kashmiri language has lost its space. The National Students Federation (NSF) of Azad Kashmir calls for independent Kashmir. Most of its activists are not

Kashmiri speaking; yet they are demanding Kashmiri language to be made their national language.

Unlike the militant groups in Indian Kashmir, who have not been able to develop alliances with democratic forces in India, the NSF of Pakistani Kashmir has been interacting with democratic parties and groups in Pakistan. While in the Indian held Kashmir, human rights groups have remained isolated from other Indian human rights groups, the students organizations and human rights activists of Pakistan held Kashmir have been able to build alliances with Pakistan's human rights movement. Some of them also actively participate in the programs of Pakistan national chapter of PIPFPD and Pakistan Peace Coalition in different cities of Pakistan.

SITUATION SINCE THE RISE OF MILITANCY

After the rise of the militant movement in the Valley in 1989, the moderates, the thinkers and the ideologues of Kashmir who could have initiated dialogues between communities and classes were either killed or forced into silence. Kashmiris who were known for their hospitality and humanism seem to have lost their capacity to help one other in times of crisis. It has been reported that a very high percentage of the population of the Valley, particularly women, is today mentally paralyzed. They suffer from immobilizing depression and need treatment.

While sections of Kashmiri human rights activists routinely highlight the violation of human rights by Indian forces, their actions remain confined only to investigation and reporting. Very few seek judicial remedy. There is virtually no humanitarian initiative for the large number of orphans, widows, and victims of torture. Even initiatives of Kashmiri women like the "Mothers of the Disappeared" have come under attack. In the early days of militancy, people who spoke of the need for reconciliation and return of the Kashmiri Pandits were seen as unpatriotic. Some of them were condemned as enemy agents and killed.

Reconciliation and unity among various religious and ethnic groups is necessary for a secular democratic solution. Since 1947, there has been no attempt to evolve a consensus on forging unity among the different entities in Kashmir. Till 1947, the

Valley people complained of suppression by the Maharaja. After 1947, people of Jammu started to make similar complaint against the government in the valley. The ruling elite has been trying to divide Kashmir into several regions on communal lines. Guns and the cries of Holy War have destroyed the cultural foundations of Kashmiriyat—the cultural ethos of having lived together for centuries.

ALLIANCE BUILDING: THE TASK OF CIVIL SOCIETY

Alliance building is an important function of civil society. A society turns to violence when it loses its capacity to dialogue with the opposition and build alliances with peacemakers across the political, social, and cultural divide. What we need is an alliance of civil society initiatives for peace and reconciliation. As the South African experience demonstrates, it is only through these alliances for peace and reconciliation that a society can hope to rid itself of colonial oppression, violence, and hatred. The communal and ethnic divide in Kashmir has to be bridged. Civil society actors and concerned NGOs of India and Pakistan have to work together with Kashmiri civil society actors and NGOs to counter the process of militarization and strengthen the forces of democratization.

The process of building solidarity between Indian/Pakistani civil society groups and Kashmiris has been hampered by the failure to recognize that just as the democratic agenda has been compromised in Kashmir, so too has the democratic agenda been compromised in India and Pakistan. For too long, the pattern has been that violations of human rights and denial of democracy in Kashmir find no echo in the national human rights communities of India and Pakistan. If that pattern is to be broken, there is need for Kashmiris to be more sensitive to democratic crisis and human rights violations in India and Pakistan. Similarly, Indian/Pakistani civil society organizations need to join efforts and strengthen the voices of Kashmiri groups.

It should be recognized that there exists a close nexus between the democratic rights of the people of Kashmir and of the peoples of South Asia, which means that the struggle of the Kashmiri people for their democratic rights cannot be separated from the South Asian people's struggle for democratic rights.

NOTE AND REFERENCE

1. Earlier versions of this essay, "Kashmir—A Willing Suspension of Reason," *Himal*, May 1999, pp. 10–21; position paper on Kashmir in the sub-commission on Kashmir in the Fifth Pakistan–India People's Forum for Peace and Democrcay, Bangalore, April 2000.

16

THE INDIAN NUCLEAR DEBATE[1]

Kanti Bajpai

The struggle for economic justice and social dignity in South Asia has focused on various internal economic, social and political conditions and practices which elevate and reward some sections of society and oppress and punish others. Much less attention has been paid to how these conditions and practices have influenced and been influenced by the state's relations with external forces, except in the general form of capitalism or imperialism. Specifically, the interaction of the regional states and the great powers with the internal struggle for justice and dignity has not been carefully and thoroughly traced through. It has been widely appreciated that there is a link between what may be termed geopolitics and the internal struggle, but the nature of the linkage has not been either theoretically or empirically demonstrated in a rigorous fashion.

I attempt here to contribute to the delineation of this linkage by asking the following question: are nuclear weapons commensurate with economic justice and social dignity? Nuclear weapons, it is often argued by stategists, are a more affordable deterrent than conventional weapons. To the extent that they are, one could argue, they are consistent with, if they do not actually promote the cause of economic justice. I shall argue, on the other hand, that nuclear weapons are not an investment in cheaper defence and that they do not therefore promote economic justice. Strategists also argue that nuclear weapons in the hands of the weak are a military equalizer and that they therefore promote a form of social dignity. I shall argue, on the other hand, that nuclear weapons retard the cause of social dignity more broadly conceived.

For the argument, it is necessary first of all to call into question the utility of a nuclear weapons capability as a deterrent. If nuclear weapons had military utility, then that might balance their economic and social dis-utility. But if it can be shown, that they do not confer any significant military benefit, indeed if it can be shown that they are militarily harmful, then the arguments for their economic and social dis-utility become decisive. My concern in this paper is with India that, over the past 25 years, has shown an interest in developing a nuclear deterrent against both Pakistan and China, her two principal adversaries.

Nuclear Weapons and Deterrence

India has two principal military adversaries—Pakistan and China. Pakistan has proven nuclear capability; and China has the third largest nuclear arsenal in the world. Both possess formidable conventional forces. India has unresolved quarrels with both, war is not an impossibility with either. In such a situation, the incentive to go nuclear is not incomprehensible. Yet, India could be secure without nuclear weapons.

Deterring Pakistan

The Indian government's declared policy is that the country is a non-nuclear weapons state, but enough information has leaked out or been allowed to lead out to signal that it is at least near-nuclear. This policy of "ambiguity," it has been suggested, has achieved a form of "non-weaponized deterrence," one that has been mimicked by Pakistan, so that the region has developed a form of mutual deterrence that promises to be stable.[2] For at least five reasons, this is a questionable proposition.

First of all, over time, keeping the nuclear option open is not likely to be credible to the other nuclear powers and may therefore seriously complicate India's strategic environment. The "neither-confirm-nor-deny" posture of half-truths, hints, calculated leaks, and genuine revelations will cumulate at some point to persuade leaks, and genuine revelations will cumulate at some point to persuade outsiders that India is virtually a nuclear power, armed with an arsenal of "short-order" weapons (that is, weapons that could be assembled and fired at short notice) and possessing missiles capable of striking well beyond the region or near-region.[3]

If so, there is every possibility that the nuclear powers will target India with their nuclear weapons. It is of course true that these powers could bring their weapons to bear against a non-nuclear India, but surely an extraordinary set of circumstances must be conjured up. However, as the impression grows that India is virtually a nuclear power, the extraordinary could very well become the normal state of affairs: India could be targeted as part of the general deterrence posture of the nuclear powers. This would very likely be the case with China (which is rumored to have missiles in Tibet, pointed at India), but also perhaps with the US and Russia. Nuclear ambiguity may also deter an equally ambiguous Pakistan, but it may expose India to several further layers of nuclear threat, thereby greatly increasing its strategic risk.

Ambiguity, in addition, may expose India to various non-nuclear threats. To persuade the Indian government to give up the ambiguity posture, the nuclear powers could exploit India's internal political problems, particularly its ethnic and religious divisions. Kashmir, in this regard, becomes a distinct vulnerability. Other punishments might include economic sanctions and technology denials. At a crucial moment in its development, these could seriously undermine the economy.

Second, while nuclear ambiguity may be "deterrence stable," it may not be "crisis stable," and therefore it is not a tenable position in the long run. Whereas uncertainty of nuclear retaliation may deter in the general course of things, in a crisis, which is an environment marked by the dangerous lack of certitudes and by shortened decision-making horizons, what is likely to be stabilizing is certainty of response. If one side or the other calculates that the other side's ambiguity is overtly ambiguous, it might decide to strike first. At a critical moment, ambiguity may give its possessor a false sense of security and its opponent a false sense of opportunity. This is why India's present position is not a stable one and why it will move gradually in the direction of an overt posture. Those who support ambiguity must therefore live with the strong possibility that in the end they are likely to lose the argument to the weaponizers.

Third, those who support ambiguity cannot draw comfort from the fact that the decay of ambiguity into outright weaponization will be in the direction of more or less permanent stability, as argued by the proponents of nuclearization. Those who argue for an overt posture—whether fully weaponized or short-order weaponized—argue that, once both sides go openly nuclear, mutual deterrence will be possible and that this will stabilize the military relationship. Against this, one can argue for the long-term imperative of abstinence. There is a fatal flaw in deterrence, and it is not simply the flaw that weaponizers recognize, namely, that if something can go wrong it will go wrong, no ifs and buts: deterrence will undo deterrence.

The argument depends on the proposition that if deterrence is built on the certainty of retaliatory punishment in the face of an attack, then over time it must be prone to decay. This is because the only way to be more or less sure that someone will carry out a threat is if they carry it out from time to time. With nuclear weapons this is not possible. Thus, the certainty of retaliation can only be approached asymptomatically: to communicate certainty of response needs ever greater investments in military capabilities; or it needs over more credible demonstrations of commitment; or both. The problem is that as capabilities and shows of commitment inflate, the opponent will have difficulty in distinguishing between a deterrence posture and a first strike posture. When that time comes, the incentive for the opponent to launch a first strike will be high. Moreover, the deterrer, recognizing this incentive, will contemplate preempting preemption, will be tempted to preempt the deterrer's preemptive preemption. And so on, in an infinite regress, till deterrence is ultimately unstable and that disarmament or abstinence is imperative.[4]

In addition, there are more "idiosyncratic" limits to nuclear deterrence in South Asia. We can see this by comparing the India–Pakistan and US–Soviet relationship. Geographically, the two superpowers were not contiguous and were not therefore prone to everyday frictions. Historically, they developed largely in isolation from each other. More importantly, they had never fought one another, and neither side harbored territorial claims against the other. After 1945, while the two were engaged in a geopolitical and ideological contest of great seriousness, at the society-to-society or people-to-people level, there was little real animosity. Militarily, from 1941 to 1945, they were allies against Fascist Germany, and, as a result, after the Second World War benefited from a history of military cooperation and military respect which helped stabilize their Cold War rivalry. In addition, geographical distance helped militarily, especially in the early years when the nuclear relationship was in its infancy and its dynamics in flux. Without missiles in their armories, strategic warning time—the time from the launch of a delivery vehicle to its arrival over the other's territory—was longer.[5]

India and Pakistan do not have these ameliorating conditions. Geographically, they are contiguous over a long border, a border that is bitterly contested by at least one side and is very much prone to everyday frictions. Historically, their development as nation-states has been ineluctably intertwined. Moreover, their history is as much a history of war as of peace, and they continue to quarrel over territory, particularly Kashmir. This rivalry is not just over territory and ideology, but is marked in addition by suspicion at a society-to-society and people-to-people level. Nor, after Independence, have the two been military allies, and, while their armed forces share a great deal, there is a fair degree of mutual contempt. Finally, strategic warning times in South Asia, even with aircraft, are measured in minutes—and with missiles will be even less.[6]

Fourth, if nuclear ambiguity is sought for deterrence, it is worth recalling what can and what cannot be deterred in South Asia. It has been argued that ambiguity generates a form of deterrence, that the uncertainty of possession of nuclear weapons is sufficient for deterrence in South Asia. It was suggested earlier that while this may be so, "crisis stability" might not be ensured by such a posture. But a more fundamental point is: what can nuclear deterrence deter?

It bears repeating that it cannot deter perhaps the most important sources of violence in the region, namely, insurgency and terrorism. Indeed, in a perverse way, it may make the region more hospitable to both. With India and Pakistan at par in their ambiguous nuclear postures, Islamabad is free to support insurgency and terrorism.[7] On the other hand, if both sides abjured nuclear weapons, such support would be exceedingly dangerous. Abstinent Pakistan would have to reckon that abstinent India might retaliate by "hot pursuit" strikes, with the promise of escalation to outright conventional war. However a strategy of conventional escalation, beyond some minimal level, becomes impossible when nuclear weapons are or may be available to the enemy.[8] In sum, nuclear weapons, declared or undeclared, have made low-intensity subversions more likely than before.

Fifth, keeping the nuclear option open as—or as part of—a deterrence posture contributes to the freezing of India-Pakistan relations. It postpones the day when the two sides must confront the fundamental causes of their quarrels and deliberate how those quarrels can be resolved short of war. And it will entrench those on both sides who have an interest in permanent enmity, thereby prolonging the region's state of war. In sum, the stability of deterrence is the stability of a cold and negative peace.

In sum, India's policy of nuclear ambiguity, often presented as a political, diplomatic, economic, military, and moral necessity and comfort, is no such thing but rather opposite.

Deterring China

The Indian government and Indian strategic analysts argue that the *raison atomique* of the Indian nuclear program is not only Pakistan but also China. Does India need nuclear weapons for China? The question presumes that China is or may be a nuclear threat, but this is doubtful.

It is argued that Chinese nuclear intimidation could occur in three kinds of circumstances. First of all, there remains the unresolved border dispute between the two countries. Second, internal instabilities in China could encourage external adventurism. As the Chinese leadership struggles to assert or retain political control, it may be tempted to use external "threats" to outmaneuver and discipline internal rivals. Third, the two countries, by virtue of their size and self-image, are likely to be perennial rivals for influence in Asia if not farther a-field.[9]

Nuclear asymmetry, it is thought, will strengthen Beijing's hand in each case. It will encourage obduracy over the border issue. Should instabilities in Tibet, and other areas of southern China tempt the leadership to "teach" India a lesson (as a way of rallying support domestically), this temptation will be reinforced by nuclear superiority. And China's nuclear confidence will enable it to enlarge its spheres of influence to India's detriment.

Each of these propositions bears examination. First, while the border dispute is unresolved in a formal sense, Beijing has got most of what it wanted out of the issue. If its primary aim was to secure the route from Xinjiang to Tibet, it long ago accomplished its goal. China is the satisfied power on the border issue, and it did not need nuclear weapons then, and does not need them now, to achieve its purpose.

Second, there is considerable room for debate over the internal–external linkage. Where internal factors truly responsible for Beijing's punitive wars against India and Vietnam? How vulnerable and unstable is China likely to be in the future? Can domestic political troubles be eased, in the new China, by external distractions? Finally, and most importantly, would war with India be credible, given that the only serious bilateral issue, namely, the border, favors China; and would it help or hurt an insecure regime or leadership to raise an India bogey in such circumstances?

Third, nuclear weapons as enhancing China's status (and the status of the other NWSs) is a constant theme in Indian thinking, but there are reasons to be skeptical.[10] China's growing stature is far more probably linked to quite different factors: the vitality and quality of its leaders; the speed with which, after 1949, the new government asserted political control and embarked on social reforms; the dramatic improvements in the quality of physical life; the willingness to use force, as demonstrated by its interventions in Tibet and Korea in the 1950s and its defeat of India in 1962; the break with the Soviets in 1958; the increasing sophistication of its conventional forces over the past two decades; the dynamism of its economy over the past 15 years; and, notwithstanding a certain measure of turbulence, overall political stability.

Nuclear weapons have not hurt China's standing in world affairs; but to ascribe Chinese status and influence primarily to nuclear weapons is untenable. The rise of non-nuclear Germany and Japan as great powers (based on economic prowess), and the decay and collapse of a nuclear-ridden Soviet Union, further challenge the linkage between nuclear weapons, status, and influence. What is reasonably evident now is that a nuclear India would be unable to match China for status and influence unless it made important economic, social, and political changes. The real "race" with China is civic, not military.

In sum, then, the notion of a Chinese nuclear threat is questionable. If we add to this the progress that has been made in India–China relations since 1988, then the likelihood of nuclear intimidation across the Himalyas seems even more remote.

NUCLEAR WEAPONS AND ECONOMIC JUSTIFICATION

One of the commonest justifications of nuclear weapons is that they are cost effective. They give states "more bang for the buck" than conventional weapons and therefore provide cheaper defence. This is a doubtful proposition. If cheaper defence is the objective, then India would be better advised to change its defence strategy from "offensive" to "defensive" defence, based on conventional weapons.

Nuclear for Conventional Weapons

The "nuclear for conventional" argument rests on the fact that the firepower of nuclear weapons cannot be matched by conventional weapons. Moreover, once they have been constructed and mounted atop delivery systems, nuclear weapons are available forever. Nuclear materials do not degrade in less than several hundreds or thousands of years, and operational maintenance consists of little more than periodic checks of their casing, firing mechanisms, and the fuels that power their delivery systems. The manpower required for this plus command and control purposes is therefore much more modest than for conventional weapons.

However, until a comprehensive accounting of the cost of nuclear weapons is available, this is a partial case at best. To be clear, an accounting of costs must include environmental hazards, a testing program, research and development, refinement of weapons, command and control, the decommissioning of older systems, and of course the very serious matter in the long run of the storage and disposal of fissile materials which have a half-life ranging from several hundred to several thousand years. The full costs of the US and the Soviet nuclear weapons programs are becoming increasingly clear, and what the world has learned so far is not reassuring.[11] A recent estimate of the environmental costs alone notes that the cleanup of US facilities which contributed to nuclear weapons production will cost between $200,000 million and $1,000,000 million, that is, 1 trillion. One trillion dollars, it should be noted, is roughly the entire annual budget of the US In 1993, the US Department of Energy spent roughly $5,000 million on environmental restoration and waste management. At this rate it will take the US 200 years to finish the cleanup![12]

Nevertheless, whatever the costs of nuclear weapons, if Pakistan goes nuclear it seems inconceivable that India would abstain for long. But, if so, it should be clear what nuclear weapons can do and what they cannot do for Indian security. Any discussion of the benefits of nuclear weapons as cost-savers must be set against their strategic uses. Can they substitute for conventional weapons in military terms? Today, and for the foreseeable future, India's greatest military threats are not the risk of outright war but proxy-war in border states—in Punjab, Kashmir, and in the Northeast. If India had nuclear weapons, could they play a role here? Clearly, they cannot deter local insurgents or infiltrators: a hammer is a poor weapon against a fly.

What nuclear weapons could do is to (*a*) deter other nuclear weapons and (*b*) deter an escalation of hostilities from insurgency and infiltration to full-scale combat. But in both cases substantial levels of conventional force will be required as a supplement to nuclear weapons. K. Subrahmanyam has said that only nuclear weapons deter nuclear weapons.[13] However, it is probably more accurate to say that, when both sides have them, perhaps nuclear weapons deter only nuclear weapons.

This is because, as argued earlier, if both sides have nuclear weapons the region is made "safe" for conventional and sub-conventional war. If so, conventional forces will continue to be vital to India's security.

The case of nuclear weapons to deter a campaign of insurgency and infiltration leading up to full-scale combat also suggests that large conventional forces will be required. To deter is to threaten unacceptable punishment on a potential attacker and thereby to prevent it from striking. Nuclear weapons of course threaten terrible punishment, so terrible in fact, that they are weapons of overkill. And everybody, including the opponent, knows that it will take considerable provocation before they will actually be used. If so, the threat of nuclear weapons use against sub-conventional and conventional attack may not be credible. To make it more credible, deterrence theorists have resorted to the notion of an "escalation ladder" which proceeds from low to higher level conventional responses and finally to nuclear strikes. The existence of a ladder signals a capacity to move deliberately towards higher levels of punishment, including nuclear, and therefore makes more credible the possibility of proceeding all the way to nuclear attack. To the extent that it makes a nuclear response more credible, an escalation ladder strengthens deterrence. In short, the exigencies of a ladder will require India to continue to invest in conventional forces.[14]

A final point to consider is that if nuclear deterrence fails, India will need conventional forces to defend. Deterrence is a psychological matter: perceptual and interpretive failures on the part of an enemy may lead to deterrence challenges. If war breaks out, and if enemy forces are fighting on Indian territory, the use of even battlefield nuclear weapons will become fraught. At that point, substantial conventional forces will be required to stop enemy advances and turn them back.

From Offensive Defence to Defensive Defence

A better way of moving towards an affordable defence posture is to reconfigure conventional forces. This can be achieved by substituting "defensive defence" for "offensive defence."[15] Since 1971, there has been a growing feeling that India should stress offensive-oriented defensive notions, that is, it should be willing to carry the fight to the enemy as a way of defending its territory.[16] This has meant two things, which have increased India's defence burden.

First, an offensive defence requires a different type of force structure. It requires a higher proportion of offensive systems such as deep penetration strike aircraft, armor, mobile artillery, and certain types of missiles. These systems tend to be more expensive. Second, and perhaps more importantly, systems such as these—whatever the intent of a country—can be misperceived. They maybe intended to form part of an offensive defence but be seen as part of a posture of offensive offence, that is, as a first-strike capacity that could spreahead a surprise attack to dismember an adversary. There is wide agreement that India and Pakistan since 1971 have moved towards offensive defence postures. The danger is that both see the ostensibly defensive intent of the other side as offensive in sprit. This is the classic "security dilemma." Each therefore counters with a build-up of offensive systems for even more defence. Each provokes the other to progressively higher levels of arms acquisitions that lead to a classic arms race. In such a race, motives and intent become increasingly shadowy, and capabilities and counter-capabilities drive defence policies.

One way out of this dilemma is to move towards more "defensive defence" postures. India can propose bilateral and multilateral discussions and agreements on postures, which signal more defensive intent. These postures would require changes in capabilities. State would move increasingly to deploy and invest in more defensive weapons systems. They would stress "defensive defence" doctrines, dispositions, and strategies. An appropriate forum for such discussions might be "cooperative security" talks at an all-Asia level in which the major Asian powers start to consider what more defensive postures, systems, doctrines, dispositions, and strategies would look like if implemented; what intentions each state harbors; and what confidence-building measures must be put in place so that intentions are clarified and the threat of surprise attack is reduced.[17] In sum, India can help initiate a move towards "non-offensiveness," defined by Bjorn Moeller as a situation in which "The armed forces should be seen in their totality to be capable of a credible defence, yet incapable of offence."[18]

This will undeniably present difficulties. Critics will question whether it is truly possible to distinguish between offensive and defensive systems and therefore between an offensive defence and a defensive defence.[19] Others will argue that intentions are always murky, no matter how much rivals and opponents may talk, and that states must prepare for the worst case based on an enemy's or rival's capabilities and not its intent or talk.

The difficulties of adopting a strategy of defensive defence should not be minimized. There are problems in clearly distinguishing between offensive and defensive forces, that is, say, between a strategic airlift capability that could sustain an invading force and one that is required for internal security purposes in a country of near-continental proportions such as India. Moreover, the intentions and motives of nations can be difficult to fathom: they may be every bit as inscrutable as that of individual human beings.

Yet, while the difficulties should not be minimized, they should not be exaggerated either. They are not insuperable. In dialogue with rivals and adversaries, India can make progress towards agreement on weapons that are more offensive and those that are less offensive. While the difficulties of judging intent and motives are undeniable, clearly we are called on to make these judgments all the time in our individual and social existences. Indeed, life would be hard to sustain without such judgements. This is so for international and military affairs too.

In sum, I would argue that through dialogue states can come closer to agreement on the nature of more defensive and less defensive weapons systems. They can also better agree on what would constitute a shift from a more defensive to a less defensive posture. In mutual capabilities, make intentions more transparent, and put in place systems which tend more often to reassure than to frighten.[20] And to the extent that it is able to do so, it can lay the basis for a more affordable defence.

Nuclear Weapons and Social Dignity

Keeping open the option to build a nuclear arsenal and going nuclear outright are both incompatible with the goals of economic justice and social dignity. I have already suggested why a nuclear capability is unlikely to give us cheaper defence and why it is therefore contrary to the prospects of economic justice. A nuclear capability is also contrary to the prospects of social dignity, by which I mean it is constructive of individual autonomy and the sense of self-worth. This is true of both nuclear options—nuclear ambiguity and outright nuclearization.

The Costs of Nuclear Ambiguity

Keeping the option open will continue to adversely affect India's domestic politics and therefore the dignity of its citizens. A "neither-confirm-nor-deny" policy—unlike abstinence or even weaponization—must perforce be built on secrecy and obfuscation, to the detriment of a tradition of public accountability indispensable in a democracy. In addition, such a policy will be to the long-term detriment of Indian science, of the nuclear program itself, and, last but not least, to the health of the Indian people.

India's nuclear program is not the only area prone to secrecy and obfuscation, but its "success" in avoiding the public gaze would contribute to a political culture of lies and evasions, which in the long term will degrade Indian democracy. This same culture of lies and evasions must harm the larger enterprise of Indian science and technology. If one of the biggest and most prestigious areas of scientific and technological endeavor becomes prone to such a culture, it is hard to see how other areas can escape the miasma. Then there are the costs to the program itself. The most extraordinary legislation has been passed to "protect" the Indian nuclear program from public scrutiny.[21] This risks digging the grave of the nuclear program. A program regulated primarily by internal scrutiny will be inefficient and dangerous, and, if and when its wastefulness and harmfulness become apparent, public reaction may be to terminate the program altogether.[22] Lastly, nuclear technology is not a forgiving technology. A shrouded program, not open to external criticism and regulation, is liable to malpractice and mismanagement, the effects of which could seriously jeopardize the health and safety of large numbers of citizens for a long time to come.[23]

The Costs of Going Nuclear

The economic and environmental costs of going nuclear are substantial, even staggering, and merit great consideration, but in addition to these material costs are at least three less tangible costs which are deleterious to an open, democratic politics and society, namely, *over-centralization, hyper-secrecy* and *gigantism*, each of which is hurtful to the dignity of citizens in ways that I have just described but which merit a lengthier and more concrete discussion because these "pathologies" will be intensified in the case of outright nuclearization.

Nuclear programs must be highly centralized. This is so because of the extremely high risks associated with the materials involved and the necessity for control and communication over their production, use, movement, storage, and disposition. If the nuclear program involves nuclear weapons, then the degree of centralization must be even greater. The command and control of these doomsday weapons must reside with the highest authority in the land, with perhaps just a handful of men and women within the authority structure. Never in human history has so few controlled the destiny of so many so completely.

Beyond over-centralization is the problem of hyper-secrecy. While the physics and engineering of nuclear reactors, power plants, and weapons and their delivery systems are no longer particularly secret there remains a very high level of secrecy over what is happening in nuclear programs. Of course the level of secrecy varies by country and type of political system, but nuclear programs are everywhere shrouded and hidden from public view. Governments and other major nuclear agencies such as the utilities dread opening up their facilities and programs to outside scrutiny. Clearly, few governments will reveal precisely how many weapons they possess and where these are located, but there is even a reluctance to reveal what is happening within civilian facilities and programs. At least part of the reason is that since nuclear technology is dual use— that is, it has civilian but also military applications—it becomes a strategic resource. But one cannot help thinking that the nuclear community, public and private, has things to hide on the economic costs and the various hazards, lapses, risks, and uncertainties associated with their product which if more widely known would jeopardize the programs.

In addition to over-centralization and hyper-secrecy is a third cost—gigantism. Nuclear facilities and programs, civilian and military, entail massiveness. They not only require enormous investments financially but also other inputs: manpower, land, water, and, ironically, energy. A nuclear weapons program increases the size of the program and facilities. Weapons, even short-order weapons which are in a near-assembles state, must be stored somewhere, dispersed so that they are not vulnerable to a preemptive strike, and regulated by a command and control structure which must have a certain degree of redundancy built into it in order to withstand internal failures of external subversion and attack. Both civilian and military programs face the problem of waste storage, often for thousands of years, which guarantees, that even if a country terminates its programs a large establishment devoted to safe storage over a considerable period of time will be necessary.

This preference or tendency towards massiveness and redundancy is hardly confined to matters nuclear. Indeed, massiveness is correlated strongly with the general trajectory of economic development for which India has opted. But, given the lethality and unforgiving nature of the technology, investing in gigantism is more marked in the nuclear sector than in perhaps any other sector. How is gigantism a political cost? Massive human systems if they are to maintain certain coherence and cohesiveness in the end must be hierarchical. They must be finely compartmentalized so that each subsystem knows and does a partial task and is not burdened with overall goals, methods, and decisions. To invest consistently in gigantism is to contribute to the psychology, culture, and ideology of hierarchy and compartmentalization, which is a psychology, culture, and ideology of obedience.

The point of course is not that nuclear programs are the sole cause of over-centralization, hyper-secrecy, and gigantism. But they are a cause. And they do aggravate these pathologies. To see this, let us imagine a situation in which the other causes are dismantled or overcome. The presence of nuclear weapons or a large-scale civilian nuclear program would remain a powerful reason for centralization, secrecy, and scale.

A deeper point is this. Excessive centralization, secretiveness, hierarchy, compartmentalization and obedience are the characteristics *par excellence* of a culture of bureaucratism and militarization. Nuclearism is in the end a culture of bureacratism and militarism that are inelegant words for an excessive preoccupation with order and violence rather than flexibility and restraint. At the limit, order produces rigidity, and violence produces death. In short, nuclearism is a form of scleroticism—what with E.P. Thompson we could call "exterminism."[24] In India, we must ask ourselves whether over-centralization, hyper-secrecy and gigantism, bureaucratism, militarism, rigidity, and violence are costs we can afford. We—and other democracies—may survive as rough and tumble pluralist democracies—but will these be commensurate with a humane society? In repeat that nuclearism itself is not the sole cause of such trends. The point though is that in any cost/benefit analysis we shall have to think more deeply about the effects of nuclear programs and weapons.

It is worth concluding these thoughts on the political and social costs of nuclear programs with some extensions to the conduct and organization of science in the shadow of nuclearism. Science as much as our political and social system is liable to the pathologies associated with over-centralization, hyper-secrecy, gigantism, bureaucratism, and militarism. The precise effects of nuclearism after 1945 on the conduct and organization as well as self-perception and ambitions of science are beyond the scope and length of this essay, but there is little doubt that the "Manhattanization" of science is one result. The Manhattan Project leading to the construction of the first nuclear weapons test and use was science most centralized, most secret, and massive. On might argue that the "success" of this dedicated program and its role in ending the war gave science a boost: if science could deliver so spectacularly, then it deserved support as never before, at least in *raison d'etat* terms. And indeed it received support worldwide as never before. But though science may have profited from—dare one say?—fallout of the Manhattan Project, Manhattanization seems contrary to a humane and humanist science. A Manhanttanized science is a bureaucratic-military machine: it is the impoverishment of the scientific imagination, and it will be the attachment of science to the state.

Science and the state will inter-penetrate, each using the other for its interests and advancement, producing a national scientific/security state.[25]

WHAT IS TO BE DONE?

If nuclear weapons are more trouble than they are worth, what can India do about the evolving nuclear arms race with Pakistan? Broadly, three types of solutions exist: multilateral; regional, and unilateral. All of these are plausible solutions, but the Indian government and Indian strategic analysts have, over the years, opposed all three on a variety of grounds. The only option India seemingly will countenance is a phased global disarmament plan which would have (*a*) the nuclear weapons states commit themselves to the complete elimination of nuclear weapons and (*b*) the near nuclear states such as India, Israel, and Pakistan to join them more or less at the penultimate stage of disarmament.

The Nuclear Non-Proliferation Treaty

One way of ending South Asia's nuclear competition is to join a multilateral structure which could ensure that once both sides give up the nuclear option this can be policed effectively. The most obvious way of doing this is for India to accede simultaneously with Pakistan to the Nuclear Non-Proliferation Treaty (NPT). While this is acceptable to Pakistan, it has been categorically rejected by the Indian government. India's case against the NPT route is mostly ethical, diplomatic, and political. Increasingly, its objections are also technical.

First, since the inception of the Treaty in 1968, New Delhi has opposed it as contrary to the norms of international society because it imposes unequal obligations on signatories. While the non-nuclear weapons powers are asked to renounce the option and to open up their facilities to international inspection, the nuclear powers are asked to renounce the option and to open up their facilities to international inspection, the nuclear powers are not constrained to dismantle their arsenals or to submit to any form of international scrutiny. India's formal position therefore is that, despite the nuclear test of 1974, it has neither exercised the nuclear option nor closed it.

Second, it is argued that no Indian government could reverse its opposition to the Treaty without serious loss of diplomatic credibility. To do a *volte face* after 27 years of steadfast opposition would undermine the reliability of India as an international partner. It would also raise questions about Indian diplomatic fortitude. If India could finally be persuaded to turn, would it not become more prone to unequal agreements?

Third, to join the NPT, it is claimed, would inflame domestic opinion and destroy any political entity that proposed accession. To accept unequal international agreements would be seen as a reversion to near-colonial political status. Public anger would topple any government that took a decision to join the NPT and might so enrage opinion as to lead a successor government to go nuclear in defiance.

Fourth, there is opposition to the NPT on technical grounds. Technically, it is being argued that there is no foolproof method, unilateral or multilateral, of preventing and policing the illicit diversion of radioactive material into nuclear weapons production. The experience of Iraq and North Korea are cited as examples. In spite of Iraqi and North Korean membership of the NPT, and in spite of IAEA certification that suggested compliance, both states violated the Treaty. In the case of Iraq, notwithstanding military defeat and three years of highly-intrusive investigations by international inspectors, there remains a concern that the full extent of the program has not yet been unearthed and that not all of it has been eradicated.[26]

There is also growing concern that the NPT as well as regional agreements and various supplemental measures are inadequate in preventing and policing the diversion of radioactive and weapons grade materials from the former Soviet Union (FSU), materials which could find their way to Pakistan. These materials plus the emigration of FSU scientists in search of employment could be used to produce nuclear weapons clandestinely.[27]

This is a powerful case. Not surprisingly, no one in India any longer seriously supports signing the NPT. At least, no one does so publicly. However, each part of the anti-NPT case can be contested.

The first response to the anti-NPT arguments is that while discriminatory agreements and institutions should indeed be avoided, India and other countries have entered into such agreements and joined such institutions when the advantages of doing so have outweighed the costs. Indian membership in the United Nations is a good instance of a cost-benefit calculus that has over-ridden the claims of universalism. The Permanent Five of the Security Council have special rights and obligations, a condition that India accepted from the inception of the UN. It did so because, on balance, it was better to have a world body than not have one. New Delhi's present position is that these special rights and obligations should be extended to include India. It is not India's position to revoke them.[28]

The fact that the NPT is attractive to the vast majority of states should also give one pause. While it is widely accepted that the Treaty is in a formal sense discriminatory, most states have nonetheless joined. If we discount the possibility that these countries are ethically blind and diplomatically naïve or craven, their accession must signify that for a very large number of countries the overall advantages of the Treaty outweigh the disadvantages including its discriminatory character.

A second response is that when the two major NWSs, the US and Russia, are making substantial progress towards disarmament, and when various "standouts" have joined the NPT, to reconsider Treaty membership may be credible diplomatically.

The destruction of US and Russia tactical nuclear weapons and intermediate forces, as well as the 50 percent cuts in strategic warheads, if carried through, will sharply reduce their inventories. Clearly, the two powers have at long last gone some way in meeting their NPT obligations. Of course, these reductions will leave enormous destructive power in American and Russian hands. Much more therefore needs to be done, but further deep cuts will be constrained by the kinds of technical and economic limits referred to earlier. Nevertheless, more cuts in nuclear weapons will likely be negotiated in the years to come. In addition, the decisions of China and France to join the NPT as NWSs, as well as South African accession to it as a non-weapon state, have strengthened the agreement. Most recently, the US—North Korea deal has prevented a potentially serious defection from the Treaty. In sum, the NPT structure is more balanced and inclusive than even before.

A third response is that public opposition to India joining the NPT is not some implacable, independent, and informed force acting on government decision-making. Public opinion in India, as elsewhere, is in considerable part moulded by political leadership and is therefore neither implacable nor independent. A stable leadership that outlined the advantages and disadvantages of joining the NPT and made a case for accession could change Indian opinion.

The larger point is that it is doubtful that public opinion in the sense of an informed mass and elite have constrained the Indian government's choices. There is no mass understanding of the issues involved. It is often suggested that this does not matter because the representatives of the Indian people, its parliamentarians, have often enough indicated their overwhelming opposition to the NPT. So too has the elite—in successive opinion surveys in its writings, and in its seminars. However, as Indian security analysts are painfully aware, whereas passions run high, sustained interest or expertise in defence matters—even amongst these groups—runs low. This does not mean that Indian MPs and the elite can be ignored; but to claim that their views are well informed is to exaggerate. India is by no means unique in respect of public apathy and ignorance on defence issues; but that is just the point.

Ignorance of defence matters and the low salience of the nuclear issue together suggest that, if the Indian government were to make a strong case for reconsidering NPT membership, opposition would not necessarily be insurmountable.

Finally, with respect to the technical problems of the NPT, it can be responded that while Iraqi and North Korean violations did indeed escape the inspection regime, surely it cannot be overlooked that both states were eventually caught. Moreover, whatever the legality and morality of the war against Iraq, it may have laid the basis for a more intrusive inspections regime. Again, while the recent US—North Korea nuclear deal has been criticized on various grounds, it is an indication that the non-proliferation effort should move in the direction of an "NPT plus" structure—constraints the former Soviet Union, this argues for greater not less multilateral regulation of nuclear programs; if the NPT did not exist, something like it would have to be invented.

A Regional Deal

India could also propose a regional accord on nuclear weapons—to limit, perhaps even eliminate them. Once again, this is acceptable to Pakistan but has been dismissed by the Indian government as "the NPT by another name." The four criticisms against the NPT and the responses to those criticisms apply here as well.

A regional agreement can be criticized on the additional grounds that, while it may have the effect of the NPT in stopping additional proliferation, it does not offer the full range of Treaty benefits. For instance, India within the NPT could be a greater force in modifying elements of the Treaty and in persuading the NWSs to fulfill their two key obligations: reducing and eventually abolishing their arsenals; and facilitating the peaceful uses of nuclear energy among the non-nuclear weapons signatories.

Perhaps the biggest advantage of an India–Pakistan agreement is that New Delhi could continue to claim that it had not retreated from its original opposition to the NPT. On balance, though, a regional agreement is probably somewhat inferior to signing the NPT. However, neither the NPT nor a strictly bilateral deal is anywhere near acceptance by the Indian government.

What seems closer to acceptance is the United States' most recent plan, an alternative regional mechanism in effect, one that is a hybrid of multilateralism and bilateralism. Washington proposes that India and Pakistan join a universal ban on (a) nuclear testing and (b) the production of fissile material. These two measures would effectively "cap" or "freeze" the nuclear arms race in the region as elsewhere. Indian joined the US and a number of other countries in co-sponsoring a resolution in the United Nations urging enactment of both measures. Neither a Comprehensive Test Ban Treaty (CTBT) nor a global fissile material ban has yet been negotiated, but India is in principle committed to both, provided that they are universal and non-discriminatory.

While the Indian government seems to have moved towards the US plan, critics in India argue that the CTBT is flawed. Central to their critique is the judgment that computer simulated testing and "zero-yield" tests are beyond the reach of a CTBT and may not be sufficiently reliable in certifying the efficacy of a weapons design. Thus, Pakistan could hide a nuclear weapons program from the NPT and could unveil it at a time of its choosing to intimidate India. Critics have also indicated a fissile material ban. They make two charges: that a ban is inequitous because it would leave the nuclear weapons states with enormous amounts of fissile material; and that banning the production of fissile material is unverifiable. This had led to a good deal of indignation in the Indian press over the US's call for India and Pakistan to join a declaration on a halt to the production of fissile material pending the enactment of a universal ban.

The critics have forced the Indian government on the defensive, but the US plan is commensurate with Indian goals and interests. A CTBT has been a long-held Indian objective. Indeed, India was the originator of the proposal, as early as 1954. More importantly, though, a verifiable halt to testing, if universal, is in India's interest because it will help check "vertical" proliferation and will prevent further environmental damage from testing. Thus, while CTBT is not a perfect solution in respect of testing, insisting on perfection risks the best becoming the enemy of the good. In addition, if computer-simulated and zero-yield tests are beyond the purview of a CTBT, it should not be forgotten that the reliability of laboratory tests is open to question: it is far from clear that the political leadership as well as the armed forces of any state will gamble with weapons that have only been certified by this sort of "quasi-testing." As for a ban on fissile material production, it is widely understood that this cannot be foolproof. Here again, though, a ban has been a long-held Indian position; and more importantly, it serves India's interest inasmuch as it slows vertical proliferation and does not require New Delhi to surrender the stocks of fissile material it has built up.

It is worth addition, in the end, that while the NPT, the complex of agreements relating to materials and personnel from FSU programs, the CTBT and the call for a fissile material ban are individually flawed, together they comprise a strong regime. It is a regime, moreover, that is consistent with the Indian goal of slowing or stopping Pakistani nuclearization. This is well enough understood in India. But it is India's calculation that the regime will or will not constrain Pakistan regardless of Indian participation in it. Thus, India could have a large slice of its nuclear cake and eat it too—the benefits of the nuclear regime without the burdens of joining it.

Unilateral Nuclear Disarmament

Finally, India could call off the nuclear arms race by unilaterally giving up the option. While this is not a policy that has much public support, it is not as unrealistic as may appear.

A variety of arguments might be advanced in support of a unilateralist position, but the most telling counter-argument is that, confronted by an India which has unconditionally and verifiably renounced nuclear weapons, Pakistan will find it extremely difficult to keep its nuclear option open, to go nuclear outright, or to remain nuclear.[29] International opinion and pressures will be exerted against Islamabad as never before. Though Pakistan can attempt to deflect international opinion and pressures by claiming that only nuclear weapons can counter India's more or less permanent superiority in conventional forces and strategic depth, this can be expected to encounter considerable opposition.

It will be argued against Islamabad that Pakistani deficiencies and fear are correctable, in at least two ways. First, Pakistan can be promised enough additional conventional arms to enable it to deter India and to defend itself should deterrence break down. Second, instead of "leveling up" the quantum of conventional forces, it is possible to "level down" so that both sides have enough defence against each other, as well as third parties and internal enemies. With its dramatic nuclear gesture, India will have opened the door to negotiating a conventional force balance that is consonant with Pakistani security needs. The Conventional Forces in Europe (CFE) agreement, signed after the Intermediate Forces Treaty, shows that this can be achieved. A South Asian balance will not be easy to construct, given that both sides have to maintain forces for other opponents and for internal security; but negotiated sufficiency and a non-provocative defence is not an impossibility either.[30]

Of the two correctives, leveling down is preferable. One of the advantages of going nuclear, it is usually argued, is that it saves expenditure on relatively expensive conventional arms. Therefore, Pakistan can object that it is cheaper to match India's conventional superiority with nuclear capability than with increased conventional capability. Leveling down to a conventional balance that satisfies both sides and which avoids a costly arms race can overcome this objection. Level-down negotiations, as suggested earlier, would focus on reducing inventories of offensive weapon systems on both sides, that is, systems which encourage thoughts of a first strike and which tend to be more expensive. To repeat, the problem of what constitutes and "offensive" weapon and what is a "defensive" weapon is a difficult one but not an insuperable one.

CONCLUSION: NUCLEAR WEAPONS AND THE MILITARIZATION OF SOUTH ASIA

Nuclear weapons cannot deter the most important threats to India's security, and to the extent that they can deter and threat this posture is prone ineluctably to decay over time. Furthermore, nuclear weapons are not an investment in affordable defence. Finally, they are incompatible with the social dignity of Indian citizens. Yet the Indian government and sections of its policy community—that is, sections of its politicians, officials, media commentators, and think-tankers—continue to argue that it is necessary either to keep the nuclear option open or to move to actual weaponization. There is on behalf of this posture an enormous propagandistic effort which has acquired plausibility and a hegemonic position in defence thinking by repetition, by the paucity of information on defence and nuclear issues (information which is controlled by the state), and by the lack of sustained interest amongst the better part of those responsible for assessing and making public policy. India could be secure without nuclear weapons, and a variety of options exist which could lead to abstinence, but these have been marginalized in public discourse by appeals to nationalism and "realism."

Undergirding Indian nuclearism, and hidden from view in a relatively open political system, is militarism. Militarism has been defined by Alfred Vagts in his classic work, as "a vast array of customs, interests, prestige, actions and thought associated with armies and wars and yet transcending true military purposes," a complex which may even hamper war aims. This complex is unlimited in its growth and may come to permeate all of society.[31] The discourse of nuclearism in India—and Pakistan is no different—is a militaristic discourse. It is a complex which, I have tried to show, tries to justify a certain approach to defence but which on strategic grounds is open to question; indeed on strategic grounds it may positively hamper certain war aims, namely, combating sub-conventional conflict. It transcends military purposes when it claims that in addition to being strategically viable it contributes to economic justice and social dignity. Moreover, this complex is part of a larger post-colonial "national security" complex that is obsessed with centralization, secrecy, and gigantism and which has come to permeate virtually all of Indian society. Any struggle for economic justice and social dignity must inevitably therefore also be a struggle against the ideology of "national security" and nuclearism.

Notes and References

1. Published in Ranabir Samaddar (ed.), *Cannons into Ploughshares—Militarization and Prospects of Peace in South Asia*. Delhi 1995.
2. For the notion of non-weaponized deterrence and its potential stability in South Asia, see George Perkovitch, "A Nuclear Third Way?," *Foreign Policy*, Fall, 1993.
3. See the view expressed in "Bundy, Crowe, and Drell—A Program for Reducing the Nuclear Danger: But No Short Road to Disarmament," in the *Carnegie Quarterly*, vol. 38, nos 3 and 4, Summer/Fall 1993, pp. 5–6, "As to the unannounced nuclear weapons states—Israel, India, and Pakistan—the cochairmen [i.e., McGeorge Bundy, Jonathan Crowe, and Sidney Drell] ask of them a greater measure of openness about their real nuclear capabilities, suggesting that each in different ways pays a heavy price for its pretense—a pretense that, in any event, has worn irritatingly thin.... The advantage of recognizing these countries for what they are is not merely a matter of dealing with reality,

as important as that is. It is also a matter of not dealing these countries as they are not."

4. There is a vast critique of deterrence. But see Jonathan Schell's *The Abolition*, London, 1984 for a thoughtful and passionate critique of nuclear weapons and deterrence. For an Indian philosopher's view, see Bimal Krishna Matilal's "Between Peace and Deterrence," in Elaine Kaye (ed.), *Peace Studies: The Hard Questions*, Oxford Peace Lectures 1984–85. London, 1987, pp. 59–82. For an Indian strategist's view, see K. Subrahmanyam, "The Myth of Deterrence," in K. Subrahmanyam (ed.), *Nuclear Myths and Realities*. New Delhi, 1981. Subrahmanyam argues that, while deterrence is a "myth," as long as others believe in its efficacy, India should use the myth to advantage.

5. This line of argumentation draws on John Lewis Gaddis, *The Long Peace: Inquiries Into the History of the Cold War*. New York, 1987, chapter 8.

6. This is a relatively controversial point, I grant. However, it seems to me that there is a good enough case to be made in support of my contention. The view that "one Pakistani is as good as ten Indians" was as marked in the Pakistani armed forces as in the public at large. On the Indian side, there has always been a sniffiness about the "feudal" style of the Pakistani officers corps, now replaced by an equal measure of ridicule about its "Islamic" character. The Pakistan army's intervention in politics has also been seen in India as sign of its lack of "professionalism."

7. Sumit Ganguly reminds me that Glenn Snyder long ago alluded to this in his formulation of the "stability–instability paradox": stability at the nuclear level would permit instability at lower levels. See his *Deterrence and Defense: Towards a Theory of National Security*. Princeton, 1961. This is hinted at also in P.M.S. Blackett, *Fear, War, and the Bomb*. New York, 1948, p. 203: "On the other hand the threat of use of weapons of mass destruction may prove far less a deterrent than an incitement of the rival power to strengthen its position by relatively unprovocative means. In fact, the obvious counter to the diplomatic use of the threat of atomic and similar weapons is the intensification of political warfare, or the actual waging of a guerilla type of war."

8. This recalls Raju Thomas' point that, if both sides go nuclear, India will have lost the advantage of more or less permanent conventional military superiority. I do not recall where Thomas made this agreement.

9. Some of these concerns are expressed by K. Subrahmanyam, "Implications of Nuclear Asymmetry," in Subrahmanyam (ed.), *Nuclear Myths and Realities*, pp. 214–15.

10. See Subrahmanyam, "India's Dilemma," in Subrahmanyam (ed.), *Nuclear Myths and Realities*, p. vii.

11. See, for instance, Clifford Singer, "Beyond Horizontal and Vertical Proliferation: Towards an Integrated Approach to Nuclear Weapons Material," in Kanti Bajpai and Stephen P. Cohen (eds), *South Asia After the Cold War: International Perspectives.* Boulder, 1993, pp. 197–201, mostly on the United States.
12. Robert B. Barker, "The Environmental Costs of the United States Nuclear Weapons Program," in Kathleen Bailey (ed.), *Weapons of Mass Destruction: Costs and Benefits.* New Delhi, 1994, p. 123.
13. See Subrahmanyam, "Implications of Nuclear Asymmetry," in Subrahmanyam (ed.), *Nuclear Myths and Realities,* p. 209: "Nuclear weapons can be deterred only by nuclear weapons."
14. It may be argued that the escalation ladder is not relevant to South Asia, that it was necessitated by the US "extended deterrence" posture which required Washington to prevent attacks on its trans-Atlantic and trans-Pacific allies. US willingness to use nuclear weapons on behalf of its allies if and when they were under conventional attack from superior Soviet or Chinese forces might not have seemed credible to Moscow or Beijing, and an escalation ladder was a way of suggesting that while the initial response would be conventional this would be part of a graduated program of responses which could culminate in nuclear weapons use from battlefied to strategic strikes. What troubled US military planners and their NATO partners was an opponent's calculation that in the end of US would not risk nuclear war to protect values outside its homeland. Proxy wars in peripheral areas such as Kashmir, Punjab or the Northeast could be seen in a similar way by India's opponents on the calculation that in the end New Delhi would not risk nuclear conflagration to defend "marginal" areas. An escalation ladder may not therefore be irrelevant to South Asia.
15. On the term "defensive defence" and its cognates such as non-offensive or non-provocative defence, see Bjorn Moeller, *Common Security and Non-offensive Defense: A Neorealist Perspective.* Boulder, 1992 and David Gates, *Non-offensive Defence: An Alternative Strategy for NATO?* New York, 1991.
16. On Pakistan's decision to move towards "offensive defense" notions, see Stephen P. Cohen, *The Pakistan Army.* Berkeley, 1984, pp. 144–7 and similarly on Indian moves, see George Tanham, "Indian Strategic Culture," *The Washington Quarterly,* 15 (Winter 1992), pp. 129–42.
17. For the notion of cooperative security, see Ashton B. Carter, William J. Perry and John D. Steinbruner, *A New Concept of Cooperative Security.* Brookings Occasional Paper, Washington D.C., 1992.
18. Moeller, *Common Security and Non-offensive Defense,* p. 151.
19. See the discussion in Moeller, *Common Security and Non-offensive Defense,* pp. 147–52.

20. Moeller, *Common Security and Non-offensive Defense*, while acknowledging the difficulties of distinguishing between offensive and defensive, nonetheless comes to a similar set of conclusions.
21. See, for instance, the Atomic Energy Act of 1948, the reconstitution of the Atomic Energy Commission (AEC) in 1958, and the AEC Act of 1962.
22. Raju Thomas argues that the nuclear weapons option is used to justify a civilian nuclear program that could at best meet only 10 percent of India's future energy needs. See his "India," in Raju G.C. Thomas and Bennett Ramberg (eds), *Energy and Security in the Industrializing World*. (Lexington, Kentucky, 1990), pp. 13–34.
23. There have been a number of accidents and failures at Indian nuclear plants since 1993. The most publicized was the fire at Narora in March 1994 that led to the temporary closing of the plant. The Indian government has apparently begun a program of cooperation with the US on nuclear safety issues. Eight US officials from the Nuclear Regulatory Commission (NRC) visited the Kaiga, Narora, and Tarapur plants in mid-February 1995. See "US Team to Visit Tarapur plants," *The Hindustan Times*. New Delhi, January 3, 1995.
24. E.P. Thompson, "Notes on Exterminism, the Last Stage of Civilisation," in *Beyond the Cold War: A New Approach to the Arms Race and Nuclear Annihilation*. New York, 1982, pp. 41–79.
25. These themes are examined and illustrated in Ashis Nandy (ed.), *Science, Hegemony, and Violence: A Requiem for Modernity*. Delhi, 1988. Especially useful are Ashis Nandy, "Introduction: Science as a Reason of State," pp.1–23 and Shiv Vishwanathan, "Atomic Physics: The Career of an Imagination," pp. 113–66.
26. P.R. Chari, "Indian Defence and Security: A Cost–Benefit Analysis of Nuclear Proliferation," in Bailey (ed.), *Weapons of Mass Destruction*, pp. 97–99 refers to the Iraqi and North Korean case in the context of the "fragility of the non-proliferation regime."
27. Chari, "Indian Defence and Security," in Bailey (ed.), *Weapons of Mass Destruction*, p. 98.
28. This is a point made also by Pran Chopra in his *India, Pakistan, and the Kashmir Tangle*. New Delhi, 1994, p. 49, rather more pungently: "... India itself discriminates in applying that criterion [non-discrimination], it is happy to be a member of the UN system in which some countries have the veto power and some not, and India would be still happier if it also acquired this discriminatory status."
29. I have examined these at some length in my essay "Nuclear Abstinence: Thinking About the Unthinkable," in David Cortright and Amitabh Mattoo (eds), *India and the Bomb*. South Bend, Indiana, 1997.

30. The notion of defensive sufficiency occupies a prominent part in the recent attempts to delineate "cooperative security." See Janne Nolan (ed.), *Global Engagement: Cooperation and Security in the 21st Century*. Washington, D.C., 1994. On an application to South Asia, see Kanti Bajpai and Stephen P. Cohen, "Cooperative Security and South Asian Insecurity," in Nolan (ed.), *Global Engagement*, pp. 447–80. On the notion of non-provocative defense, see Moeller, *Common Security and Non-offensive Defense* and Gates, *Non-offensive Defence: An Alternative Strategy for NATO?*
31. Alfred Vagts, *A History of Militarism: Civilian and Military*. (Place of publication not cited: Meridian Books, 1959), p. 13.

17

SUB-REGIONAL DIALOGUE IN THE EAST AND THE NORTHEAST—A NEW WAY TO COOPERATE[1]

Paula Banerjee, Sanjoy Hazarika, Monirul Hussain, and Ranabir Samaddar

Almost all of the outstanding issues between India and Bangladesh continue to be related to disputes along the common border. This paper puts forth a few suggestions for successful negotiation of the immigration problem that is also linked to the larger issue of enhanced sub-regional communication and trade.

THE PROBLEM

Both India and Bangladesh have proved woefully inadequate in dealing with the reality of the border between the two countries. It is ironic that the border which was drawn by the British in 1947 to rationally reorganize the political space in the region, has eventually not only generated its own irrationality, but has also created many new problems for the region. The border, with its long history of movements between people, cultures, beliefs, ideas, and customs was completely unreal from the beginning. Land on both sides of the border was mostly cultivable and was locked and there were farms that were within 40 yards of zero point on either side. Perhaps the most important characteristic of the border was that in many cases it was not contiguous. There are 53 rivers in the region that make functioning of the border more complicated. Almost all of India's disputes with East Pakistan related to this border, mostly involving rivers (Report of the Indo-Pakistan Boundary Disputes Tribunal,

1958). The dispute over the boundary between Murshidabad and Rajshahi was a typical example of these initial disputes where even the tribunal decided that the demarcation of the line made by the boundary commission "... is found to be impossible." Even more problematic was that each country had its enclaves within the boundary of the other, meaning that the border was rife with potential for problem.

After the liberation of Bangladesh it was hoped that the border would lose much of its potential for creating disputes and enmity with the improvement of bilateral relations. Sadly, even after 25 years of the birth of Bangladesh, almost all the outstanding issues between India and Bangladesh continue to be related to the common border. These include sharing of water-resources of common rivers, CHT, demarcation of maritime boundaries and the ownership of South Moore/Talpatty Island, illegal crossborder activities, illegal migration, Berubari corridor and the granting of entry/exit facilities. Convictions about the sanctity of the border are weaker in this region than elsewhere in India.

Efforts to curb the movement of people and goods, including timber, cattle, textiles, electronic goods, sugar, medicine and kerosene, have failed. Out of a combination of despair and political pressure, the Government of India has built barbed wire fencing on parts of both Assam and the West Bengal sides of the border. In South Bengal sector alone 358 km and in Assam 159 km of fencing program has been sanctioned. Other measures such as regular patrolling and check posts continue. But these have not stemmed the flow of either people or goods; indeed, it is no secret that border guards on either side accept and demand bribes from those seeking to cross illegally. As a result of the influx, the size of which is difficult to estimate, a constant state of tension exists, in Assam in particular and other states of the Northeast as well as between migrants, perceived migrants and the host communities. If one is to accept that migration is a natural human phenomenon that occurs in varying degrees world wide, one must also accept the fact that few countries in the world have successfully contained it, be it a super power like the United States or a small country like Germany. Again, if one is to go by the premise that immigration, especially illegal immigration cannot be stopped, one must go a step further and say that it can only be contained or regulated. Or rather, it can be negotiated through a process of meaningful economic activities, exchanges, regulatory mechanisms, and above all through dialogue.

The problem of crossborder migration is sometimes complicated by religious factors. Either the minorities look to the option of taking shelter in the neighboring country exasperated with majoritarian insensitivities, or remain potential refugees or illegal migrants. During 1972–93, a total number of 4,125,576 people arrived in India from Bangladesh. Out of that a total of 836,524 overstayed (difference between the immigration and emigration figures). Of them 538,501 were Hindus (GOI data).

SOME POLICY SUGGESTIONS

In terms of the Indian side of the border, particularly on the eastern side of Bangladesh, the following are some specific suggestions that require inputs from the legal specialists for improvement and better implementation. These are suggestions that will need much more study and detailed work.

(1) A system of identity cards acceptable to local population, particularly those living on the border in the eastern and the Northeastern region has to be ensured.

(2) While the system of visas for nationals of either country will continue, for those who cannot or do not want to use the visa system for economic and quasi-economic reasons, a specific, time-bound legal system sanctioning their presence in the host area for mutual economic benefit of both sides, legal and acknowledged, has to be devised. We can take the specific case of the border Indian district of Dhubri that shares both a river and land border with Bangladesh. The process of acquiring a passport (for which one has to travel eastward in an opposite direction, to the capital city of Guwahati) and a visa (for which one has to travel again to Calcutta) are both cumbersome and time-consuming. It is therefore, often tempting to simply cross the contiguous border "unofficially" by paying some money to the *dalals* or brokers who arrange for a quick and safe crossover for almost a paltry sum. A less cumbersome and more practical system of arranging for both passport and visa in the region will

help in turning many such "unofficial" bordercrossing into legal entrance and thus help in a meaningful monitoring and negotiation of the phenomenon.

(3) This will involve the development of a scheme to allow migrants to come legally into the region on the basis of work permits issued by a Central Work Permit Authority with the backing of the relevant state set up by an Act of the Parliament, with specific clauses involving the officials of the local state and village-level administrators who will act as checks and balances to each other ensuring that no one group becomes too powerful so as to be able to bend the system. This may be worked out in association with the Home Ministry as well as Ministry for Law and Company Affairs. A retired Supreme Court/High Court judge may head such a panel and a member of the National Human Rights Commission (NHRC) may be associated with it.

(4) Since the permits are intended to discourage illegal migration, and promote healthy economic cooperation at sub-regional and local level of both sides, the priliminary step may be that the permits be issued to groups (of say, 20 or so) rather than to individuals. It should be allowed in the following fields: agricultural operations at harvest time; construction; boat-building; fishing, and allied activities. The work permits could be issued at the border at posts set up for this purpose by cells that would include a representative of the District Magistrate. The members include one senior member of the local panchayat or village council system; a police officer; a member of an NGO or some other public organization; a representative of the labor board; and a labor; with one of these five being a woman. Since the border is long, a system of such posts needs to be worked out either situating them at existing check posts or around them.

(5) The permits may be issued on the spot after verification of the following documents: (*a*) the identity of the applicant(s) as proof of nationality/residency; (*b*) a clear statement on the place he/she will be residing for a maximum of next one year (work permits will be given for a maximum of one year to begin with) and the name of the employer who or whose representative must be present for the issue of the permit with supporting documents from his side; (*c*) a document of undertaking signed by the employer stating the employer's responsibility for the

immigrant group/individual and his/her duty to report to the local authority (preferably local labor board) three times in a year; at the time of arrival to register; after six months to reconfirm their presence; and at the time of departure at the end of the year. If the permit is to be extended, it can be done by the District Commissioner (DC) or the Labor Commissioner of the relevant district, for a period not exceeding another two years; (*d*) the work permit will carry the photograph of the permit holder and will be laminated with his thumb impression/ signature on the document to prevent misuse of the same; (*e*) the permit holders will have no voting or political rights but will have access to courts of the host country if their civil rights are injured in any way and will be permitted to receive payment for services at the same level as local workers and repatriate their savings to their home country; (*f*) the entire arrangement will also give due consideration to the rights of local citizens while making use of a dynamic human resource.

(6) For the Indo-Bangladesh border, an autonomous binational commission can be formed to act as a flexible instrument for formulating strategies of cooperation. Such a commission will form temporary working groups of local parallels as existing between West Bengal/Assam/Meghalaya/India and Bangladesh on matters of land-holdings, employment, social and economic resources and formulate policies based on commonalities and the market. Border demography, settlement problems in border areas, ethnic divisions within the region, viability of developing environmental provisions to convert the area into a self-sustaining unit with linkages to both countries will be ascertained by groups set up by the commission, the ultimate goal being to hand over local administration to largely de-centralized administrative units which can work with greater competence and stability in comparison to the vested interest groups and consequently the promotion of an atmosphere of greater understanding between two countries and also in the sub-region. Keeping in mind the enormous problems of surface communications suffered by the Northeast Indian states, it is strongly recommended that Bangladesh seriously considers the allotment of exit/entry visa facilities that will allow them to travel to other parts of the Indian mainland through Bangladesh territory. Bangladesh will generate substantial revenue from

this traffic. It is recommended that such exit/entry visa facility be available to Indian nationals who are residents of the seven Northeast Indian states—Tripura, Mizoram, Manipur, Meghalaya, Assam, Nagaland, and Arunachal Pradesh—for a period of four days. In case of transport problems due to unforeseen calamities such as floods the visa may be extended for another three days. The total duration of the exit/entry visa should not be for a period of more than seven days. Bangladesh already has a mission in Agartala that can be empowered to issue the exit/entry visas on the basis of an agreed amount of foreign exchange endorsement. In issuing such visas the Bangladesh mission may be guided by the permanent address of the visa applicant's passport.

(8) The proposed passenger bus service between Kolkata and Dhaka should be extended to Agartala and if possible to Silchar and Guwahati. This will provide cheap means of transport to residents in the area.

(9) To facilitate legitimate growth in Indo-Bangla border trade, customs and banking formalities of both countries should be simplified through direct interaction between the Chambers of Commerce in Bangladesh and those in Northeast India. Existing border area markets locally called as *hat*, should be identified to develop legitimate border trade.

LARGER POLICY ISSUES

A successful negotiation of the immigration question is linked to the larger issues of enhanced sub-regional communication and trade. Though this calls for a separate paper, here we present some broad issues.

(1) In today's world, it is appropriate to emphasize commonalities, the need for greater cooperation and the need to abandon an "isolationist mind-set", particularly in the backdrop of the partition of the subcontinent which has put both India and Pakistan/Bangladesh into serious economic disadvantage apart from the immense human cost that it has involved. The economy of East Pakistan remained blocked as remained that of India's Northeast. Minus East Pakistan/Bangladesh, the distance between the east and the Northeast increased substantially, thereby acutely burdening the region with a

quasi-permanent state of underdevelopment and underdeveloped communication. Experts have pointed out that the road distance between Kolkata and Agartala is about 2,000, longer than the distance between Kolkata and Mumbai. However, bulk commodities can be transferred from Kolkata or Haldia by ship along the coast to Chittagong port in Bangladesh, thereafter taken by Bangladesh railroad to Akhaura, adjacent to Agartala, and finally transported by Indian trucks to various destinations in the Northeast, with the cost of transportation reducing drastically and the revenue of the Chittagong port increasing. India and Bangladesh, particularly the entire sub-region will gain consequently. Bangladesh can gain handsome royalty for the use of Chittagong port and the railway between Chittagong and Akhaura. This will help Bangladesh set off the current adverse balance of trade with India and have a trade surplus with the neighboring states of the sub-region. Bangladesh does not have enough goods for export to India, but can export services to the region. Then again, this traffic will improve the berthing facilities at Chittagong. The additional traffic to Akhaura will open up employment opportunities along the route. The units of the sub-region enjoying common facilities can undertake partial burden to construct berths at Chittagong port dedicated to the traffic, and also railway wagons and may also save foreign exchange.

(2) Another alternative is the reactivation of river traffic between Kolkata and Assam through the Sundarbans and the Bangladesh river system. There was considerable traffic on this route until 1965, when it was closed. On paper this route was revived after the independence of Bangladesh in 1971. But it has remained on paper only because of lack of investment necessary for maintaining a navigable channel all the year round, and because of inertia. According to experts, the river route is navigable all through the year from Kolkata up to the river port Ashuganj on the Meghna, or even up to Karimganj. The distance between Ashuganj and Agartala is only about 40 km. What is needed is the activation of this route with advice and help from inland water transport experts of both the countries and also from Germany, the Netherlands, and France, which have traditionally used inland water-borne traffic. What is lacking is the political will in this region to give effect to this concept.

With Haldia, Kolkata, Chittagong, Akhaura, Ashuganj, and Karimganj becoming the pivotal points of the coastal and rail routes the entire sub-region will gain enormously. We may think of the coordination of the roads also with the opening of the new Jamuna Bridge. What is principally needed is a fresh outlook that does not regard the common border and the common river as a burden but an asset to the entire region, i.e., the sub-region.

(3) The two countries as well as the units in the sub-region must give up its old attitudes, and must get away from the habit of mutual suspicion, and treat questions of security or espionage as of lesser consequence to the prospect of economic cooperation between the two countries, and particularly in the region. Once the two countries as well as the units in the region decide on improvement of trade, utilization of common resources, arrangement of transit, and mutual cooperation in investment, they will realize that political differences are of secondary importance. In short, to strengthen the communication network we need in the first place a sub-regional perspective before we adopt a metropolitan outlook symbolized by an Asian highway that covers India (West Bengal and the Northeast) and Bangladesh and can be utilized for the maximum benefit of the entire region. The truth is that the Asian Highway can bring economic improvement in the region only when it is linked with a network of local communication systems of rail, road, and water transport.

(4) The improvement of air transport is also crucial here. Not being a member of the IATA, the Biman (Bangladesh Airline) has its freedom and advantage to operate at a lower rate than most other international airlines. Once the Guwahati airport turns international, the Biman will have easy access to Guwahati, the gateway to the Northeast. Besides operating passenger services, it can have cargo services and hence can export/re-export certain goods from Assam/Northeast to the international market rapidly.

(5) Trade relationship can be augmented further when units in the sub-region have access to each other's markets. In this context it is important to note that most of the trade now is conducted illegally depriving both the Government of Bangladesh and its neighboring states. In such illegal trade, private traders

have built a nexus with some of their government officials and corrupt politicians, which has to be countered at all cost.

(6) Some new items may be taken up for trade: to take the example of the Northeast, the Meghalayan oranges and pineapples (which may be exported to Bangladesh and thence to Europe and the Middle East), in both raw and processed forms, so also the ginger, a kg of which costs Rs 120 in Dubai whereas the same costs Rs 10 in Guwahati. The famous Bangladeshi *jamdaani* and other high quality saris will have good market demand in Assam. Assam, in turn is famous for her *paat* and *mugaa* silks that could be sent to Bangladesh markets. Trade between India/Assam and Bangladesh has not increased substantially despite 12 years of South Asian Association for Regional Cooperation and the operationalization of South Asia Preferential Trading Agreement. What is needed today is a fast track approach and equity in trade. Trade relations lead to improvement of relations on a broad scale, like exchange of cultural troupes, artists, litterateurs, journalists, academics, researchers, and others.

(7) Finally, a joint sub-regional project to study the problem of borders and immigration should be initiated soon with a stipulated timeframe to complete the study. Admittedly, hurdles are there and pose a challenge to our collective intellectual capacity. They also impel us to negotiate the problem of borders and immigration in the broader context of economic cooperation, sub-regional cooperation, cultural dialogue, and human security in this part of the globe, which can hardly afford to remain an island in a fast-changing world.

NOTE AND REFERENCE

1. Working paper in the sub-regional dialogue initiated by the Bangladesh International Institute of Strategic Studies, Dhaka, on cooperation in the East and the Northeast of South Asia, and published in the *Economic and Political Weekly*, 4 September 1999, pp. 2549–51.

18

LITERARY SENSITIVITIES ON WAR, EXODUS, AND PARTITION

Subhoranjan Dasgupta

EPIC AS PREFACE

By "literary sensitivities" we mean in this context those emotions or feelings which war or warlike disposition or warlike attitude incites in creative writers and how these subjective reactions ranging from horror to pathos, disgust to sorrow are objectified in literary texts. I would like to begin from the epic, often designated as unsullied, heroic poetry. In fact, the popular impression is that in the ancient age war was valorized uncritically and this uncritical admiration received a fulsome expression in the epic. For example, when we recall the *Mahabharat* we tend to ignore almost everything else in favor of Arjuna's archery or Bhima's prowess with the mace. But that is a false reading of the text. For, the explicit critique of war even in these so-called heroic texts celebrating battles is embedded in the verse itself. It is difficult to bypass it.

Let us ignore for a moment the combats in *Kurukhestra* in order to concentrate on the *Streeparba* that follows. In this section, Gandhari, Bhanumati and other women who lost their sons and husbands have gone to the battlefield after the war is over. And what do they see:

> A great terror strikes on reaching the field
> Vultures and jackals are shouting hoarse
> Ghosts are dancing with heads in hands
> Dogs are feasting on flesh and blood
> Blood-spattered, the women move slowly.[1]

Then we are struck full by that gruesome detail which would have shocked even Luis Bunuel:

> Many trace their husbands after a long search
> They try to fix eagerly heads on shoulders.[2]

These lines (a rough translation from Kashiram Das's *Mahabharat*' done by me) are self explanatory. They associate the much-vaunted *Dharmayuddha* with a terrible outcome.

Streeparba has an apocalyptic quality about it. It rips open the soil of *Kurukhestra* and lays bare the vicious fruits of war. By doing so, it challenges the logic of Krishna: "Even when you fight, you do not fight for the spoils." Hence, the debate on war and peace in this epic is not confined to the text of *Gita* only, it is present in other sections as well. When one evaluates this debate with the entire text in mind, one concludes with Yudishtira:

> Friendless am I, what shall kingdom give
> Where is heroism in killing brothers and friends.
> I shall go where Duryodhan has gone
> Where brother Karna, valiant Drona have gone....
> I have deprived the earth of the brave
> I have sinned and I am afraid.[3]

On the one hand, we hear this lacerating self-condemnation of Yudishtira—war left him an eternal loser—and, on the other, we hear the wails of Gandhari and Bhanumati merging with the laments of Subhadra, Uttara, Kunti, and Draupadi. Agonies of the victor and vanquished formed one single piercing cry. Therefore, to the epic poet, war was one catastrophic experience that uprooted everything that fell on its course. Even the so-called Holy War left *Dharmaputra* Yudishtira an unholy sinner. In his own words, "I have committed endless crimes." He is the *other* opposed to all, Krishna included. Buddhadeva Bose wisely directed our attention to the sensitivity of this lonely moralist in his *Mahabharater Katha*.

Modern Intonation

Once we decipher this corrective inheritance of literary sensitivity starting from the epics, we realize that the inversion attempted in the same epics as a paradigmatic disguise or artifice, namely offer war as a noble deed, has its modern equivalent too. Anyone who has seen the documentaries of Leni Riefenstahl would understand what is meant. Her films show how the Nazis tried to accomplish a total inversion of the value system by propagating war as peace and vice versa. Leni's Hitler clamored for peace as the war machine steeled itself. In his poem *The Command of Warmongers* Ali Sardar Jafri detailed this stupendous distortion:

> Think of the smell of blood and gunpowder as perfume
> The command now is to regard wounds as fresh flowers
> Take the pleasure of an embrace from death
> And think of the sword's curve as the beloved's form
> Call war peace and peace war;
> Consider the prick of the thorn the same as that of a flower
> The wealth of the tearful eye is common everywhere
> Consider tears a cup of crime;
> Give the spirit of Satan the name of Gabriel,
> Think of lies as God's command, the prophet's word.[4]

—(Translated from Urdu by Carlo Coppola and Munibur Rahman)

The inbuilt irony of this poem makes it clear that the deliberate inversion is imposed as a command whose repetition does create a hellish impact at times. The hammered order—"call war peace"—becomes a part of the acquiescing self and soon an entire nation starts marching to it. Thus a second and fake actuality, but actuality nonetheless, is produced. Ali Sardar Jafri witnessed this debased reality in other words, the advance of Fascism. Yet, as a poet, it was his obligation to blast the ghostly bubble by concluding with an artifice that had to crumble under its own deceptive weight:

> Give the spirit of Satan the name of Gabriel
> Think of lies as God's commands, the prophet's word.

The distinctively modern tone in the structure of feeling or reaction around war entered when Ali Sardar Jafri chose the inversion of truth as his theme. This is the ironic accent, not without poignancy, which Wilfred Owen, perhaps the most eloquent war-poet of this century, introduced to cement the friend and enemy, killer and the killed in one indivisible sweep of agony in the poem *Strange Meeting*:

> I am the enemy you killed, my friend.
> I knew you in this dark; for so you frowned
> Yesterday through me as you jabbed and killed.
> I parried; but my hands were loath and cold.
> Let us sleep now.[5]

Neither Homer nor Vyasa explored such subtleties of psycholinguistic inversion or *self/other* dichotomy. The typical modern sensibility, aware of the disruptive power of language and of the impressionable nature of the human psyche, attended to these intonations in its complex reactions to war. Accordingly, the black and white emotions of epic sensitivity swaying between admiration and disgust were replaced by intricate sensitivities that combined lament and irony, truth and untruth in one expression.

The poet's comrade in this battle against war was his beloved. Inspired by the poetry of Paul Eluard and Louis Aragon who merged love and resistance in their idiom of revolt against Nazi occupation of France, Bengali poets like Bishnu De and Subhas Mukhopadhyay created their own Diotimas. While Bishnu De discovered freedom and peace in the figure of Ophelia:

> Your eyes hint forth freedom—far birds flying up in the sky,
> In your fist the snows of peace, scatter once in drop of rain,
> Let the heart fly to heaven....[6]

—(Ophelia)

Subhas Mukhopadhyay pledged to accompany his consort who promised egalitarian peace in the poem *I am coming*:

> I look at the sky
> Your face
> I closed my eyes
> Your face
> Silencing the thunder you are
> Calling me.[7]

This peace, won after an intense strife against the enemies of promise, is synonymous with life, our only refuge. In order to establish it, the poet-protagonist advanced pushing away darkness with his bare hands. Obviously the path was not smooth. The "warmongers" in Ali Sardar Jafri's poem obstructed and to them the poet said:

> Who has raised arms? Remove
> Who has raised barriers? Break
> I am bringing peace
> Throughout the world
> Tumultuous, irresistible peace.[8]

Here we encounter the Marxian vision of a classless peace shot through with tremors of unrest. This is not the dead peace of sepulchres. The beloved, Elsa or Subhadra, inspired the poet and both joined hands to reinstate peace after defeating those who wanted to desecrate it. Consequently, the surge of protest–challenge–resistance was an intrinsic element of this quest for a tranquillity that was tumultuous. Even before the outbreak of the First World War, the entire Marxist tradition in theory and praxis underlined its worth. A poem such as this opens the floodgates of memory—we recall the heroic figure of Rosa Luxemburg running from one assembly to another to lash out against the impending war, we recall the resolute though tragic resistance of the German Communists against Fascism, we recall Antonio Gramsci in his prison and, finally, the movement launched by our poets and painters in this subcontinent. In short, the committed search for a just and durable peace is an indispensable legacy of 20th century Marxism. To deny its worth in the name of "salvation army" peace in a Fukuyama era deprived of ideology would amount to a gross falsification of history. For a student of art and literature in particular, to forsake it would mean dismissing a whole body of imperishable creative sensitivity on war and exodus—the art of Kathe Kollawitz, the poetry of Paul Eluard and Samar Sen, the drama of Bertolt Brecht and the fiction of Akhtaruzzaman Elias.

Even when genuine and durable peace was denied, a poet like Birendra Chattopadhyay did not give up the quest for Utopian peace. Indeed, his mock-lyrical vision of the latter sharpened by accents of lament underlined the essential deprivation. This poet-activist, who protested stubbornly against state oppression of every kind, castigated desecrators of peace in his poems and dreamt of dwelling in the distant moon when he found that peace was not to be in this planet. The sarcasm was evident in his choice of the blessed realm. In the poem *Against War* he wrote:

> Let us go to the land of moon
> If there is time let us offer moon,
> More valuable than gold, a national anthem.
> Then when the moon withers, when gradma's tale ends
> We shall calculate anew. Like Agastya we shall
> Suck dry the land of Saturn, Jupiter, Mars,
> We peaceful men.
> To live we need a six feet stretch of land.[9]

This caustic tone and evocation of another world as an illusory substitute is not the predominant intonation in poets' reactions to war. Lyrics, generally, depend more on piognancy and fervor, anger and despair as emotional correlatives. This tonal spectrum was set by Wilfred Owen who died in the battlefield with Tagore's *Gitanjali* in his pocket.

Partition and Exodus

With the collapse of Nazi Germany, Kollawitz and Brecht's country was divided into two; east and west. Partition, then, was either the outcome of a full war or it could also be caused by the warlike disposition of two groups and their animal-brutality proceeding hand in hand with pernicious politics, for example, the Partition of Bengal and Punjab. Partition, again, could foment exodus of two kinds. One, single or collective efforts, frantic and despairing, to cross over barbed wires as depicted by Margarethe von Trota in her film *Alexaznderplatz* or massive, multitudinous transfers of population associated with trauma and terror as recorded by Ritwik Ghatak, S.M. Sathyu, Govind Nihalni, and Nemai Ghosh in their films. Taken together, war and partition in this century prompted massive migrations, which dehumanized millions. While the epigraph from Gunter Grass to this essay focused on the macrocosmic landscape of this nightmarish journey, Adil Mansuri singled out the individual, broken and battered, as the microcosmic victim of the entire process in his poem *When the Injured Sun Opened His Eyes*:

When the injured sun opened his eyes here
He was blinded by the flash of daggers.
Clouds of faithlessness thundered;
As we went out of our homes, our homes were wiped out.
The link-line of soul and body was disconnected
And the hands raised for prayer were slashed.
Blood ties were reduced to ashes
And the ashes concealed words of introduction
It was difficult to recognize the hazy spots:
There were flames in the distant horizon
And conflagration shooting out of the night's body.
Numerous ants were crushed on the roads,
The startled pigeon on the window was scared of his voice.
Now there are neither doors nor walls in between
And no place on earth to keep your feet on.
Fill up the mirages with tears;
Irrigate the wilderness of migration.

—(Translated from Urdu by Pritish Nandy and Ain Rasheed)[10]

When confronted with this reality or even while recollecting it, the creative writer hardly had a choice. He realized that he had "no place on earth to keep your feet on"—hands raised for prayer were slashed. Hence his reaction was unequivocal condemnation. Even the so-called sops, which the Partition was supposed to bring turned stale and sour. They were nothing more than mirages created by the instrumental reason of politics to waylay and inflame people. Instead of offering a new home as promised, Partition broke the hitherto single home into ruinous fragments, dividing the Self into innumerable vengeful Others. It scissored the bond or link which thereafter turned into memory—hymnic and elegiac at the same time.

The castigation, in literary terms, was not univocal. It was prompted either by the elegiac memory of homes broken and lives uprooted, and, to that extent suffused with nostalgia, or it was simply harsh and merciless. While the reminiscences of Bengalis who were forced to leave East Bengal (compiled in the collection *Chhere Asa Gram*) belong to the former category, Sadat Hasan Manto's stiletto-sharp sketches are examples of the latter. Those who had left their villages evoked the hymnic world lost forever and voiced the condemnation in lyrical letters. There was even a strain of illusion in their evocation of the past but even that was better than the lashes of actuality. In fact, this castigation was spiritual in essence because it refused to discover the enemy in the assaulting *other*. Consider, for instance, this fragment of remembrance: "A group of Bihari people, villagers from Bihar ... had become people of this village, sharing our soul.... Are they still there in my village? In our childhood we noticed that the Muslims' joy at Durga Puja was not any less than ours. As in the Hindu households, new clothes would be bought in their houses too. Muslim women would go from one neighborhood to another to see the images of Durga."[11] When one reads a tender remembrance like this, one feels like judging Partition and Exodus as a gruesome accident that defied the human course of events.

Sadat Hasan Manto, who was a witness to the unfolding of the horror, assaulted the reality of Partition with a vengeance that outstripped even the vengeance displayed by Hindus and Muslims. He mocked and ridiculed, stabbed and pounded in rage till agony emerged from the actual scenario. This was the other side of literary sensitivity that did not have a second to lose for a golden past or elegiac recapitulation. On the actuality in all its sordidness mattered. Manto's cynical disgust prompted an unforgettable dialogue in *Mistake Removed*:

Who are you?
And who are you?
Har Har Mahadev, Har Har Mahadev!
Har Harr Mahadev!
What is the evidence that you are what you say you are?
Evidence? My name is Dharm Chand, a Hindu name.
That is no evidence
All right, I know all the sacred Vedas by heart,
test me out.
We know nothing about the Vedas. We want evidence.
What?
Lower your trousers.
When his trousers were lowered, there was
Pandemonium 'Kill him, kill him'.
Wait, please wait ... I am your brother ... I swear
By Bhagwan that I am your brother.
In that case why the circumscision?
The area through which I had to pass was
Controlled by our enemies, therefore, I was forced
To take this precaution ... just to save my life ...
this is the only mistake, the rest of me is in order.
Remove the mistake.
The mistake was removed ... and with it Dharam Chand.[12]

This fragment etches the horrible deed in as few words as possible. The skeletal dialogue compels the reader to ponder and he concludes that Partition and Exodus was one related act of vicious insanity. Like, or with Manto, he aspires for that intrinsic sanity which admits no difference between a penis with a foreskin and one without.

As if to protest against this rupture between the *self* and the *other*, Manto's *Toba Tek Singh* refused to accept either India or Pakistan and Samresh Bose's protagonists in the short story *Adab* found themselves tied in the natural bond of love. In the words of Manto, Toba Tek Singh "screamed and as officials from the two sides rushed towards him, he collapsed on the ground ... on one side, lay India and behind more barbed wire, on the other side, lay Pakistan. In between, on a bit of earth that had no name, lay Toba Tek Singh.[13] By refusing to vacate his no-man's land Toba Tek Singh rejected Partition and Exodus. Manto's ideal sensitivity deciphered the irrepresible rebel in him. In the different emotional backdrop of *Adab*, a Hindu worker and a Muslim boatman surrounded by screams of "Bande Matram" and "Allahu Akbar," clung close to each other. Both said, "No, we are no longer men, we have turned into sons of bitches. Only sons of bitches bite one another like this."[14] Their confession cutting across the divide condemned the essence of Partition that interpreted the agony of the *other* as the jubilation of the *self*.

Indeed, the psycho-sadistic ballast of the politics of Partition earned a fitting rebuff in the Literature of Partition. Creative sensitivity refused to identify the Other's paroxysm as the Self's exultation. After studying the Urdu literature on Partition, Aijaz Ahmad confirmed, "Out of the thousand of poems, short stories and even novels written in the Urdu language, say, between the Pakistan Resolution of March 1940 and the Indo-Pakistani war of October 1965, there is not even one which has, by any critical standards whatever, any sort of literary merit and that celebrates the idea of Pakistan ... when we consider this very broad spectrum of literary productions, on both sides of the border, the sheer absence of a literary text which is pro-Pakistani in sentiment seems most remarkable and indicative of a certain consensus of perspective."[15] This is the defiant consensus of creative sensitivity on Exodus and Partition.

On the eastern side, the celebrated novelist Akhtaruzzaman Elias condemned the Partition of Bengal in the same unequivocal manner. Refusing to discover the "new dawn" in the homeland of Bengali Muslims, he asserted, "My father like many other members of the educated Muslim middle class of that time earnestly wanted that Muslim boys and girls should keep pace with their Hindu counterparts, that they live with equal dignity. But, let us not forget, these Muslim boys and girls belonged to a particular class. Hence, only the progress of this middle class was aspired for. But the movement they unleashed in order to fulfill this aspiration simply cannot be approved. The Partition of 1947 was so catastrophic, so deplorable, so heartrending and meaningless that we are realizing it more everyday."[16]

Elias' critique acquired its creative articulation in his novel *Khowabnama* where he showed how the dream of Pakistan was deceptive to the core. Against the unending reiteration of the Muslim League's promise that Pakistan would liberate the oppressed Muslim peasantry from the clutches of zamindari tyranny, he posited the disbelief of the loner Choto Mia who refused to accepted that the "social responsibility of the Muslim zamindar" would blossom once Pakistan came to being. According to Choto Mia, the rule of the Muslim League in Bengal "had only famine to offer as its achievement." Moreover, his query, which exposed the duplicity of Partition politics in one revelatory flash, went unanswered, "All the bigwigs of your League are rich people and zamindars. If you expel them how can you ensure the survival of the party?"[17]

There is a distinct Marxist component in Elias' verdict. He denounced Partition and the exodus for that very reason which made both look so attractive to the Muslim middle class. The much-vaunted Muslim homeland offered no relief to him because the exploited majority continued to toil and suffer even after the break-up. In order to highlight his ideology of genuine classless liberation, he opposed Partition with Tebhaga, though the latter was doomed to defeat. A stirring passage in the novel where he portrayed the do-or-die defiance of peasants against landlords, asserted his politics. This redemptive politics invested with the halo of victory-in-defeat guided his creativity: "The jotedars have come with the police. Trains filled with police are spreading out in every station. They come down like Cholera, like Small Pox. Peasants attack them with their scythes and sickles. The scoundrels gasping for breath cannot find the path to escape."[18]

In contrast to this explicitly political accent, Elias' friend Kayes Ahmed, himself a refugee, emphasized the psychic and metaphysical nightmare of homelessness. Almost recalling Ritwik Ghatak's resolutely emotional opposition to Partition, Kayes Ahmed in his novel *Nirbasito Ekjan* described Partition as the "freedom to be a refugee." His protagonist (or alter ego) cogitated, "What is the meaning of refugee? *Udbastu*. That means he who has no home. But I do have a home. Still I am a refugee, because I am countryless.... So, this freedom that we have gained after driving out the English—this Hindustan and Pakistan—is it to produce refugee.... Is this the name of freedom.... Who are those who maneuvered and manipulated to turn human beings into refugees after so many years?"[19]

Kayes Ahmed's uprooted psyche tolerated no compromise. His rejection of Partition was so compulsive that he even regarded members of his next generation as alien and rootless, "Rabeya will give birth to a child after some months. As the child—boy or girl—will be born with my identity, will grow and live, so I too with a false identity will survive among thousands and die with the same false identity."[20] After reading Elias' *Khowabnama* and Kayes Ahmed's *Nirbasito Ekjan* we conclude that these are texts of commitment that expose and indict the politics and psychology of Partition in unforgiving terms.

> There was a land of mangoes, jackfruits
> Where one could get soaked to the skin
> Returning home in rain then faintly tremble,
> Or bask in the sun after the fog cleared
> There was a land-yours, mine, our forefathers'?
> Some suddenly halved this land of love into two.
> They who did it wrenched the stem of the dream
> Which danced like the upper end of the gourd,
> Dream of the people.
> They shook violently the roots of the land
> And people were flung about who knows where,
> None kept account of who perished who survived.
> Residents of Bikrampur landed on Gariahata crossing
> Some came to Phultali from Burdwan,

> Some fled to Howrah from Jessore,
> From Netrokona to Ranaghat,
> From Murshidabad to Mymensingh,
> The outcome was inevitable
> Like when you release a wild bull in a flower garden
> Two parts of the land stretch out their thirsty hands
> Towards each other. And in between the hands
> Stands the manmade filth of religion, barbed wire.[21]

When these overwhelming experiences of partition, war, exodus, migration, dislocation agitate the creative mind, the creed of humanism with or without the specific Marxian component is a force strong enough to challenge the negative in the literary text. This retaliation is articulated to pay homage to the principle of life which rages against the dying of light (Dylan Thomas) even when the nameless protagonist perishes on the path. That is what peace is all about: *to recognize and revere the basic human right of the battered individual to live.* All wars fought in this world since the days of epics, all partitions and all migrations have not been able to throttle this human voice that is recorded in the literary sensitivity of the poem *At the Border* written by Alokeranjan Dasgupta. The martyr in this lyric is the archetypal Everyman who defies the cycle of violence and exile, bloodshed and exodus to anoint the human and his home with immanent sanctity:

> At that moment he stood up; if he so desired
> He could demolish all the barriers of convention.
> I trample ice and sun to touch him
> And find he is nowhere.
> Or did he carry freedom to the utmost limit
> On his bodily frame, gaunt with martyrdom?
> Failing to find his own name amongst the banished,
> He died for all refugees.

NOTES AND REFERENCES

1. Kashiram Das, "Streeparba" in *Mahabharat*. Calcutta, 1993, p. 289.
2. Ibid., p. 289.
3. Ibid., p. 301.
4. Ali Sardar Jafri, "The Command of Warmongers" in Pritish Nandy (ed.), *Modern Indian Poetry*. New Delhi, 1974, p. 37.

5. Wilfred Owen, "Strange Meeting" in F.T. Palgrave (ed.), *The Golden Treasury*. London, 1965, p. 452.
6. Bishnu De, "Ophelia" in Samir Dasgupta (ed.), *Selected Poems*. Calcutta, 1972, p. 13. The poem has been translated by Bishnu De himself.
7. Subhas Mukhopadhyay, "*Ami Ashchi* (I am coming)," in *Srestha Kabita*. Calcutta, 1970, p. 45; translated by the author of this essay.
8. Ibid.
9. Birendra Chattopadhyay, "*Judher Birudhe*" in *Srestha Kabita*. Calcutta, 1970, p. 77; translated by the author of this essay.
10. Adil Mansuri, "When the injured sun opened his eyes," in *Modern Indian Poetry*, p. 27.
11. Dakshinaranjan Basu (ed.), *Chhere Asa Gram*. Calcutta, 1975, pp. 8–13.
12. Sadat Hasan Manto, "Mistake Removed" in *Partition*. New Delhi, 1991, pp. 16–17; translated from Urdu by Khalid Hasan.
13. Sadat Hasan Manto, "Toba Tek Singh" in *Kingdom's End*. New Delhi, 1989, pp. 11–18; translated by Khalid Hasan.
14. Samaresh Bose, *Adab*. This unforgettable story has found its deserved place in many selections and anthologies.
15. Aijaz Ahmad, "In the Mirror of Urdu: Recompositions of Nation and Community, 1947–1965," in Aijaz Ahmad, *Lineages of the Present*. New Delhi, 1996, pp. 210–11.
16. *Lyric Volume 8*, Akhtaruzzaman Elias Number, Dhaka, April 1992, p. 132; edited by Ezaz Yusufi.
17. Akhtaruzzaman Elias, *Khowabnama*. Calcutta, 1996, pp. 99–100.
18. Ibid., p. 318.
19. *Kayes Ahmed Samagra*. Dhaka, 1993, p. 97.
20. Ibid., p. 98.
21. Taslima Nasreen, "*Bhanga Banga Desh*" in *Behula eka bhayichilo bhela*. Dhaka, 1993, p. 15, translated by the author of this essay.

19

BETWEEN REVENGE AND RECONCILIATION[1]

Rajeev Bhargava

I

The morning of 16 August 1946 saw the beginning of what came be described as the "Great Calcutta Killing" in which about 4,000 people were killed and another 11,000 injured. Trouble was already brewing for sometime. "There was fear about, and fear in India means trouble," Francis Tuker, a colonial army officer, had written in April.[2] But the magnitude of the tragedy caught everyone unawares. The "intensity of the hatred let loose and the savagery with which both sides killed each other" surprised everyone. Soon people began re-describing the killing as civil war and the foreboding of "impending terrible disasters" began to grip collective imagination. The local English daily, *The Statesman,* in a lament claimed that Calcuttans desperately needed "psycho-therapy on a mass scale."

Gandhi arrived in Calcutta in August 1947, on the very day of the first major sabotage of a train in Punjab and declared that his "head hung in shame at this continuous recital of man's barbarism." When, Suhrawardy, the Muslim League Chief Minister of Bengal, pleaded with him to stay on in Calcutta and see it through in times of trouble, Gandhi insisted he would do so only if Suhrawardy agreed to live with him in a local, riot-hit Muslim *bustee*. Gandhi knew that the breakdown of trust between the two communities was the principal cause of the violence and therefore that this "experiment" by him, a Hindu, would be crucial for winning back the trust of ordinary Muslims. Chastened by the violence he had personally witnessed,

Suhrawardy agreed. Hindus, on the other hand, reacted to this proposal with horror. How could Gandhi live with a known Leaguee in the midst of Muslims who had had slaughtered Hindus? However, Gandhi's argument and charisma eventually prevailed. Communal violence was halted. Hindus and Muslims flocked to Gandhi with their grievances, pleading innocence and pinning the entire blame for violence on members of the other community or on the *goondas*. Gandhi predictably asked everyone to "turn the searchlight inwards", and to accept collective responsibility for evil.

For a while the ploy worked. This experiment of rebuilding trust between two estranged communities had effected a remarkable catharsis. Collective ill-will was not suppressed but Gandhi had succeeded in transforming it into mutual goodwill. The explosion of communal harmony was intense but short-lived, however, forcing Gandhi to undertake a fast unto death. Now people began to respond with greater resolve: peace demonstrations were held, resistance groups to prevent killings were formed, civil servants joined in the fast and even goondas offered to submit to any penalty Gandhi wished to impose on them. Peace returned but Gandhi did not stop his fast. His objective was to bring about not merely a temporary truce but a lasting peace dependent in his view on a real change of heart. Only when the worst offenders within both communities pledged to forgive one another, reconcile their differences, and vowed to lay down their lives for communal amity did Gandhi break his fast. Hindus who had earlier cried for the blood of Muslims now agreed to protect them. Calcutta began to witness a more stable peace. By all accounts, "a truly wonderful victory over evil had been achieved."

My objective in recalling this slice of Indian history is to draw attention to something that holds a lesson for all societies. Clearly, any society needs to pull back from barbarism when it has lapsed into it; it must immediately restore peace. After arresting the current round of violence, it must ensure a way out of the cycle of revenge and self-destruction, and prevent the recurrence of evil. For Gandhi, this cannot be achieved by forgetting or repressing grievances. These must first be allowed full expression and then tamed by "confronting the goonda we harbor within." We must own up collective responsibility for the evil that has been generated. This alone helps reconcile differences, and rebuild communal harmony—our final objectives. In Gandhi's view, this then is the structure of moral action in the aftermath of evil:

BARBARISM—restoration of peace—expression of grievances—their truthful assessment—the acceptance of collective responsibility for evil—forgiveness—RECONCILIATION. (A society where formerly estranged members are morally reconciled may be called a fully decent society.)

In what follows, I endorse this broadly Gandhian structure of moral action in the aftermath of evil. Nonetheless, a number of questions remain to be asked. For instance, it is worth asking how a stable peace could have been restored in Calcutta in the absence of Gandhi. Impressed by the "magician," the Congress leaders urged Gandhi to go to civil war-stricken Punjab. He never managed to go there, but confronted with evil on a much larger scale, would Gandhi have succeeded? How would a society not blessed with a Mahatma, without moral saints, find a way out of barbarism? What other mechanism can perform roughly the same function? Do societies anyway not require *institutions* for a more stable harmony between two radically differing communities that have been at war with one another? It is one thing to stop violence and quite another to get people to talk to one another, to induct everyone into the process of negotiation. Which institution can perform this function? In Calcutta, the killers were known to the victims but in situations where victims have disappeared without trace, where the basic facts are not known, institutions must do more than become vehicles of collective catharsis? What more will an institution need to do in such situations? I believe that even societies that have had the benefit of moral saints require institutions to perform similar and related functions, particularly when they have faced evil on a large scale. A South African style Truth and Reconciliation Commission is one such institution that could contribute to the realization of the Gandhian structure of basic moral action in the aftermath of evil. However, the principal argument of my paper is that their function is more limited. In one way, Truth commissions do more than what is suggested by the Gandhian structure—they help unearth the truth—but overall, they aim to achieve results that are less-and therefore, more modest—than what is suggested therein. This is why, in a way, I also seek to modify the structure. In my view, the structure can be realized only by a complex set of institutions, and in stages, not immediately.

II

In order to amplify this point I wish to introduce and fully flesh out a distinction implicit in the account given above—the distinction between what I call a barbaric and a minimally decent society. A minimally decent society is governed by what I call minimally moral rules. A complete break down of such rules characterizes a barbaric society. In this context, what makes these rules moral is their capacity to prevent evil and not their ability to promote a particular conception of the good life, including a substantive conception of justice. Such rules embody a commitment to abjure violence and include negative injunctions against killing and maiming one another. It follows that a violation of such rules is an act of grave immorality. It is of course true that acts of grave immorality can be committed within minimally decent societies. Consider the case of a serial murderer, say Jack the Ripper, who murdered several persons by slitting their throats and mutilating their bodies with the consummate skill of an expert in human anatomy. Such evil acts can occur in minimally decent societies, within a moral order that is reflected at least partly in the law. The offender can be brought within due process of law and punished in proportion to the crime. But the situation in barbaric societies is qualitatively different, for here the scale of evil is much greater and the potential of the criminal justice system to deal with it far less adequate. Such a situation is beyond legality, and has even crossed a threshold beyond which moral notions are virtually inapplicable. This is a monstrous universe, exemplifying pure and unadulterated evil. Sri Lanka, Afghanistan, Rwanda, and former Yugoslavia provide the most recent examples. But for Indians, the partition of the subcontinent that left more than half-a-million dead and many more dispossessed remains a vivid, festering example of that madness. Accounts of partition reveal this collective insanity. Here is a sample:

My earliest memory is of a hot summer day in Delhi in 1948. I remember that as I unlocked the door to our house, I saw, stretched out on the steps below, the body of a man. He was lying face down. The man's limbs were in disarray, his clothes were soaked in blood and the sun had begun to darken his skin. Earlier in the day the man had sought shelter in our house. He was a Muslim trader who had been chased into our locality by violent men seeking revenge for blood spilled in Pakistan. The man had tried to reach our house ... but he was killed before he could knock at our door ... I have never since forgiven that day. It taught me that a group of people—any people—in their religious passion or tribal pride can always go mad; and that after a time they can relapse into madness again. I became conscious of the fact that the world which most of us had chosen to create, and in which I would have to grow up, was neither safe nor brave. The partition had broken the covenant that men must make with men, castes with castes, religions with other tolerant religions, without which our survival is always precarious and our enslavement to some barbarian is certain. Over the years, I came to realize that my recollections of those days were not private obsessions with the horrific. Similar incidents, known to others, had become a part of their experiential world. My own memories acquired a density and detail from the narratives of a variety of different people. My aunts told me of properties burnt, my grandfather about friends lost; a massacre witnessed, about the public mutilations of women. I grew up trying to understand the problem of evil and to explore the possibilities of magnanimity in such a world as ours.[3]

It is important to recognize the scope and depth of evil, its reach, and what all it destroys. In barbaric societies, it is not public morality alone that is ruined. Evil here has a way of spilling over not only from the public into the private domain but of pervading our intimate realms. Friends, lovers, members of the family can all be complicitous in crime. No one may be presumed innocent. The very distinction between friend and enemy, between those one loves and those one hates intensely is erased. The sociologist, Veena Das reporting on victims of the massacre of Sikhs in Delhi in 1984 talks of how the traumatic violence of the crowd suddenly revealed to one of its victims the fragility of her kinship universe.[4] Shanti, the victim, disclosed that "It was my own *mama* (mother's brother) who had advised my husband to hide. He revealed the hiding places of the Siglikar Sikhs to the leaders of the mob. He bartered their lives for his own protection. Go and see his house. Not even a broken spoon has been looted." Such personal betrayal is not uncommon in these times. The misfortune of a life without love, of complete friendlessness, surely one of the great evils that can befall human beings, as also rancor and bitterness among siblings was not uncommon, for instance, when India was partitioned.[5]

More importantly, evil eventually ensnares the victim. Typically, in barbaric societies, the very distinction between victims and perpetrators is obliterated. In societies with prolonged phase of barbarism, everyone is trapped in an escalating cycle of revenge. It is true of course that even in ordinary situations, it is normal for the victim to experience the impulse to retaliate, to want to punish the perpetrator of crime and get even. However, in barbaric situations, where a downward spiral of violence is firmly set in motion, vengeance invariably leads people to excesses. The retaliatory impulse gets a momentum of its own and forces people to exact more than is necessary. Acting disproportionately, in a manner that is intrinsically hideous, victims too become hateful creatures who routinely create new victims.

The association of the concept of evil with the idea of original sin and more generally with theology is one reason why secular-minded western philosophers are reluctant to give it the attention it deserves. But its neglect is due also to post-war euphoria—a general sense of well being through out the industrialized world, and a motivated lack of interest in theorizing the great injustices of colonialism and its destructive consequences in the non-western world. Stuart Hampshire is among a handful of philosophers who has reflected on this issue and not surprisingly, the Second World War, in particular the horror of the Nazi regime compelled him to do so: "I learnt how easy it had been to organize the vast enterprises of torture and of murder, and to enroll willing workers in this field, once all moral barriers had removed by the authorities. Unmitigated evil and nastiness are as natural, it seemed, in educated human beings as generosity and sympathy…. Once notions of fairness and justice are eliminated from public life and from people's minds and a 'bombed and flattened moral landscape' is created, there is nothing that is forbidden or off limits, and the way is fully open to natural violence and domination" (p. 69).[6] 'One now witnesses

Evil: "a force not only contrary to all that is praiseworthy, admirable, and desirable in human lives but which is actively working against all that is praiseworthy and admirable" (p. 67). For Stuart Hampshire, such evil cannot be prevented by substantial conceptions of justice over which there may be little agreement in society. He argues that in such situations what is required is *basic procedural justice*. This procedural justice is part of "a bare minimum that is entirely negative and without this bare minimum as a foundation no morality directed towards the greater goods can be applicable and can survive in practice" (p. 72). Justice, in this view, involves fair procedures of negotiation, a sort of machinery of arbitration that forms the basis for the recognition of untidy and temporary compromises between incompatible visions of a better way of life (pp. 72–78). It is a means of enabling different conceptions of the good life to coexist and as far as possible to survive without any substantial reconciliation between them and without a search for the common ground. This coexistence is possible by virtue of a restraint accepted by everyone on unmeasured ambition, on limitless self-assertion and on the obsessive desire for an everlarger slice of the cake and because people involved in even the fiercest of disputes are prepared to recognize the need to balance argument against argument, concession against concession. Basic procedural justice makes possible a minimally decent life, which has a value independent of any wider conception of the good. Its principal objective, in Hampshire's memorable phrase, is to prevent "madness in the soul" (p. 189).

It follows from what I have said above that barbaric societies are characterized by the breakdown not only of elementary moral injunctions but also of basic procedural justice. (Indeed, basic procedural justice is part of what I have called minimal morality.) Conversely, a minimally decent society is one where basic moral injunctions and procedural justice prevail. How do societies recovering from barbarism arrive at a minimally decent order? In my view, they must do so in two distinct stages. In the first stage, violence ceases probably because people have had enough of evil. In the second stage, basic procedural justice is restored and thereby also the process of negotiation between groups previously at war with one another. This then is the first suggested modification to the Gandhian schema: in the immediate aftermath of evil, in the period of brief reprieve from violence, an institution to consolidate basic procedural justice is desperately required. The Truth commission is an institution that performs this role. Its primary function is to help societies transit from barbaric to minimally decent societies, particularly by stabilizing a system of basic procedural justice. This it does by publicly establishing that grave wrongs have been committed in the past, and where this is already public knowledge, by showing why this was done. By responding to the needs of victims and by getting perpetrators to acknowledge responsibility for crimes, Truth Commissions build the trust and confidence crucial for restoring basic procedural justice and thereby reinstate a minimally decent society.

In a minimally decent society former victims are not reconciled with their former oppressors nor are groups with inherited hostilities towards one another reunited. If so, the primary objective of a truth commission is not reconciliation but the institution of a minimally decent society. It does not however, rule out a future cancellation of estrangement. Indeed, a truth commission creates conditions for a third stage of future reconciliation. It may do this by fixing collective responsibility in the appropriate way, and in so doing, changing the ideological climate that facilitates as far as possible, former oppressors to shed prejudice and for victims to regain their self respect. Since victims experience retributive emotions, truth commissions may permit their controlled expression and also help victims to eventually overcome them. When this happens, truth commissions may also be seen as *facilitating* mechanisms of forgiveness and reconciliation. So, my suggested modification of the Gandhian schema is this:

BARBARISM—truce (stage 1)—recall of grave injustice and expression of grievances, and restoration of basic procedural justice i.e., a minimally decent society (stage 2)—(The function of TRCs is to help societies move from stage 1 to stage 2, i.e., they must aim to help realize a minimally decent society)—acceptance of collective responsibility—forgiveness—RECONCILIATION (stage 3) (TRCs may facilitate conditions favorable to stage 3, to forgiveness and reconciliation).

As is evident, my intention is not to reject the Gandhian schema. However, I do claim that, no simple, linear movement exists from barbarism to a state of moral reconciliation, to full decency. Rather, it is necessary to transit through a complex of three stages. In stage 1, a highly frail and temporary truce prevails that may easily collapse generating a fresh burst of violence. With help from appropriate institutions such as the Truth Commissions, we then move to stage 2, to a minimally decent society. A sufficiently prolonged period of minimal decency may eventually create facilitating conditions for stage 3, for forgiveness and reconciliation, and therefore, to a fully decent society.

III

A number of points still need clarification. First, the term "society" refers to a human collectivity that may be a small configuration within a community, a large community within a society, a large political order such as the nation state consisting of interacting communities or indeed the entire world order or a part thereof. So, as I have used the term "society," it is possible for there to exist a minimally decent social formation within a larger barbaric society and likewise, for there to be a barbaric social formation within a larger minimally decent society. One of the cases I mention below, the massacre of Sikhs in Delhi in 1984 is a barbaric social formation on a relatively small scale. Its existence did not imply that the whole of India had turned barbaric.

Second, the phrase "minimally decent" implies that the best available ethical standards in a society, even by its own lights, remain unrealized. A minimally decent society is not free of exploitation, injustice or demeaning behavior. It may not even embody political equality. Yet, it is a social order where almost every voice is heard, some visibility for everyone is ensured in the political domain and, even the most marginalized and exploited are part of negotiation, howsoever unequal the conditions under which it takes place. There remain asymmetries in such a society, but it is not asymmetrically (or symmetrically) barbaric. On the other hand, in a barbaric society, where basic procedural justice is dismembered, the entire mechanism of negotiation and arbitration has vanished. Usually, the violation of norms of procedural justice begins with the politically motivated deployment of excessive force. In the early stages of regression into barbarism, gross violation of basic rights, i.e., physical intimidation, torture, and murder, even massacres occur on a fairly large scale; active deliberation and opposition is brutally terminated. This initial use of massive force may eventually make physical coercion more or less redundant, as indifference and submissiveness are routinely generated in a depoliticized environment. The noteworthy point here is that in either case, the demise of basic procedural justice is a *political* evil, which creates political victims. If the collapse of basic procedural justice brings about what may be described as political death, then clearly its restoration marks the political rebirth of members of a society. This helps explain why, by making the restoration of basic procedural justice their primary objective, Truth Commissions focus primarily on the rehabilitation of political victims.

Third, in saying that minimally moral rules are universally endorsable, I deny relativism—the view that the validity of *all* moral rules is culture-relative; but not in the familiar way. The familiar strategy of denial is to abstract from all traditions, cultures, and social roles and reach an archimedean point where universal moral rules are waiting to be discovered. I follow Michael Walzer in holding the view that every contextually bound, thick morality has an in-built set of thin, universalist moral norms because many terms within a moral tradition have both a maximal and a minimal moral content.[7] If so, people do not have to abstract from their moral tradition in order to reach a universal, minimalist morality. Rather, access to it can be had from within. Nor is the idea of minimal morality tied to some version of cold, dry, proceduralist reason commonly in use within many liberal conceptions. On the contrary, as Walzer persuasively argues, thinness and intensity go together. Minimal morality is "close to the bone" which is why there is universal revulsion at the sight of evil, why evil arouses our passion almost everywhere, in any context.

A final point worth making is this: When transiting from a barbaric to a minimally decent condition, societies are beginning their ascent from hell, are taking the first faltering steps away from a situation of gross injustice on a massive scale brought about probably by people with profoundly deadened moral sensitivities. When it comes to a society standing precariously on the threshold of moral restoration, it is important that we look at it bottom-up rather than top-down. I mean that we must remain firmly anchored in low-level ground realities and begin our search for relevant moral principles from here. We must not first reach out for high, near perfect ethical standards only to subsequently judge ground realities with their help. And, in the ground reality of such societies, the only reasonably certain thing is a diffuse agreement that enough of evil has been wrought and that relief from it is urgently required.

It is important to fully understand the significance of this. It does not mean that enmity or estrangement has ceased between victims and perpetrators or between conflicting groups. Nor even that they have begun to view each other with equal respect. However, it does mean that a space has opened up for a new order on terms not entirely unfavorable to all political actors, that a temporary reprieve from civil war or tyranny exists as also the hope that this can be prevented in future. It also means that force has begun to give way to negotiation, and, although relations of force characteristic of barbaric societies are not totally dismantled the process has begun to loosen their tenacious grip.

Normally, such transitional moments emerge out of a settlement in which former oppressors refuse to share power unless guaranteed that they will escape the criminal justice system characteristic of a minimally decent society. Alternatively, it typically arises because former victims do not fully control the new order they have set up and lack the power to implement their own conception of justice. However, such transitional moments can also come about by other routes. It is entirely possible that former oppressors are comprehensively vanquished but current victors, victims of the previously existing barbaric society refuse on moral grounds to avenge themselves, or fully implement the conventional criminal justice system. In short, former victims refuse on moral grounds to don the mantle of victors, something someone like Gandhi might well have done.

In question here are transitional situations of extreme complexity, replete with moral possibilities including, of course, with grave moral danger. The danger is obvious: victims may forever remain victims and their society may never cease to be barbaric. But what is often missed is that seeds of moral progress are also present herein because former victims are saved the awesome responsibility of wielding absolute power and therefore may escape the devastating consequences of being corrupted by its use. As a result, the possibility is foreclosed that past wrongs will be annulled only by fresh acts of equally excessive wrongdoing. Instead, we are presented with the possibility of confronting past wrongs by means other than the use of force or the willful manipulation of the criminal justice system. So, what may begin as mere political constraint opens up moral possibilities and it is these possibilities that lend moral weight to mechanisms like the Truth Commission.

IV

I have claimed that basic procedural justice prevents limitless, negative self-assertion and gives everyone an effective voice in political negotiation. Therefore, in order to break the cycle of revenge, former victims must be inducted into a system of basic procedural justice equipped with a mechanism of arbitration. Persuading them back into the system is, however not easy. Understandably, victims experience deep resentment and hatred towards those responsible for their misery. Besides, a numbing of emotions is at once a symptom and a constituent of their general disengagement from the world. An effective voice in the political process is impossible unless former victims regain self-confidence and renew trust in beneficiaries, perhaps even direct perpetrators of past atrocities, now also part of the negotiations. In short, victims cannot do without confidence and trust-enhancing mechanisms. Now, without public recognition of wrong done to them in the past, former victims are hardly likely to regain self-confidence in themselves or trust in others. Unless they break their silence, narrate their version of events and contest public lies, they will not see procedures of negotiation as just. To have an effective political voice, they must recover their voice more generally. Truth Commissions, I contend, are precisely such mechanisms by which the submerged voice of victims is retrieved. Given this connection between Truth Commissions and basic procedural justice, it is not difficult to see why they are necessary for the transition to stage 2.

This claim about the role and significance of Truth Commissions is not entirely uncontroversial. Even those who abjure revenge disagree on how a transition to a fully decent society must be made. Some, advocating a strategy of silence and forgetting, wish to skip stage 2. Others, disclaiming collective responsibility and forgiveness, reject stage 3. In what follows, I try to meet these objections. In this section, I try to rebut the claim that stage 2 is unnecessary. In the next section, I argue against the view that stage 3 is redundant.

Against the argument that truth commissions are necessary in societies transiting from barbaric to minimally decent societies, one counter-argument frequently leveled is that truth commissions inherently do more than is required in such situations. Those who hold this view inundate the victim with advice to check emotions. Rather than tell publicly and remember past injustice, victims are exhorted to forget. They are asked to contain hatred, overcome resentment, in short to condone or immediately forgive. Revenge to which resentment may lead them, they are told, is unbecoming of civilized people, full anyway of terrible consequences for society. These critics draw a distinction between the felt needs of the victim and the real needs of the entire community and suggest that the two often run against one another. Instead of focusing on the past, the victim is told to think of the future. In brief, on this view truth commissions are dangerous or at best, unnecessary. Is this view correct? Is it more appropriate in these circumstances to forget?

Among former perpetrators, a motivated forgetfulness of their own wrong doing, accompanied with the hope that former victims will quickly forget past suffering is not uncommon at a time when asymmetries of power are in the process of being dissolved. In this context, calls to let bygones be bygones, to wipe the slate clean or start afresh, work unabashedly in favor of perpetrators of crime. In any case, most calls to forget disguise the attempt to prevent victims from publicly remembering in the fear that "there is a dragon living on the patio and we had better not provoke it."[8] But it is doubtful if this is a good strategy for repairing wounds or achieving reconciliation. When a person is wronged, he is made not only to suffer physically but also is mentally scarred, the most injurious of which is the damage to his sense of self-respect, if he is left with any residue of it. As Jeffrie Murphy points out, when a person is wronged he receives a message of his marginality and irrelevance.[9] The wrong doer conveys that in his scheme of things the victim counts for nothing. Since self-esteem hinges upon critical opinion of the other, the message sent by the wrongdoer significantly lowers the self-esteem of the wronged. In these circumstances, the insult and degradation inflicted constitutes a deeper moral injury. The demand that past injustices be forgotten does not address this loss of self-esteem. Indeed, it inflicts further damage. Asking victims to forget past evils is to treat them as if no great wrong to them has been done, as if they have nothing to feel resentful about. This can only diminish them further.

Forgetting specific instances of past wrongs does not appear to achieve the desired objective anyway—a point to which Jeremy Waldron has drawn our attention, "When we are told to let bygones be bygones, we need to bear in mind also that the forgetfulness being urged on us is seldom the blank slate of historical oblivion. Thinking quickly fills up the vacuum with plausible tales of self-satisfaction, on the one side, and self-deprecation on the other."[10] Beneficiaries of injustice then come to believe that gains accrue to them due to the virtue of their race or culture and victims too easily accept that their misfortune is caused by inherent inferiority. The call to forget reinforces loss of self-esteem in the victim. Furthermore, moral injuries that are neglected petrify demoralization in the victim. Under these conditions, past perpetrators feel that they can get away with murder and grow in confidence that such injuries can be inflicted without resistance even in future. Therefore, rather than prevent, forgetting ends up facilitating wrong acts. If so, it is difficult not to conclude that proper remembrance alone restores dignity and self-respect to the victim.

A proper remembrance is critical if wounds of the victim are to be healed. It is also necessary to fulfill the collective need of a badly damaged society. This view comes up against a pervasive social condition as well as against a famous argument by Hobbes. It is an uncomfortable fact that while societies remember their heroic deeds they suppress memories of collective injustice. Recall Ernest Renan's remark that nations are constituted by a great deal of forgetting. In a perceptive essay, Sheldon Wolin wonders if collective memory is an accomplice of injustice and whether by its silence on collective wrongs, it does not signify the very limits of justice.[11] But he also asks if a society can ever afford to remember events in which members feel tainted by a "kind of corporate complicity in an act of injustice done in their name." Can France remember the Saint Bartholomew massacre; America, its civil war; or India, its Partition? Can these horrific events be remembered by being represented in civic rituals? One philosopher who thought collective forgetting necessary was Thomas Hobbes. Suppression of memories of past wrongs was essential because if society is treated as a building made of stones then some stones that have an "irregularity of figure take more room from others" and so must be discarded (p. 37). Hobbes's covenant was a device to incorporate social amnesia into the foundation of society. Commenting on this, Wolin remarks that for Hobbes a necessary condition of social amnesia is the dehistorization of human beings.

Is dehistoricization possible? I think not. "Muslims" invaded India in the 12th century but for many Hindus, Muslims continue to be invaders who may kill, destroy and convert them. The conquest of Quebec by the English happened more than two centuries ago but for Quebec nationalists their nationalist project "involves a reconquest of the conquest." A large part of nationalist agenda all over the world, Ignatieff rightly reminds us, is about settling old scores.[12] In so many countries people remarkably similar in essential respects appear to go at each other's throat simply because once upon a time one ruled over the other. A simple strategy of forgetting has simply not worked. Only an appropriate engagement with the past can make for them a livable common future. It is true of course that one must guard against cosmetic remembrance. An engagement with the past must take place simultaneously at the level of gut, reason, and emotion. If not properly addressed grievances and resentments resurface. Oddly, animosity between groups is sustained even when it goes against their current interests. This happens because emotional reactions ingrained in the human mind remain insensitive to altered circumstances and are bequeathed from generation to generation.[13] Like property, animosities are inherited too!

Nonetheless, former victims and fragmented societies eventually need to get on with their lives rather than be consumed by their suffering. Perhaps victims need to forget just about as much as they need to remember. People who carry deep resentment and grievance against one another are hardly likely to build a society together. Therefore, to ask people to forget is not entirely unreasonable. I believe timing is the essence of the issue here. Forgetting too quickly or without redress, by failing to heal adequately, inevitably brings with it a society haunted by its past. One can't forget entirely, too soon, and without a modicum of justice. Clearly, while some forgetting at an appropriate time is necessary, a complete erasure is neither sufficient nor desirable for healing or for the consolidation of a minimally decent society. Moreover, while specific acts of wrongdoing need to be forgotten eventually, a general sense of the wrong and of the horror of evil acts must never be allowed to recede from collective memory. Such remembering is crucial to the prevention of wrongdoing in the future. I conclude that without a proper engagement with the past and the institutionalization of remembrance, societies are condemned to repeat, re-enact and relive the horror. Forgetting is not a good strategy for societies recovering from prolonged barbarism. The recognition of this is the *raison d'être* of Truth commissions and also one of the virtues of the Gandhian schema.

V

What is the relation of Truth commissions to the rest of the Gandhian schema? Can they realize the structure in full? My view is that though they may facilitate the realization of stage 3, they must not aim to do so. However, critics find flaws in the very idea of a passage through stage 3. Two criticisms are fairly common. First, that the notion of collective responsibility is incoherent. Second, that forgiveness is morally inappropriate.

To begin with, my use of the word responsibility is less to do with strict legal or moral liability and linked more with what men and women decide to do. Our decision to perform this or that action is connected by a loose, not always explicit or fully conscious, practical reasoning to our beliefs and desires. I avoid discussing the vexed question of whether or not beliefs and desires are mental states or occurrences. Even if this is so, an important question remains about how their content is to be individuated, their meaning fixed. For me, what these beliefs and desires are about, their meaning is determined by social practice, by collective actions rather than individual mental acts of people.[14] If this is so, and if our decision to act is constitutively linked to these irreducibly social beliefs and desires, then it follows that, in part, our decisions are social too and so therefore is responsibility. I share Larry May's view that most of our responsibilities are shared rather than uniquely our own.[15] When such a social view on conceptions of self and agency is taken, the domain of moral responsibility expands beyond what a person directly causes. Moreover, just as social beliefs cause individual action, just so they cause an interlocking set of actions involving several individuals. If that is so, groups, indeed entire collectivities can be held responsible for various harms. I also agree with May that guilt and blame must be seen to lie on a continuum that also contains shame, remorse, regret and the feeling of being tainted (p. 35). From this brief account it follows that for me, groups can be held morally responsible for wrongs and individuals can partake that responsibility.

It is possible though not necessary that when individuals as members of a group publicly acknowledge their crime, they also admit to their role in a collective wrong. This is not something they always know of before matters are brought in the public. An individual may not have a sense of responsibility for wrongdoing when in reality he should. Alternatively, he may feel exclusive responsibility and therefore excessive guilt for a wrong of which he has only shared responsibility. The act of making something public is not merely to reveal what is known already to each person in private. It is to come to the realization of a fact about ourselves that was not properly known at all. Normally, the recognition of such collective responsibility is accompanied by feelings of shame, regret or remorse. People qua members of a group may also feel morally tainted. Ignatieff makes the telling Freudian point that something may be confronted in one's head without it being confronted in one's heart or guts. This self-confrontation that takes place at the level of feelings is critical for a deeper change in one's attitudes. Since such encounters with the self are painful, they may be referred to as punishment of the soul, a form of deeper punishment neither noticed by the penal system nor by standard conceptions of retributive justice. Punishment of the soul is critical, affective self-confrontation before radical conversations in identity occur; an acknowledgement not of the wrong one has done but the wicked person one is. It is only when such changes take place on a large scale, and the moral climate of a whole society is altered, that people, particularly former oppressors, shed their prejudices, and former victims begin to regain a deeper, more stable sense of self-respect. Surely this is necessary for reconciliation.

Under altered circumstances, when evil and suffering is publicly revealed, remembered and even acknowledged by the perpetrator, should the victim respond with forgiveness? Is forgiveness morally appropriate? If so, what justifies it? Is acknowledgement of responsibility of the crime sufficient for forgiveness? What is it anyway to forgive? It is a fact that victims experience deep, enduring hatred and resentment towards the wrongdoer as well as feelings of revenge towards him. Commonly viewed, forgiveness is the forswearing of these resentments, a determined overcoming of hatred and anger towards a person who has inflicted moral injury.[16] One frequently cited reason in favor of forgiveness points towards the negative qualities that inhere in the very emotions of hatred and resentment. A decent, morally upright person, it is said, simply shouldn't have such emotions, in part because by holding persons rather than being held by them, these emotions inhibit proper judgment and undermine autonomy and, by virtue of their raw motivational power, are likely to drive a person to commit an equally immoral act. For instance, one may be swept, it is argued, by feelings of revenge inconsonant with moral systems in the modern world.

Reasons that require forgiveness because of its productive role in eliminating such emotions are unconvincing, however. For a start, there is nothing wrong inherently in feelings of hatred and resentment. "Proper self-respect," observes Jeffrey Murphy, "is essentially tied to the passion of resentment. A person who does not resent moral injuries done to him is almost necessarily lacking in self-respect."[17] It follows that resentment is valuable by virtue of its link with something we all value, namely self-respect. It is terribly odd for a self-respecting person not to resent violation of rights or the seizure of unfair advantage of his labor. Likewise, there is nothing wrong in hatred towards those wholly identified with an immoral cause or responsible for an immoral practice. Distinguishing it from simple hatred—an intense dislike for a strongly unpleasant object, accompanied by an equally strong desire to eliminate it, Jean Hampton calls this moral hatred.[18] Hatred is moral when moved by moral indignation, conjoined with the desire to defeat the ideology of the offending person in the name of a fundamental moral principle. Such moral hatred may be experienced towards neo-Nazis or towards those South African whites who perpetrate or justify violence against blacks. These *retributive emotions* are essential not only for the preservation of self-respect but also for the stability of the moral order in society.[19] If the only ground for forgiveness is that retributive emotions are intrinsically wrong or harmful, then surely forgiveness is unjustified.

If victims who experience moral hatred and resentment must not feel in the wrong then why in the first place overcome these emotions and forgive? The answer is that a refusal to forgive often betrays insensitivity to altered circumstances, to a change in the condition or character of the wrong doer. Murphy lists five grounds for forgiveness, three of which are relevant for our purposes.[20] When the perpetrator repents, undergoes humiliation or has in turn suffered enough, it may well be appropriate to forgive him, especially since such forgiveness does not diminish the self-esteem of the victim. Indeed, under these circumstances, the act of forgiveness may enhance the self-respect of the victim and contribute towards precisely the kind of healing required in such circumstances. When a person acknowledges the wrongness in his act and the role it played in causing harm to the victim and when, in admitting its immorality he ceases to endorse it, indicating thereby that he is with the victim in condemning all acts of this kind, he initiates the process of restoring parity with the victim. It may become morally appropriate now to forsake hatred for the person and resentment towards his past actions. Likewise, subsequent to punishment and suffering the perpetrator may be sufficiently humbled to cause the victim to alter his view of the wrong doer. Much the same is true for someone who admits guilt through an apology. In short, if restoration of a moral parity between self-respecting individuals is desirable and if forgiveness contributes to its realization, then it is morally appropriate to forgive.

If forgiveness is to result from the repentance of the perpetrator, to flow from the punishment of his soul, and if this is conditional upon the recognition of collective responsibility, then it follows that a truth commission cannot *aim* to bring about forgiveness. Nor must reconciliation, dependent upon a deeper change in people's identity, be part of its stated objectives. It is of course true that such fundamental changes can eventually occur as a by-product of the activities of a truth commission and therefore it may certainly be seen to create conditions for future reconciliation. Nonetheless, given the time frame of truth commissions, it is too much to expect them to bear the burden of getting people to forgive or to reconcile with one another.

However, this is not usually the reason why truth commissions are criticized. It is sometimes accepted that a truth commission can get people to forgive but then pointed out that this is morally questionable. Critics frequently attack the very idea of forgiveness. One well-known argument against forgiveness is that it is deeply tied to Christian morality, at any rate that it takes us beyond ordinary morality into the domain of high religion. Victims in South Africa have complained bitterly that the justification of forgiveness derives from a particular moral vision with which they do not identify and therefore it is not incumbent upon them to heed the plea to forgive. Others object that forgiveness must come from within and only the victim has the proper standing to do so. One can't forgive under compulsion nor can others forgive on behalf of the victim. A third criticism of forgiveness is that it has the effect of erasing wrongdoing, that it is an invitation to reconcile with rather than conquer evil.[21] Finally, it is also argued that the plea for general amnesty with which it is linked can only lead to enraged victims opting for personal acts of vengeance. The demand for forgiveness on this view can only exacerbate the settling of scores outside the rule of law.

Within Christianity, it is widely recognized that since the propensity to wrongdoing is pervasive, forgiveness should be generally available too. As original sinners, we seek forgiveness from God. As sinners in our day-to-day existence, we must seek forgiveness from each other. It is therefore undeniable that Christianity provides an important source for the justification of forgiveness. However, from the availability of a virtue in one religious tradition, it hardly follows that it is unavailable in others.[22] More importantly, atheistic humanism must have place for forgiveness too. Even unbelievers can and should admit that in the course of living our lives we wrong others, particularly those about whom we care deeply. If we care about people we have wronged we would certainly want them to forgive us. Indeed, a humanist must accept that at the heart of the human condition lies a radical fallibility that it is futile to try to totally overcome. We need forgiveness from each other, alas, because without God-like features we often commit wrong and because there may be no God to forgive us. As Murphy notes "we do all need and desire forgiveness and would not want to live in a world where forgiveness was not regarded as a healing and restoring virtue."[23] Furthermore, the domain where this virtue is exercised needn't only be private. We need and expect forgiveness even within the wider public domain. Therefore, I am not entirely convinced with the view that forgiveness is exclusively tied to one religious tradition or that unbelievers have no need for it.

The criticism that forgiveness bypasses the act of wrongdoing is not justified either. To forgive is not to convert a wrong into right. It is not to justify the wrong done. Nor is it identical with excusing the wrong done, as when one excuses a child for causing some harm on the ground that he can't really be held responsible for it. The process of forgiveness begins only after proper recognition of wrongdoing and is conditional upon it. Since the wrong is not simply white washed, to forgive is not to compromise with evil. Nor does forgiveness entail amnesty. Forgiveness is not to be confused with mercy.[24] This confusion may well have lain at the heart of the earliest formulation of the objectives of the South African Truth Commission. Reasons for forgiveness are not automatically reasons for mercy. A victim may forgive the perpetrator but not thereby free him of legal accountability. Conversely, he may, out of compassion, reduce punishment for the wrongdoer but not forgive him. Finally, forgiveness is not a virtue in all contexts and is appropriate only when it is consistent with the dignity and self-respect of the victim. The good of the community cannot provide reasons for unconditional forgiveness. A perpetrator cannot be forgiven if he does not repent, for without proper repentance, he may repeat his crime. Nor can the evidence of repentance be a mere expression of regret or remorse. It must also be expressed in deed, by reparative actions directed at victims. This is what Gandhi meant when he insisted that Hindus who only the other day were crying for the blood of Muslims must offer protection to them. Furthermore, the victim may not forgive if he retains the feeling that his suffering is not properly acknowledged. If there is no forgiveness from within, "then the door is open to private acts of vengeance and retribution."[25] Given these qualifications, in principle there appears nothing inappropriate or wrong in the Gandhian strategy of reconciliation via acknowledgement of collective responsibility and forgiveness. The basic idea that animates it is correct, even though as I have argued, Truth commissions must modify the schema and aim to achieve much less than what is envisaged by it.

NOTES AND REFERENCES

1. Originally appeared under the title, "Restoring Decency in Barbaric Societies," in Robert Rotberg and Dennis Thompson (eds.), *Truth v Justice*. Princeton and Oxford, 2000.
2. Dennis Dalton, "Gandhi during Partition: A Case Study in the Nature of Satyagraha," in C.H. Phillips and Mary Wainright (eds), *Partition of India: Policies and Perspectives 1935-1947*. London, 1970.
3. Alok Bhalla, *Stories about Partition in India*. New Delhi, 1994.
4. Veena Das, "Our Work to Cry: Your Work to listen" in Veena Das (ed.), *Mirrors of Violence*. Delhi, 1990.
5. Urvashi Butalia, *The Other Side of Violence: Voices from the Partition of India*. Delhi, 1998.
6. Stuart Hampshire, *Innocence and Experience* Cambridge, 1989.
7. Michael Walzer, *Thick and Thin: Moral argument at Home and Abroad*. London and Notre Dame, 1994.
8. Tina Rosenburg, *The Haunted Land*. London, 1995.
9. Jeffrie,G. Murphy and Jean Hampton, *Forgiveness and Mercy*. Cambridge, 1990.

10. Jeremy Waldron, "Superseding Historic Injustice," *Ethics*, 3, 1992.
11. Sheldon Wolin, *The Presence of the Past*. Baltimore and London, 1989.
12. Michael Ignatieff, *Blood and Belonging*. London, 1994.
13. David Hume, *Political Writings*. Cambridge/Indianapolis, 1994.
14. Rajeev Bhargava, *Individualism in Social Science*. Oxford, 1992.
15. Larry May, *Sharing Responsibility*. Chicago and London, 1992.
16. Jeffrie, G. Murphy and Hampton, op. cit.
17. Ibid., p. 16.
18. Ibid., pp. 79–81.
19. John Mackie, *Persons and Values*. Oxford, 1995.
20. Jeffrie, G. Murphy and Hampton, op. cit., p. 24.
21. Mahmood Mamdani, "Reconciliation without Justice", *South African Review of Books*, CIV, 1996.
22. M.K. Gandhi, *Collected Works of Mahatma Gandhi*, CXXXVI. New Delhi, 1982.
23. Jeffrie, G. Murphy and Hampton, op. cit., pp. 30–31.
24. Jeffrie, G. Murphy and Hampton, op. cit., p. 34.
25. Tina Rosenburg, op. cit.

FURTHER READINGS ON THEMES IN PEACE STUDIES

DEFINING PEACE STUDIES

[Modern western writings on peace seem to have taken Immanuel Kant as their point of departure. His writings (as well as those of John Rawls influenced by him) however generated a lively political debate (otherwise known as the Liberal–Communitarian debate) and divided contemporary political theory literally down the middle. Much of the contemporary communitarian theory focuses on the problem of making peace in a multi-community society. In Amitai Etzioni's phrase, the problem there is to create "a community of communities." A part of the liberal theory has concentrated on the quantitative aspects of their argument and underlines the importance of simulation and mathematical models for explaining conflicts and also avoiding them. There is reason to believe that the modernist historiography of peace is increasingly under fire in recent times. The writings of such post-modernist thinkers as, Jean-Francois Lyotard and others have played a vital catalytic role in evolving a new historiography of peace in the West. The forces of globalization have also contributed to a certain reinforcement of what we have called the micro-traditions of peace. While these theoretical interventions predominantly in the West have made room for a review of the autochthonous peace traditions in South Asia, Peace Historiography here finds it difficult to fully absorb their implications for reasons not unknown to us. Unfortunately, the historical-anthropological writings of the subaltern historians do not take the post-colonial experience into account, though of course many of them have concentrated on the historical encounter between Western modernity and our autochthonous peace traditions. Since subaltern historians have a tendency of writing people's histories in moments of conflict, it is not as much sensitive to the imperative of re-narrating their peace traditions. Historiography of the indigenous people in post-colonial South Asia is still at its infancy. The hybrid nature of the peace discourse in South Asia has received some, though very sketchy, attention. The writings of Sheldon Pollock, R.S. Khare, Vijay Prashad, and Gerald James Larson in recent times are noteworthy in this connection. The works on the anthropology of reconciliation and understanding—though have a tradition of their own in the West, are highly scattered and sporadic in this region. The writings of F.G. Bailey, Bernard Cohn, and McKim Marriott—among many others, may be mentioned in this regard.]

Abrams, Irwin, (ed.), *Peace 1981–1990*. Singapore, 1997.
Alexayevich, Parel A., *People Rise Against War*. Moscow, 1983.
Banerjee, Nikunja Vihari, *Towards Perpetual Peace*. Shimla, 1980.
Barnaby, Frank, *Prospects for Peace*. Oxford, 1960.
Bertrand, Maurice, *The Third Generation World Organization*. Dordrecht, 1989.
Booth, Ken and Moorhead Wright, *American Thinking about Peace and War*. Sussex, 1978.
Dawar, John, *Nuclear Weapons, the Peace Movement and the Law*. Basingstoke, Hampshire, 1986.
Donald, C.F. Daniel and Bradd C. Haynes (eds), *Beyond Traditional Peace-Keeping*. New York, 1996.
Dunn, Ted (ed.), *Alternatives to War and Violence*. London, 1963.
Einstein, Albert, *Einstein on Peace*; ed. by Otto Nathan and Heinz Norden. New York, 1960.
Flagel, John Carl, *The Moral Paradox of Peace and War*. London, 1941.
Fremgsmyr, Torre (ed.), *Peace 1981–1990*. Singapore, 1997.
Gaither Jr., Rawan H., *The Social and Economic Foundations of Peace*. Delhi, 1957.
Galtung, Johan, *Peace by Peaceful Means: Peace and Conflict, Development and Civilization*. London, 1996.
Gillett, Nicholas, *War Against War*. London, 1965.
Gourevitch, Boris, *The Road to Peace and Moral Democracy: An Encyclopedia of Peace*. New York, 1955.
Gress David, *Peace and Survival*. Stanford, Calif, 1985.
Hancock, W.K., *Four Studies of War and Peace in this Country*. Cambridge, 1961.
Horowitz, Irving L., *War and Peace in Contemporary Social and Philosophical Theory*. London, 1973.
Kant, Immanuel, *Perpetual Peace*; ed. with Introduction by Lewis White Back. Indianapolis, NY, 1957.
Kumar, Mahendra, *Current Peace Research in India*. Varanasi, 1968.
Lentz, Theodore F., *Towards a Science of Peace*. London, 1955.
Martin, Charles E., *The Politics of Peace*. Stanford, California, 1929.
Miller, Paul R., *Negotiating Peace: War Termination as a Bargaining Process*. Princeton, 1983.
Murty, K. Satchidananda, *The Quest for Peace*. Delhi, 1986.
Murty, K. Satchidananda and A.C. Bouquet, *Studies in The Problems of Peace*. Bombay, 1960.
Mushkat, Mario'n, *The Third World and Peace: Some Aspects of the Inter-relationship of Underdevelopment and International Security*. New York, 1982.
Reeves, Emery, *The Anatomy of Peace*. London, 1946.
Rochou, Thomas, *Mobilization for Peace: The Nuclear Movements in Western Europe*. London, 1988.
Rothschild, Robert B., *Peace for our Time*; trans. from French by Anthony Rhodes. London, 1988.
Rustow, Eugene V., *Law, Power and the Pursuit of Peace*. Lincoln, 1969.

Sondhi, Madhuri, *The Making of Peace: A Logical and Societal Framework according to Basanta Kumar Mallik*. New Delhi, 1985.
Veblen, Thorstein, *An Inquiry into the Nature of Peace and the Terms of its Perpetration*. New York, 1964.
Walker, R.B.J., *One World, Many Worlds: Struggles for a Just World Peace*. Boulder, Colorado, 1988.
Wehr, Paul, *Conflict Regulation*. Boulder, Colorado, 1979.
Weizsacker, Carl F., *The Politics of Peace: Economics, Society and the Prevention of War*; trans. from German by Michael Shaw. New York, 1978.

NUCLEAR POLITICS OF THE INDIAN STATE

Agarwal, Prasanta, *India's Nuclear Development: Plans and Policies— A Critical Analysis*. New Delhi, 1998.
Bidwai, Praful and Achin Vanaik, *South Asia on a Short Fuse: Nuclear Politics and the Future of Global Disramament*. Delhi, 1999.
Chatterjee, Partha, "How We Saved the Bomb and Later Ruled it," *Economic and Political Weekly* (Mumbai), XXXIII (24), 13 June 1998, pp. 1437–41.
Chatterjee, Shibashis, *Nuclear Non-Proliferation and the Problem of Threshold States*. Calcutta, 1999.
Chengappa, Raj, *Weapons of Peace*, New Delhi, 2000.
Ganguly, Sumit, "India's Pathway to Pokhran II: The Prospects and Sources of New Delhi's Nuclear Weapons Program," *International Security*, vol. 23, no. 4, 1999, pp. 148–77.
Ghosh, Amitava, *Countdown*. New Delhi, 1999.
Hogarty, Devin T., "South Asia's Big Bangs: Causes, Consequences and Prospects," *Australian Journal of International Affairs*, vol. 53, no. 1, 1999, pp. 19–29.
Mattoo, Amitabh (ed.), *India's Nuclear Deterrent: Pokhran II and Beyond*. New Delhi, 1998.
Mohan, Sulakshan, *India's Nuclear Leap*, New Delhi, 2000.
Patil, V.T. and N.K. Jha (eds), *Peace and Cooperative Security in South Asia*. New Delhi, 2000.
Perkovich, George, *India's Nuclear Bomb*. New Delhi, 1999.
Ram, N., *Riding in a Nuclear Tiger*. New Delhi, 1999.
Subrahmanyam, Raju (ed.), *Nuclear India*. Delhi, 2000.
Vanaik, Achin, "Crossing the Rubicon," *Economic and Political Weekly* (Mumbai), XXXIII (24), 13 June 1998, pp. 1433–36.

WOMEN AND PEACE

Afshar, Hak and Carolyne Dennis (eds), *Women and Adjustment Policies in the Third World*. London, 1992.
Alonso, Harriet Hyman, *Peace as Women's Issue*. Syracuse, 1993.

416 Further Readings on Themes in Peace Studies

Alonso, Harriet Hymar, *The Women's Peace Union and the Outlawry of War, 1921–1942.* Knoxville, 1989.

Alternatives, special issue, Feminists Write International Relations, vol. 18, no. 1, 1993.

Anderson, Gillian (ed.) *Women and Peace: A Practical Resource Pack.* London, 2000.

Bennet, O. (ed.), *Arms to Fight, Arms to Protect.* London, 1995.

Berkin, Carol R. and Clara M. Rovett (eds), *Women, War and Revolution.* New York and London, 1980.

Bhasin, Kamla, Ritu Menon and Nighat Said Khan, *Against All Odds.* New Delhi, 1994.

Bhasin, Kamla and Ritu Menon, *Borders and Boundaries: Women in India's Partition.* New Jersey, 1998.

Bhutalia, Urvashi, *Other Side of Silence: Voices from the Partition.* New Delhi, 1998.

Boulding, Elise (ed.), *New Agendas for Peace Research: Conflict & Security Reexamined.* Boulder, 1992.

Burguieres, Mary, "Feminist Approaches to Peace: Another Step for Peace Studies," *Millenium*, vol. 19, no. 1, 1990, pp. 1–18.

Derrida, Jacques, "Women in the Beehive: A Seminar," in A. Jardine and P. Smith (ed.), *Men in Feminism.* New York, 1987.

Enloe, Cynthia, *Bananas, Beaches and Bases: Making Feminist Sense of International Politics.* London, 1989.

——, *Does Khaki Become You? The Militarisation of Women's Issues.* London, 1983.

Ferris, E.G., "Women as Peacemakers," in *Women, Violence and Nonviolent Change.* Geneva, 1996.

Gok, Alice and Greenham Gwyn Kerk, *Women Everywhere: Dreams, Ideas and Actions From the Women's Peace Movement.* London, 1983.

Grant, Rebecca and Kathleen Newland (eds), *Gender and International Relations.* Bloomington, 1991.

Harris, Adrienne and Ynestra King (eds), *Rocking the Ship of State: Toward a Feminist Peace Politics.* Bloomington, 1989.

Jayawardane, Kumari, *Feminism and Nationalism in the Third World.* New Delhi, 1986.

Jean, Berthke Elshtain, *Women and War.* Brighton, 1987.

Leonardo, Micaela di, "Morals, Mothers and Militarism: Anti-militarism and Feminist Theory," *Feminist Studies*, vol. 11, no. 3, 1985, pp. 599–617.

MacDonald, Sharon, Perl Holden and Ardener Shirley (eds), *Images of Women in Peace and War: Cross-cultural and Historical Perspectives.* London, 1987.

Mohanty, Chandra, Ann Russo and Lourdes Torres (eds), *Third World Women and the Politics of Feminism.* Bloomington, 1991.

Petkin, Hanna F., *Fortune is a Woman: Gender and Politics in the Thought of Niccolo Machiavelle.* Berkeley, Los Angeles and London, 1984.

Pierson, Ruth Roach (ed.), *Women and Peace: Theoretical, Historical and Practical Perspectives.* London, New York and Sydney, 1987.
Randall, Vicky, *Women and Politics: An International Perspective.* London, Macmillan and Chicago, 1987.
Ruddick, Sara, *Maternal Thinking: Towards a Politics of Peace.* London, 1990.
Shiva, Vandana, *Ecofeminism.* Halifax and London, 1993.
Sinha, Mrinalini (ed.), *Feminism and Internationalism.* Oxford, 1999.
Stiehm, Judith, *Arms and Enlisted Women.* Philadelphia, 1989.
Sylvester, Christine, *Feminist Theory and International Relations in a Postmodern Era.* Cambridge, 1994.
Tickner, J.A., *Gender in International Relations: Feminist Perspectives on Achieving Global Security.* New York, 1992.

BORDER STUDIES

Anderson, J., and O'Dowd L., "Borders, Border Regions and Territoriality: Contradictory Meanings, Changing Significance," *Regional Studies*, vol. 33, no. 7, 1999, pp. 593–604.
Anderson, M., "The Political Problems of Frontier Regions," *West European Politics*, vol. 5, no. 4, 1982, pp. 1–17.
Anderson, M., and E. Port (eds), *The Frontiers of Europe.* London, 1998.
Baker, S., "Punctured Sovereignty, Border Regions and the Environment within the European Union," in O'Dowd L., and T. Wilson (eds), *Borders, Nations and States.* Aldershot, 1996, pp. 19–50.
Barjak, F., "Entrepreneurial Decisions with Spatial Impact at the East German Borderlines," in Eskelinen, H., et al., *Curtains of Iron and Gold, Reconstructing Borders and Scales of Interaction.* Ashgate, 1999.
Benito, G., and G. Gripsrud, "The Expansion of Foreign Direct Investment: Discrete Rational Location Choices or a Cultural Learning Process?" *Journal of International Business Studies*, 1992, pp. 461–76.
Tilburg Berg, E., "National Interests and Local Needs in Divided Setumma, Myths and Reality," in Karelia Eskelinen, H., et al., *Curtains of Iron and Gold, Reconstructing Borders and Scales of Interaction.* Aldershot, 1999.
Boer, E. de, *Personal Transport and Active Space. Dutch German Cross Border Networks*, ERSA, Zurich, Switzerland, 1996.
Boggs, S.W., *International Boundaries: A Study of Boundary Functions and Problems.* New York, 1940. Brednikova, O., "Smuggling of Ethnicity and 'Other' Russians: Construction of Boundaries," in Eskelinen, H., et al., *Curtains of Iron and Gold, Reconstructing Borders and Scales of Interaction.* Aldershot, 1999.
Brocker, J., "How Do International Trade Barriers Affect Interregional Trade?" in A.E. Andersson, W. Isard and T. Puu (eds), *Regional and Industrial Theories.* North-Holland, 1984, pp. 219–39.

Broek, J.O.M., "The Problem of 'Natural Frontiers'," *Frontiers of the Future*. University of California, Committee on International Relations, Berkeley, 1941, pp. 2–20.

Cadwallader, M., "Problems in Cognitive Distance and their Implications for Cognitive Mapping," *Environment and Behaviour*, 11, pp. 559–76.

Canter, D., and S.K. Tagg, "Distance Estimations in Cities," *Environment and Behaviour*, 7, pp. 59–80.

Cappellin, R., "Interregional Cooperation in Europe: An Introduction," in R. Cappelin and P. Batey (eds), *Regional Networks, Border Regions, and European Integration*. London 1993, pp. 1–20.

Castells, I.M., *The Rise of the Network Society, The Information Age: Economy, Society and Culture*. Cambridge, MA; Oxford, UK, 1996.

Cheshire, P., "Explaining the Recent Performance of the European Community's Major Urban Regions," *Urban Studies*, 27, 1990, pp. 311–33.

Church, A. and P. Reid, "Transfrontier Cooperation, Spatial Development Strategies and the Emergence of a New Scale of Regulation: the Anglo-French Border," *Regional Studies*, vol. 29, no. 3, 1995, pp. 297–316.

———, "Cross-border Cooperation, Institutionalisation and Political Space Across the English Channel," *Regional Studies*, vol. 33, no. 7, 1999, pp. 643–55.

Clark, C., et al., "Industrial Location and Economic Potential in Western Europe, *Regional Studies*, 197–212.

Clark, T., "National Boundaries, Border Zones, and Marketing Strategy: A Conceptual Framework and Theoretical Model of Secondary Boundary Effects," *Journal of Marketing*, 58, 1994, pp. 67–80.

Clement, N., "The changing Economics of Borders and Border Regions," in J. Scott et al. (eds), *Border Regions in Functional Transition, European and North American Perspectives*. Regio, Series of the IRS, 9, pp. 41–52.

Duchacek I.D., Latouche D, mabd stevebsib G., *Perforated Sovereignties and International Relations: Transsovereign contacts of subnational governments*. Westport C.T., 1988.

G. Newman, D., "The Spatial Manifestation of Threat: Israelis and Palestinians Seek a 'goo' boundary", *Political Geography*, 14, 689–706.

Forsberg, T. (ed.), *Contested Territory: Border Disputes at the Edge of the Former Soviet Empire*, Aldershot, U.K., 1995.

Frijda, N., "Emotions, Cognitive Structure and Action Tendency," *Cognition and Emotion*, 1, 1987, pp. 235–58.

Gallusser, W.A. (ed.), *Political Boundaries and Coexistence*, Berne, 1995.

Ganster, P., A. Sweedler, J. Scott and W. Dieter-Eberwein, (eds), *Borders and Border Regions in Europe and North America*, San Diego, California, 1997.

Geenhuizen M. van, et al., "Transborder European networking: Shifts in corporate strategy?" *European Planning Studies*, vol. 46, no. 6, 1996, pp. 671–82.

Giaoutzi, M., L. Suarez-Villa and A. Stratigea, "Spatial Information Aspects and Communication Barriers in Border Areas," in Ratti, R. and, S. en Reichman, (eds), *Theory and Practice of Transborder Cooperation*. Basel and Frankfurt am Main, 1993.

Giersch, H., "Economic Union between Nations and the Location of Industries," *Review of Economic Studies*, 17, 87–97.

Gijsel, P., M. de Janssen, H.J. Wenzel and M. Woltering (eds), *Understanding European Cross-Border Labour Markets*, Issues in Economic Cross-Border Relations, Metropolis, Marburg, 1998, pp. 165–82.

Goertz, G. and P. Diehl, *Territorial Changes and International Conflict*, London, 1992.

Golledge, R.G. and R.J. Stimson. *Analytical Behavioural Geography*. New York, 1987.

Gould, P. and R. White, *Mental Maps*. Harmondsworth, England, 1974.

Hansen, N., "Border Regions. A Critique of Spatial Theory and European Case Study," *Annals of Regional Science*, 11, 1–14.

———, "The Economic Development of Border Regions," *Growth and Change*, 8, 2–8.

Hansen, N., "International Cooperation in Border Regions: An Overview and Research Agenda," *International Regional Science Review*, vol. 8, no. 3, 1983, pp. 255–70.

Hartshorne, R., "Suggestions on the terminology of political boundaries", *Annals of the Association of American Geographers*, vol. 26 no. 1, 1936, pp. 56–57.

Harvey, D., "From Space to Place and Back Again: Reflections on the Condition of Postmodernity," in J. Bird et al., *Mapping the Futures, Local Cultures, Global Change*. London, 1993.

———, *The Condition of Postmodernity: An Enquiry into the Origins of Cultural Change*. Oxford, 1993.

Heigl, F., "The Border as a Sociological, Social or National Phenomenon—the Anthropogenous Region," in Strassoldo R. and G.D. Zotti, *Cooperation and Conflict in Border Areas*. Milan, 1982, pp. 215–34.

Hofstede, G., *Culture's Consequences*. London, 1980.

Houtum, H. van and F. Boekema, "Regions Seen as Laboratories for a New Europe: The Applicability of the Flexible Specialisation Model," in Van Dijck, J.J.J. and J. Groenewegen, *Changing Business Systems in Europe, an Institutional Approach*, Brussels, 1994, pp. 85–109.

Houtum, H. van, The Development of Cross-Border Economci Relations; a Theoretical and Empirical Study of the Influence of the State Border on the Development of Cross-Border Economic Relations between Firms in Border Regions of the Netherlands and Belgium. Tilburg, 1998.

Huth, P., *Standing Your Ground: Territorial Disputes and International Conflict*. Ann Arbor, 1996.

Illeris, S., *Urban and regional development in Western Europe in the 1990s: Will Everything Happen in the London-Brussels-Frankfurt-Milan* "anana," (mimeo).

Janssen, M., "Obstacles and Willingness for Cross-Border Mobility: The Dutch-German Border Region," in Gijsel, P., M. de Janssen, H.J. Wenzel, and M. Woltering (eds), *Understanding European Cross-Border Labour Markets. Issues in Economic Cross-Border Relations*, Metropolis, Marburg, pp. 143–64.

Jones, S.B., *Boundary-Making: A Handbook for Statesmen, Treaty Editors and Boundary Commissioners*, Washington D.C., 1945.

Karelia Eskelinen, H., et al., *Curtains of Iron and Gold, Reconstructing Borders and Scales of Interaction*, Ashgate, 1999.

Kolossov, V.A., *Ethno-Territorial Conflicts and Boundaries in the Former Soviet Union*. International Boundaries Research Unit, Durham, England, 1992.

Liikanen, I., "The Political Construction of Identity: Reframing Mental Borders in Russian," in H. Eskelinen, I. Liikanen, and J. Oksa (eds), *Curtains of Iron and Gold: Reconstructing Borders and States of Interaction*. Aldershot, 1999.

Losch, A., *The Economics of Location*. New Haven, 1940, 1954.

Mackay, J.R., "The Interactance Hypothesis and Boundares in Canada," *Canadian Geographer*, no. 11, 1958, 1–8.

Martinez, O., *Border People: Life and Society in the U.S.–Mexico Borderlands*. Tuscon, USA, 1994.

Martinos H., and A. Caspara., *Cooperation between Border Regions for Local and Regional Development*. Brussels, 1990.

Minghi, J.V., "Boundary Studies in Political Geography," *Annals of the Association of American Geographers* 53, 407–28.

Monnesland J., and B. Moen, "The Role of Regional Development in Cross-border Programmes," Imatra, Finland, 1997.

Murphy, A., "Emerging Regional Linkages within the European Community: Challenging the Dominance of the state," *Tijdschrift Economische en Sociale Geografic (Journal of Economic and Social Geografie)*, vol. 84, no. 2, 1993, pp. 103–18.

Murray, P. and L. Holmes (eds), *Europe: Rethinking the Boundaries*. Ashgate, 1998.

―――― (eds), The role of regional development in cross-border programmes, Workshop Borders and Border regions, Imatra, Finland, 1999.

Newman D. and A. Paasi, "Fences and Neighbours in the postmodern World: Boundary Narratives in Political Geography," *Progress in Human Geography*, vol. 22, no. 2, 1998, pp. 186–207.

Newman, D. (ed.), *Boundaries, Territory and Postmodernity*. London, 1999.

Nijkamp, P., P. Rietveld and I. Salomon, "Barriers in Spatial Interactions and Communications: A Conceptual Exploration," *Annals of Regional Science*, vol. 24, no. 4, 1990, pp. 237–52.

O'Down, L., *Negotiating State Borders; A New Sociology for a New Europe?*, Inaugural lecture, Queen's University, Belfast.

O'Down L.J. Corrigan, and T. Moore, "Borders, National Sovereignty and European Integration: The British–Irish case," *International Journal of Urban and Regional Studies*, vol. 19, 1995, pp. 272–85.

O'Dowd, L. and T. Wilson, "Frontiers of Sovereignty in the New Europe," in O'Down L. and T. Wilson (eds), *Borders, Nations, and States*. Avebury, 1996, pp. 1–18.

Paasi, A., "Boundaries as Social Practice and Discourse: The Finnish–Russian Border," *Regional Studies*, vol. 33, no. 7, 1999, pp. 669–80.

———, *Territories, and Consciousness: The Changing Geographies of the Finnish–Russian Border*. Chichester, 1996.

Perkmann, M., "Building Governance Structures Across European Borders," *Regional Studies*, vol. 33, no. 7, pp. 657–67.

Pratt, A.C., "Discourses of locality," *Environment and Planning*, A. 23, pp. 257–66.

Prescott, V., *Political Frontiers and Boundaries*, Chicago, 1987.

Ratti, R., "Spatial and Economic Effects of Frontiers: Overview of Traditional and New Approaches and Theories of Border Area Development," in Ratti, R., and S. en Riechman (eds), *Theory and Practice of Transborder Cooperation*. Basel and Frankfurt am Main, 1993a.

———, "Strategies to Overcome Barriers: From Theory to Practice," in Ratti, R., S. en Reichman, (eds), *Theory and Practice of Transborder Cooperation*. Basel and Frankfurt am Main, 1993b.

Rietveld, P. and L. Janssen, "Telephone Calls and Communication Barriers: The Case of the Netherlands," *The Annals of Regional Science*, vol. 24, 1990, pp. 307–18.

Romann, M., "Divided Perception in a United City: The Case of Jerusalem," in Boal, W., and D.N. Livingstone, *The Behavioural Environment, Essays in Reflection, Application and Re-evaluation*. London, 1989.

Rumley, D. and J.V. Minghi, (eds), *The Geography of Border Landscapes*. London, 1991.

———, "Introduction: The Border Landscape Concept," in Rumley, D., and J.V. Minghi, *The Geography of Border Landscapes*. New York, 1991.

Schofield, C.H. (ed.), *Global Boundaries*. World Boundaries, Vol. I. London, 1994.

Schofield, C.H. and Schofield, R.N. (eds), *The Middle East and North Africa*. World Boundaries, Vol. II, London, 1994.

Scott, J., "European and North American Contexts for Cross-Border Regionalism," *Regional Studies*, vol. 33, no. 7, 1999, pp. 605–17.

Shapiro, M.J. and H.R. Alker (eds), *Challenging Boundaries: Global Flows Territorial Identities*. Minneapolis, 1996.

Shields, R., *Places on the Margin: Alternative Geographies of Modernity*. London and New York, 1991.

Wilson, T. and H. Donnan (eds), *Border Identities: Nation and State at International Frontiers*. Cambridge, U.K., 1998.

Zotti, G.D., "Transnational Relations in a Border Region: The Case of Fruili-Venetia Julia" in Strassoldo R., and G.D. Zotti, *Cooperation and Conflict in Border Areas*, Franco Angelli Editori, Milan, pp. 25–60.

Literary Sensitivities and Peace

[The selected reading list that follows is only indicative of the available corpus of literary tracts on peace. Drawing on two streams of anti-war literature, western and eastern—the subcontinent in particular—this list acts as the entrance to that ever-increasing collection which explores and addresses the destructive futility of war. By beginning with the epic, we have stressed the continuity of this literature that travels back to ancient times. Even in those days, contrary to popular impression, war was looked upon as a scourge. Almost each and every military exploit was counter-pointed by an elegy that revealed the tragic consequence of this exploit. Achilles and Priam weeping together at the end of the *Iliad* is perhaps the most moving example of the elegiac woven into the heroic strain. While the tradition of protest flowed down through the centuries, it flowered in the last before and after the First World War. For the first time, in this phase, creative writers and thinkers assembled together to condemn war and chauvinistic nationalism as related evils. The initiative was taken in the West—in France, Germany, and England in particular—and its impact was felt in our region as well. The impact was nurtured and it prompted an outburst of anti-war creativity in 1930s and 1940s under the banner of anti-Fascist resistance. What is remarkable to note is that in the present phase, writers, especially poets and dramatists, have traversed the full-circle and are drawing their anti-war themes from the *Mahabharat*. Here too, Rabindranath showed the way by writing the two poetic dramas 'Karna Kunti Sangbad' (Karna Kunti Dialogue) and *Gandharir Abedan* (Gandhari's Appeal). This rediscovery of the epic and classical literature as a medium of protest has its equivalent in the West as well. Moreover, this contiguity explains why the two streams have been brought together in this list. Sartre's "The Trojan Women," which is an adaptation of Euripides' play and Dharamvir Bharati's *Andhyug* (Blind Age) delivered the same message.

Epics

Goethe J.W., *The West-eastern Divide*. London, 1944
Homer, *The Iliad*. Harmondsworth, 1964
Homer, *The Odyssey*. Harmondsworth, 1964
Das, Kashiram, *Mahabharat*. Calcutta, 1993
Virgil, *The Aenid*. Harmondsworth, 1964

Novels

Boll, Heinrich, *The Bread of Our Early Years*. London, 1957
Boll, Heinrich, Adam, *Where Art Thou*. London, 1955
Grass, Gunter, *The Tin Drum*. New York, 1961
Grass, Gunter, *Cat and Mouse*. New York, 1963

Grass, Gunter, *Dog Years*. New York, 1964
Heller Joseph, *Catch-22*. London, 1965
Hemingway, Ernest, *For Whom the Bell Tolls*. Harmondsworth, 1954
Hemingway Ernest, *A Farewell to Arms*. Harmondsworth, 1956
Mailer Norman, *The Naked and The Dead*. New York, 1968
Remarque, Erich Maria, *All Quiet on the Western Front*. London, 1954
Remarque, Erich Maria, *The Road Back*. London, 1931
Roy Sabitri, *Badwip/Delta*. Calcutta, 1972
Tolstoy Lev, *War and Peace*. London, 1911

Plays

Aristophanes, *Lysistrata*. New York, 1969
Bernhard, Thomas, *Heldenplatz*. Frankfurt um Main, 1989
Bharati, Dharamvir, *Andhyug*. 1954
Bose, Buddhadev, *Sangkranti*. Calcutta, 1976
Brecht, Bertolt, *Mother Courage and Her Children*. London, 1994
Brecht, Bertolt, *The Resistible Rise of Arturo Uri*. London, 1994
Brecht, Bertolt, *Schweyk in the Second World War*. London, 1994
Chattaraj, Asim, *Itihaser Atma*. Calcutta, 1999
Das Sisir, *Aloukik Sanglap*, Calcutta, 1996
Sartre, Jean Paul, *The Trojan Women*. New York, 1969

Short Stories

Boll, Heinrich, *Children are Civilians Too*, New York, 1970
Boll, Heinrich, *Absent without Leave and Other Stories*, New York, 1968
Crane, Stephen, *The Red Badge of Courage and Other Stories*, New York, 1965

Poetry

Owen, Wilfred, *The Collected Poems of Wilfred Owen*. New York, 1963
Rosenberg, Isaac, *Collected Poems*. London, 1949
Sassoon, Siegfried Lorraine, *Collected Poems*. London, 1961
[Bengali Poets Bishnu De, Subhas Mukhopadhyay, Samar Sen, Birendra Chattopadhyay have written eloquently against war. Urdu poets such as Ali Sardar Jafri, Kaifi Azmi, Adil Mansuri castigated war in their poetry. These are to be found in representative selections and anthologies.]
Bishnu, De, *Kabita Samagra I and II*. Calcutta, 1990
Mukhopadhyay, Subhas, *Sreshta Kabita*. Calcutta, 1968
Chattopadhyay, Birendra, *Sreshta Kabita*. Calcutta, 1970
Sen, Samar, *Samar Sen-er Kabita*. Calcutta, 1987

Essays and Critical Writings

Adorno, T.H., *Minima Moralia*. London, 1974
Graves, Robert, *Goodbye to All That*. London, 1929
Mailer Norman, *Why Are We in Vietnam*. New York, 1967
Tagore, Rabindranath, *Nationalism*. London, 1917

About the Editor and Contributors

Editor

Ranabir Samaddar belongs to the critical school of political readings in India. He is the Director of Calcutta Research Group, Kolkata and was earlier the founder-director of the Peace Studies Program at the South Asia Forum for Human Rights, Kathmandu. He has worked extensively on issues of justice and rights in the context of conflicts in South Asia.

His particular researches have been on migration and refugee studies, the theory and practices of dialogue, nationalism and post-colonial statehood in South Asia, and technological restructuring and new labor regimes. He has recently completed a three volume study of Indian nationalism, the last one titled as, *A Biography of the Indian Nation, 1947–1997*. His work on the *Paradoxes of the Nationalist Time* written in the context of the history of independence movement in Bangladesh has challenged the prevailing accounts of the birth of nationalism purely in cultural terms. His most recent work is *Refugees and the State: Practices of Asylum and Care in India, 1947–2000* (edited).

Contributors

Kanti Bajpai is presently Headmaster, The Doon School, Dehra Dun. Earlier, he was Professor of International Politics at Jawaharlal Nehru University, New Delhi where he taught from 1994 to 2003. His most recent book is *Roots of Terrorism*.

Paula Banerjee specializes in diplomatic history. She now works on themes related to borders and boundaries in South Asia, and women in conflict situations. She is at the Department of South and South East Asian Studies, University of Calcutta,

Kolkata. Her book on Indo-US relations is titled, *When Ambitions Clash*.

Gautam Kumar Basu is a professor of International Relations at the Jadavpur University, Kolkata. He is a specialist in comparative politics. He is the author of *The State, Development and Military Interventions*.

Rajeev Bhargava is a professor of Political Science at the Delhi University, Delhi. He is the author of *Individualism in Social Science: Forms and Limits of a Methodology*. He is also the editor of two well-known volumes, *Secularism and Its Critics*, and *Multiculturalism, Liberalism, and Democracy*.

Sanjukta Bhattacharya chairs the Department of International Relations at the Jadavpur University, Kolkata. She has written on various aspects of forced migration and the humanitarian response. She has co-edited *Perspectives on India's North East*.

Tapan K. Bose is the secretary general of the South Asia Forum for Human Rights. He has worked for long in defence of human rights in Jammu and Kashmir. He is also well known as the director of several noted documentaries.

Subhas Chakraborty is a historian and teaches at the Presidency College, Kolkata. He is the author of important historical essays on the district of Darjeeling, West Bengal. Besides he specializes in European history.

Samir Kr Das teaches Political Science at the University of Calcutta, Kolkata. He works on ethnicity and conflicts. He is the author of two important books, *ULFA: A Political Analysis* and *Regionalism in Power: The Case of Asom Gana Parishad*.

Subhoranjan Dasgupta is a well-known literary critic and a journalist. He is now a researcher at the Institute of Development Studies, Kolkata. His doctoral dissertation was published as an acclaimed volume, *Dialectics and Dream*. He is also a well-known researcher on the partition the East in 1947.

Barun De, a widely respected senior Indian historian, is a specialist on Central Asia. He was the founder director of the Centre for Studies in Social Sciences, Calcutta, and later he was the founder director of the Maulana Abul Kalam Azad Institute of Asian Studies, Calcutta. He has authored several significant historical essays in his long career.

Partha S. Ghosh is a Professor at the Omeo Kumar Das Institute of Social Change and Development, Guwahati. He has authored numerous publications on the political history of conflicts in South Asia and has worked extensively on forced migration. Among his publications is *Ethnicity versus Nationalism*.

Brian Gorlick is a specialist in international law and in particular on humanitarian law. He is a functionary in the UNHCR, now in Sweden; earlier he was in India and looked after the work of legal protection.

Asha Hans is Professor and Head of the Department of Political Science, also the Director of the School of Women's Studies, Utkal University. She has been a recipient of Fulbright and Kathleen Ptolemy awards for her work on the refugees.

Sanjoy Hazarika is Consulting Editor of *The Statesman*, editing its Northeast Page. He is also Research Professor at the Centre for Policy Research, New Delhi. For long he was a correspondent for The New York Times (1981–1996). He has authored numerous books, including the acclaimed *Strangers of the Mist* and *Rites of Passage*.

Monirul Hussain is a professor of Political Science at the Guwahati University, Gauhati. His works on the Assam Students movement are widely read. Among his works is *The Assam Movement*.

Irene Khan, a specialist in international human rights and humanitarian law, had been for long a senior functionary in the UNHCR and worked in several capacities in India, Kosovo, Geneva, and elsewhere. Currently, she is the secretary general of the Amnesty International.

INDEX

A

Abdullah, Sheikh, 165, 166
Afghan situation, 195
Afghanistan: change in the political scenario in, 120; Soviet intervention in, 245
African Charter on Human and Peoples Rights (1981), 94, 257
agitation, anti-Sikh, 166
Agni, 55
Ahmed: Fakhruddin Ali, 301; Kayes, 387
Ahom, 210
Akbar, M.J., 161, 166
Aksai Chin, 176, 186
Alavi, Hamza, 61
All Arunachal Pradesh Student's Union (APSU), 311
All Parties Hurriyat Committee, 331
Allan, Charles, 218
ambiguity, nuclear, 56, 57, 341, 343, 351
American Convention on Human Rights, 257
Amnesty International, 169
Anderson, Benedict, 216, 286
Anthony Giddens, 26, 313
Aragon, Louis, 380
arms control: confidence building and, 56; conventional, measures, 57
Asamiya: colonial suppression of, 300; colonial suppression of the, language, 300; hatred of the, ruling class, 309; historical capacity of the, nationality, 305; nationalism, 302; nationality, 304; nationality in colonial Assam, 302; official imposition of the, language, 307; ruling class, 304, 306
Asamiyaization, process of, 305
Ashokan Empire, 207
Asian-African Legal Consultative Committee, 192, 203
Asom, 210
Assam Gana Parishad rule in Assam, 241
Assam movement, institutionalization of the, 305
Assam: accord, 240; education in, 300; pre-colonial society in, 296; reactivation of river traffic between Kolkata and, 374; size of pre-colonial, 297
asylum: policy changes, 198; policy on, for Afghan refugees, 198; protection of the rights of, seekers and refugees, 99; refugee protection in countries of, 192; refugees in the country of, 200; seekers from neighboring countries, 97; temporary, for the refugees in the ASEAN countries, 194; to the Dalai Lama, 186
attack, diversionary, 53

authoritarianism: 83, 222;
frontier-style, 220; landlord-cum-chieftain style, 220
Awami League, Sheikh Hasina's, 64, 323
Azad Kashmir: 268, 269, 270; National Students Federation (NSF) of, 335; Pakistani, 335

B

Balibar, Etienne, 142
Baluchistan Peoples Liberation Front (BPLF), 246
Bandyopadhyay, Hiranmoy, 160
Banerjee: Nikunja Vihari, 26; Paula, 141, 143, 173, 368
Bangladesh: 51; democracy in, 243; infiltrations into India, 250; issues between India and, 368; liberation movement, 232; liberation of, 152, 369; liberation war, 232, 243; migrating from, 163; out-migration from, 240; secession of, 227
Bangladeshi, migration of, Muslims, 51
Bara Hoti, Chinese "trespass" in, 179
Barthes, Roland, 37
Basu, Gautam Kr, 72
Bentham, Jeremy, 84, 86, 88
Bhagabati, A.C., 301
Bhandari, Nar Bahadur, 239
Bhargava, Rajeev, 319, 390
Bhartiya Janata Party, 64
Bhasin, Kamla, 268, 270
Bhattacharjee, Bijon, 322
Bhattacharya, Sanjukta, 145, 254
Bhutto, Zulfikar Ali, 173

Birdi, J.P., 280
Bismarck, 110
Bodo Security Force (Bd.SF), 310
Bodo: leadership of the, movement, 312; militants, 312, 313; movement for Bodoland, 312
Bodoland Autonomous Council (BAC), 312
border: between India and Nepal, 235; compulsions of the, 186; continuing insecurities over the, 82; control, 222; cooperative, management, 320; cost of protecting the, 141; crossing, unofficial, 371; democratization of, management, 320; demography, 372; dispute between India and China, 175; disputes, 182, 185; female combatants from across the, 278; histories of, 142; Indian preoccupation with its, 180; Indian rigidity over the, question, 183; India–Pakistan, 262; Indo–Bangladesh, 372; interpretation of the Sino-Soviet, 185; issue of, 185; militarization of, 184; negotiations between India and China over, issues, 178; origin of South Asian, 174; politics of, 147, 178, 186; politics of, in South Asia, 175; problem of, and immigration, 376; sanctity of the, 184; settlement problems in, areas, 372; settlements of, disputes by arbitration, 184; Sino-Indian, 176, 180;

Sino-Soviet, 185; troop reductions along the, 46; unresolved, disputes of the 19th century, 182; war in Kargil, 141; women on the, 282; women's position in the, areas of India, 268
Bose: Buddhadeva, 378; Tapan K., 320, 323
Boulding, Kenneth, 38, 39, 42, 62
boundaries: and borders, 175; demarcation of maritime, 369; India's traditional, 181; international, between India and Pakistan, 183; new, in women's lives, 272; notion of, permeability, 148; of the LoC, 277; of the Simla Convention, 177
Bouquet, A.C., 25
Brecht, Bertolt, 381
brinkmanship: 58; sub-strategic, 59
Bull Hedley, 39, 41, 42
Bunuel, Luis, 378
Butalia, 268

C

capital flows, control of international, 130
capital, liberalizing, movement, 75
capitalism, emergence of, 297
capitalist nations, aggressive, 74
Cartagena Declaration on Refugees, 192
Chakma: Accord, 265; rehabilitation, 265; rehabilitation process, 265
Chakrabarty: Dipesh, 153; Sudhir, 152

Chakraborty, Subhas Ranjan, 103
Chambers of Commerce, 61
Chappell, David, 142
Chattopadhayaya: Birendra, 321, 381; Brajadulal, 208
Chaudhuri, Salil, 322
Chavan: S.B., 241; Y.B., 182
China: 44; agreement between India and, 177; friendly relations with, 194
Chinese nuclear intimidation, 344
Choucri, Nazli, 227
citizenship: 156; certificates, 158
civil society: gap between the state and, 83, 84; permanent visibility in the, 88; Task of, 337
civil war, victims of, 256
civilian: casualties, 255; non-combatants affected by war, 146; population, 145
Clausewitz, 154, 155, 156
Clavero, Bartolomé, 136
Cohn, Bernard, 216
Cold War: conflicts during the, 255; end of the, 44; rivalry, 343
colonial transformation, 299
colonialism: British, 302; internal, 169; oppression of, and feudalism, 299; penetration of British, 297
Committee Against Torture, 96
Committee for Initiative on Kashmir, 169
Committee on the Rights of the Child, 96
communalism, politicization of, 232
communication, and consultation, 65

Communism, 113
Communist Party of
  Yugoslavia, 113
Comprehensive Plan of Action
  for Indo-Chinese Refugees in
  Southeast Asia (CPA), 192,
  261
Comprehensive Test Ban
  Treaty (CTBT), 48
confidence-building measures
  (CBM), 46, 49
conflict: and violence, 314;
  armed, 257; Asamiya–non-
  Asamiya, 300; causes of
  ethnic, in Northeast, 314;
  ethnic, 234, 276; ethnic,
  and violence, 309; ideological, 254; in Kargil, 147;
  India–Pakistan, 44; Indo-
  Pakistani, 179; laws on
  non-international armed,
  257; low-intensity, 156;
  minority, 254; non-
  internationalized armed,
  258; political solutions to,
  situations, 179; population
  movements and interstate,
  226; post-Partition, 276;
  Sinhala Tamil, 233; temporary postponement of, 27;
  with Pakistan, 276
Congress, 333
Congress party, defeat of the,
  in India, 227
*Convention Against Torture and
  Other Cruel, Inhuman or
  Degrading Treatment or
  Punishment* (1984), 93
*Convention Against Torture and
  the Convention on the Rights
  of the Child*, 192
*Convention on the Elimination
  of All Forms of Discrimina-
  tion Against Women*, 93
*Convention on the Elimination
  of Discrimination Against
  Women* (1979), 93
*Convention on the Elimination
  of Racial Discrimination*
  (1965), 93
*Convention on the Non-
  Applicability of Statutory
  Limitations to War Crimes
  and Crimes against
  Humanity*, 94
*Convention on the Political
  Rights of Women*, 93
*Convention on the Prevention
  and Punishment of the
  Genocide*, 94
*Convention on the Prevention
  and Punishment to the Crime
  of Genocide* (1948), 93
*Convention on the Prohibition
  of Military or any other
  Hostile Use of Environmen-
  tal Modification Techniques*,
  257
*Convention on the Prohibition
  of the Development, Produc-
  tion, and Stock-piling of
  Bacteriological (Biological)
  and Toxin Weapons and their
  Destruction*, 257
*Convention on the Rights of the
  Child* (1989), 93
*Convention on the Suppression
  and Punishment of Apart-
  heid*, 93
*Convention relating to the
  Status of Refugees*, 193
*Convention relating to the
  Status of Stateless Persons*
  (1954), 93
Conventional Forces in Europe
  (CFE) agreement, 361
cooperation, notions of trans-
  boundary, 149

counter insurgency: operations in Kashmir, 328; operations in Upper Assam, 313
Curzon, Lord, 173
Czernin, Count, 111

D

Dalai Lama, His Holiness the XVth, 26
Danicic, 109
defense: defensive, 348, 349; ignorance of, matters, 358; offensive, 53, 348, 349
democracy: 113; Calvinistic campaign of, 121; corruption of, 221; liberal, 113; manifestation of international, 131; survival of, 88
deterrence: 39; absence of a, posture, 58; at the level of nuclear and conventional war, 59; by denial, 53; hegemony and, 42; nuclear weapons and, 340; nuclear, 348; nuclear, in South Asia, 342; problem of, at the substrategic level, 58; recessed, 55; stable mutual, 58; strategic level, 59; substrategic, 59
Deuskar, Sakharam Ganesh, 215
Devi, Jeera, 284
Dhar, 269
Didda, Queen, 270
disarmament, unilateral nuclear, 361
disinvestments: of PSUs, 83; of state enterprises, 75
Displaced Persons (Compensation and Rehabilitation) Act, 1958, 263
dispute: bilateral political, between India and Pakistan, 195; Sino-Indian border, of 1962, 185; territorial, 173
distribution, question of, 87
Disturbed Areas Act, 148
Djilas, Milovan, 114
domestic laws: 202; international treaties and, 199
Dostam, General, 213
Drèze, Jean, 78
Durand Line, 174, 186, 213, 218
Durand, Sir Mortimer, 174, 176

E

East India Company, 77
Eastern Europe: 103; construction of a new political geography in, 106; political developments in, 105
East–West CBMs, 49
economic cooperation, prospect of, 375
economic development, benefits of generalized, 51
economy: laws of classical political, 85; liberalization of the, 81; logic of classical political, 85; move towards market, 78, 87; neo-classical political, 82
education: 77; health and, 78; higher, 78; patterns of, expenditure, 78; spread of, and communication, 42
educational institution, admission to, 78
Ekka, Balamdina, 284
Elias, Akhtaruzzaman, 381, 386
Eluard, Paul, 380, 381
Embree, Ainslie, 155
enemy, female representation of the, 279
Enloe, Cynthia, 146

equality, sovereign, 21
ethic: of ultimate ends, 127; Kantian sense of, 322; of war strategy, 36
European Convention for the Protection of Human Rights and Fundamental Freedom (1969), 94, 257
Europeanization, process of, 110
Everest, Sir George, 217
Exchange: functional and economic, between India and Pakistan, 61; systems, 40
exodus: of East Pakistan refugees to India, 233; sensitivity, on and Partition, 385

F

federalism, negation of, 231
Ferdinand: assassination of Franz, 111; Franz, 110
fertilizer subsidies, 81
feudalism, decline of, 297
fissile material, ban on, production, 360
foreign direct investment (FDI), 80
foreign: investment, 80; technology, 80
forgiveness: demand for, 409; justification of, 410; mechanisms of, and reconciliation, 397; process of, 410; reasons for, 410; reasons for unconditional, 411
Foucault, Michel, 322
frontier, Sino-Indian, 177

G

Galbraith, John Kenneth, 181
Gandhi Peace Foundation, 32

Gandhi: 123, 391, 392; assassination of Rajiv, 234; Mahatma, 322
Ganges, Mahakali and, water sharing, 51
Ganguly, Sumit, 154, 157, 166, 168
Gellner, Ernest, 216
gemeinschaft (community), 30
Geneva Convention, 125
Geneva Peace Accord, 195
Ghatak, Ritwik, 382
Ghising, Subhash, 158, 239
Ghosh: Nemai, 382; Partha S., 143, 163, 226
Gill, Stephen, 73
Giuliani, Carlo, 130
Glenn, 53
global humanitarian, commitment to, principles, 203
globalization: 23, 75, 126, 133; of society, 223; specific history of, 129
Goa, Indian occupation of, 180
Gorlick, Brian, 92
Gottman, Jean, 142
governance: connection between, and "government", 23; good, 75
government: funds, 79; policy of inviting foreign multinationals, 80; of Abdul Gayoom, 50; reliance on, funds, 79
Gramsci, Antonio, 381
Gray, Chris Hables, 154, 155
Gromchevsky, Captain, 176
Gromyko, Andrei, 183
growth: economic, 50; of the British Empire, 248; population, 242
Grujic, Jevrem, 107
Guha, Amlendu, 296
Gujral Doctrine, 50, 52

Index

Gupta Empire, 207
Gurkha National Liberation Front (GNLF), 158, 239

H

Haas, Ernst: 59, 60; neo-functionalism, 60
habits, connection between *values, institutions,* and, 63
Hampshire, Stuart, 395, 396
Handicap International, 261
Hare Krishna sect, popularity of the, 24
Harkat ul-Ansar, 49
health: spending, 81; medical and public, 77
hegemony: 39; limits of, 52; regional, 180, 181
Hill Tribal Population after Independence, 307
Himalayan security, Indian concerns about, 50
Hindu Mahasabha, influence of the, 220
Hindus in the Sunni-dominated valley, 272
Hindutva, 64
Hirtze, 74
Hitler, 113
Hobbes, 21, 403
Hobsbawm, Eric, 216, 134
Hogan, Michael, 258
Holdich, Sir Thomas, 218
Hore, Somenath, 322
Horowitz, Irving, 129
Hsien, Fa, 208
Human Rights Commissions, 94
Human Rights Committee, 96
human rights: 92; accession to, instruments, 198; activists of Pakistan held Kashmir, 336; concepts and refugee law, 256; development of, principles, 96; erosion of civil liberties and, 32; guarantees, 258; importance of the international system of, protection, 94; international attention to, violations, 95; international system of, protection, 95; international, instruments, 93, 98, 192; international, treaties, 93; Kashmiri, activists, 336; laws, 258; of individuals, 92; promotion of, standards, 96; protecting and assisting victims of, violations, 92; refugee problem in the context of, 92; safeguard against, abuses, 200; safeguarding, and refugee protection, 97; treaties, 99; victims of, violations, 92; violations of, 203, 337
humanitarian law: 256; beginning of, 256

I

Ikhwan-ul-Muslimoon, 169
immigration: control, 200; illegal, 369
India: and its neighbors, 65; Kashmir's inclusion in, 161
Indian and Pakistani Defence Secretaries, 326
Indian leadership of the Asian and African "block", 179
Indian Muslim League, 332
Indian National Congress, 301, 332
Indian Nuclear Debate, 339
India–Pakistan: crisis of 1987, 44; issues, 46
Indo-Pakistan Boundary Disputes Tribunal, 368

Indus Rivers Treaty (1960), 60
infiltration: evidences of Bangladeshi, 240; Bangladeshi, 240; insurgency and, 348
insiders, powerful, 49
institutionalization, of remembrance, 405
instrument of accession, 324
insurgency: movements, 185; Naga, 310
integration, value, 20
integrative relationships, 41
Integrative systems, 40
integrity: preservation of Indian security and, 194; territorial, 51
interest of Super Powers in South Asia, 179
internal affairs, non-interference in India's, 52
internal dynamics in Iran and Iraq, 120
internally displaced persons (IDPs), 95, 255
International Bill of Rights, 93
International Commission of Jurists (ICJ), 244
International Convention on the Elimination of All Forms of Racial Discrimination, 93
International Covenant on Civil and Political Rights (1966), 93
International Covenant on Economic, Social and Cultural Rights (1966), 93
International Covenants on Civil and Political Rights, 257
International Labor Organization, 80
international law, principle of customary, 191

international life, Kantian vision of, 62
Islami Jamhoori Ittehad (IJI), Nawaz Sharif's, 64
Islamic connections, Pakistan's, and credentials, 46
Islamic order, canons of the new, 275
Ispahani, Mahnaz, 213, 219

J

Jafri, Ali Sardar, 322, 379
Jumma problem, 221
Jurisprudence, Anglo-Saxon system of, 24
justice: cause of economic, 339; criminal, system, 400; conventional criminal, system, 400; economic, 363; goals of economic, and social dignity, 350; internal struggle for, and dignity, 339; struggle for economic, 339, 363; violation of norms of procedural, 399
justification, nuclear weapons and economic, 346

K

Kargil: cease-fire, 328; conflict, 280, 286; confrontation between Indian and Pakistani forces in, 328; contextualizing women's position in the, conflict, 276; ceasefire in, 328; Importance of, 331; liberation war in, 331; war, 142, 320, 328, 331; war in the, sector of Kashmir, 329; war widows, 283; women in the, war, 286; women of, 286

Kashmir Hindu and Buddhist
  Mahasangh, 333
Kashmir: 176; accession of, to
  India, 48; building peace in,
  323; desire of the people of,
  320; dispute, 325; imbroglio,
  164; independence movement, 335; Indian Position
  on, 326; Indo-Pakistan war
  on, 325; long-term involvement in, 164; movement in,
  326; nationalist discourse
  in, 285; nexus between the
  democratic rights of the
  people of, 337; nuclear
  weapons and, 49; Pakistan
  occupied, 184; Pakistan's
  claim on, 166; Pakistan-
  held, 335; Pakistani, 335;
  Pakistani position on, 327;
  perpetrating war-like
  situations in, 169; present,
  problem, 272; quarrel and
  proliferation, 48; question,
  179; trained militants in,
  275; women across borders
  in, 268; women's position in
  the history of, 269
Kashmiri: civil society, 333; leaders of, national movement,
  332; marginalization of women
  in, politics, 286; Muslims,
  334; narrative of nationalism,
  286; national identity, 273;
  national movement, 332; nationalism, 332, 333, 334;
  Pandits, 332, 334; self-determination movement, 334;
  women, 270, 275
Kashmiriyat, concept of, 332
Kaul, General B.M., 181
Kaveri dispute, 249
Khaleda Zia's Bangladesh
  Nationalist Party (BNP), 64

Khan: Ayub, 180; Chengiz, 217;
  Irene, 144, 190
Khomeini revolution, 44
King, Martin Luther, Jr., 123
Kissinger, Henry, 136
Koirala, Girija Prasad, 86
Kokrajhar, Santhals of, 313
Krishna, Sankaran, 125
Krishnamachari, T.T., 182
Kurfi, Dr Bashir, 131
Kyi, Aung San Suu, 221

L

Ladakh, repercussions in, 181
Lahore Declaration, 326
Lattimore, Owen, 142
Lebanese rightist forces, 125
Legal Regime for Refugee
  Care, 92
Leimgruber, W., 147
life: political way of, 65; South
  Asia's political way of, 66
Line of Control (LoC), 272, 325
Lokshahi Hakk Sangathana, 169

M

Macmahon Line, 218
Macpherson, B., 86
Maldives security, 50
Malthus, Thomas Robert, 248
Manhattanization, 354
Mansuri, Adil, 382
Manto, Sadat Hasan, 383, 384
Maratha migrants, 214
Masood, Ahmad Shah, 219
mass destruction, modern
  means of, 254
Matsyanyaya, 28
May, Larry, 406
Mcgowan, William, 86
mediation, Indian attitude
  towards third party, 184

Menon, 268, 270
Menon, Ritu, Krishna, 181
methods, Eurocentric, of dividing people, 143
middle class, entrepreneurial, 66
migration: cross-border, motivated economic concerns, 190; cross-national, 228, 246; confusion with economic, 199; forced, 264; illegal economic, 199; India–Pakistan, 264; of tribal population, 300; peasant, 162; politics of Interstate, 228; probability of return, 157; problem of cross-border, 370; task force on, 237
militancy, support of sub-national, in Pakistan, 58
militant movement, rise of the, 336
militarism: 73, 74, 363; and security, 144; external, 34; Marek Thee's definition of, 74; of state, 143; possibilities of, in South Asian countries, 73; subtle, 29; third world, 129
militarizaion: 354; growing, 32; internal, 34; of state power, 222
military: demarcation between civilian and, affairs, 74; dynamics of, regimes, 84; history of, cooperation, 343; Indian, and economic power, 50
Mill, James, 84, 88
Miller, Joseph, 74
minimalist state: emergence of a, 72; role of, 72
ministry, emergence of a non-Congress, 87

Misra, Udayon, 148
Missile Technology Control Regime (MTCR), 46
Mitrany: David, 59; scheme, 60
Mizo insurgency, 310
modernity: 162; advent of, 25, 26; peace characteristic of, 27; peace under conditions of, 27; Western framework of, 26
Moeller, Bjorn, 349
Mohajir issue in Pakistan, 264
Mohajir Quami Mahaz (MQM), 264
monopoly, over the legitimate instruments of coercion, 160
Montesquieu, 132
moral laws, Kantian concern for universal, 23
Morris, Benny, 128
Movement for the Restoration of Democracy (MRD), 245
movement: of people and goods, 369; of population, 226, 243; of the Vedic peoples, 209; women's, 277
Mujahideen: Pakistani, 277; supporters of the, in Pakistan, 328
Mukherjee, Dr Radha Kumud, 211, 212, 216
Mukhopadhyay, Subhas, 380
Murphy, Jeffrey, 403, 407, 409, 410
Murty, K. Satchinanda, 25
Muslim League, 333
Muslim Liberation Front, 169

N

Narain, Madhav Rao, 214
Narayan, Jai Prakash, 183
nation formations, histories of, 142

National Commission for Women, 283
National Defense System (NDS), 121
National Human Rights Commission (NHRC), 94, 371
National Human Rights Commission of India, 198
National Hydro-Power Corporation (NHPC), 76
national security, pervasiveness of the, lobby, 182
National Socialist Council of Nagaland (NSCN), 308, 310
National Textile Corporation, 76
National Thermal Power Corporation (NTPC), 76
nationalism: 117, 362; anti-colonial, 216; claims, 166; cultural, 287; facile interpretations of, 146; Indian, 297; pan-Indian, 298; present-day Kashmiri, 274; regional, 298; Sinhala–Buddhist, 247; understanding of, 287
nationalist character, of the Indian state, 167
nationalist discourse: widow's place in the, 286; women across borders and the, 285
nation-state, concept of the, 217
natural selection, process of, 160
Nedic, General, 115
NEFA, 181
negotiation: and arbitration, 399; of the immigration question, 373
Nehru–Liaquat Pact, 262
neo-ethics, 135

neo-functional theory, 61
neo-functionalists, 60
neo-realism, 135
neo-Zapatism, 131
Nepal: 50, 51; demographic invasion of, 237; economy in, 86; legal Indian migrations to, 235; naturalized citizen of, 238
Nepalese, Assam's, population, 238
Nepali Congress and communists, 64
Nepali National Commission on Population, 237
Nepali: legal, migrations to India, 235; in India, 239; politics, 86; terrorism, 235
new world order, 75
newly industrializing countries (NICs), 83
Nihlani, Govind, 382
Nixon, 179
non-aggression, policy of, towards the aliens, 25
Nonaligned Movement, leadership of the, 180
non-alignment, policy of, 194
non-governmental organizations: 79; criticism against, 79
Non-Proliferation Treaty (NPT), 45
non-refoulement, principle of, 191
non-weaponization, costs and benefits of, 55
Northeast, topography of, 293
Northeast, violence in India's, 292
nuclear incrementalism, 55
Nuclear Non-Proliferation Treaty (NPT), 46, 355
nuclear powers, 56

nuclear threats, deterrent system based on conventional and, 53
nuclear weapons, 58, 346
nuclearism: 354, 363; effects of, 354; Indian, 363
nuclearization: 351; Pakistani, 361; proponents of, 342

O

Obrenovic, Milosh, 110
Okey, Robin, 108
Open Skies agreement in Europe, 49
Operation South Sudan, 260
Organization of African Unity Convention, 97
outsiders, powerful, 43
Owen, Wilfred, 379, 382

P

pacifism, 33
Packenham, 161
Pakistan: aggression committed by, 183; deterring, 340; dismemberment of, 233; election of Nawaz Sharif, in, 1997, 66; international opinion against, 58; nuclear arms race with, 355; official history of, 152; official talks between India and, 329; regime, 242; registered Afghan refugees in, 245; relationship with, 46; survival of, as a sovereign state, 159; talks between India and, 327; trade, 330
Pakistan's national integrity, 246
Pakistan's nuclear and missile program, 46

Pakistani: general elections, 64; Indian border, 176; infiltrations, 241; making of the, state, 167; reports of, espionage agents, 242
Pakistan–India Peoples Forum for Peace and Democracy, 330, 331
Palacky, 108
Palghat Tamils, 215
Parbatya Chattagram Jumma Saranarthy Kalyan Samity, 265
Paris Commune, 125
Paris Peace Plan on Cambodia, 195
partition: 175, 177; and exodus, 382; and shifting identities, 270; duplicity of, politics, 386; feminist interpretations of, 268; Independence and, 303; of British India, 220; refugees, 193; victims of, 279
Pax Britannica, establishment of, 28
peace: agenda of, 35; and stability on China's Southwestern border, 45; as functional and economic interaction, 38; audit of, in South Asia, 20; breakdown of, in the region, 147; cold, 39; deterrent, 38, 53, 66; established through the formation of nation-states, 22; evolution of, studies, 19; experts, 32; fostering, in South Asia, 45; functional, 66; functionalist path to, 59; hegemonic, 43; histories of, 153; inclusion of, studies, 22; Indian, studies, 35; integral philosophy of, 26;

440 Index

integrative, 66; micro-traditions of, 28; minimalist, 39; modalities of, 29; modernity and the indigenous, traditions, 28; narratives of, and war, 319; Nehru's involvement in the Korean, process, 179; Notions of, 38; pathway to, 42; perpetual, 38; positive intervention for, 149; professional, researchers, 32; program of, education, 33; prospects of a functionalist, 66; *reasons to make*, 20; researchers, 147; South Asian, 64; South Asian, historiography, 27; South Asian, studies, 35; sufficient condition for, 21; textbook on, studies, 37; threats to, 23; traditions of South Asia, 27; traditions, 29; triumphalism, 28; types of, 38; uneasy, 27; voices for, 330; working, system, 59
peacemaking by threatening, 39
People's Liberation Army (PLA), 308
Peoples Union for Civil Liberties (PUCL), 169
Peoples Union for Democratic Rights (PUDR), 169
Peoples' Revolutionary Party of Kangleipak (PREPAK), 308
permanence, myth of, 207
Phadikar, Shri Prabhas, 215
policy, frontier, 174
political power, potential of an ethical interrogation of, 134
politics: and pronouncements of the Pakistani government, 230; communalization of, 232; current phase of global, 129; economics over, 62; interaction between demographic issues and, 227; intermeshing of the Sri Lanka Tamil, 234; model of criminalizing, 86; pre-partition Muslim, 230; South Asian, 187
population: categories of, movements, 229; cross-border, movements, 190; large-scale, movements, 151; massive displacement of, 262; movements, 144, 147, 151, 210, 226, 229, 235, 242, 244; phenomenon of cross-border, movements, 228; pressure, 159; size of, movements in Asia, 201; trans-border, movement, 157; war-like situations and, movements, 157
Power Grid Corporation Limited (PGCL), 76
power: redistribution of, 82; threatening, 40; trans-national centers of, 162
Pradhan, Dr Kumar, 206
Praja Parishad, 333
Princip, Gavrilo, 123
Prithvi, 55
privatization: 75, 76, 79, 82; concept of, 72, 84, 87; government policy of, 79; of agricultural lands, 75; of public enterprise, 81; preference for, 87; programs, 79
privatized society, 85
Protection of Human Rights Act (1993), 94
protection: against unlawful expulsion or detention, 98; concept of international, 191; legal basis of, 255

Proudhon, 73
psychology, rise of a militarist, 35
public opinion in India, 358
public sector enterprises, non-plan budget support to, 76

R

Rajachakravartin, coronation of the great, 28
Rao: B. Subba, 216; Balaji Baji, 214
rapprochement, Sino-Indian, 187
Rashtriya Samaj Sudhar Sangastha (RSSS), 238
Rashtriya Swayam Sewak Sangh, 220
Rawls, John, 22
Ray, Annada Shankar, 207
realignment of the Third World countries economies, 75
realism, 362
reconciliation, policy of, 116
re-democratization, trend of, 84
reforms: initiated by the government, 80; introducing structural, 75
refoulement: deportation and, of refugees, 199; protection from, 98
Refugee Convention, 21
refugee: absence of a definition of a, in the law, 199; awareness of, protection issues, 96; basic rights of, 190; burden of Asia, 194; cross-border nature of the, problem, 191; definition, 191, 196; domestic legislation on, 202; East Pakistani, 263; enforceability of domestic, institutions, 96; ethnic affinities between the host community and, 197; flows out of Vietnam, 194; formulation of policies on, 145; from West Pakistan, 263; handling of the, 329; harmonization of, policies, 202; inconsistent and discriminatory treatment of, groups, 199; inflow of Afghan, into Pakistan, 245; influxes of, 97; international obligations on, 203; international protection to, 193; international standards on, protection, 203; international, instruments, 202; international, law, 92; international, regime, 99, 190, 193, 194; international, regime in Asia, 193; lack of procedures to identify, 199; legal protection of, 201; means of strengthening, protection, 202; militarization of, populations, 259; model, community, 264; movements, 190, 219; origin of the international system of, protection, 92; population in India, 97; precondition for, to return home, 203; presence of Tibetan, 244; preventing, problems, 203; principles of, protection, 99; problem in South Asia, 145; problem, 196, 201, 246; problems and ethnic stress, 220; problems confronting Asian countries, 196; problems in Asia, 193; procedure for determining, status, 199, 201; protecting the rights of, 190; protecting, against expulsion, 198;

protecting, in exile, 203; protection of, 94, 190, 192, 198, 201, 202; regional agreement on, 196; rehabilitation, 259; relevance of the, rights, 203; respecting, protection, 201; response to, problems in Asia, 201; rights of, 203; Rohingya, 197; solutions to the Indo-Chinese, problem, 195; South Asian, protection regime, 145; specific legal framework for, 197; Sri Lankan Tamil, in India, 234; Sri Lankan, 234; Tibetan, 244, 264; Tibetan, crisis, 194; Tibetan, in India, 244; Vietnamese and Laotian, 195; Vietnamese, camp, 195; West Pakistan, 262
regime: authoritarian, 84; differentiation between civilian and military, 72; military, 74; totalitarian, 113
Registration of Claims (Displaced Persons) Act, 1956, 263
rehabilitation: 255; discrepancies in the, efforts, 261; efforts, 266; of victims, 145; of Victims in war-torn societies, 254; of victims of conflict in war-torn societies, 255; program in Cambodia, 261; reconstruction and, 261; sustainable, 145
relations: freezing of India–Pakistan, 344; India–Pakistan, 65, 230; Indo-Pak, 232; Sino-Indian, 186
relationship: between governments and UBHCR, 191; between local and foreign capital, 77; between the state and its people, 161; India–Pakistan, 60
relative gains problem, 61
relativism, 399
Remarque, Erich Maria, 321
Renan, Ernest, 404
repatriation: assistance to individuals, 266; principle of voluntary, 198; voluntary, 196, 201
republicans, anti-Bonapartist polemics of the, 73
resentment, towards the wrongdoer, 407
responsibility: collective norms of, 126; ethic of, 127; moral principle of, 20
retribution, private acts of vengeance and, 411
Riefenstahl, Leni, 379
Rights: Economic, Social and Cultural, 257; socio-economic, 196
riots: anti-Tamil, 233; Hindu–Muslim, 232; incidence of Hindu–Muslim, 232
Robinson, Pat, 124
Roman Empire, 104
Roman Empire, decline of the, 104
Rose, Leo, 158
Rousseau, Jean-Jacques, 256
Roy: A.K., 77; Olivier, 219
Rudolph, 162

S

Salal Dam agreement (1978), 60
Salisbury, Lord, 174
Samaddar, Ranabir, 119, 156, 167, 368

Sathe, Sheo Bhat, 215
Sathyu, S.M., 382
security: amalgamated, community, 62; dilemma, 40; India's goal of national, 180; internal, requirements, 57; national, 363; pluralistic, community, 62, 63, 65
Selden, Mark, 127
Sen: Amartya, 78; Samar, 381
separatism: Baluch, 246; Bengal, 231
Settar, Prof. S., 216
Shastri–Sirimavo Pact, 243
Simla Agreement of 1972, 50, 142, 272
Sikdar, Radhanath, 217
Singh: Lal, 218; Maharaja Hari, 323; Ram, 218; V.P., 222
Sisson, Richard, 158
social dignity, nuclear weapons and, 350
society: barbaric, 398; institution of a minimally decent, 397; minimally decent, 393, 396, 400
solidarity: international, 203; process of building, 337
South Asia Preferential Trading Agreement, 376
South Asia: coalition politics in, 86; formation of state system in, 151; hegemonic peace in, 49; impediments of the existing peace historiography in, 28; indigenous peoples of, 26; international attention on border politics in, 141; legal framework for protecting refugees in, 97; Militarization of, 362; Neo-Liberalism and democracy in, 72; Peace Audit on, 38; rigid borders in, 186; transparent nuclear environment in, 56; urban people in, 81
South Asian Association for Regional Cooperation (SAARC), 159, 376
South Asian Free Trade Regime, 20
Srinivas, M.N., 216
St. Augustine, 19
state discourse: concept of, 160, 162; distinction between state formation and, 162
state formation: process of, in modern India, 162; project of, 160; withdrawal of, 80
Stein, Aurel, 218, 219
Subrahmanyam, K., 55, 347
subsidies: food, 81; Indian fertilizer, 81
Suhrawardy, 390, 391
Super Power: 179; rivalry, 178
Szechenyi, 107, 108

T

Tagore, Rabindranath, 212
Tai Ahom, 210
Tamil Brahmins, migrations of, 214
Tashkent peace process, 276
tax reforms, 75
tea plantations, British-owned, 300
Thapar, General P.N., 181
The Mahabharata, 19
The Peloponnesian War, 19
Thimayya, General, 181
Thompson, E.P., 354
threat: of diversionary attack, 54; systems, 40, 57; to Indian democracy, 87; to Sri Lankan security, 50

Thucydides, 154
Tibet: question, 179; road connecting Sinkiang and, 177
Tibetan settlement program, 194
Tibet–Nepal treaty, 177
Tilly, Charles, 160
Timur, Amir, 217
Tito, death of, 116
trade: Basic, theory, 81; benefits of, and commerce, 42; India and Pakistan, 61; Indian, with Sri Lanka, 52; relationship, 375
transformation, sustainable socio-economic, 79
transition: after Indian independence, 221; to a market oriented society, 83
Tripura Volunteer Force (TNV), 308
Trota, Margarethe von, 382
Truth Commission, 401, 409
Tudjman, 115
Tuker, Francis, 390
Tulasidhar, Dr U.S., 77

U

U.S.: hegemonism on China's Peripheries, 47; non-proliferation policies, 48; policy towards South Asia, 47
UNHCR: international assistance from, 194; international monitoring by, 200; presence of the, 200; role of the, 200
United Liberation Front of Asom (ULFA): 308, 310; anti-statism of the, 169; emergence of the, 305
United Nation Children's Fund (UNICEF), 254

United Nations Commission on India and Pakistan (UNCIP), 324
United Nations Conference on Trade and Development, 82
United Nations Convention, accessions to the, 197
United Nations Covenant on Civil and Political Rights (CCPR), 192
United Nations High Commissioner for Refugees (UNHCR), 95, 191
United Nations Human Rights Committee, 192
United Nations Relief and Works Agency (UNRWA), 259
United Nations Transitional Authority in Cambodia (UNTAX), 261
United Nations, Indian membership in the, 357
Universal Declaration of Human Rights (1948), 93, 95
Ustashi, 115

V

Vagts, Alfred, 363
Vaishnavism, 26
Versailles Treaty, 73
victim: felt need of the, 402; nationality of the, 196; voice of, 401
Vienna Declaration, 94
Vienna World Conference Human Rights, 94
Vietnam War, 125
Vlasto, A.P., 104
Voters' identity cards, 158

W

Walzer, Michael, 399

war: and military establishment, 36; and war-like situations, 152; between states, 145; civil, 156; devastating effects of, 145; experience of, 36; first Indo-Pak, 168; histories of, 153; history of, and negotiations, 271; in South Asia, 159; increasing costs and miseries of, 42; India's, with Pakistan, 183; India-Sri Lanka, scare, 50; Indo-Pak, 152, 157; internal armed disputes or non-internationalized civil, 258; issue of protection against effects of, 255; limited, and developing countries, 36; modern issues of, and peace, 173; nature of, 254; nuclear, 44; of Bourbon and Habsburg succession, 217; of national liberation, 258; outbreak of, 42; polarization and, 43; postponement of, 29; problematic nature of, and peace, 154; protesting against, and its causes, 320; proxy, 156; psychological support to, 33; re-integration of the victims of, 260; shadow of, studies, 34; Sino-Indian border, 178; total, and the great powers, 36; widows, 283
warfare: biological, 125; chemical, 125; gas, 125

war-like situations, 153, 156, 158, 168, 169
warlordism, 222
Warner, Daniel, 127
war-torn areas, quality of lives of people in, 145
water tax, 81
weaponization: outright, 55; progress towards, 56; short-order, 55; virtual, 55
weapons: battlefield nuclear, 348; conventional, 346; costs of nuclear, 347; non-nuclear, signatories, 359; presence of nuclear, 353
Weber, Max, 30, 127
Weiner, Myron, 163
welfare: family, 77; state system, 82
West Bengal, post-partition, 161
Western Liberal tradition, 73
widowhood: Hindu constructions of, 284; public shame of, 284
Williams, Raymond, 322
Wolin, Sheldon, 404
women on the LoC, 282
Women's International War Crimes Tribunal, 128
World Bank, 81

Z

zamindar, social responsibility of the Muslim, 386
Zebunissa, 288
Zia-ul Haq, 245
Ziua-ur-Rahman, 242